Joe Graedon's
The New People's
Pharmacy

Drug Breakthroughs of the '80s

Joe Graedon's The New People's Pharmacy

Drug Breakthroughs of the '80s

by Joe Graedon
and Teresa Graedon

BANTAM BOOKS
TORONTO • NEW YORK • LONDON • SYDNEY • AUCKLAND

ATTENTION

The health and drug information contained in this book has been obtained by careful review and analysis of the scientific literature and through personal interviews with knowledgeable health experts. However, many of the issues discussed are controversial in nature. Because individuals respond differently to medications, there is no way to know exactly how any given person will react to the medicines discussed. Every reader is strongly advised to consult with his or her physician before starting or stopping any medicine, and before implementing any of the therapies discussed in this book. Most important, any side effects should be reported promptly to a physician.

JOE GRAEDON'S THE NEW PEOPLE'S PHARMACY
A Bantam Book

*Published simultaneously in hardcover and trade paperback by Bantam
February 1985*

Library of Congress Cataloging in Publication Data

Graedon, Joe.
  Joe Graedon's The new people's pharmacy.

  Includes bibliographical references and index.
  1. Pharmacology—Popular works.   2. Drugs—side effects.
3. Drug trade.   4. Consumer education.   I. Graedon,
Teresa, 1947–   .   II. Title.   III. Title: New people's pharmacy
RM301.15.G72   1985   615'.1   84-45186
              ISBN 0-553-05072-9
              ISBN 0-553-34134-0 (pbk.)

Published simultaneously in the United States and Canada

*Bantam Books are published by Bantam Books, Inc. Its trademark,
consisting of the words "Bantam Books" and the portrayal of a rooster,
is Registered in the United States Patent and Trademark Office and in
other countries. Marca Registrada. Bantam Books, Inc., 666 Fifth
Avenue, New York, New York 10103.*

PRINTED IN THE UNITED STATES OF AMERICA

FG   0 9 8 7 6 5 4 3 2 1

THIS BOOK IS DEDICATED TO:

WILLIAM P. PINNA
Friend, adviser, and miracle-worker who
helped make it all happen

DR. JERE GOYAN
A visionary leader and champion of people's
right to drug information

SID GRAEDON
Who gave us tremendous insight into
the world of publishing

HELEN GRAEDON
Who gave us the support and love we needed

LOU WOLFE
Who has had ongoing faith in our ability and
was willing to take a risk

DR. DEAN EDELL
A kindred spirit who communicates about
health better than anyone else we know

ACKNOWLEDGMENTS

A few dedicated souls helped us complete this book, with both their insight and their hard work. Special thanks go to:

Brian Weiss, a loyal friend and colleague who was always there when we needed him most;

Dr. David McWaters, whose expertise was truly invaluable at the critical moments;

Dr. Ralph Scallion, one of the smartest, most insightful physicians we have ever known, and a heck of a nice guy to boot;

Dr. Stanley B. Levy, our favorite dermatologist, who helped out with some very important and practical advice;

Gail Schmidt, an unusual woman with great integrity, enthusiasm and joie de vivre;

Dawn Taylor, who helped get us up to speed in the early days.

Carole Dombach, a noble assistant who got into the trenches with us and kept working right up to the last sentence.

AUTHORS' NOTE

Many other individuals have contributed to our work in one way or another. We'd like to thank:

Dr. Tom Ferguson, a self-care advocate and friend who lends us inspiration and helps us keep our priorities straight;

Dr. Robert Day, a great talent scout and compatriot;

Dr. Phil Lee, who blazed the path before it was popular;

Dr. Milt Silverman and Mia Lydecker, wonderfully kind people who opened their hearts to us and provided the best example of all;

Gary Collins, a special kind of television host who gave us the insight and courage to tackle this kind of book;

Dr. Robert Mendelsohn, a wonderful heretic and ally who never fails to surprise us;

Cliff Butler and Warren Jones, special pharmacists who take care of us as well as their customers;

Brad Miner, a fine editor who gave us lots of support and encouragement;

Jennifer Sedwick and Kevin Stack, who came through for us in the crunch;

Dr. Roger Williams, a special kind of clinical investigator who truly cares about quality research;

Dr. Steve Leighton, a physician dedicated to the concept of informed self-care;

Dr. Ruby Wilson, who furthered our collaboration and careers;

Dr. Tad Smith, a brilliant researcher but not such a great judge of character—thanks for the memories;

Dr. Linda Hart, whose sparkling intelligence and insight helped point us in the right direction;

John Doorley, a heck of a nice guy who always managed to find someone for us to talk to;

Dr. Pat Barry, a clear thinker and powerful ally for more enlightened health policy;

Carolyn Glynn, a bright and innovative leader within the pharmaceutical industry;

Ed Nida and Faye Peterson, FDAers who were willing to help provide information on almost any occasion;

Dr. Bob Temple, who came through with some candid information at a critical moment;

James Russo, a joy to know and a noble representative of the pharmaceutical industry;

Mara Gabriel, a professional who always arranged an interview when it was needed most;

Dr. Trudy Elion, just plain spectacular;

Dr. Pedro Cuatrecasas, a brilliant scientist and superb administrator;

Dr. Dannie King and Dr. Ron Keeney, helpful and accessible researchers who provided straightforward answers to tough questions;

Phil Schwartz, a graceful compromiser who went the extra mile and then some;

John-Henry Pfifferling, an all around nice guy who would give you the shirt off his back;

Sir James Black, a pharmacological innovator who is definitely one of a kind;

Dr. Robert Powell, a superb researcher who provided us with state-of-the-art information on drug interactions;

Dr. John Cello, who provided insight into the world of GI drugs;

Dr. William Parmley, who provided insight into the world of cardiovascular drugs;

Drs. Marcia and Ricardo Hofer, who have given us encouragement, advice and great food for over a decade;

Dr. Bonnell and Betty Frost, who provided love and support all the way through.

There are many more people who have given us insight, assistance, inspiration, and support. Thanks to:

Shirley Abbott, Leo Ars, Dennis Bailey, John Barth, Judy Burnham, Kathy Beaty, Molly and Frederick Bernheim, Meg Bogen, Jeannette Boudreau, Chuck and Alice Cambron, Betye Carey, Meade Christian, Betty Clark, Margaret Clark, Steve Clements, Belita Cowan, Louise Cook, Richard Crout, Ron Culp, Ben and Mary Daitz, Marvin and Carol Davidson, Helen De Barbieri, Fred and Janet D'Ignazio, Jim Eason, Jeff Ellinger, Larry Ferber, Jill and Issy Figueroa, Judi Fitzpatrick, Andi, Karro, and Jim Frost, Fernando Galindo, Robert Gilgor, Diane Glynn, Leo and Luce Goldstein, David and Alena Graedon, Eva and Jim Greenberg, Kathe Gregory, Bill Grigg, Joanne Hall, Ed and Joy Hill, David and Carol Hogue, Robert Johnson, Michael Kahn, Devva Kasnitz, Ed and Aleka Leydon, James Lynch, Fran Lynn, Magdaline Mack, Sarah Madry, Shirley and Steven McConnell, Will and Deni McIntyre, John & Christopher McLachlan, Duffy Miller, Susan Moldow, Michael Naimark, Barney Nietschmann, Melva Okun, Sam Putnam, Harry Philips, Wayne Pines, Barbara Pinna, Allan Priaulx, Tom Pritchard, Leah and Carl Rakosi, Joanne and Warren Reich, Jerry Rosen, Joseph Saba, Eva Salber, Lynn Scallion, David and Marty Sedwick, Tom Smigel, David Sobel, Susan and Allen Spalt, Carol Stack, Richard Surwit, Hank and Vicki Swain, Dan Waits, Jack Ward, Ellie White, Redford Williams, Leo Waldenberg, and Sid Wolfe.

CONTENTS

CHAPTER 1   WE'RE IN TROUBLE NOW!   1

Bye-Bye, PPI: The FDA Gives Up on Patient Package Inserts
▪ The Popular PDR: More Patients than Physicians Read the
Doctors' Drug Bible ▪ Prescription Super Bloopers: Just What
Did the Doctor Order? ▪ Myths and Misconceptions About
PPIs ▪ The Amazing FDA Flip-Flop: Letting the Fox Guard
the Henhouse ▪ Drug Lag: Fact or Fiction? ▪ The Thalidomide
Tragedy ▪ **Selacryn** Strikes Out ▪ The **Oraflex** Calamity:
Lilly Loses Luster ▪ Did Dishonest Doctors Test Your Drug? ▪
Getting Zapped by **Zomax** ▪ Surviving the Coming Drug
Revolution.

CHAPTER 2   DRUG ADVERTISING IS HAZARDOUS TO YOUR HEALTH   35

Advertising Prescription Drugs: **Clinoril** Creates Confusion—
and Cash ▪ The Dog-and-Pony Drug Show: **Nasalide** and
Naprosyn ▪ **Zovirax**: Help for Herpes is Here ▪ **Oraflex**: Eli
Lilly's House of Cards Comes Crashing Down ▪ The New
and Improved Medicine Show ▪ FTC: Does It Stand for Federal Trade Commission or Forsaking The Consumer? ▪ Doctors Buckle Under Badgering ▪ Dealing Drugs to Doctors ▪
Too Much Medicine.

CHAPTER 3   THE NEXT MIRACLES OF MEDICINE   63

The New Drug Revolution ▪ A History Lesson: The Fabulous
Fifties, Sobering Sixties, and Stagnant Seventies ▪ The Excit-
ing Eighties ▪ Sniffing Your Way to Birth Control ▪ A is for
Apple and Aphrodisiac: LHRH, Yohimbine; L-Dopa, and

Parlodel ▪ Sex and the Fat Rat ▪ Opiates and the Brain ▪ B is for Bashful, Baldness, and Balderdash ▪ Biotechnology and Blue Sky: Unlocking the Body's Secrets: Interferon, Interleukin-2, Immune Stimulators, Monoclonal Antibodies, and Wound Healing.

reading All Lead to Errors ▪ Is Your Doctor Giving You High Blood Pressure? ▪ Do-It-Yourself Blood Pressure Readings: Electronic Wizardry Makes It Easy! ▪ Mild Hypertension: The Gray Zone Gets Grayer ▪ Hurting More than Helping?: MRFIT Raises Doubts ▪ Depletion & Disruption with Diuretics ▪ Replacing Potassium—The Plot Thickens ▪ The Sodium Controversy: Stickier than You Thought ▪ Cashing Out on Caffeine ▪ Simple Non-Drug Steps to Success ▪ Gone Fishin': Learning to Relax ▪ Evaluation of Home Blood Pressure Devices ▪ Table: Blood Pressure Medicines.

CHAPTER 8 COPING WITH PAIN

Pain Relief—Too Often, Too Little or Too Late? ▪ The Private Experience of Pain ▪ Measuring Pain: Easy as Capturing Moonbeams ▪ Fear of Addiction ▪ How to Treat Something With Nothing: The Placebo Response ▪ How the Brain Fights Pain: Endorphins and Enkephalins ▪ Treating Pain With Pills ▪ Aspirin and Acetaminophen: **Anacin, Anacin-3, Tylenol, Datril,** and **Panadol** ▪ When Aspirin Won't Work: **Dolobid, Motrin, Rufen, Naprosyn, Clinoril, Anaprox, Feldene, Tolectin, Nalfon, Tylenol No. 3, Empirin No. 3, Fiorinal No. 3, Darvocet-N, Percodan, Talwin, Demerol, Dilaudid, Dolophine,** and morphine ▪ Watch Out for **Phenergan** ▪ Banishing Pain: The Non-Drug Alternatives ▪ Pain Clinics, Biofeedback, TENS, Behavior Mod, Acupuncture, Hypnosis ▪ The Future of Pain Relief.

CHAPTER 9 BEHIND THE SCENES WITH OTCs

Nonprescription Drugs Make Snake Oil Look Good ▪ The FDA's 21 Year Review ▪ Without Prescription But Not Without Power ▪ OTC Dangers for Children ▪ Pregnant Women Beware ▪ Questions About PPA Still Alive ▪ The Big Switch: From Prescriptions to OTC ▪ Informed Self-Care: The Wave of the Future.

CHAPTER 10 A PRACTICAL GUIDE TO DRUGS OF THE 1980s

A Revolution in Acne Treatment: **Accutane** and Those Amazing Retinoids ▪ The Quiet Breakthroughs in Allergy and Asthma: **Beconase, Vancenase, Nasalide, Beclovent, Vanceril, Proventil, Ventolin, Theo-dur, Slo-phyllin** ▪ An Antibiotic

Worth Knowing: **Ceclor** ▪ Another NSAID for Arthritis: **Feldene** ▪ Cutting Back on Cigarettes with **Nicorette** ▪ A New Cholesterol Lowering Drug: **Lopid** ▪ Fighting Fungi with **Nizoral** ▪ Going After Gallbladders with **Chenix** ▪ Help for the Heart (and Maybe the Ears) with **Tonocard** ▪ Motion Sickness Magic: **Transderm-Scop** ▪ **Parlodel** for Parkinsonism ▪ Sedatives and Sleeping Pills: **Centrax**, **Halcion**, **Paxipam**, **Xanax** ▪ **Zyderm** for Your Wrinkles.

LIST OF TABLES AND ILLUSTRATIONS

HOW TO USE THIS BOOK

This book is meant to be read and enjoyed. Hopefully, you will find facts that will amuse, surprise or astonish you. While it's not a drug dictionary and does not review every medication on the market, we hope that nevertheless it will be of practical reference value as well. We have tried to include in the tables some of the most important new drugs currently available, with information on their uses, side effects, precautions, and interactions. Anyone taking a drug—prescription or over-the-counter—needs to become informed about it. Although no publication can substitute for good communication among patients, pharmacists, and physicians, we hope this book will help you become a more knowledgeable consumer.

CHAPTER 1

We're in Trouble Now!

Bye-Bye, PPI: The FDA Gives Up on Patient Package Inserts ▪ *The Popular PDR: More Patients than Physicians Read the Doctors' Drug Bible* ▪ *Prescription Super-Bloopers: Just What* **Did** *the Doctor Order?* ▪ *Myths and Misconceptions About PPIs* ▪ *The Amazing FDA Flip-Flop: Letting the Fox Guard the Henhouse* ▪ *Drug Lag: Fact or Fiction?* ▪ *The Thalidomide Tragedy* ▪ **Selacryn** *Strikes Out* ▪ *The* **Oraflex** *Calamity: Lilly Loses Luster* ▪ *Did Dishonest Doctors Test Your Drug?* ▪ *Getting Zapped by* **Zomax** ▪ *Surviving the Coming Drug Revolution.*

When Terry and I finished *The People's Pharmacy–2* we really believed we had seen the last of writing books for a good while. It did not seem likely that anyone would need another *People's Pharmacy.* The number of prescriptions filled in drugstores was declining steadily, and people appeared to have grown more skeptical of drug advertising and more cautious about popping pills.

Best of all, the FDA (Food and Drug Administration) was on the verge of initiating a program of PPIs (Patient Package Inserts) that would at long last provide much-needed drug information to millions of Americans every time they got a prescription filled. We figured that these mandatory leaflets—describing the proper uses, risks, and side effects of prescription medications—would make future books on drugs virtually unnecessary, and we couldn't have been more delighted. Boy, were we wrong!

Our crystal ball didn't warn us that there would be an incredible about-face at the FDA. It also failed to predict that around the same time the FTC (Federal Trade Commission), which is responsible for protecting people from misleading and deceptive drug advertising, would be hobbled, hamstrung, and otherwise sandbagged. The powerful pharmaceutical industry emerged with more influence in Washington than it had ever had before and rejoiced that its intensive lobbying had resulted in revision of the drug-approval process. In short, a regulatory system once almost immune to outside influence was politicized and insidiously weakened. The American public was getting shafted and didn't even know it.

Bye-Bye, PPI

In 1975 the FDA finally woke up to the fact that patients desperately wanted to know more about the drugs their doctors were so casually prescribing. A modest proposal was conceived that would have required drug companies to supply informational brochures describing drug actions, side effects, and dangerous interactions in easy-to-understand language for a handful of basic medications. Naturally the feds couldn't simply go with a good idea. They had to seek comments, convene panels, commission studies, and generally futz along at a snail's pace. But finally, five years later, the bureaucrats concluded that PPIs were indeed a good idea.

Patricia Harris, then Secretary of HHS (Health and Human Services), announced with great fanfare that by the spring of 1981 inserts would be required for ten drugs or classes of drugs. These included such frequently prescribed medications as antianxiety agents like **Valium** (diazepam), **Librium** (chlordiazepoxide), and **Tranxene** (clorazepate); digitalis heart medicine such as **Lanoxin** (digoxin); diuretic drugs used to treat high blood pressure, like **HydroDIURIL** (hydrochlorothiazide) and **Dyazide** (hydrochlorothiazide and triamterene); ampicillin antibiotics; an ulcer medicine called **Tagamet** (cimetidine); an anticonvulsant for epilepsy, **Dilantin** (phenytoin); a cholesterol-lowering agent, **Atromid-S** (clofibrate); and the pain reliever **Darvon** (propoxyphene).

Ultimately this pilot program would have been expanded to include hundreds of different drugs. Although the value of supplying relevant information with such medications seems self-evident, the folks in Washington felt compelled to marshal their statistics in support of the program.

> **Studies show that about 40 percent of the prescriptions given to patients each year may not be taken correctly, often because the patient does not understand the effects of the medication. Misuse may prolong illness, lead to serious adverse drug reactions, costly visits to the hospital or to the doctor's office, and cause needless suffering.**
>
> **Every year the Food and Drug Administration receives between 10,000 and 12,000 reports of adverse drug reactions, but these numbers constitute only a small fraction of an estimated *six million people in the U.S. each year who are affected by adverse drug reactions*.**
>
> **Many of these could be prevented or minimized by giving patients more information about their prescription drugs. [Emphasis added][1]**
>
> **—Patricia Harris, Secretary of Health and Human Services, September 10, 1980.**

You would think that such a reasonable concept would meet with approval from everyone—especially pharmaceutical manufacturers, pharmacists, and physicians. After all, how could anyone be against a program designed to cut down on errors in taking drugs and to warn patients about serious side effects? We're talking apple pie and motherhood, right? Wrong! You guessed it. Not only did drug companies, druggists, and doctors come out against PPIs, they did so with a vengeance.

The first argument was money. According to these "health professionals," PPIs would cost too much. No matter that serious adverse reactions might be prevented or lives saved. The manufacturers argued that it would be far too expensive to print and distribute the brochures. And the pharmacists complained bitterly about the burden of stocking and handing out PPIs. The FDA countered these arguments with some cost/benefit analyses of its own.

> **FDA estimates that the cost of increased health care and lost productivity as a result of inappropriate use of the 10 drugs or drug classes, may range from $400 million to $800 million a year . . . if patient package inserts reduce this misuse by only 10 percent, the $40 million to $80 million in savings would be significantly greater than the $21 million annual cost of the project.**
>
> **We estimate that the total cost of the preparation, printing and delivering of patient package inserts to patients will be no more than 18 cents each.**[2]

Imagine: 18 cents to warn someone about a serious side effect—information that might save a life—and the price was too steep! And let's be honest; you and I know who would really have paid—the patient. The cost would have been passed on, as it inevitably is. But who would have complained? For a measly 18 centavos you could have been forewarned of dangerous side effects and drug interactions. And if the cost of the inserts were spread out to include all prescriptions sold, the price would have dropped to 1½ cents. Now *that* would have been a real bargain!

But expense wasn't the only argument. Oh, no! The biggest sticking point was authority. Doctors and druggists saw the mandatory leaflets as muscling in on their privileged turf. Physicians often take the condescending attitude that "we know what's best for our patients, so don't meddle!" A letter we received from an angry physician in Philadelphia typifies this mind-set: "Practicing medicine in the old days was much easier when patients were not bombarded with unnecessary medical information from various mediums [sic] both written and visual and were more accustomed to following their doctor's instructions than to questioning them.'' Another doctor, James A. Lundquist, M.D., expressed much the same opinion in a letter to the editor of *Medical World News*.

> It is impossible to inform the uninformable. It is my experience that patients in general do not listen to what is told them, do not understand what they read, and are simply confused by the information provided. With the limited use of PPIs by government order, it has been my experience that patients generally resent such inserts and do not want to be bothered with reading them. There are exceptional cases, however, in which the patient does read them in detail and is disturbed by the description of risks of taking the drug. Not all the risks mentioned are real; some are apparently imaginary. . . .
>
> The use of patient package inserts—existing or proposed—is utterly ridiculous, useless, time-consuming, and costly. It is certain, too, that in some cases the inserts will deter the patient from taking a necessary medication and thus be harmful to the patient in the long run.[3]

I can't begin to tell you how angry that letter makes me! The arrogance, unmitigated gall, and general insensitivity of such an epistle is beyond my comprehension. But Susan M. Anderson, a medical librarian, puts it more rationally than I could. She replied to Dr. Lundquist in the letter section of *Medical World News*.

> Dr. Lundquist's assertion that "it is impossible to inform the uninformable" is highly insulting to any consumer who cares enough to question any health-care provider on regimens, tests, or drugs prescribed. His generalization that patients do not listen, do not understand, and only end up confused is simply not true. Many consumers do listen and do care about their health and treatment. Though they may be confused, they welcome the opportunity to learn through such methods as PPIs.[4]

Amen! Contrary to what Dr. Lundquist believes, it is clear that most people want more, not less, information about their medicine. And they're willing to pay for it. One of the perennial best-sellers in bookstores across the country is the so-called *PDR (Physicians' Desk Reference)*, even at a hefty price of over $25. It is also one of the most popular books in public libraries. Though it's been called the doctors' "drug bible," an FDA-commissioned survey shows that probably more patients than physicians read the *PDR*.[5]

Now that popularity with patients might not seem too surprising unless you already know that the *PDR* has an incredibly complicated indexing system that makes it hard to track down any information. Furthermore, once you do locate what you're looking for, you find it written in a medical mumbo jumbo that's not easy to understand. Worse yet, all side effects, whether they are common or ridiculously rare, are usually lumped together, with no way for the uninitiated to sort them out.

Why would droves of patients spend time and money on such a book? The answer is simple. Although two recent surveys show that doctors and pharmacists think they're doing a good job providing drug information, patients are not at all convinced that they are getting the facts they need.[6,7] One national pollster under contract to the FDA talked to over a thousand patients who had received prescriptions within the preceding two weeks. The researchers found that only 6 percent of the people reported that their doctors had given them any written information, while a mere 15 percent received something in writing at the pharmacy.

I can almost hear you suggesting that the explanations might have been given verbally, while the patient was in the doctor's office. But Louis Harris, one of the pollsters, noted that "surprisingly few physicians report that they tell their patients what the medication is and what it is used for."[8] The doctors spent somewhere between two and six minutes talking with each patient about the four drugs considered in the study, while pharmacists averaged less than two minutes. That's hardly enough time to pronounce the name of some of the drugs, let alone give instructions for their use or warnings about possible problems and interactions. In fact, three out of four patients were not told anything concerning drug side effects in the doctor's office.

How in the world, then, can physicians kid themselves into believing they are doing a great job communicating? The reason is that very few patients—only 2 to 4 percent of those polled—asked questions, leading most doctors to think that people are satisfied with such information as they're now getting. But the real reasons they're not asking questions, patients say, have more to do with fear, confusion, uncertainty about what to ask, or respect. Some even worried that they might be considered insolent. And no wonder: a surprising number of physicians get downright hostile when you start asking questions.

Prescription Super-Bloopers

When they do make an attempt to communicate, far too many physicians are unable to provide verbal instructions and cautions in language that can be understood. Printed PPIs would help with this problem and alleviate the difficulties caused by ambiguous or illegible prescriptions, which often lead to serious drug-taking errors. Although medication mistakes and adverse reactions are not well reported (few practitioners are willing to volunteer that they gave out inadequate instructions or that a patient got sick from a prescribed drug), Michael Cohen, an assistant clinical professor of pharmacy at Temple University, has reported one particularly harrowing example.

> The patient was suffering an ache in his right ear and the doctor prescribed Lidosporin, a combination antibiotic-local anesthetic.
>
> It was a simple remedy, except that in the doctor's prescription there was no period after "R" (for right), and the person administering the drug read it as "Rear."
>
> The patient received three drops of the drug Lidosporin in his rectum three times before the error was discovered. Perhaps he immediately should have questioned why he was receiving rectal medication for an earache, but then, in case after case, patients—and nurses, pharmacists, and other physicians—do not question prescriptions.[9]

And Cohen remarks:

> The chief fault is that doctors' illegible handwriting is regarded as a joke. But the joke's on the patients, who too often are receiving improper medication, and sometimes dying from it.[10]

It's pretty hard not to chuckle when you hear about someone mistakenly getting ear drops in the rear. Fortunately such an error is unlikely to to be life-threatening; but it should never have happened in the first place. If the physician had taken a few extra seconds to clearly print this prescription in full and inform the patient what was being recommended, the accident could have been prevented. Nurses, too, have a responsibility to communicate clearly. Cohen cites another classic screwup.

> A patient was to go for gallbladder surgery in the morning. In the evening before surgery, the patient was shaved and told to take a shower. For the shower, the preoperative protocol called for Phisohex to be used. Nurses poured Phisohex soap from a gallon container into a styrofoam cup. Bringing it to the patient, who was still in bed, the nurse said, "Here's your cup of Phisohex," as she placed it on the night table. The patient drank the Phisohex.[11]

Mistakenly drinking **Phisohex** cleaner one time probably won't lead to long-term complications, but you can bet that it tasted terrible and probably didn't do much to reassure the patient about his impending surgery. Professor Cohen has, however, uncovered far more serious errors. One patient, for example, received a strong iodine solution (**Lugol's solution**) in her eye instead of orally because a hastily scribbled Latin abbreviation was interpreted incorrectly.[12]

In another case of illegibility a patient suffering from constipation was given a sleeping pill called **Doriden** (glutethimide) instead of the laxative **Doxidan** (docusate and danthron).[13] Another report tells of a 70-year-old woman with arthritis who received the diabetes drug **Tolinase** (tolazamide) instead of the anti-inflammatory medicine **Tolectin** (tolmetin) which was actually prescribed.[14]

You may think such mistakes are inconsequential, but far from it. The woman who got the diabetes drug instead of her arthritis medicine developed pseudoinsulinoma—a serious condition that mimics excessive insulin production. We are not told what happened to the patient who was given a sleeping pill instead of a laxative, but such an error could be extremely serious, especially if it happens to an older person in a nursing home; the resulting sedation and lethargy might have led to a false diagnosis of senility.

Such mistakes are not isolated events. Professor Cohen states that the medication-error rate in some hospitals and nursing homes can be as high as 12 percent. And it's not a whole hell of a lot better at your neighborhood drugstore. The truth is that pharmacists have just as much trouble making sense out of a doctor's chicken scratches as you do. Sure, they can decipher the Latin code that some physicians still like to cling to, but when it comes to trying to make sense out of an illegible scrawl, they're no better at it than anyone else.

An editorial in the professional journal *American Druggist* lays it on the line.

> **A mysterious affliction, *malagraphicis medici*, causes pharmacists to fill prescriptions incorrectly, possibly endangering the lives of patients. The name of the disease is fictitious, but its ravages are real. We're referring, of course, to the poor handwriting of physicians.**
>
> ***More than half of the pharmacists who responded to a questionnaire published in* American Druggist *said they had made errors in dispensing because of doctors' sloppy writing.* One shudders at the dimensions of such a silent, continuing disaster! Imagine the injuries inflicted on unsuspecting patients! Imagine the lawsuits against doctors and pharmacists if these injuries come to light![15]**

Can you believe that? Half the pharmacists polled admitted that they had made mistakes because they had misread a prescription. Here are some selected comments by those who responded to the questionnaire.

A former employer was sued for $250,000. He dispensed a similar sounding drug by error and the patient got pregnant.

A dermatologist, notorious for his almost unreadable Rx's, once told me on the phone that if I couldn't read the Rx, I should give it back to the patient and tell him to take it elsewhere! In two years of practice near his office, I saw hundreds of his Rx's and never found even one which I could read in its entirety.

Gave *Librium* [a sedative] once for *Indocin* [an arthritis drug]. Thank God the patient happened to be on *Librium* anyway, so not too much harm was done.

Many times when I question the doctor about his own handwriting, he doesn't remember what the medicine should be.

I know of a pharmacist who dispensed *Paregoric* [a diarrhea medicine] instead of Panmycin [an antibiotic]—and refilled it twice![16]

Enough said! Actual examples of illegible prescriptions are worth far more than a thousand words. Thanks to one of my favorite pharmacists, I was able to obtain some real winners in the doctors' chicken scratching sweepstakes. Even ignoring such Latin symbols as q.i.d. (four times a day), p.r.n. (as needed), or p.c. (after meals), I think you will discover why pharmacists often have a hard time deciphering prescriptions.

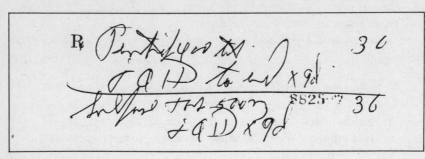

What he wrote:

Pentids 400 tabs.36.
1 qid to end × 9 d
Sulfose tab 500 mg36.
1 qid × 9 d

What he meant to tell the pharmacist:

Dispense 36 tablets of Pentids 400, with directions reading:
Take one tablet four times a day for 9 days.

Dispense 36 tablets of Sulfose 500 mg. with directions reading:
Take one tablet four times a day for 9 days.

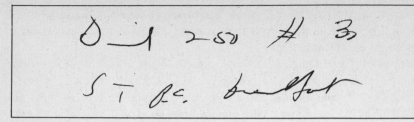

What he wrote:

Diuril 250 # 30
Sig.: One tablet p.c. breakfast

What he meant to tell the pharmacist:

Dispense 30 Diuril 250 mg. pills, with directions reading:
Take one tablet after breakfast.

But why don't pharmacists telephone doctors when they can't read the damn Rx? Ah, but they do! Almost one-fourth the pharmacists surveyed admitted that they had to make at least one call a day to verify an unreadable prescription. The trouble is that sometimes the doctor's signature is so illegible that they may not know whom to contact. Hospital prescription forms usually don't have the doctor's name printed on them.

Even when pharmacists do call, the doctor will not always come to the phone or return the call promptly. Almost one-fourth of the physicians mentioned waited hours before they responded to a query, and 3.6 percent ignored the pharmacists' pleas entirely. This study reported that when doctors were confronted with a concern about an illegible prescription, half were indifferent, 22 percent were defensive, and 14 percent became downright angry, as if the problem were the pharmacist's fault. Perhaps worst of all, pharmacists report that "M.D.'s tend to treat our calls as jokes! After all, how can you question an M.D.?"[17]

Well, I'm here to say that illegible prescriptions are not a laughing matter. Your doctor wouldn't be amused if your check was so hard to read that the bank refused to cash it. You **MUST NOT** ever accept a prescription that you cannot easily understand. Before you leave your doctor's office, ask the nurse to print or type the words of the prescription right under the chicken scratches. And for double protection, have the generic name (scientific name) of the medicine included along with the brand name.

Finally, ask your doctor to use English instead of an outdated Latin code. The most respected pharmacology text in the world, *Goodman and Gilman's The Pharmacological Basis of Therapeutics*, is crystal clear in its instructions to medical students: "The directions to the patient should always be written in English. The use of Latin abbreviations, such as . . . '1 cap t.i.d.a.c.' [one capsule three times a day before meals], serves no useful purpose."[18] If you can read and understand the prescription, you will be doing your pharmacist a favor; at the same time you will be protecting yourself from the possibility of a serious mistake that might be life threatening.

But even if you manage by some miracle to get a legible prescription and the pharmacist fills it correctly, you are only halfway home. Remember, if your doctor and druggist are similar to the ones in the FDA survey we mentioned, the chances are good that you won't have received crucial instructions or precautions. No one knows how many errors patients make at home because their doctors failed to provide adequate information, but the numbers must be staggering.

Myths and Misconceptions About PPIs

Patient Package Inserts would have gone a long way toward eliminating these problems, but as we pointed out earlier, the medical profession fought this program tooth and nail. Besides insisting that people would merely throw away the brochures without reading them, a great many doctors and pharmacists maintained that the mere mention of side effects constitutes a self-fulfilling prophecy that can produce psychosomatic symptoms in patients or scare them out of taking needed medicine.

According to this argument the power of suggestion is so strong that if you tell a man his high blood pressure medication might cause impotence, he will have sexual difficulties even when the drug itself is not responsible. If you tell a woman her arthritis drug could cause stomach pain or diarrhea, you will increase the likelihood that she will experience these adverse reactions.

While it's undoubtedly true that the power of suggestion can be very strong for some people, that realization is no justification for witholding information. Such an approach implies that ignorance is bliss. If the patient is unaware of side effects, they won't happen. Horsefeathers! That's what I call the head in the sand approach.

I've always objected to this sort of thinking for a couple of reasons. For one thing, it's incredibly condescending and assumes that people are incapable of understanding very much of anything. For another, it's based on preconceptions and prejudice. Doctors pride themselves on their rationality. They like to think they make logical decisions based on scientific facts. But the truth is, doctors are just like everyone else. They can be just as biased and inflexible as the rest of us, and nowhere is this more apparent than in their attitude on package inserts.

During the time the FDA was trying to make up its mind whether or not PPIs could work, the agency commissioned the prestigious Rand Corporation to conduct a thorough investigation. In 1978 the researchers started a study that was to involve 1,821 men and women and over 2,000 prescriptions. The cost to the FDA for this three-year effort was

$525,000. The results of the research knocked down most of the arguments drug companies, doctors or pharmacists were making against PPIs:

Misconception 1: Patients don't want more drug information. They'll just throw away PPIs.

Rand Results: About 70 percent of patients said they read the PPI (more among first time users of the drug). About half of the subjects said they kept the PPI for reference, and 20 to 30 percent said they read it more than once.

Misconception 2: Only intellectuals, hypochondriacs and flakes will read PPIs.

Rand Results: We found no evidence that PPIs are read only by an information-seeking elite; the less educated were just as likely to read them as anyone else.

Misconception 3: Patients are too easily confused. They can't understand or make use of drug information.

Rand Results: People who received PPIs could answer more questions correctly about how to use the drug, its interactions and contraindications, than those who did not get PPIs. . . . Patients reported that PPIs helped them to understand their drugs, to follow their doctors' advice, and to know when to take their drugs. The less educated respondents rated the PPIs the most useful.

Misconception 4: Information about side effects will scare patients out of taking needed medicine.

Rand Results: Few respondents changed their mind about whether to take a drug after reading the PPI. Only three of more than 2,000 prescriptions dispensed with PPIs were returned for a refund.

Misconception 5: Patients are susceptible to suggestion. Just mention a side effect and they'll experience psychosomatic symptoms.

Rand Results: PPIs did not generally increase reports of side effects. People did not "imagine every side effect" listed in the leaflet.[19,20]

The Amazing FDA Flip-Flop

Now, you would think the Rand report would have made the folks at the FDA jump for joy. After all, the results confirmed the value of package inserts and pulled the rug out from under the physicians, pharmacists, and pharmaceutical manufacturers who had been fighting the program. But it turned out that the report was a big embarrassment to the feds. Hard as this may be to comprehend, the big boys at FDA were not at all pleased to hear that PPIs could be successful.

Wait a minute—that doesn't make any sense. The Rand study was commissioned by the FDA, and the results supported the value of the original program. What happened? In the interim, the ship of state changed hands and course. A new administration, less committed to consumer awareness, took over. Heavy lobbying by the American Pharmaceutical Association, the American Medical Association, the National Association of Chain Drug Stores, and numerous pharmaceutical manufacturers was directed at the new team.

Needless to say, these pressure groups looked on the idea of PPIs with horror and did everything in their power to kill it. And were they ever successful! On December 22, 1981, just four months after the Rand report proved they worked magnificently, PPIs were zapped and laid to rest. Without any explanation the "new" FDA concluded that informational brochures "have significant limitations and impose unreasonable constraints on the health care system."[21] Wham, bam, no thank you, ma'am! Years of work and careful planning went down the tubes almost overnight.

The bureaucrats' idea of a better way to provide drug information was to invite the AMA (American Medical Association) and the drug companies to get into the act. The AMA proudly announced that Eli Lilly, Upjohn, and the Mead Johnson Foundation would ante up some big bucks for a PMI (Patient Medication Instruction) program, and Ciba-Geigy announced its own $1 million plan to develop ways of helping consumers learn about prescription drugs. The idea was that physicians would buy and hand out little AMA drug brochures, and everything would be hunky-dory.

But relying on doctors to provide drug information voluntarily is, if memory serves me, how we got into this mess in the first place. Early reports on the AMA's program were hardly encouraging. Four months after the AMA sent out a mailing to 400,000 M.D.'s and D.O.'s (osteopaths) announcing its patient-information program, only 16,000 docs had responded.[22] Just in case your calculator isn't handy, let me tell you that amounts to a response of less than 5 percent. So much for the "honor system."

Even if physicians were willing to supply patients with these AMA-sanctioned pamphlets, would that be enough? The original PPI program would have been run by the FDA, and all the material would have been carefully analyzed for accuracy and clarity. Having drug companies and the American Medical Association supply advice and instructions without FDA oversight sounds suspiciously like asking the foxes to guard the henhouse.

Even though the FDA publicly applauds the AMA initiative, some staffers have serious reservations. Insiders have admitted that there are serious flaws in the AMA leaflets.[23] One source in the agency confided that they "downplayed side effects quite a bit."[24] In some cases important information has been left out. For example, instead of stating directly that long-term use of tranquilizers like **Valium, Librium, Ativan,** and **Tranxene** can sometimes lead to *very* uncomfortable withdrawal symptoms in up to 44 percent of users if the drug is discontinued abruptly, the PMI handles this issue with kid gloves.

> **Your doctor may want you to gradually reduce the amount you are taking before stopping completely, since your body may need time to adjust. If you have taken this medicine in high doses or for a long time, this may take several weeks.**[25]

Sometimes even "several weeks" may not be enough. One group of investigators discovered that patients suffered such withdrawal symptoms as insomnia, "depersonalization," sadness, lack of appetite, "worrying over trifles," difficulty concentrating, pessimistic thoughts, muscular tension, agitation, hostility, and unsteadiness even when the dosage was reduced gradually.[26] It's hardly any wonder that a CYA (Cover Your A—) statement at the end of each AMA brochure reads, "The information in this PMI is selective and does not cover all the possible uses, actions, precautions, side effects, or interactions of this medicine." Do you begin to wonder if something is fishy somewhere?

You're on Your Own

The death of the PPI program was just the first in a series of changes in the FDA's attitude that spell serious trouble for consumers. Unlike many other federal agencies, the Food and Drug Administration used to be relatively immune to power politics and outside influence. The relationship between drug-industry executives and federal regulators has generally been adversarial—as it should be. Although pharmaceutical manufacturers obviously want to make good medicine, their primary goal is to make as much money as possible, while the goal of the FDA is to make sure that drugs are as safe and effective as possible. Quite often these different objectives have led to conflict.

But in the early 80s, all that has changed. A tilt in favor of industry at the highest level of the federal bureaucracy radically altered the nature and independence of the agency. Insiders on the Washington scene described the relationship between the pharmaceutical industry and the FDA as "less troublesome" and "more cordial," stopping short of calling it downright cozy. A number of officials who had a reputation for independence were fired or reassigned to less important posts.[27–29] Politics, not science, became the name of the game, and some scientific advisers were being recommended more for their ideology than for their academic credentials.[30]

For all intents and purposes, by 1982 the FDA was no longer making all its own decisions, and political appointees sympathetic to industry were calling the shots on some crucial issues. One disgruntled ex-FDA staffer confessed to us that the agency was "getting out of the regulatory business—not giving a damn about safety. Consumers are at greater risk. FDA is more interested in speeding new drugs through."[31]

Drug Lag: Fact or Fiction?

Widespread complaints that thousands of Americans are dying unnecessarily because drugs available abroad can't be purchased here may indeed have led the FDA to change its priorities on new drug approvals. For years pharmaceutical manufacturers have been moaning and groaning about a drug lag, claiming that many medicines already widely used in Europe are unavailable in the United States because of excessively strict regulations. If only the rules were relaxed, they insisted, drug approval would be quicker, and everything would be peachy keen. Arthritis victims would suffer less pain, heart patients might live longer, and people with asthma could breathe more easily. From the industry viewpoint, the great benefit of these new drugs far outweighs any risk of serious adverse reactions. How fast they forget!

In 1956 a most extraordinary new sleeping pill, called **Contergan,** was introduced in West Germany. The drug was extremely popular with both doctors and patients, and it quickly became the most widely used "hypnotic" on the market. The phenomenal success of the new sleeping pill was attributed to its high degree of safety. Whereas sedatives and tranquilizers previously available could be lethal in overdose, **Contergan**, even at relatively large doses, produced little or no observable toxicity.[32] One expert familiar with the medication reported:

> **The drug was thought to be so safe that for a time it was available without a prescription in Germany and was widely used in hospitals, mental institutions, and homes. In a liquid form, designed for children, the drug became "West Germany's baby sitter." Ironically it proved effective in combating nausea due to pregnancy and was used to give many a pregnant woman a good night's sleep.[32, 33]**

The West German manufacturer quickly realized that **Contergan** was a hot number, and the drug was licensed and marketed throughout Europe under a variety of brand names. But the really big market was in the United States. The William S. Merrell Company of Cincinnati recognized the drug's potential and, after buying the United States license, submitted it to the FDA on September 12, 1960, under the name **Kevadon**.

The person at the FDA who was responsible for reviewing this New Drug Application was Dr. Frances Kelsey. She was new at the agency but eminently qualified, having a medical degree as well as a Ph.D. in pharmacology. Dr. Kelsey was not impressed with what she read. For one thing, she felt that the scientific studies supporting the drug's effectiveness were incomplete. More important, she had reservations about the drug's safety. On November 10, 1960, two months after receiving the application for **Kevadon**, Dr. Kelsey wrote a letter to the drug company stating in part, "The chronic toxicity data are incomplete and therefore, no evaluation can be made of the safety of the drug when used for a prolonged period of time."[34]

Needless to say, the drug company was not pleased to hear that the FDA wanted more data. It had been expected that with the drug's wide popularity and a four-year track record in Europe, **Kevadon** would have clear sailing into the American market. But questions were raised by a report in the *British Medical Journal* which linked long-term use of the drug to possible peripheral neuritis (a nerve disorder of the hands and feet).[35] Dr. Kelsey was also asking for evidence that the drug was not dangerous when used during pregnancy.[36]

When it became apparent that there would be a delay in approving this wonderful new drug, Merrell started to get anxious. According to Dr. Kelsey, "other firms had on occasion applied pressure," but she noted that "in no instance was it as severe as with this application."[37] Representatives of the company repeatedly called and visited the FDA in an attempt to persuade Dr. Kelsey and her superiors that the drug was safe. But without adequate proof, the feds held their ground, and one year later had still not approved **Kevadon** for use in the United States.

As you can imagine, this "drug lag" had the drug company really ticked off. According to one investigator, Richard McFadyen, the company decided to go on the offensive.

> **Early in September [of 1961] Merrell mounted an all out campaign to persuade the FDA to release the drug by mid-November in preparation for the Christmas market. Clinical investigators were brought in by Merrell to try to persuade Dr. Kelsey and other FDA officials of the effectiveness of the drug and of its safety especially in comparison with barbiturates. But the evidence was still inadequate as to whether the drug would be harmless to the fetus.[38]**

Before the FDA could knuckle under to the increased pressure, a startling and tragic thing happened. On November 30, 1961, the pharma-

ceutical manufacturer announced that the drug was being abruptly withdrawn from the West German market. The reason: women who took this
medication during their pregnancy were giving birth to children with
incredible malformations. By the summer of 1961 it was clear that
Europe was in the middle of an epidemic. Babies born with "seal limbs,"
missing ears, and severe defects of the digestive tract were cropping up
all over.

By now I'm sure you've guessed the generic name of this mystery
medicine. The thalidomide tragedy was at last revealed, five years after
the drug had first been introduced in West Germany under the name
Contergan and one year after Merrell submitted it to the FDA for
approval under the name **Kevadon**.

It is estimated that over 8,000 children were born with birth defects as
a result of exposure to thalidomide.[39] Besides having missing or stunted
limbs, many children suffered deafness, visual problems, heart defects,
spinal abnormalities, and urinary-tract complications. Those babies are
now young adults, and their painful existence is a constant reminder that
drugs can occasionally have unpredictable and tragic consequences.

But, you may ask, what does that horrible disaster have to do with
me? After all, thalidomide was never marketed in the United States.
Well, yes and no. Thanks to Dr. Kelsey and her colleagues at FDA,
Kevadon wasn't approved, and we were spared the incredible suffering experienced in Europe. But we're going to let you in on a little-
known fact. Unbeknownst to the FDA, Merrell had provided samples to
over 1,000 physicians in the United States. They in turn had given out
over 2.5 million tablets to approximately 20,000 patients, 624 of whom
were pregnant.[40] While it isn't clear how many victims there were in this
country, Merrell has settled at least ten cases out of court. We were
lucky—but not quite lucky enough.

Lots of pharmaceutical manufacturers and even politicians who express concern about what they consider a drug lag dismiss thalidomide
as a quirk, insisting that another such disaster is impossible. And rather
than praise the regulators for preventing untold suffering, they often
criticize the agency for still using this incident as an excuse to perpetuate
bureaucratic indecisiveness. In the past, FDA staffers responded to this
kind of attack by insisting that it took time to carefully evaluate a new
drug application. If you want to detect rare but dangerous side effects,
you sometimes have to be patient.

The untold story of practolol is a perfect example. Here was a heart
drug with great promise. Introduced in Great Britain in 1970, it apparently offered a triple whammy—control of irregular heartbeats, relief
from angina pain, and a lowering of blood pressure. Practolol had an
advantage over its rival **Inderal** (propranolol) in that it did not affect
the lungs and could be used by patients with asthma. Physicians were
enthusiastic. But four years later doctors began to realize that something

was dreadfully wrong. Some people who were given practolol suffered severe skin rashes, hearing loss, permanent visual damage, and serious inflammation of the lungs, heart, and abdominal cavity. At least 1,000 patients were seriously harmed.[41] An editorial in the *British Medical Journal* tried to rationalize the problem.

> The practolol syndrome was not detected until the cumulative experience with the drug had totalled one million patient years. This delay occurred because practitioners were not aware of the syndrome and so were not looking for it or recognising it. Furthermore, wide-scale use of a drug seems to be necessary before unexpected and unpredictable adverse reactions can be recognised.[42]

This surprisingly candid confession by the medical profession really nails the problem. When side effects of any medication haven't been "officially" recognized, doctors quite often discount patients' complaints as being unrelated to the drugs they are taking.

Fortunately for people in the United States, practolol never made it across the Atlantic. We were spared another tragedy because of the "drug lag." But the times they were a-changin', and as pressure to speed up the drug-approval process mounted, our luck began to run out.

Selacryn Strikes Out

In May 1979 the Smith, Kline & French pharmaceutical firm announced with great fanfare the introduction of an important new medicine for high blood pressure. **Selacryn** (ticrynafen) was a diuretic with a difference. Unlike other "water pills," such as **HydroDIURIL** (hydrochlorothiazide) and **Lasix** (furosemide), which raise uric-acid levels, **Selacryn** actually lowered this substance in the body. That might not sound like such a big deal, but for hundreds of thousands of gout victims with high blood pressure the new drug represented a real breakthrough. High uric-acid levels can bring on a painful attack in joints or even cause kidney stones in susceptible individuals.

The FDA thought the new medicine sounded pretty exciting and gave it priority status. Instead of being subjected to the usual three or four years of review, **Selacryn** zipped through on the "fast track" in eighteen months, partly because it had been marketed in France for three years with no evident safety problems.

Shortly after Americans started taking the new blood-pressure medicine, however, reports of serious liver damage started cropping up. Instead of forwarding this critical information to the FDA within 15 days as required by law, SmithKline apparently chose to delay notifying the

agency of these cases for months. This lag cost Dorothy Beaseley her
life. In an interview for "60 Minutes", reporter Mike Wallace questioned
the physician who had prescribed **Selacryn** for her high blood pressure without any inkling that it could be dangerous.

> MR. WALLACE: Could Mrs. Beaseley's death have been pre-
> vented?

> DOCTOR: I think it could have been.
> MR. WALLACE: How?
> DOCTOR: With earlier knowledge that this drug could cause
> liver damage. Just one month, I think, would have saved
> her life. Unfortunately, when she had a relapse there was
> no bringing her back.

> MR. WALLACE: Didn't [it] occur to you when you put her back
> on the drug after she came out of Lakeshore Hospital that
> maybe Selacryn was the culprit?

> DOCTOR: Absolutely not because I went back and read the
> literature. Nothing. Nothing in the literature that was avail-
> able to United States physicians. . . .

> MR. WALLACE: Do you feel no sense of personal responsibility
> in all this?

> DOCTOR: Yes, you have to feel a sense of personal responsibility.
> There's loss of a life and it's devastating. It's a tragedy. It's
> a tragedy to the family, to the children, to the husband, to
> the brothers and sisters of this young woman. Under differ-
> ent circumstances she may not have received this drug.[43]

Dorothy Beaseley died on January 30, 1980—two weeks after
Selacryn was abruptly pulled from the market. Unfortunately the
banning of the drug came too late to save her life. While Dorothy
Beaseley's doctor may have felt some responsibility for her death, Smith-
Kline must also have felt accountable. The drug company settled with
her family "in the $350,000 range."[44] But Dorothy Beaseley's death
was by no means the only tragedy resulting from **Selacryn**. When
the dust settled, the FDA had reports of almost 1,000 adverse reactions,
"60 of them deaths."[45]

Selacryn caused a hepatitislike reaction. People became jaundiced
and weak, they became nauseous and lost weight. A doctor who
himself took the drug described his reaction to a single pill.

> I had a shaking chill, a temperature, a bad stomach. I just
> felt absolutely terrible. I was totally beat. I had such lack of

energy that I could hardly lift a razor to my face to shave and
if a patient had told me that I would have found it hard to
believe. I had never been ill before in my life.[46]

When this physician contacted SmithKline to report his side effects
and ask if they could be related to **Selacryn,** the company apparently denied "that his problem had anything to do with the drug,"[47]
despite the fact that there were reports of liver damage even before
Selacryn was marketed. It was this kind of stonewalling that delayed removal of this medication and probably resulted in unnecessary
deaths.

It also got the company into hot water. In June 1984 federal prosecutors followed the FDA's recommendation and took the unprecedented
step of filing criminal charges against the company and four of its
executives. After a three-year investigation, the prosecutors became convinced that people at SmithKline had known of many instances of liver
damage, but failed to alert the FDA or the public to the hazards the drug
posed.

Apparently, the company first heard of the drug's link to liver problems in French patients as early as May of 1979, the very same month it
introduced **Selacryn** in the United States. It's shocking to think that
Dorothy Beaseley and others like her might still be alive if the FDA had
received this information promptly.

By now we would have expected critics of the drug lag to keep their
mouths shut, but they're still yipping, even though Americans are beginning to catch up with their European counterparts. Instead of suffering
for lack of new medicines, we are beginning to die because of them.

The Oraflex Calamity

And the trend continues. On April 20, 1982, the Eli Lilly Company
proudly announced FDA approval for the marketing of **Oraflex** (benoxaprofen), "a new direction in antiarthritic therapy." The official press
release stressed the safety of this once-a-day drug. The company
emphasized that **Oraflex** had been "well accepted" in the United Kingdom since 1980 and that it was also available in Denmark, West Germany,
South Africa, and Spain. A blitz of radio, television, and newspaper
reports made the drug appear to be much better than existing arthritis
drugs. One authority on medical breakthroughs, for example, praised
Oraflex on a popular radio show.

It has three amazing properties. First, it is much more potent
a pain-killer than aspirin. Two, you can take it in large quantities and there's no gastrointestinal bleeding. . . . But three,

and most miraculous of all, benoxaprofen seems to actually reverse the joint damage caused by arthritis inflammation.[48]

Although there was little if any evidence to support such enthusiasm, guess what happens when that kind of announcement is made in print or on radio or TV? Right! Thirty million arthritis victims perk up and pay attention. Patients all over the country started demanding that their doctors give them a prescription for this wonderful "breakthrough medicine." After only 21 days on the market, 64,000 **Oraflex** prescriptions were filled, to the tune of $1,300,000.[49] After a little more than two months that number had climbed dramatically, and almost 500,000 people had tried the new drug. Then the shit hit the fan!

In May of 1982—about the same time Lilly was patting itself on the back for the successful launch of **Oraflex**—British physicians were reporting severe side effects and some deaths associated with the drug.[50-53] People were dying from liver or kidney damage, gastrointestinal bleeding, or perforated ulcers. On August 4, 1982, the drug was outlawed in Britain, and on August 5, after pressure from the FDA, the Eli Lilly Company agreed to withdraw the drug from the United States market. The toll in Britain after almost two years on the market: 4,000 adverse reactions and 96 deaths.[54] After less than three months in the United States: untold adverse reactions and 43 deaths.

What makes this story even more incredible is that some Eli Lilly executives knew about serious adverse reactions, including at least 29 deaths, before the drug was approved for marketing in the United States. And the company failed to tell the FDA about the problem.

The gory details leaked out later. *"Sixty Minutes"* did one of its inimitable hatchet jobs on the way the whole **Oraflex** scandal was handled. Mike Wallace introduced the story.

MR. WALLACE: **Oraflex was going to make millions for the Eli Lilly Company. That was in May of 1982. But what the American public didn't know while it was being bombarded with praise for Oraflex was that there were some dark secrets in the drug's recent past. That while some were hailing it as a wonder drug in the United States, there were people overseas who were cursing it. Like Kathleen Grasham of Norwich, England. Her mother, Grace, took Oraflex on the advice of her doctor. She was 82 years old and the fittest 82-year-old he had ever seen. But after five days on Oraflex, she suddenly began to fail.**

What happened?

MS. GRASHAM: **Well, there were the digestive disturbances first and they were really quite serious and the next day an** absolutely appalling skin rash and a very high fever. She said "It's very difficult to describe. I feel as if I'm on fire all over." Then on the day following that, she became confused and she was admitted to the hospital with suspected renal failure.

MR. WALLACE: And how long after that did she pass away?

MS. GRASHAM: Six days.

That early warning of danger came in February 1981, over a year before **Oraflex** hit the United States market. It wasn't the only red flag; Dr. Hugh Taggart, a physician in Belfast, Northern Ireland, watched five patients die, all within the space of a few months.

MR. WALLACE: Is there any doubt in your mind, Dr. Taggart, that it was the Oraflex that caused the deaths of these individuals?

DR. TAGGART: Absolutely no doubt at all. This was a particularly unique and unusual damage to the liver particularly, which has not been described for other drugs. Some other drugs do cause liver jaundice, but not exactly the same as this particular drug.

MR. WALLACE: So it was the Oraflex, you are satisfied?

DR. TAGGART: Yes.[55]

Dr. Taggart did not sit on this information. He told the British equivalent of our FDA, he told the British subsidiary of the Eli Lilly Company, and he started writing up his cases and concerns for publication in the *British Medical Journal*.[56] But while drug-company executives back in Indianapolis were fully aware of these disturbing developments in Europe, they said nothing to the United States Food and Drug Administration.

Eli Lilly officials maintain to this day that they did nothing wrong—either legally or ethically. The company has steadfastly insisted that no reporting to the FDA was necessary because the deaths that occurred in Europe were to be "expected" from drugs like **Oraflex**.[57] Because I was shocked when I learned that Lilly "expected" so many people to die, I got in touch with an FDA official to get the agency's opinion. When I told him that Lilly still maintained that its drug was no different from any of the other arthritis agents, he was caught off guard. He responded that "between you and me, it takes a lot of balls to say that."

Another argument the Indianapolis pharmaceutical manufacturer has used in its defense is that officials didn't have to report overseas deaths because they were the responsibility of a foreign subsidiary. And that, furthermore, United States regulations don't require notifying the FDA of deaths of non-American patients under some conditions. A different FDA spokesman had an equally candid reply to this tack: "Horseshit!"

It will probably be up to the courts to decide who, if anyone, was at fault. There has been talk of a probe by the Justice Department and of a grand-jury investigation. As of this writing, one civil lawsuit has been settled. A jury in Columbus, Georgia, "found Eli Lilly responsible for the death of an 81-year-old woman" and awarded "$6 million in damages to the woman's son."[58] According to the company, approximately 250 other individuals or families have also filed lawsuits.

The final chapter in the **Oraflex** disaster was written a few days before Christmas of 1983. That's when Eli Lilly notified the FDA and the 534 doctors still authorized to prescribe **Oraflex** experimentally that the drug was associated with an "increased incidence" of liver cancer in mice. At that point the company told physicians to immediately stop providing **Oraflex** to anyone and gave up all hope of ever bringing the drug back to the marketplace. A story that started with a very big bang in the spring of 1982 thus ended with scarcely a whimper over a year and a half later.

Are you starting to wonder how a drug like this gets on the market *before* all the studies have been completed? You're not the only one. Representative Ted Weiss, chairman of the House subcommittee that monitors the FDA, has suggested:

> **Oraflex is but one of numerous medicines that the agency has released to the market in the face of warnings from its own scientists "that they had not been adequately tested for their cancer-causing potential."[59]**

Enough already! How does all this happen? How do we end up with a thalidomide tragedy, a **Selacryn** problem, and a crisis like the one caused by **Oraflex** if tens of millions of dollars are spent testing each new medication for years and years before it is marketed? If the FDA has been doing such a good job that it's been accused of overregulating the drug industry, how is it that Americans are still vulnerable to drug disasters?

For one thing, drug companies don't always tell the feds everything they know. Dr. Sidney Wolfe, Director of the consumerist Health Research Group, discovered not only that Eli Lilly kept foreign information from United States authorities, but that the company also kept United States data from British regulators.

> **It is now clear that Lilly Vice-President, Dr. Ian Sheddon, lied in a May 29, 1982 article in the *British Medical Journal* in which he stated categorically that "no jaundice" had been seen in the 2200 patients given the drug in the U.S. prior to marketing.**

We have obtained summaries of 5 cases of jaundice in women in the U.S. which occurred *prior to approval of Oraflex.*

Not only did these people have jaundice caused by Oraflex, but four had simultaneously developed serious kidney failure.

It is quite likely that Oraflex would have been banned even earlier in the U.K. had this information about the U.S. cases of jaundice and kidney damage been promptly brought to the attention of the British Government drug authorities.[60]

But, you may wonder, why didn't the FDA discover this problem independently? Most people believe that the Food and Drug Administration actually does extensive safety research on all new drugs itself. The truth is, though, that the agency does virtually no drug testing of its own. Instead, it relies almost exclusively on data supplied by the drug companies. As a result, every medication sold should be labeled:

"CAUTION: THIS PRODUCT WAS APPROVED BY THE FDA ON THE BASIS OF TESTS IT DID NOT CONDUCT, DATA IT DID NOT ANALYZE, AND RESULTS IT CANNOT GUARANTEE. YOU ARE PART OF AN ONGOING DRUG EXPERIMENT."

Dedicated workers at the FDA do scrutinize each new drug application carefully. But they have to rely on the basic data supplied by the manufacturer. What the FDA doesn't know can hurt you.

Did Dishonest Doctors Test Your Drug?

Before a new medicine can be given to people, it first has to be administered to laboratory animals to make sure it doesn't cause birth defects or result in some other horrendous side effect. A drug company has two choices—it can do the work itself, or it can contract with any of several hundred private labs that specialize in this sort of "preclinical" research.

With tens of millions of dollars riding on the outcome, there can't help but be pressure to "clean up" the results. And sometimes companies give in to that temptation. The largest of the private labs, IBT— Industrial Bio-Test—was one of the worst offenders. The FDA first became nervous about IBT's research reports when an agency pathologist, Dr. Adrian Gross, happened to review a new drug application at random. What he found led to a scandal that has shaken the whole pharmaceutical-testing process to its foundation.

When government scientists began examining the company's original data, they discovered reports that had been doctored in the crudest ways. Studies were cut short, and tumors and animal deaths were underreported.

Dr. Gross found "that a great portion of the animals weren't examined at all. They were too rotten. When they died, instead of doing an autopsy, IBT just let them decompose."[61] In drug-safety studies, dead rats can tell many tales, but not if you let them lie around too long.

Even more incredible, rats that had presumably died in one study were listed as participating in a later one. Dr. Gross viewed this discrepancy with a jaundiced eye and wrote, "We do not really believe in animals coming back to life after death."[62]

IBT was hired to test both over-the-counter and prescription drugs, as well as compounds used in herbicides, insecticides, food additives, cosmetics, water treatment chemicals, soaps, and other household chemicals. We now know that a large number of these tests were either invalid or altered. It's shocking that many compounds still in use today were approved on the basis of fraudulent data. Both the EPA (Environmental Protection Agency) and the FDA are caught in a bind because they aren't even sure which chemicals need further testing to tell whether they are safe.

And the IBT data isn't the only problem facing the FDA. "Irregularities" have been found in the research of other labs as well. But even more frightening is the fraud that has been uncovered in drug studies on human test subjects. As Dr. Edward G. Feldmann of the American Pharmaceutical Association has pointed out, clinical drug testing is basically a "cottage industry."

> **Even the largest companies conduct very little clinical research themselves. Traditionally, such testing is done by independent clinical investigators affiliated with universities, or teaching hospitals, or operating as very small testing laboratories.**[63]

At least 14,000 doctors around the country have been hired by pharmaceutical manufacturers to test drugs on their patients. While I have little doubt that most physicians are conscientious and honest, there is proof that some are not.

Take the case of Dr. Ron Smith. He was a clinical investigator for a number of major companies including Sandoz, Lederle, Upjohn, and Marion Laboratories. According to the magazine *Mother Jones*, he occasionally practiced the "flush method" of drug research—apparently "hundreds of capsules had been 'tested' in the Smith toilet."[64]

Dr. Ron Smith isn't the only one. When FDA investigators called another physician, Dr. James Scheiner, for a routine inspection of his drug-testing records, he told an incredible story. In the two weeks between the notification letter and the FDA's actual visit, he said, his office had been broken into no less than three times.

During the first break-in, the doctor said, vandals had thrown most of the pertinent drug study records into a whirlpool bath; they were so water soaked, he said, he had to throw them away. In the second break-in, he told them, a fire had started mysteriously in the X-ray room, destroying other documents. During a third break-in, Scheiner said, he had been attacked, struck in the head with a piece of pipe, and suffered a laceration of the scalp and cerebral concussion.

The investigators checked the story with the police department, which expressed skepticism that the break-ins had occurred. For one thing, their investigation indicated that Scheiner had been the last person seen to leave the X-ray room before the fire, and it started about six minutes after he left. Further, police analysis of the piece of steel identified as the weapon used to attack the doctor revealed only one palm print—Scheiner's.[65]

When the FDA's investigators examined the data that had somehow survived these "accidents," they discovered "serious discrepancies—differences in patients' ages, sexes, diagnoses, and the medications they were taking (which could have skewed the test results). Most of the patients contacted for statements denied they had participated in any drug studies."[66]

Then there is the case of a gynecologist, Harvey Levin. Over four years he was paid $140,000 to test drugs for Bristol-Meyers, McNeil, Ortho, Sterling, and Pennwalt. He was charged with 19 counts of falsifying clinical-test results and submitting false data to the FDA through the drug manufacturers. Dr. Levin pleaded guilty to 2 of the 19 counts as part of a plea-bargaining arrangement and received a sentence of one year and one day in jail.[67] One of the drugs he "tested" was **Zomax** (zomepirac), a painkiller that was later removed from the market because of reports that it had caused some life-threatening allergic reactions.

Some of the clinical investigators who have been caught fudging data have been prominent researchers, highly respected in their fields. Dr. Wilbert S. Aronow is a heart specialist who had been an outside adviser to the FDA for six years. He also served as a consultant to other federal and state agencies and advised the American Heart Association and the American Medical Association's Department of Drugs. He is a past president of the Veterans' Administration Association of Cardiologists and has published over 200 articles in medical journals. Dr. Aronow is a heavy-weight.

He also tested drugs. According to one FDA official, he carried out a "vast number" of studies, and some were "heavily relied upon by industry in support of claims of efficacy."[68] But apparently someone at the FDA became suspicious when Aronow's results looked "too good to be true.''[69] After reviewing Dr. Aronow's research on **Minipress** (prazosin) and four additional drugs, the FDA noted:

> **"Aronow discarded 'most of the raw data' while failing 'to maintain adequate and accurate case histories.' It also cited 'serious discrepancies' between hospital records and his sometimes handwritten case reports."[70]**

Investigators found that records were lost, unavailable, and in some cases, unbelievable. Apparently Dr. Aronow did nothing illegal, since no court case was filed, but the FDA did bar him from future testing of drugs on humans.

No one really knows how many physicians who perform clinical investigations have fudged their data. Fraud and carelessness may be isolated events, or they might be just the tip of the iceberg. One reporter interviewed Mary Miers, a staff official at the National Institutes of Health. She said that before 1980 phony research appeared rarely, with cases of fraud coming up "perhaps once every other year."[71] But more recently such cases "are cropping up so often they can't be dealt with as isolated events."[72]

What is alarming is that even in the face of these cases, the FDA proposed relaxed drug-approval requirements. In the new spirit of cooperation between government and industry a major effort was initiated to get new drugs on the market faster.[73-75] Drug companies would be allowed to substitute summaries for the complete data they used to submit, and some products would be cleared solely on the basis of foreign research. While I have no doubt that these changes may speed up approval, they could make it even harder for an understaffed FDA to prevent abuses and to track down dishonest doctors and labs. As a result, drugs of questionable safety and effectiveness may continue to be approved for marketing.

According to the Naderesque Health Research Group, a dramatic drop in regulatory action has already become evident.[76]

> **There has been a 66.4% decrease in total FDA law enforcement actions (regarding food, drugs, medical devices and other FDA regulated products). . . .**
>
> **This drastic decrease in government policing of the industries FDA is supposed to regulate is an open invitation to drug companies and food companies to violate Federal law, thus risking the health and lives of 230 million Americans.[77]**

It may be years before the damage is undone, and even then things may never be the same at the FDA. The blush is off the rose . . . the virgin has been violated. This is not to say the agency was ever perfect.

Goodness knows I have knocked the feds over and over for not living up to their responsibility to protect the public from unsafe and ineffective drugs. But not long ago the Food and Drug Administration was respected for its independence. Science, not politics, was the basis for decision making.

Now, because the rules have been changed, it is highly unlikely that we can ever return to the "good old days," when the FDA did its work without worrying about political influence. In practical terms this means that politicians, not scientists, may very well decide what chemicals are safe. The American public could easily be exposed to potentially hazardous food dyes, preservatives, and medications because the people calling the shots may be less interested in facts and more easily swayed by industry.

Getting Zapped by Zomax

Even if the agency were independent again and drug company research were flawless, rare but dangerous side effects could easily be missed. Few people realize that during the testing phase only a thousand to two thousand volunteers ever receive a new medication. Unless it is relatively common, a serious adverse reaction may not be discovered during the official testing period. Only after a drug has been approved by the FDA and released to an unsuspecting public does the real "testing" get done. It may take years and hundreds of thousands of innocent human guinea pigs before unexpected but life-threatening side effects are finally uncovered.

That's what happened with **Zomax**. It was introduced in October 1980 with a great promise: "**Zomax** is the first nonaddicting pain reliever proven significantly more effective than aspirin and as effective as narcotic painkillers."[78] The manufacturer advertised it as the "After-Aspirin" painkiller, effective against arthritis, headaches, backaches, toothaches, sprains, strains, fractures, sore muscles, and almost anything else that might hurt.

Zomax (zomepirac) sounded fantastic. Here was a drug that was as good as potent narcotics but was not addicting. One physician went so far as to say that "**Zomax** represents the wave of the future," while others used words like "impressive" and "exceptional efficacy and safety."[79] With a send-off like that, it's no wonder the drug caught on fast. Over the next two and a half years over 15 million people received the painkiller. Tens of millions of dollars poured into the Johnson & Johnson Company coffers.

But a cloud started forming on the horizon 17 months after the medication had been approved. That was when the drug company first heard that a patient had died from a severe shocklike reaction called anaphylaxis.

Everything quieted down for a while, but over the next year three more **Zomax**-associated deaths were reported. On March 3, 1983, a Syracuse, New York, television station reported that "a number of area residents had suffered allergic reactions to the drug. One resident, Jack Yoffa, an obstetrician, said he went into shock while driving his car, some 60 seconds after taking **Zomax** for a back ailment."[80]

Publicity was immediate, and the following day—March 4, 1983—the company withdrew **Zomax** from the market admid growing reports that life-threatening allergic reactions were indeed a possibility in susceptible individuals. When the dust settled, the FDA discovered 10 deaths and over 2,000 allergic reactions associated with the "After-Aspirin" pain reliever. Side effects ranged from itchy hives and difficulty breathing to irregular heart beats, swollen body parts, and anaphylactic shock.

All the hoopla forced federal staffers to reexamine earlier data with a fine-tooth comb. In the process they discovered that when low doses of **Zomax** had been given to rats, the animals developed cancer. This finding led some investigators to wonder whether **Zomax** should have ever been approved in the first place.

So why did it take over two years and 15 million patients for the FDA to wake up to the fact that they had a serious problem on their hands? Once again, we are reminded that relatively rare adverse reactions can be hard as hell to catch. Shocking as it may sound, there is no organized system to monitor adverse drug reactions once a medication has been approved by the FDA. The only way serious or unexpected side effects are reported is when physicians voluntarily notify the drug company or the feds—something a lot of doctors are unwilling to do.

There is also a catch-22 here. If a patient reports an unusual side effect—difficulty breathing or a burning sensation in the mouth, say—the doctor looks up the drug in his *PDR* and, finding no reference to such adverse reactions, reassures the patient that they couldn't be caused by the medicine. That gets the doctor off the hook, and leaves the patient concerned and frustrated as to what is producing the unpleasant symptoms.

Even when a doctor does take the time to notify the FDA that he has encountered a serious or unexpected adverse drug reaction, it does not follow that the feds will move at anything other than a snail's pace. Dr. Edward Feldmann, Vice President for Scientific Affairs of the American Pharmaceutical Association, describes what *doesn't* happen after an adverse-reaction report is filed.

> **The apparent general supposition on the part of the public, members of Congress, and many members of the health care professions is that an alarm is immediately triggered, the FDA springs into action, and the drug is immediately whisked off the market. In essence, a reaction is assumed that would be comparable in speed and effectiveness to that expected**

from our national military defense in the event of a nuclear attack.

Obviously, however, even under the best of circumstances and even under ideal operating conditions, no adverse reaction system will work that well.

So, how well is the present FDA system working?

The answer appears to be: Not very well. In fact, rather poorly indeed.[81]

The bottom line here, my friend, is that in a very real sense you're on your own! And never, ever forget that drugs can and do cause serious side effects every day. At the end of 1983 it was reported that "One of every 30 hospitalizations in the United States is the result of an adverse response to medication. In addition, about 30 percent of all medical patients who are in a hospital develop at least one adverse drug reaction, 10 percent of which are life-threatening."[82]

Those numbers should come as no surprise. We are more than ever an overmedicated society. Dr. Hershel Jick, a professor at Boston University and one of the world's most knowledgeable drug epidemiologists, was reported at his eloquent best.

"Exposure to drugs in our country is staggeringly high," he says. As outpatients, 75 million U.S. adults take one or more drugs at least once a week. And the average hospital patient receives 9 or 10 drugs during his stay. Other countries use far less; in Scotland the average is 4.6 drugs per hospital stay. Jick says, "One method of cutting down on adverse reactions is to cut down on drug use."[83]

Surviving the Coming Drug Revolution

By now you're probably swearing to yourself that you'll never take a new medicine as long as you live. In fact, you may be tempted to throw out every pill in the house after all the horror stories we have just related. But you'd be making a *big* mistake. We are on the verge of a drug renaissance that will knock your socks off. Medical treatment will never be the same. For one thing, an incredible number of new drugs is being tested, and these will provide more effective therapy than many existing medications. Better yet, these compounds will have far fewer side effects than do traditional remedies. Even more impressive are the breakthroughs reported from laboratories across the country.

Would you believe that a baldness remedy could be right around the corner? How about help for herpes, a cure for the flu, or a pill to make weight loss effortless? Could you get interested in a drug that might improve your memory as you got older? What about a cure for acne, relief from asthma and allergy, or a medication that would reverse some of the ravages of rheumatoid arthritis? You bet your sweet banana you'd be interested!

And if you were unfortunate enough to have a heart attack, you'd want a drug that could reverse it almost instantly. Wouldn't it be nice to say good-bye to ulcers forever? Millions who suffer from ringing in the ears, an almost unbearable affliction, would celebrate the approval of a drug that could end their constant torment. People with chronic pain would certainly cheer if someone came up with an effective, nonaddicting analgesic. Sound too good to be true? It's not! Some of these drugs are already on your pharmacy's shelves. Others are in the pipeline or are being tested right now.

If all this news seems exciting, keep reading. There's a whole lot more just around the bend. Because of the incredible advances in biotechnology, drug companies are reinventing the wheel. What I mean to say: they have discovered that the body is infinitely complex in its ability to make crucial chemicals to heal itself. Things like interferon, interleukin-2, epidermal growth factor, human growth hormone, endorphins, and countless other biochemicals that occur naturally are being harnessed through the revolutionary processes of genetic engineering. When you cut yourself, it would be great to speed the healing process and make the wound disappear almost overnight; epidermal growth factor and related compounds might make this possible before the decade is over. What's more, if ever there is to be a cure for cancer, researchers are convinced that it will come through modulation of the body's own immune system. And that's just the beginning.

Whoa, Nelly! What the hell is going on here? You're probably asking yourself if Graedon just flipped his lid. One minute I'm warning about the dangers lurking in the drugstore, and the next I'm announcing the coming miracles in medicine. Something smells funny here.

Well, I have to admit that all this does seem complicated and contradictory, but it really isn't as crazy as it sounds. Yes, there are problems because of the new partnership between the FDA and industry; and yes, there have been examples of fraud in testing; and yes, consumers are at greater risk without Patient Package Inserts. But at the same time breakthroughs in understanding have led to an unprecedented number of exciting new medications, many of which will make life easier for millions of Americans.

In the coming chapters we're going to provide you with a candid, up-to-date, in-depth analysis of the advances in drug development. Some items are scary, others impressive. By the time you finish, you may end up knowing as much or more about some of these new medications as your doctor does. Without guidelines, however, taking these new medications could be a little like skipping through a mine field with blinders on. But do not fear, our goal is to make you a knowledgeable consumer, so you can take a greater role in your own health care. There will be lots of tables to help you use these drugs as wisely as possible. Remember, information is your best protection when it comes to swallowing any drug, especially a new one!

References

1. Harris, Patricia. Statement on Patient Package Inserts. *HHS News*, September 10, 1980, p. 1.

2. Ibid, p. 3.

3. Lundquist, James A. "Patients Don't Want to be Bothered with PPIs." *Medical World News* 22(21):95, 1981.

4. Anderson, Susan M. "Some Patients Like PPIs." *Medical World News* 22(25):88, 1981.

5. "FDA Says *PDR* a 'Most Surprising' Source of Patient Information." *PMA Newsletter* 25(34):1–2, 1983.

6. Miller, Roger, W. "Doctors, Patients Don't Communicate." *FDA Consumer* 17(6):6–7, 1983.

7. Morris, Louis A. "A Survey of Patients' Receipt of Prescription Drug Information." *Medical Care* 20:596–605, 1982.

8. "FDA-Sponsored Survey Reports 37 Percent of Physicians Provide Informational Materials." *F-D-C Reports* 45(21):T&G–4, 1983.

9. Cohen, Michael R. "Prescriptions a Health Hazard." *The Sunday Record* (Middletown, N.Y.), Aug. 2, 1981, syndicated by INA.

10. Cohen, Michael R. "Medication Error Reports." *Hospital Pharmacy* 15 (Oct.): 5–25, 1980.

11. Cohen, Michael R. "Error 176—Phisohex at Bedside." *Hospital Pharmacy* 16:398, 1981.

12. Cohen, Michael R. "Error 179—Confusion with Use of Latin Prescription Terminology." *Hospital Pharmacy* 16 (Aug):448, 1981.

13. Cohen, Michael R. "Prescriptions a Health Hazard." INA, Philadelphia, Aug. 2, 1981, syndicated.

14. Ahlquist, D. A., Nelson, R. L., and Calloway, C. W. "Pseudoinsulinoma Syndrome from Inadvertent Tolazamide Ingestion." *Ann. Intern. Meds.* 93:281–282, 1980.

15. Siegelman, Stanley. "Scribbled Rx's By MD's Result in RPh Errors; Many Patients End Up With Wrong Medication." *American Druggist* 187(5):3, 1983.

16. American Druggist Questionnaire. "Verbatim Comments by RPh's About Doctors Who Scribble." *American Druggist* 187(5):64–68, 1983.

17. Ibid.

18. Swinyard, Ewart A. "Principles of Prescription Order Writing and Patient Compliance Instruction." in *Goodman and Gilman's The Pharmacological Basis of Therapeutics* (6th ed.), Goodman, Louis, S. and Gilman, Alfred (eds.) New York: Macmillan, 1980, p. 1663.

19. Rand News Release. "People Read Drug Inserts—Few Return Drugs Because of Warnings." August 25, 1981.

20. Rand Corporation PPI Study. Submitted August 25, 1981, pp. 1–38.

21. *HHS News* pp. 81–20. Dec. 22, 1982.

22. In Brief. "AMA's Patient Medication Instructions." *FDC Reports* 45(3):T&G8, 1983.

23. "FDA Finds Some Weaknesses in Physician PPIs." *Drug Topics* 126(18):15–16, 1982.

24. Personal Communication, FDA staffer.

25. "Benzodiazepines." *Patient Medication Instruction Sheet* 012, 1982.

26. Tyrer, Peter. "Gradual Withdrawal of Diazepam After Long-Term Therapy." *Lancet* 1:1402–1406, 1983.

27. "Crout/Finkel Era Ends at Bureau of Drugs." *Washington Drug Letter*. 14(12):1–3, 1982.

28. "Ex-FDA Associate Com. for Public Affairs Wayne Pines Was Not Target of Conservative 'Hit List,' HHS Chief of Staff Newhall Tells House Investigators." *F-D-C Reports* 44(28):9, July 12, 1982.

29. "Ouster of Pines Shows Hayes' Weak Position." *Washington Drug Letter*. 14(20):1–2, 1982.

30. Russell, Cristine. "Some at FDA Fear Politics Tainting Science." *Washington Post* June 6, 1982, p. 1.

31. Personal communication, Wayne Pines, ex-associate commissioner of public affairs at FDA.

32. McFadyen, Richard E. "Thalidomide in America: A Brush with Tragedy." *Clio Medica* 11(2):79–93, 1976.

33. Taussig, Helen F. "The Thalidomide Syndrome." *Scientific American* 207(2):30, 1962.

34. McFadyen. Op. cit., p. 80.

35. Florence, A. Leslie. Letter to the Editor. *British Medical Journal* Dec. 31, 1960, p. 1954.

36. McFadyen. Op. cit., p. 82.

37. The Humphrey Hearings, Part 1, Aug. 13, 1962, p. 75.

38. McFadyen. Op. cit.

39. "$50 Million Mistake." *Newsweek* August 13, 1973, p. 40.

40. McFadyen, op. cit., pp. 85–86.

41. Editorial. "Compensations for Unforeseen Adverse Drug Reactions." *Lancet* vol 1:788, Apr. 9, 1977.

42. Editorial. "Hazards of Non-Practolol Beta Blockers." *British Medical Journal* vol 1 (6060):529, Feb. 26, 1977.

43. "The Bad Drug." Interview with Mike Wallace "60 Minutes". February 7, 1982.

44. Trade and Government Memos. "SmithKline Response to '60 Minutes' Selacryn Broadcast." *FDC Reports* 44(7):T&G6–7, 1982.

45. Walton, Mary. "The Drug SmithKline Doesn't Talk About." *Today Magazine* Sunday, February 21, 1982, p. 30.

46. "The Bad Drug." Op. cit.

47. Ibid.

48. Broadcast Excerpt. "The Bob Grant Show." WMCA-AM Radio, New York. July 27, 1981, 4:13 P.M.

49. "Feldene-Oraflex Successful Launches Show NSAID Market Growth, PDS Says." *F-D-C Reports* 44(25):9, 1982.

50. Taggart, H. M., and Alderdice, J. M. "Fatal Cholestatic Jaundice in Elderly Patients Taking Benoxaprofen." *Brit. Med. J.* 284:1372, 1982.

51. Diffey, H., and Hindson, C. "Side Effects of Benoxaprofen." *Brit. Med. J.* 284:1630, 1982.

52. Goudie, B. M., et al. "Jaundice Associated With the Use of Benoxaprofen." *Lancet* 1:959, 1982.

53. Prescott, L. F., and Leslie, P. J. "Side Effects of Benoxaprofen." *Brit. Med. J.* 284:1783, 1982.

54. Mintz, Morton. "Eli Lilly Tells of Oraflex Link to Cancer in Tests." Los Angeles *Times* (The Washington *Post* News Service) December 24, 1983, Part I, p. 3.

55. "The Oraflex Story." "Sixty Minutes", April 17, 1983.

56. Taggart, op. cit.

57. Mintz, Morton. "Lilly Officials Knew of Deaths Before U.S. Approved Drugs." *Washington Post*, July 22, 1983, p. A8.

58. Richards, Bill. "Jury Rules Eli Lilly Responsible for Death of Woman, 81; Sets Damages at $6 Million." *The Wall Street Journal*, November 22, 1983, p. 7.

59. Mintz, Morton. "Eli Lilly Tells of Oraflex Link to Cancer in Tests." The Los Angeles *Times* (Washington *Post* News Service), December 24, 1983, Part I, p. 3.

60. Letter to John D. Dingell, Chairman of House Committee on Energy & Commerce from Dr. Sidney M. Wolfe and Allen Greenberg of Health Research Group. Aug. 17, 1982, p. 3.

61. Foster, Douglas, and Dowie, Mark. "The Illusion of Safety Part One: Poisoned Research." *Mother Jones* 7(5):38–49, 1982.

62. Ibid.

63. Feldmann, Edward, G. "The 'Weak Link' in New Drug Research." *J. Pharmaceut. Assoc.* 72:463, 1983.

64. Ibid.

65. Ballentine, Carol. "Lies Add Up to a Year in Prison." *FDA Consumer*, May 26, 1982, pp. 26–27.

66. Foster, op. cit.

67. Morris, Betsy. "Doctor Pleads Guilty to Falsifying Results of Painkiller Tests." *The Wall Street Journal*, March 1, 1983, p. 4.

68. Mintz, Morton. "FDA, Citing Phony Evidence, Bars Drug Tests by Researcher." *Washington Post*, March 23, 1983, p. A23.

69. Ibid.

70. Ibid.

71. Ibid.

72. Ibid.

73. Schorr, Burt. "FDA Chief Hayes Says He Wants to Inject More Speed into Drug-Approval Process." *The Wall Street Journal*, Aug. 12, 1981.

74. "FDA Plans to Speed Approval of New Drugs as Early as Spring '82." *The Wall Street Journal*, September 17, 1981.

75. "Panel Recommends that FDA Quicken New-Drug Approval." *The Wall Street Journal*, April 30, 1982.

76. "HRG Blasts 66% Enforcement Drop." *Drug Topics* 126(18):24, 1982.

77. Letter to John D. Dingell, op. cit.

78. Evans, John. "Zomax: Important Advance in Non-Narcotic Pain Relief." Press Release, McNeil Pharmaceuticals.

79. Ibid.

80. "Johnson & Johnson Suffers Second Blow in 5 Months with Zomax's Link to Deaths." *The Wall Street Journal*, March 7, 1983, pp. 7.

81. Feldmann, Edward G. "Adverse Drug Reactions—A Continuing Problem." *J. Pharmaceut. Sci.* 72:585, 1983.

82. Biomedicine. "Bad Reactions for Drugged Country." *Science News* 124:392, 1983.

83. Ibid.

CHAPTER 2

Drug Advertising Is Hazardous to Your Health

Advertising Prescription Drugs: **Clinoril** *Creates Confusion—and Cash* ▪ *The Dog-and-Pony Drug Show:* **Nasalide** *and* **Naprosyn** ▪ **Zovirax***: Help for Herpes is Here* ▪ **Oraflex***: Eli Lilly's House of Cards Comes Crashing Down* ▪ *The New and Improved Medicine Show* ▪ *FTC: Does It Stand for Federal Trade Commission or Forsaking The Consumer?* ▪ *Doctors Buckle Under Badgering* ▪ *Dealing Drugs to Doctors* ▪ *Too Much Medicine.*

By now we've scared you with tales of drug disasters and tantalized you with promises of medical breakthroughs. Perhaps you're feeling a little bit confused; or maybe you're wondering what the big deal is. Common sense suggests that if you want to avoid serious and unexpected side effects from some new drug, just don't be the first one on your block to try it. Let someone else be a guinea pig for a few months. Once the dust has settled and doctors have had a chance to evaluate the new medicine— then you can sign up.

Sounds good; but believe me, it's a lot easier said than done. If you begin to go bald at the age of 27 and your professional and social life starts to suffer, you might be more than willing to say damn the torpedoes, full speed ahead; any drug that promises to restore your glorious locks will probably be met with open arms. Or what if you suffer from arthritis? Anyone who has a hard time getting out of bed in the morning because of stiff joints will be very interested in the latest anti-inflammatory agent. Anything that's supposed to give greater relief immediately captures headlines and eager volunteers.

Advertising Prescription Drugs

And therein, dear reader, lies a tale. Once upon a time, not so very long ago, the makers of prescription medications called themselves "ethical drug firms" to distinguish themselves from peddlers of snake-oil nostrums. They prided themselves on their promotional practices, which targeted only the doctors, who would be prescribing their medicines. Until recently no drug-company executive in his right mind would have considered promoting prescription drugs directly to consumers; such a method didn't seem logical or cost-effective. In fact, most manufacturers were tight-lipped, preferring to keep a low profile. Inquiries from the press about new prescription products were often met with a standard "no comment."

But the whole situation has changed almost overnight. Already faced with a barrage of advertising claims about what makes laundry whiter, whether butter is better, or which deodorant is driest, patients now get the chance to ponder if **Zovirax** is indeed the answer for the discomfort of herpes, if **Rufen** can help their arthritis, or if **Nasalide** will subdue their stuffy nose.

What's unique about this situation, of course, is that while you can run right out and buy a box of Whito detergent or a can of No-Drip deodorant, you can't stroll to the pharmacy and request a tube of **Zovirax**. The advertising is aimed at you, but the *prescription* still has to be written by your doctor. And he may not be particularly anxious to hear a layman's advice on what to prescribe.

Merck Sharp & Dohme was one of the first major firms to break with tradition by taking a prescription drug public. When the company received approval in 1978 to market the new arthritis medicine, **Clinoril** (sulindac), it embarked on an ignoble experiment. Not content merely to take out ads in medical journals and arm its sales reps with samples for doctors, a media blitz was arranged to inform the public about this so-called breakthrough medicine. Company officials confessed that they themselves were amazed at the incredible interest shown by the press. In fact, they were a little too successful.

Patients who heard about this new "wonder" drug started contacting their doctors. But Merck had blundered badly. The press releases for public consumption were distributed even before the company had notified physicians about the new arthritis medicine. Doctors were furious. Nasty letters to the editors of medical journals expressed an outrage rarely seen in such stodgy publications as the *New England Journal of Medicine*.

> Recently, a new non-steroidal anti-inflammatory agent produced by Merck Sharp and Dohme was promoted heavily to the public via the media of television, radio, and newspaper. Most physicians, including rheumatologists, were not prepared for the onslaught of telephone calls and patient inquiries concerning this new drug, Sulindac. Most physicians practicing primary medicine had no knowledge of this compound. . . .
>
> Patients with arthritis have enough difficulty dealing with widespread quackery available to them in this day and age.

> **They should not have to be exposed to "blitz" attacks by drug companies.** [1]

You would think that with that kind of outrage, the executives at Merck would rethink their promotional policies. The last thing a drug company wants to do is alienate doctors. But then they saw the bottom line: **Clinoril** took off like a shot. Although the drug offered little if any improvement over existing arthritis medications, it quickly outpaced rivals like **Naprosyn** (naproxen), **Nalfon** (fenoprofen), and **Tolectin** (tolmetin). Doctors may have been furious, but their anger didn't stop them from writing prescriptions. During its first year on the market there were more new prescriptions filled for **Clinoril** than for any other arthritis medicine available.

Bolstered by this kind of success, the folks at Merck decided to take their advertising even more directly to the consumer. This time they were pushing **Pneumovax,** a pneumonia vaccine for older people. The ad appeared in a number of newspapers, *Modern Maturity Magazine,* and *The Reader's Digest:* "Over 65? Under medicare, you are now eligible for protection against a potentially serious health hazard." Recognizing that everyone loves to clip coupons, the reader was encouraged to "Tear out this coupon and show it to your physician."

> **Dear Doctor:**
>
> **Please inform this patient whether or not he or she is an appropriate candidate for vaccination with Pneumovax (Pneumococcal Vaccine, Polyvalent, MSD) under Medicare coverage.**

Not surprisingly, quite a few "dear doctors" were shocked to find coupon-waving patients demanding a pneumonia vaccine. But once again the program worked—and to drug-company executives, that *is* what really matters.

When there was little demand for the company's expensive new hepatitis-B vaccine (**Heptavax-B**), Merck took a different tack. Recognizing that the gay community might offer a worthwhile target, the company offered to bankroll the American Liver Foundation in an "unusual ad effort" at arm's length, so to speak. Full-page spreads appeared in 87 magazines under the bold headline, "**An open letter to the gay community on hepatitis B.**" The text announced the availability of the vaccine and encouraged its use, signing off with, "This message is brought to you as a public service by The American Liver Foundation." What the ad didn't say was that it had been paid for by Merck with a grant of $200,000 to the foundation. [2]

Merck's success wasn't lost on the competition. Other drug companies may have been critical of such commercialism, but they started thinking about doing much the same thing. Using another advertising gimmick designed to appeal to consumers, Boots Pharmaceuticals followed the lead of the appliance and automobile industries by offering a rebate on each bottle of their prescription antiarthritic drug **Rufen** (ibuprofen). A little tag on each bottle carried a message.

> **Dear Consumer:**
>
> **Boots Pharmaceuticals, with your physician and pharmacist, would like to help lower the cost of your medication.**
>
> **When you fill out and send in this coupon you will receive a $1.50 rebate, and Boots will contribute 25¢ to arthritis research.**[3]

Not content with a mere rebate, the president of Boots Pharmaceuticals, John Byer, decided to go on a 15-city publicity tour. This media marathon was unabashedly designed to "generate lay press coverage of the company's consumer rebate program."[4]

Once again physicians were indignant. Dr. William O'Brien responded to this direct-to-the-consumer promotion in the pages of the *New England Journal of Medicine*.

> **Boots' promotional kit clearly suggests that if this campaign succeeds, other drugs will be promoted by similar means. Unfortunately, when the lure of rebates to patients, rather than therapeutic appropriateness, becomes the basis for prescribing, any gains are much more likely to be commercial than medical.**[5]

The Dog-and-Pony Drug Show

Little did Dr. O'Brien realize how right he was. Drug-company executives were eager to hop on a bandwagon that was rapidly gathering speed.

Lyn Christenson, Manager of Communications Programs for the Syntex corporation, has admitted that when it comes to marketing drugs "a new day has dawned—all the rules were changed after **Clinoril**." When Syntex Laboratories launched its new allergy spray, **Nasalide** (flunisolide), the company hired a public-relations firm to put together a fancy brochure for distribution to the media. But that wasn't all. It recruited a physician, Dr. Miriam Stoppard, to crisscross the country making appearances on Syntex's behalf. Dr. Stoppard wasn't just any old doctor; she was extremely attractive and delightfully British. Better yet, she had the kind of media experience that would make a PR firm drool.

> **Physician, business executive, author, journalist, television reporter, and commentator—Miriam Stoppard, 44, retired**

from active business life July 31, 1980, as Managing Director of Syntex Pharmaceuticals Ltd., Maidenhead, England.[6]

Dr. Stoppard had already proved herself once before for Syntex. During a previous tour of the United States she had "interviews with over 100 print and broadcast reporters in 20 U.S. cities about [the] recent discovery of the cause and effective treatment for painful menstruation." Not surprisingly, Syntex had a vested interest in this topic too, since one of its hottest drugs, **Naprosyn,** is one of those "effective treatments."

This kind of road show scares me. Although Syntex officials insist that they are "informing, not promoting" when they send out Dr. Stoppard to appear on radio and television, the line between the two intentions is a fine one. Nonprofessionals may not realize that the charming, informative physician who is bringing them up to date on the latest allergy treatment is actually representing a drug company with a hot new product to sell.

Another example of how "all the rules have changed" came soon after the Burroughs Wellcome Company received approval to market **Zovirax,** a prescription drug for herpes infections. The company itself did no direct-to-consumer advertising, but drugstores did. One large pharmacy chain took out full page newspaper ads with the headline: **Help for Herpes is Here.** Another chain bannered the headline. **New break thru for Herpes sufferers.** Almost as an aside (in much smaller print) the ad mentioned that **Zovirax** is "available on written or oral prescription only."

When contacted about the ad heralding that "Help for Herpes is Here," Burroughs Wellcome at first claimed to be "shocked!" and not responsible. But after due consideration an executive of the company changed his tune.

> We believe that prescription drugs should be advertised to health care professionals, but we find ourselves in a changing environment and we also must respond to increasing demands of consumers and the media for information about health care products. We are in favor of providing accurate information to the consumer, and pharmacy ads like this one may contribute to this effort.[7]

Now that sounds pretty reasonable. Everyone is for accurate information about health-care products. But accuracy in advertising is not something drug companies have been known for. All you have to do is turn on the tube to see commercials that are barely believable. It doesn't matter much whether the products are supposed to heal hemorrhoids, correct constipation, or cure the common cold, the airwaves are filled with misleading and deceptive promises.

If you're like me, you would probably prefer not to watch someone complaining about problems of gas or bad breath. But at least those are minor discomforts, and we have all learned to live with such silliness on television. Are you ready for prescription-drug advertising on the tube? Can you imagine some actor simulating a heart attack and begging for **Brand X**? How about somebody doing a "before and after" sequence to show the wonders of **Threeblindmycin** in curing the clap?

As ridiculous as these examples are, prescription-drug advertising on TV is already occurring in some parts of the country and will no doubt spread like crabgrass. One ad that has been aired on the Cable Health Network makes a pitch for a new form of nitroglycerin from the Ciba-Geigy Corporation.

Transderm-Nitro: Fishing

Video	Audio
Long shot boat on pond, two men are fishing	ANNCR: Doctor, have you ever wondered what happens after you prescribe medication? SOUND: gentle lapping of water, interrupted by:
Cut to closeup watch on wrist as man's hand clicks off the alarm	SOUND: Bleep, bleep of alarm wrist watch. 1ST MAN: (Quietly): You're scaring the fish.
Two shot	2ND MAN: Time for my nitroglycerin pill.
First man pats his chest *Show patch on chest here*	1ST MAN: You take those? 2ND MAN: Well, what else is there to take? 1ST MAN: Well, my doctor just prescribed Transderm-Nitro, nitroglycerin *patches*. Look.
First man pats his chest *Show patch on chest here*	ANNCR: Doctor, your angina patients don't have to be tied to the clock.
Closeup product on man's chest	ANNCR: Now there's Transderm-Nitro. A simple 10-second application helps protect your angina patient, with 24-hour sustained blood levels. . . .

Video	Audio
Cut to medium shot. First man playing a fish	With Transderm-Nitro, there's less concern about noncompliance, because they're more likely to use it. . . .
Closeup Patch 5	Transderm-Nitro, NITROGLY-CERIN—from CIBA.[8]

Now I have to admit that this kind of TV ad is relatively benign. Nevertheless, it does make me nervous. The potential for abuse is incredible. Consider this humorous view of the future brought to you by the one and only Art Buchwald. The scene: a doctor's office. A patient is badgering his physician to provide a prescription for an imaginary drug called **Carraflex**.

> PATIENT: **I don't know, Doc. I respect you, but Orson Welles knows a lot about medicine. And Robert Young has played a doctor on TV for years. And as far as Ricardo Montalban goes, I'm not one of those people who think a guy is a lousy M.D. just because he speaks with an accent. Besides, Carraflex sponsors the L.A. Dodgers baseball team and I want to show my gratitude.**

> DOCTOR: **You're going to have to get another doctor if you want a different prescription.**

> PATIENT: **That's what they said in the TV commercial. "If your M.D. is not clued in on the miraculous medical benefits of Carraflex, find yourself a doctor who is." Then they gave a toll-free number for people to call to find the name of the doctor nearest you who is willing to prescribe Carraflex.[9]**

Buchwald's column is funny, of course, but this goofy scenario would never fly in the real world. No "ethical" pharmaceutical manufacturers would ever push prescription drugs as aggressively as the makers of OTC (over-the-counter) remedies do. At least let's hope not, but don't count on it.

When Eli Lilly launched its hot new arthritis drug **Oraflex,** it pulled out all the stops with an "estimated $12 million advertising blitz."[10] The public relations firms prepared a dog-and-pony show that put all previous publicity extravaganzas to shame. First, they sent out over 6,000 slick press kits, each containing an 8 × 10 glossy photograph and brochures to suggest that **Oraflex** was something really special—"A new direction in antiarthritic therapy." The impression was given that the drug was more effective than other anti-inflammatory agents.

Studies conducted with the drug in laboratory animals indicate that it may work differently from other drugs currently
available for arthritis. One of the ways Oraflex appears to
work is by inhibiting the migration of certain white cells in
the blood stream to the sites of arthritis inflammation. In
animal studies, Oraflex has been shown to arrest the development of arthritis.[11]

Equally important to arthritis victims was the suggestion that the drug
was safer than other nonsteroidal anti-inflammatory agents—"It has a low
rate of serious gastrointestinal side effects sometimes associated with
antiarthritis medication."[12]

The press kits were just the appetizer. The main course was served up
at a huge press conference at the Waldorf-Astoria Hotel in New York.
According to one observer, "Lilly officials played up Oraflex's possible
role in reversing the effects of arthritis, leaving many reporters with the
mistaken impression that it was the only compound with such benefits."[13]

Hundreds of newspapers around the country heralded the arrival of
this new "wonder" drug. Some writers went so far overboard as to
imply that Oraflex might be an arthritis cure. Not to be outdone, hundreds of radio and television stations joined the bandwagon. And the
networks swallowed the bait, too. The "ABC Evening News" offered the
following.

Medical news now. A breakthrough in the treatment of
arthritis, this nation's number one crippling disease affecting
some thirty-one million Americans. While there's still no cure,
there's a new drug on the market which not only reduces the
pain of arthritis, but may actually stop the progression of the
disease.[14]

But just in case someone might have missed the news, Lilly and its
PR firm "then dispatched Lilly scientists to tout the medicine to smaller
newspapers and broadcast outlets."[15]

The response from the public was immediate and enthusiastic. Everyone and his brother wanted a prescription for Oraflex and doctors were
swamped with calls. *The Wall Street Journal* reported that "prescriptions
for Oraflex jumped to 55,000 a week from 2,000—bringing the manufacturer close to $1 million a week in new revenue."[16] Once again drug-
company executives marveled at the power of direct-to-consumer publicity.

Of course the house of cards that Lilly built soon came crashing
down. Scientists complained that Oraflex really wasn't any more effective than most of the other arthritis drugs already on the market. And as
reports started filtering in that people were dying from kidney and liver
failure while on Oraflex, any claims that the drug was safer than other
arthritis medicines were quickly dispelled. And as we pointed out in

Chapter 1, this "new direction in arthritis therapy" was unceremoniously withdrawn from the market a few months after it had been introduced.

The moral of this sad tale: don't count on "ethical" drug firms to tell the truth, the whole truth, and nothing but the truth when they are promoting their fancy new prescription drugs. And don't believe everything you read in the newspapers or a book—the author could well have been snookered by a PR firm or some drug-company flack.

Books that promise a fountain of youth if you take estrogen hormones, safe relief from arthritis through cortisone, or quick weight loss with the latest fad diet are hardly objective sources of information. If something sounds too good to be true, it probably is. Check the story out carefully through as many references and professionals as possible, and *always* use your rubber ducky detector—QUACK, QUACK, QUACK!!!

Finally, and most important of all, don't be taken in by publicity, coupons, commercials, or rebates. Drugs are big business. So what else is new? The snake-oil peddlers of the nineteenth century could have told you that. The difference between the 1890s and the 1980s is one of sheer magnitude.

The New and Improved Medicine Show

Nowadays Americans shell out well over $20 billion per year, and pharmaceutical manufacturers spend hundreds of millions of dollars to get you to buy, Buy, **BUY**! Ad agencies and PR firms are hired to apply their marketing wizardry. They have signed up such people as Pat Boone to push pimple remedies, while they drafted Roger Staubach to convince people to spell relief **Rolaids**. And now they are promoting prescription drugs directly to you, so you'll bother your doctor until he prescribes the latest arthritis medicine or allergy treatment.

Such hard-sell maneuvers are commonplace in marketing detergents and toilet paper, but drugs aren't commodities like watches or cars. If you make a mistake and purchase a watch that doesn't keep good time, you either return it or kick yourself for being a dumb consumer. You lose a few bucks, but no real harm has been done. But if you make a mistake and buy the wrong medicine, you could be risking your life. For example, that seemingly harmless cold remedy that's supposed to "get you going" could interact with some blood-pressure medications to stop you cold.

The medicine-show magnates of the last century used some pretty crude selling techniques to peddle their colored water and alcohol. All they needed was a couple of Indians on the back of a covered wagon to dance and shout, while a plant in the audience miraculously recovered after swigging the foul-tasting concoction. The drugs may not have lived up to their billing, but they weren't likely to do very much serious damage either. And people didn't expect too much in those days. After all, they were a self-reliant lot, who rarely counted on anyone in Washington to look out for their welfare.

Today pharmaceutical manufacturers and their ad-agency hype artists come equipped with market surveys, demographic analyses, computer readouts, professional actors, prime time, and "real" drugs in their over-the-counter products. Side effects are also real. And now that powerful prescription medicines are being advertised to consumers, the number of serious adverse reactions may become higher than ever. Unfortunately the average consumer has no way of knowing whether the drug being advertised could hurt more than it may help.

Who Are the Feds Protecting, Anyway?

Now wait just one second. Whatever happened to the Food and Drug Administration? Aren't there supposed to be people in Washington protecting us from prescription-drug advertising? Quite right—in the good old days, like ten years ago. But remember, things at the agency have changed dramatically. The new FDA appears to encourage prescription-drug advertising. In a speech to the Pharmaceutical Advertising Council, the Commissioner "seemed to give the green light" by stating that:

> **We may be on the brink of the exponential growth phase of
> direct-to-consumer promotion of prescription products . . .
> business competition is good medicine for all consumers, ill
> as well as healthy. The firms whose products we regulate
> have a good track record of cooperation in exploring the
> frontiers of copywriting. You may assume that I look forward
> to seeing the latest promotional innovations. There will al-
> ways be much worthwhile to communicate.**[17]

That makes me gag! I think it should be clear that consumers won't be able to count on the FDA for protection from pharmaceutical promotion. But what about the Federal Trade Commission? Even if the FDA isn't up to the job, surely the folks at the FTC will monitor all forms of advertising to make sure that we aren't exposed to deceptive or misleading garbage. Wrong again. An editorial in *The Wall Street Journal* titled "Lean Closer, Kiss me" reveals a new philosophy at FTC as well.

> **The new chairman of the Federal Trade Commission, James
> Miller, gave his first press conference the other day, and the
> Naderites undoubtedly went chalk white. For Mr. Miller voiced
> "strong reservations" about the commission's long-standing
> requirement that companies substantiate advertising claims,
> asserting that it adds needless costs that are passed on to
> consumers.**[18]

Another editorial in *The Wall Street Journal* titled "Regulatory Mouthwash" goes into even greater detail.

> **James C. Miller III, chairman of the Federal Trade Commission, wants to give the FTC a taste of its own Listerine. To curb abuses of its power to regulate deceptive advertising, he wants to subject the FTC to a set of procedural burdens and paperwork requirements that will fatten the pocketbooks of economists and Washington lawyers.**
>
> **Mr. Miller is proposing a stricter statutory definition of "deception." Before the FTC could challenge an ad, it would have to show that "reasonable" customers would be deceived and that the ad causes some kind of material "injury."[19]**

No foolin', folks, those are the chairman's words—"material injury." Just because an ad is misleading and deceptive is no reason to get upset. Before the commission can take action, you would have to prove that the commercial could contribute to "some kind of material injury." And what exactly does that mean? How many bodies will it take to establish "material injury"?

Advertisers aren't dummies. They know there's no one looking over their shoulders now. Pick up the Sunday supplement of almost any newspaper, and you'll be able to read about some "amazing discovery" for instant weight loss. One I saw last week had a huge headline.

> **I had been overweight for ten years so. . . . My friends could hardly believe their eyes when they saw me lose 56 lbs. in only 6 weeks![20]**

The ad featured one of the most incredible sets of before-and-after photographs I have ever seen. "Monica Lee" looks tired, dumpy, and depressed in her shapeless size-sixteen dress while her "after" photo shows her beaming energetically in a sleek, revealing size-seven leotard. The ad goes on to claim that the amazing Japanese weight-loss tablet "melts down pounds like fire melts down ice!"[21]

Then there was the mail-order advertisement for a "simple pill for your bedroom." The banner headline read:

> **Limp Useless Manhood Rises Firm And Proud Again: Doctor Reports Amazing "Bone Up" Breakthrough *Can Raise A Man's Penis For Sex, Any Time, At Any Age![22]***

These sorts of incredible claims are just the tip of the iceberg. There are people making money on the gullibility of victims of cancer, arthritis, psoriasis, and almost any other chronic ailment. And it should be clear by now that you can't look to Washington for help.

Doctors Buckle Under Badgering

But what about doctors? Surely you can count on them to counteract the drug company razzmatazz. Before you sit back and relax, though, take a look at an editorial titled "Lessons from the Benoxaprofen [**Oraflex**] Affair" published in the British medical journal, *Lancet*.

> The launching of benoxaprofen [Oraflex] was accompanied by an intensive marketing campaign, which, judged by the number of patients treated, was highly successful. . . . Shortly after benoxaprofen was launched, general practitioners complained that their patients were demanding treatment with the new drug; again, doctors should be able to resist pressure of this sort.[23]

But doctors sometimes buckle under pressure from patients, even though they know better. It is pounded into medical students' heads that antibiotics are worthless for colds or the flu, and yet every year during flu season prescriptions for these drugs skyrocket, often because patients ask for penicillin or tetracycline. We received one heartrending letter that illustrates what can happen when a doctor gives up on his responsibility.

> My niece has suffered from bursitis for years and has tried all sorts of pain relievers without much success. When she heard about a new drug called Feldene, she called her doctor and asked for a prescription.
>
> I guess he was a little reluctant, but my niece is persistent, and eventually he went ahead and called in a prescription over the phone. At first she was pleased as punch because the pain disappeared like magic. But then she developed severe burning, itching, and a red rash all over her body.
>
> At first her doctor thought it was caused by a bug bite or some virus and she kept taking the Feldene. Then she developed stomach pain, nausea, and diarrhea along with the rash. By that time the doctor began to suspect Feldene was the culprit and stopped the medicine. The rash slowly went away but it was too late for her stomach. She developed a bleeding ulcer. Her problems with bursitis pale in comparison to the trouble she's had with Feldene. I wish her doctor had been less willing to prescribe it.

Doctors *should* be more cautious about prescribing drugs, but often they have a notion that if they don't hand out a prescription, the patient will feel cheated. Like so many others, this myth has little basis in fact.

A study of over a thousand patients at Johns Hopkins Medical School found that people who did not receive prescriptions were actually more satisfied with the outcome of the medical visit than were those who got them. According to this study, a prescription appears to be a "poor substitute" for time and attention.[24]

To be fair, though, people who have been seduced by sexy slogans can be very insistent. Patients who aggressively demand advertised medications can put the doctor in an awful bind. If he refuses to prescribe a drug he is unfamiliar with, he risks antagonizing his patients or losing them to another practitioner.

Only a few years ago such problems didn't exist. Many doctors silently supported the secret drug lag in this country. No, not the kind of drug lag we talked about in the first chapter, but rather the months or years between the time a new drug was first marketed and the time it became widely prescribed. Doctors used to be more conservative in adopting new products. There were a basic dozen or so medicines they prescribed regularly. When a doctor reached into his black bag to pull out a high blood pressure drug or an arthritis treatment, he felt the confidence of long familiarity. When something new came out, the doctor had plenty of time to read up on it, check in with colleagues, and ease into using it slowly. But today it seems as if a new blood pressure drug, pain reliever, anti-inflammatory agent, antidepressant, or antibiotic becomes available almost every month. In some cases the patient has heard about and started demanding these products even before the doctor knows what they are.

Despite these pressures, you'd expect most doctors to see through and resist the drug companies' high-powered promotional campaigns. Many probably do, but a surprising number get snookered. In that editorial about the **Oraflex** affair, the editors of *Lancet* had some tough words for their colleagues.

> **[D]octors are too often either ignorant of the hazards of a particular drug or incapable of making a reasoned judgement concerning its risks and benefits. Most of us will have witnessed instances of illogical, inappropriate, or dangerous prescribing . . . and the remarkable efficacy of the marketing of benoxaprofen seems to confirm that medical men and women are highly susceptive to advertisements.[25]**

Dealing Drugs to Doctors

Like it or not, doctors are human, just like everyone else—maybe too human. Page through almost any medical journal, and you will find advertisements that will shock you. Not because they are filled with gory pictures, but because the ads are often so simplistic that they would insult the intelligence of the average dodo bird. And talk about sex! There are more than a few naked ladies found between the pages of respected journals.

One woman smiles mysteriously as she stands in her altogether, advertising **Transderm-V** (scopolamine), a motion-sickness medicine worn behind the ear as a small adhesive disk. Another naked woman stares seductively out at the doctor from the Garden of Eden. In her hand is an apple, and the caption over her head reads—"At long last . . . relief for the pain of primary dysmenorrhea" (menstrual cramps). It's not clear whether the message is that women have been suffering cramps all this time because of some original sin or whether the doctor will be richly rewarded if only he prescribes **Ponstel** (mefenamic acid) for her cramps.

Playing upon classic stereotypes, Lederle Laboratories portrays young sailors being led astray by scantily clad hookers to advertise **Minocin** (minocycline) for gonorrhea. In another ad the doctor is told that a sweet young thing in a short slip with a forlorn look on her face has "been feeling more pain than pleasure." On the following page we are told that for urinary tract infections "in sexually active women **Macrodantin**" (nitrofurantoin) is the choice. It must have worked, because now our lovely lass has a broad smile on her face and looks ready to boogie. She's seen in a slinky evening gown, snuggling up to her honey as he stares down at her cleavage.

Even though such ads in medical journals are likely to catch a male doctor's eye, they are only the tip of the promotional iceberg. The real action takes place behind closed doors in the doctor's office. Ask the marketing director of any major drug company what sells the product, and he will tell you that it's the detail man.

The name *detail man* comes from his responsibility for making sure that the doctor knows the relevant *details* about his company's drugs. Actually the term *detail man* is fading fast. For one thing, more and more women are being hired these days and "detail woman" just doesn't have the right ring. For another, drug companies are doing their best to give these folks a professional image. The term *pharmaceutical representative* or *medical representative* is in. And rather than "detailing" drugs, the emphasis these days is on "imparting accurate information."

Some drug companies even have so-called super-reps or "health science associates," who do nothing more than answer questions, supply scientific papers, and help set up studies in teaching hospitals. All this activity certainly sounds respectable. But whatever they are called, make no mistake; these are *salesmen* and *saleswomen,* pure and simple. One regional manager for a major pharmaceutical firm unabashedly admitted to me that sales reps "are working for one basic reason, and that is to sell the product—you betcha. That is the primary function—that is our job!"[26]

What are these people like? Over the years I have had an opportunity to meet a number of sales reps. Many were disenchanted and cynical about doctors and were willing to give me some information about their tactics.

Carol is a vivacious blonde in her early thirties with a sparkle in her eye. She is good-looking, self-assured, and assertive without being pushy. She dresses stylishly, with only a hint of seductiveness. Carol admits that despite her training, she's no pharmacologist. But, she goes on, "I don't have to be. I never get to talk about that intricate biochemical stuff with doctors. It's my people skills, not my knowledge, that makes me good at what I do."

When I inquired if the doctors asked her tough questions about the mechanism of action of new drugs, she laughed and replied, "You're too idealistic. They like seeing me—I'm a break in their day." And to the query if being a woman influenced her effectiveness, she replied, "Definitely! Even though you don't socialize with them, you *can* get their attention." Some of the reps do socialize, however. Carol described one of her associates as "sleazy—not professional. She comes on to the doctors, winking and blinking—she's flirting instead of working."

But Carol *was* a hard-working professional. She set sales records in her territory, and after only two years she was earning a $28,500 salary, with a hefty bonus on top. The more of her drugs the doctors she visited prescribed, the more money she made. And she had lots of tricks for getting them to help her surpass her sales objectives.

Carol was particularly proud of her special projects. She would throw three or four major dinner parties and clinical conferences a year for physicians in her territory. Her company sponsored all-expenses-paid affairs at fancy restaurants. Some "expert" might be flown in from out of town to bring the doctors up to date on hypertension or infectious disease. Everything was supposed to be very objective and scientific, but Carol always managed to get in a subtle pitch for her company's products.

She talked disdainfully of how some doctors took advantage of the drug company's generosity. "They're mostly interested in the dinner. They will bring their girlfriends or wives without even asking permission. If you wait till after the dessert to bring on the speaker, they either walk out or are too drunk to care. To keep their attention you have to make sure you present the talk between the salad and the entree."

Carol finally burned out. She got tired of waiting for hours in doctors' offices, pushing free drug samples, trying to talk doctors into prescribing "me-too" drugs of marginal value, and constantly striving to surpass her "objectives." She threw in the towel. Instead of detailing drugs to doctors, she's now selling surgical supplies. Please don't go out looking for Carol. She is a composite of several reps I talked to over the last several years. But the quotes are all taken from actual conversations.

There are approximately 25,000 drug detailers roaming this country, knocking on the doors of about 225,000 doctors. Just in case you don't have your calculator handy, that boils down to just about one sales rep for every nine doctors. Incredible! What that means is that doctors are the targets of an intense, one-on-one promotional campaign that is virtually unrivaled in any other industry. Only the makers of perfumes and breakfast cereals outspend drug companies when it comes to pushing their products.[27]

And believe me, drug detailers are good at what they do. They should be; they get paid very well. According to *The Wall Street Journal*, Merck forks over between $25,000 and $50,000 a year to each of its sales reps, depending upon years of service and productivity.[28] And that doesn't even count what it costs to keep these folks on the road. "The visits are expensive; their costs are estimated at from $11 to $80 for each call. Detailmen average about 150 calls to physicians each month."[29]

All this activity adds up to far more than $1 billion each year that drug companies spend just to keep these folks knocking on doctors' doors. If you then throw in all the free samples, snazzy brochures, books, notepads, pens, pencils, paper weights, calendars, magazines, grants, trips, seminars, free meals, ads in medical journals, and goodness knows what else—the total begins to boggle the mind.

To put it all into perspective, consider this. The entire yearly budget for the Food and Drug Administration is less than $400 million. That may seem like a lot, but keep in mind the agency must guard all the food processed in this country to make sure it isn't adulterated or tainted. The agency must also analyze new drug applications, monitor vaccines, and generally police the entire pharmaceutical industry. Drug companies spend more than three times the FDA's total budget just promoting their products to physicians. Is it any wonder the FDA sometimes feels like the little Dutch boy, holding its federal finger in the dike while the water pours over the top?

Even one aspect of this onslaught—promotional mail—is already overwhelming and seems to be getting worse fast. Dr. Roger A. Breslow of Utica, New York, saved all of the unsolicited mail (much of it from pharmaceutical companies) he received during 1982; it made an impressive pile that weighed over 500 pounds.[30] Another physician, commenting on Dr. Breslow's letter, issues an urgent call.

> **We seem to be witnessing the appearance of a major threat to the health of physicians, postal-delivery workers, garbage collectors, and trees; the exponential growth of junk mailings. . . . The rate of increase between 1970 and 1978 was 7.18 kg [15.8 lbs.] per year; between 1978 and 1982 it rose to 30.93 kg [68 lbs.] per year. . . . Given recent trends . . . we should all expect to be receiving at least 15,000 kg [33,000 lbs.] of junk mail yearly by 1990. . . .**
>
> **Fellow physicians, let us stem this tide before we are buried beneath it. Our forests, postal carriers, and garbage collectors will be forever grateful.[31]**

Then there are all those medical meetings. Almost any doctor who wants a tax-deductible vacation can scan the lists of conferences and conventions; there's bound to be one at a desirable location almost every month of the year—it's only a matter of scheduling. And while there, he can count on picking up lots of lovely "souvenirs." I asked a physician who was attending an annual professional meeting to keep a diary of all the free giveaways and perks he was offered during the conference. Here is his report.

> In response to your questions re: what kinds of items were given by the various drug companies to visiting physicians and their guests, they were as follows: tote bags, T-shirts, hats, pens, marking pencils, notepads and portfolios, various brochures, literature, reprints, games, and the *Guiness Book of World Records*.
>
> The usual sample of drugs was available, along with a variety of cosmetics in well-designed gift packages. Available free of charge at various booths were orange juice, Sanka coffee, carbonated beverages, and a variety of chocolate candies. One booth was set up with phones for free long distance calls to the doctors' offices or homes.
>
> In addition to the various hospitality suites [with "open" bars], one drug company bought out the entire Saturday night performance at the Chicago Auditorium of a cabaret-type show. The Art Institute of Chicago was open for the doctors one evening, and included a very generous buffet of hors d'oeuvres and various wines. A wine and cheese party was set up for 4,000 people two evenings, and one evening the Field Museum had a reception followed by a private showing of the Shanghai Exhibit.

Drug companies even provide all-expenses-paid trips for certain doctors—and sometimes for their families—to attend conferences in places like Disney World, Paris, Venice, Hawaii, or the Dominican Republic. But occasionally these benefits have unforeseen side effects that are far from beneficial, as reported in the San Francisco *Chronicle*.

> Three doctors survived a harrowing brush with death . . . when giant waves swept them off the deck of a fishing boat into the icy ocean outside the Golden Gate. . . .
>
> The ill-fated salmon fishing trip was organized and paid for by Hoechst, the multinational West German firm, as a way to promote the company's pharmaceutical products among Bay Area surgeons.[32]

Who do you think pays for all these freebies? As usual, the costs are eventually passed on to you, the consumer. You pay a lot more for your medicine because of all the expensive attention devoted to influencing doctors' prescribing patterns.

But does it work? Do these highly educated, hard-nosed doctors really fall for a pitch by some little ol' drug peddler who leaves free samples and pretty calendars? You're damn right they do! According to Dr. Jean Abel Cramer, a New Jersey dermatologist, "A detail man can really sell a doctor a drug these days. It wasn't always so, but they've become more sophisticated, better-trained, and smarter."[33] Research by *The Wall Street Journal* supports Dr. Cramer's observations.

[P]romoting drugs to doctors these days is much like selling soap to consumers: It's all in the marketing. Indeed, the very survival of a drug in today's highly competitive marketplace often depends as much on a company's marketing talents as it does on the quality of its medicine.[34]

Most doctors would vehemently deny such allegations. I have yet to meet a practitioner who admits he looks at ads in medical journals or relies on detail men for drug information. Physicians would like to believe that they prize scientific objectivity above all else, and they scorn the idea that they would be influenced by advertising of any sort.

But pharmaceutical manufacturers are definitely *not* in the charity business. The billions they spend on doctors pay handsome dividends. A former marketing-plans manager for Eli Lilly, Peter Sichrovsky, admits as much.

The doctors are influenced . . . because no company . . . wouldn't [sic] spend one single dollar without being sure that they get at least double, or three times, as much back. So every pen, every small gift to the doctor, reminds him of the company, reminds him of the drug.[35]

A Harvard Medical School researcher recently confirmed what the sales managers have always known. Dr. Jerry Avorn and his colleagues set out to discover objectively which had a greater influence on doctors' prescribing patterns—scientific sources or drug advertising. Two categories of drugs were selected for study: **Darvon**-type pain relievers and vasodilators (medications which, in theory, increase blood flow to the brain and the extremities). Dr. Avorn and his team picked these compounds because there is little evidence in the medical literature to support their use. Writing in *The American Journal of Medicine,* the Harvard researchers offered their commentary on these compounds:

Advertisements for these drugs [the vasodilators] are the major current sources of the misinformation that mental failure

in the elderly is the result of inadequate blood flow—a concept now abandoned by neurologists and internists alike.[36]

And as for **Darvon** and its relatives, the writers point out, they are no stronger than aspirin, though they may cost more than ten times as much. Any doctor who has been keeping up with the scientific literature ought therefore to think twice before prescribing such medications. But the study found that about half the doctors in the sample believed that **Darvon**-type drugs were stronger than aspirin and 84 precent "often or occasionally found themselves prescribing Darvon."[37] Equally shocking was the discovery that 71 percent of the doctors incorrectly believed that senility was caused by reduced blood flow to the brain and that almost one-third thought vasodilating drugs were "useful in managing confused geriatric patients."[38]

Now these doctors were no dummies. Many probably had some affiliation with Boston's medical schools or teaching hospitals. In a sense these guys were the cream of the crop. That's why the conclusions of this study are so damning and why the team found the findings "even more scary."[39]

> **Though primary care doctors here think academic sources and experience dictate their prescription decisions, a Harvard poll shows they're most influenced by ads and detail people.**
>
> **"In the absence of mandatory postgraduate education or recertification, pharmaceutical advertising has become the major source of continuing education for the American physician,"** says head researcher Jerry Avorn (M.D.), an assistant professor of social medicine and health policy at Harvard.
>
> **"Advertising's influence is so pervasive that doctors often aren't aware of it."[40]**

ZAP! Nailed between the eyes, scraped, salted, and hung out to cure. So what's so surprising about that? A lot of folks have been saying pretty much the same thing for years—but they were going mostly on gut feelings. To my knowledge, this is the first time a doctor set out to study his colleagues in a scientific manner and to resolve the issue once and for all. And boy, did he do it! It scares me to think that so many practicing physicians rely more on advertising and detail people than on journal articles and scientific meetings.

How do the detailers feel about their influence? You'd think they'd be tickled pink. After all, the proof of the pudding is in the pudding. Pharmaceutical representatives are obviously serving doctors some mighty tasty tidbits these days, and the doctors appear to be eagerly lapping them up. On the other hand, sales reps don't want to be too obvious.

They're proud of their ability to persuade, but since most doctors prefer to believe they're immune to salesmanship, it has to be done with subtle skill.

And indeed, detailers are skillful. Most, if not all, have college degrees, and many even have training in such health-related fields as nursing and pharmacy. They are given several weeks to several months of training about the drugs they will be promoting, plus lots of input on how to interact with physicians. They're taught how to turn the tables on an aggressive doctor and make him feel defensive. A doctor who doesn't prescribe the company's products becomes a challenge; just as a used car salesman will work on a reluctant customer, the detailer will pull out all the stops to convert the skeptical M.D. into a believer. But it's a soft sell. The one thing drug detail men don't want doctors to find out is how effective they really are. An editorial in *Pharmaceutical Representative* tells it all. In his own words I bring you the publisher, Mr. William M. McKnight, responding to one of my newspaper columns.

> The column was titled, "The People's Pharmacy." I needn't mention the author's name—he's already well enough known for his two consumer-oriented books of the same title. The gist of his article was that doctors count on drug manufacturers' promotional efforts (bravo for stating the obvious!). But he also said that some physicians "rely more heavily on advertising than on published scientific research for their drug information," and implied that pharmaceutical representatives sometimes deliberately mislead doctors.

> When my pulse had dropped below 130, I took the column in hand again and read on. The author proceeded by saying that companies are more interested in selling drugs than in conveying information, that irresponsible advertising has led to the overutilization of estrogen hormones, pain relievers, and antianxiety agents. . . .

> I had to wonder whether the "people's pharmacist" had any idea of what goes on during a typical call, if he knew that the promotional literature distributed by sales reps is almost always accompanied by reprints of articles from scientific journals—articles that discuss the pros *and* cons. . . .

> We've heard a lot in recent years about taking the "business" out of health care. Is that realistic? . . .

> We're in business, and darned proud to be, too.[41]

On that issue Mr. McKnight and I are in complete agreement. I certainly concur that he and his colleagues are most definitely "in business,'' and I'm not surprised that he's proud of his accomplishments. The more drugs a detail man gets the doctor to prescribe, the better the overall sales and the more bonus money he makes. But as far as I'm concerned, doctors have no business relying on these folks for their prescribing information. I wouldn't want a neurosurgeon to learn his surgical technique from the person who sells him scalpels. If a doctor can't find the time to look up a new drug in the scientific literature, he shouldn't be handing it out to his patients.

But according to Dr. William J. Kane, addressing the American College of Clinical Pharmacology, "There is a tendency among physicians to use any new therapy they can get their hands on. The physician gets a kick out of prescribing the latest drug. It makes him feel up to date on the latest technology."[42]

Too Much Medicine

As it is, Americans swallow too damn many pills. That's not just my opinion, that's the opinion of Dr. Jere E. Goyan, Dean of the University of California, San Francisco School of Pharmacy, and past Commissioner of the FDA. He has repeatedly stated that many prescriptions are medically unnecessary.

> I would be willing to bet that we could get along with about half the number of prescriptions that are written each year. We Americans are given to overeating, to overdrinking, to oversmoking, and to underexercising. If anything goes wrong, we expect to be able to go to a doctor and get fixed up with a chemical.
>
> I've talked to a lot of physicians who tell me that they don't think they are doing their job as a physician unless they give the patient a prescription. I've also been told by other physicians that it is the easiest way to bring their consultation to an end and move on to the next patient.[43]

Unfortunately the problem is getting worse, not better. During the 1970s there was a glimmer of hope. Each year doctors seemed to be writing fewer prescriptions, and people were swallowing fewer pills. The number of prescriptions filled in pharmacies was 1,518,462,000 in 1973.[44] By 1979 the number had dropped by over 100 million prescriptions, to 1,365,858,000.[45] Still a mind-numbing figure, but at least the trend was in the right direction.

But in 1980 everything changed. For the first time in six years doctors started prescribing more drugs than before, and by 1981 we were back up to the 1.5 billion mark once again.[46] Another source suggests that in

1982 almost 1,966,217,000 "scripts" were written by physicians.[47] That's as close to two billion as you can get without going over the top.

If such big numbers blow your mind, let me help. Those figures break down to over four (perhaps as many as eight) prescribed medicines for every man, woman, and child in this country each year.[48] Seeing as how a lot us don't take any drugs at all, that means there are quite a few folks out there taking far more than four. Remember that "75 million U.S. adults take one or more drugs at least once a week."[49]

The cost of medicine has been soaring, too. In 1976 the average prescription price was $5.22.[50] By 1982—only six years later—the price per prescription jumped to $11.51, an increase of 120 percent.[51] But arthritis patients have fared far worse; they now pay more than $14 per prescription.

Collectively we now spend much more than $25 billion on prescription and nonprescription drugs. Just in case you're curious, at last count we shelled out over $16.1 billion on Rx's, $1.2 billion on vitamins and tonics, and $6.2 billion on OTCs.[52,53] And then there are the hidden billions spent for medications dispensed in hospitals.

Why the sudden upsurge in drug taking? Experts say it's partly because we're getting older. The graying of America means that people are living longer, and along with extended age come chronic ailments that require medicine, such as arthritis, high blood pressure, and heart disease.[54] There has also been an alteration in philosophy at the FDA. A profound proindustry tilt has led to changes in the drug-approval process and more new medications are appearing on pharmacy shelves every month. And you can bet the new drugs cost a lot more than the old ones. Between 1980 and 1983 the amount spent on arthritis medicine jumped from $.5 billion to over $1 billion, partly because of all the new (and more expensive) anti-inflammatory agents that have sprung up lately like mushrooms after a rain.

Last but not least is the power of promotion. Many major drug makers have increased their advertising budgets and hired more detail people. For example, "In the past two years, Merck has increased its sales force by 55 percent to 1,400 largely to help promote the company's surge of new-product introductions."[55] And as we have clearly seen, far too many physicians fall prey to the salesman's pitch.

So there you have it. You're on your own more than ever before. There are more new drugs than ever before, but the FDA is understaffed and less capable of monitoring them. Drug companies have become more aggressive in their promotion and advertising, but the Federal Trade Commission has been retreating from its responsibility to protect us from misleading and deceptive ads.

The moral of this story? Watch out for yourself; you won't get a lot of help from the government. And don't necessarily count on your doctor to ride to the rescue. If he's following in the footsteps of his colleagues, he's listening to the detailers and writing more prescriptions than ever.

The situation sounds desperate. But it doesn't mean that you have to give up taking medicine for good. As we said in the first chapter, there are a lot of valuable new drugs in the pipeline, and many of them are important advances that will improve the quality of life for millions of people.

But in order to take advantage of them without risking life and limb, you will have to become more self-reliant. Learn more about the drugs you swallow. Don't be afraid to ask questions of everyone—the doctor, the nurse, and the pharmacist. Take notes, no matter how smart you are; you may forget important instructions and warnings unless you write them down. And don't stop there; seek additional sources of information. We will do our best in the following pages to bring you up to date on all the hottest developments in the world of drugs, but we can't hit every detail. Look for at least one of the references we list at the end of this chapter, and before you swallow any new pill or potion, make sure you find out all you can about it.

For Self-Protection: Books About Medicines

1. *Physicians Desk Reference (PDR)*
   Box 58
   Oradell, NJ 07649
   Price: approximately $26.00

This is certainly the most complete book on the market when it comes to listing side effects and dosage information. There are even lots of pretty pictures of pills, so you can look up your own particular potion.

Unfortunately, there are some major problems with this book. First, it has the craziest damn indexing system you will ever find. Drug companies must pay to get their drugs listed (this book *is* glorified advertising). So, unlike most reference books that put the drugs in alphabetical order, here the pharmaceutical manufacturers are listed in alphabetical order. As a result the medications are spread higgledy-piggledy throughout the book in no particular order.

Second problem: the book is written in medical mumbo-jumbo. The information is nothing more than the official FDA package insert that comes with each bottle of medicine. The result is chaos.

Third problem: there is often no way to tell which adverse reactions are common and which are rare. This adds to the confusion when you see a list of 50 or 60 scary side effects following a particular drug. Some may have only occurred once in 25,000 patients, but you'll never know by reading the *PDR*.

Finally, the book is expensive. But given all its disadvantages, the *PDR* is still the most complete and standard reference on the market. If you want to know what your doctor is reading, go ahead and splurge on a copy or locate one in your public library.

2. *Advice for the Patient (USPDI; vol. II)*
   The United States Pharmacopeial Convention, Inc.
   12601 Twinbrook Parkway
   Rockville, MD 20852
   Price: approximately $22.00

The U.S. Pharmacopeial Convention is a nongovernmental but nevertheless quasiofficial organization that sets the official standards of strength, quality, purity, packaging, and labeling for medical products in the United States.

Several years ago the folks at USP got into the consumer publishing business. Their "Dispensing Information" book was initially aimed at health professionals, but they later brought out a version called *Advice for the Patient*. It is very comprehensive and much more logical than the *PDR*.

The book lists side effects as "more common, less common, or rare," which gives you some idea of what you are up against. There are also cautions about drug interactions.

I can certainly recommend this book, but people have told me that they find it hard to use. It is written in a very stuffy medical style, even though the authors have tried to eliminate all the big words. Another drawback—it's not cheap.

3. *The Essential Guide to Prescription Drugs*
   James Long, M.D.
   Harper & Row Publishers, Inc.
   10 East 53rd Street
   New York, NY 10022
   Price: approximately $9.00 in paperback

Now this is definitely a good buy for the money. The book is extremely complete, providing both United States brand names as well as Canadian listings. It tells you who should *not* take a particular medicine, which can be critical information.

Dr. Long lists the side effects two ways—"natural, expected, and unavoidable," vs. "unusual, unexpected, and infrequent." Not a perfect system, but as good as any other on the market. He also provides lots of excellent cautions and warnings and tells you which other drugs may interact with your medicine to cause problems. Overall, this is an excellent reference book and well worth the investment.

4. *The Pill Book*
   Dr. Harold Silverman
   Bantam Books, Inc.
   666 Fifth Avenue
   New York, NY 10103
   Price: approximately $4.00

Another excellent choice. Although *The Pill Book* is not quite as comprehensive as the other references listed, it does give you all the critical information, including side effects, dangerous interactions, cautions, and warnings. There is even a section with color photographs of tablets and capsules, so you can identify your particular drug the same way you would if you bought the *PDR*. Another advantage is its handy size. Unlike James Long's oversized paperback, *The Pill Book* is compact and easy to stash.

5. *The People's Pharmacy (currently being revised)*
   St. Martin's Press, Inc.
   175 Fifth Avenue
   New York, NY 10010
   Price: approximately $15.00

6. *The People's Pharmacy–2*
   Graedon Enterprises, Inc.
   P.O. Box 31788
   Raleigh, NC 27622
   Price: approximately $6.00

I always hate to toot my own horn, but many folks have told me they find both these books useful. To answer your first question, no, they aren't the same book merely revised. Each is quite different with material that does not overlap. *The People's Pharmacy* discusses such issues as allergy, asthma, contraception, drug interactions, and stocking your medicine chest. *The People's Pharmacy–2* includes information about drugs used to treat women, older people, and children. There is also a comprehensive discussion of vitamins and arthritis therapies.

These books are not "references" in the classic sense. Unlike the preceding books, they aren't "dictionaries." My books are meant to be read and enjoyed. They are also intended to serve as sources which people can refer to from time to time to look up side effects or dangerous drug interactions. I would like to believe they will complement the book you are now reading.

References

1. Solomon, Sheldon D., et al. "Complaint about Promotion of New Anti-Arthritic Drug." *N. Engl. J. Med.* 300:203, 1979.

2. "With Vaccine Use Lagging, Merck Opted for Anonymous 'Outreach.' " *Medical World News* 24(2):64–65, 1983.

3. "Boots President Byer Aims to Stimulate Patient Demand for Branded Ibuprofen, Rufen, Through Multi-City Publicity Tour; $1.50 Consumer Rebate Offered." *F-D-C Reports* 43(38):3–4, 1981.

4. Ibid.

5. O'Brien, William M. "Alleged Direct Promotion of Prescription Drugs to Consumers." *N. Engl. J. Med.* 306:181–182, 1982.

6. Press Kit from Russom & Leeper public relations firm. Biographical Information on Miriam Stoppard, M.D.

7. Personal communication, Peter Howsam, Director of Marketing, Burroughs Wellcome Co; 1982.

8. "Ciba-Geigy Ads Appearing on Cable Health Network's 'Physician's Journal Update.' " *F-D-C Reports* 45(28):11, 1983.

9. Buchwald, Art, cited in Krieger, Lisa. "Prescribers' Pens are Target of Ads for the Public." *Medical World News* 24(2):59–69, 1983.

10. "Oraflex Case Spurs Congress to Denounce FDA Drug Regulations." *Medical World News* 24(23):86–87, 1983.

11. "Oraflex, once-a-Day Arthritis Treatment, Cleared for Marketing." *News of Lilly* April 20, 1982.

12. Ibid.

13. Waldholz, Michael. "Drug Firms Seeking Publicity To Popularize New Medicines." *The Wall Street Journal,* July 22, 1982, p. 23.

14. Taken from a news clip rebroadcast on "60 minutes," April 17, 1983.

15. Waldholz. Op. cit.

16. Ibid.

17. Quoted in "Dr Hayes Sees More Rx Ads Directed at Consumer." *American Druggist* 185(4):29, 1982.

18. Editorial. "Lean Closer, Kiss Me." *The Wall Street Journal,* November 9, 1981.

19. Editorial. "Regulatory Mouthwash." *The Wall Street Journal,* May 12, 1982.

20. Advertisement, St. Petersburg *Times,* January 9, 1984, p. 16A.

21. Ibid.

22. National American Pharmacal mail-order advertisement for VBE-21 vitamins.

23. Editorial. "Lessons from the Benoxaprofen Affair." *Lancet* 2:529–530, 1982.

24. Wurtman, Steven A., et al. "Do Prescriptions Adversely Affect Doctor-Patient Interactions?" *Am. J. Pub. Health* 71:1358–1361, 1981.

25. "Lessons from the Benoxaprofen Affair.", op. cit.

26. Drug-company source.

27. Strelnick, Hal. "What They Don't Know Can Hurt You." *Heal/PAC Bulletin* 13(6):6, 1982.

28. Waldholz, Michael. "Pill Purveyor: How a 'Detail Man' Promotes New Drugs to Tennessee Doctors." *The Wall Street Journal*, November 8, 1982, p. 1.

29. Altman, Lawrence K. "The Drug Touters." Reprinted in "This World", San Francisco *Chronicle*, August 15, 1982, p. 17.

30. Breslow, Roger A. "Junk Mail." *N. Engl. J. Med.* 308:1168, 1983.

31. Connors, Joseph M. "More on Junk Mail." *N. Engl. J. Med.* 309:673–674, 1983.

32. Pereira, Joseph. "3 Rescued After Waves Engulf Boat." San Francisco *Chronicle*, February 21, 1983, p. 1.

33. Waldholz. Op. cit.

34. Waldholz, Michael. "Pill Promoters: Marketing Often Is the Key to Success of Prescription Drugs." *The Wall Street Journal*, December 28, 1981, p. 1

35. Sichrovsky, Peter. Interviewed on "Panorama," January 17, 1983, British Broadcasting Corporation.

36. Avorn, Jerry; Chen, Milton; and Hartley, Robert. "Scientific Versus Commercial Sources of Influence on the Prescribing Behavior of Physicians." *Am. J. Med.* 73(July):4–8, 1982.

37. Ibid.

38. Ibid.

39. Quoted in Jacobs, Paul. "Prescribing Drugs: The Hard Sell." Los Angeles *Times*, Dec. 29, 1982, Part I, p. 5.

40. "Physicians' Prescribing Habits. Doctors Don't See Power of Drug Ads." *Medical World News* 23(19):19–20, Sept. 13, 1982.

41. McKnight, William M. Editorial. "The 'People's Pharmacy': It'd Be Empty, But For Us." *Pharmaceutical Representative* 11(9):4, September, 1981.

42. Kotulak, Ronald, and Van, Jon. "They Write, Patients Suffer: Many Doctors Suffer 'Rx Fever.' " Chicago *Tribune*, October 9, 1980, p. 1.

43. Ibid.

44. National Prescription Audit in Continuing Education. "1977: Top 200 Drugs: Total Number of Rx's Slumps Again for the 4th Year in a Row." *Pharmacy Times* 44(4):41–48, 1978.

45. "Rx's Rise 3.8% Boosted by a 10.8% Jump in Generics." *Pharmacy Times*, April, 1982, pp. 23–32.

46. Ibid.

47. Consumer Expenditure Study. "Prescriptions." *Product Marketing* 12(8):12, 1983.

48. "Survey Says 58% of Population Gets Rx in Year, or 4.3 Rx's Per Person." *American Druggist*, May, 1982, p. 33.

49. Biomedicine. "Bad Reactions for Drugged Country." *Science News* 124(25):392, 1983.

50. "Generic Prescribing Hits All-Time High Regional Survey Indicates." *Drug Topics* 122(12):14–15, 1978.

51. Glaser, Martha. "Rx Drug Sales Bloom Despite Economic Climate." *Drug Topics* 127(8):34–45, 1983.

52. *Product Marketing*. Op. cit.

53. "35th Annual Report on Consumer Spending." *Drug Topics* 126(13):3–70, 1983.

54. "Why the Rx Upsurge? New Drugs, Easier Regs, and More Oldsters." *Medical World News* 23(19):18–20, Sept. 19, 1982.

55. Waldholz, 1982. Op. cit.

CHAPTER 3

The Next Miracles of Medicine

The New Drug Revolution ▪ A History Lesson: The Fabulous Fifties, Sobering Sixties, and Stagnant Seventies ▪ The Exciting Eighties ▪ Sniffing Your Way to Birth Control ▪ A is for Apple and Aphrodisiac: LHRH, Yohimbine, L-dopa, and **Parlodel** *▪ Sex and the Fat Rat ▪ Opiates and the Brain ▪ B is for Bashful, Baldness, and Balderdash ▪ Biotechnology and Blue Sky: Unlocking the Body's Secrets: Interferon, Interleukin-2, Immune Stimulators, Monoclonal Antibodies, and Wound Healing.*

Are you sick and tired of gloom and doom? Fed up with federal failures? Frustrated by physicians' indifference? Freaked out by pharmaceutical fraud? Filled with self-righteous indignation? Relax; here's where we ease up and declare a temporary truce. Put your feet up for a few minutes, and prepare for some *good* news for a change.

We are in the midst of a pharmacological revolution. It has been a quiet revolution—no blood and guts, and very little publicity, which is surprising, given the profound influence it is having on people's lives. If you haven't heard much about this revolution, perhaps it's because the drug industry has a vested interest in convincing legislators and the public that we are suffering and dying for lack of new drugs available in other countries. Maybe they have spent so much time and energy complaining about a drug lag caused by excessive government regulation that they can't very well start bragging about the extraordinary advances being made.

A History Lesson

The truth is that we have already seen some incredible drug developments over the past several years, and the future holds even greater promise. Not since the "fabulous fifties" have there been so many important new breakthroughs. In that decade the "antis" arrived. We saw the proliferation of life-saving antibiotics, pain-relieving anti-inflammatory agents, and antipsychotic drugs that helped put an end to straitjackets, wet sheets, and padded cells in mental institutions. Antidepressants became available and for the first time offered psychologically depressed patients an alternative other than suicide or electric shock treatment.

Diuretics and antihypertensive agents introduced in the 1950s held out hope of prolonging the lives of patients with high blood pressure, while oral anticoagulants helped prevent blood clots from reforming and causing strokes and heart attacks. Oral diabetes medicine offered an alternative to insulin. Antituberculosis drugs virtually put an end to TB sanatoriums. Polio vaccine spared millions the anguish of paralysis or death. And the development of the birth-control pill promised its users the pleasures of passion without the penalties.

None of these breakthroughs was without hazards, however, and during the "sobering sixties" the thalidomide disaster dramatized drug dangers in a most painful way. Public outcry and congressional scrutiny led to greater caution and slowed the headlong rush to license new compounds. Then came the "stabilizing seventies"—or, as some people called them, the "stagnant seventies." It was a period of gradual growth. Patients became less eager to pop pills and instead started weighing drug benefits against risks. Pharmaceutical manufacturers retrenched and, while griping about FDA regulations, invested hundreds of millions of dollars in basic research. That investment is now paying off.

The Exciting Eighties

It's hard to believe we are in the middle of a spectacular pharmaceutical renaissance. No proclamations have been issued, no trumpets have sounded, and few people realize it's been happening. Even doctors seem unaware of the full extent of the incredible drug developments taking place all around them. But even if this revolution has been low-key, the ramifications are nothing less than mind-boggling. An extraordinary number of new drugs have recently been approved, are in the pipeline, or are being tested. They will change your life or that of someone you know in a profound way.

Let's get down to basics. For openers there either are, or soon will be, more effective treatments, with fewer side effects, for people with arthritis, depression, angina, high blood pressure, acne, allergy, asthma, backaches, and ulcers. Breakthroughs in the treatment of the flu, herpes, senility, psoriasis, obesity, osteoporosis, baldness, and the common cold are here or are within sight. There is even hope that several new compounds may provide safer and more effective contraceptive protection.

Take LHRH, for example. Those four little letters don't sound very sexy but they could turn out to be the hottest thing in contraception since the 1960s. Even better, an LHRH compound could pay a big bonus by stimulating sexuality. You heard me—a *real* aphrodisiac!

Sniffing Your Way to Birth Control

The "exciting eighties" may be aptly named as much for developments in sexuality as for anything else. And if anything deserves a renaissance, it's got to be contraception. Let's face it, birth control is a bummer. The Pill is effective, but the price of such protection is high. The fear of such adverse reactions as increased blood pressure, heart attacks, and strokes has prevented many women from using oral contraceptives, especially as they get older.

The IUD (intrauterine device) has its own problems—cramping, heavy monthly flow, and a risk of infections (pelvic inflammatory disease, or PID). Diaphragms are a drag, and spermicidal foams and jellies are messy. In addition, lots of women complain that diaphragms reduce sexual sensitivity. The contraceptive sponge (**Today**), impregnated with a spermicidal chemical, has been controversial because preliminary reports linked it to toxic-shock syndrome. Although only several women were affected, at this writing the issue remains unresolved; however, the sponge does not appear to be any more effective than traditional spermicidal contraceptives—diaphragms, foams, jellies, and suppositories. That leaves good old-fashioned condoms. Mother always said not to go out without your rubbers, but condoms too cut down on sensation, and they're not 100 percent foolproof. It would be fair to say that there hasn't been any significant advance in birth control in over twenty years.

Enter LHRH—luteinizing hormone-releasing hormone. This natural substance plays an important role in regulating fertility, but it can also prevent ovulation and sperm production as well as induce menstruation.[1-6] Researchers have been busy creating hundreds of compounds (1,500 at last count) that mimic LHRH, and some of the key players believe that these substances may lay the foundation for a contraceptive revolution.

Unlike the Pill, which affects almost every cell in the body, LHRH has a much narrower physiological action and produces far fewer adverse reactions. It would be a little like comparing the effects of a shotgun blast with those of a peashooter. And you will probably be able either to swallow a pill or inhale LHRH with a nasal spray.

Early research suggests that LHRH compounds may have a wide range of contraceptive benefits.[7] Used every day, the nasal spray would prevent ovulation and mimic birth-control pills, hopefully without their side effects. A woman who has intercourse only occasionally—say once or twice a month—may not want to use birth control daily; in such a case LHRH may serve as a safe morning-after contraceptive. And if a woman misses her period, she may be able to use LHRH to induce menstruation.

Some LHRH compounds may even have important therapeutic benefits—for example, in the treatment of premenstrual syndrome and endometriosis. The latter can be an incredibly painful condition, which occurs when the cells which line the uterus (endometrium) start growing where they don't belong—in the vagina, bladder, ovaries, or rectum. During every menstrual period the whole abdomen can ache terribly, and monthly flow can be quite heavy. Endometriosis can also cause infertility. Preliminary research suggests that LHRH may be one of the most effective and safest approaches to this problem. It may also be of value in treating ovarian cysts and possibly even hirsutism—an embarrassing excess of facial and body hair.

So how long do we have to wait before we can try this new contraceptive? Syntex started testing a compound in 1977, and Hoechst Laboratories has been investigating an LHRH nasal spray in Sweden since 1978. Preliminary studies there have shown an impressive degree of contraceptive protection (equivalent to the Pill), with virtually no serious side effects.[8] About the only complaint has been mild nasal irritation from the spray itself. Wyeth and Abbott are also in the running.

Dr. Brian Vickery, who has headed Syntex's preclinical research, can barely suppress his enthusiasm, as he showed in one interview.

> **"This is *the* most exciting drug in my working life." Vickery hopes to receive FDA approval for use of the drug as a contraceptive toward the end of this decade and he believes approval for combating cancer could come earlier.**
>
> **Syntex is hardly alone in researching LHRH, however, and Vickery admits "we're in a race with other competitors to be first to the market."[9]**

An article in the *British Medical Journal* echoes Dr. Vickery's enthusiasm with the conclusion that "LHRH agonists are our brightest hope for a new approach to contraception and offer challenges for treatment of sex-hormone related disorders."[10]

Although initial studies on human subjects have been very encouraging, everyone is gun-shy these days. And a darn good thing, too! Because early reports touting the safety of oral contraceptives gave people a false sense of confidence, today researchers are far more cautious. Before LHRH is released, it will have to pass some pretty high hurdles. But unless some undiscovered hazard shows up, my best guess is that within two to three years you will find at least one LHRH compound on pharmacy shelves.

A Is for Apple and Aphrodisiac

Until recently few researchers were willing to study the effects of drugs on human sexuality. After all, what respected scientist wants to be labeled a flake by his colleagues? Even in our "enlightened" age studies of sexuality are considered somewhat suspect by the medical profession. Another reason no one has been particularly anxious to undertake such work is that the news has been mostly bad.

A surprising number of commonly prescribed medications have been reported to cause reduced libido, impotence, frigidity, or inability to achieve orgasm. Doctors and drug companies don't like to talk about this problem, for fear that it will scare patients out of taking needed medicine. And they seem equally reluctant to engage in comprehensive studies to uncover the true scope of these complications.

But even if most researchers have pretty much ignored the adverse sexual side effects of drugs, a few courageous investigators have started looking at the opposite side of the coin—aphrodisiacs and drugs to reverse impotence. Dr. Robert L. Moss is a respected neuroendocrinologist at Southwestern Medical School. He has been testing one tailor-made LHRH compound that, he believes, can stimulate sexuality.[11,12] After administering it to laboratory animals, he observed increased libido and greater sexual contact.

Dr. Moss has also noted a sexually activating effect in men. After giving LHRH to 50 impotent men he noted some benefit in approximately 60 percent.

> The spectrum of improvement ranged from very slight to dramatic. Some men simply reported feeling sexy and then obtained an erection several hours later. Others became very sexually aroused, obtaining an erection almost immediately after the injection.[13]

Other researchers have confirmed Dr. Moss' observations. A team of investigators in Munich, Germany, carried out a four-week double-blind* controlled experiment with an LHRH nasal spray. They found that a number of impotent men benefited and that the increase in sexual potency lasted up to six weeks "*after* discontinuing the administration of LHRH."[14-16] Not only do some of these compounds offer hope as contraceptives, then, but others may also restore sexual function or act as aphrodisiacs. There is even strong evidence that they may play an important role in treating breast and prostate cancer.[17-20]

As exciting as these LHRH substances may be, they are still mostly experimental and won't be widely available for several more years. Naturally there had to be a catch. But lest you think I've just been

*In a double-blind controlled study, some patients get an active drug, while others receive an indistinguishable but inert placebo. Neither the experimental subjects nor the investigators know who's getting what until the study ends and the code is broken.

pulling your chain with tantalizing tales of enhanced sexuality, let me hasten to add that several other possibilities are available.

If LHRH is at the cutting edge of contraceptive research, yohimbine represents a step back in time. This ancient herbal remedy comes from the bark of the African yohimb tree and has long had a reputation among tribesmen as a restorer of sexual potency. Naturally scientists scoffed at such a claim, and the FDA rejected yohimbine for use in over-the-counter preparations. But new research suggests that this is one folk remedy that might have some validity.

Dr. Alvaro Morales is an associate professor of urology at Queen's University in Ontario, Canada. He became interested in some of the unique characteristics of yohimbine and started evaluating its usefulness in the treatment of impotence. While not all his patients were helped, a surprisingly high number (43 percent) did note some improvement, and more than one-fourth experienced a return of complete erections and orgasms.[21,22]

This isn't the first time yohimbine has been shown to be effective. Occasional reports in the medical literature have noted beneficial effects, and even the famed heart surgeon Dr. Christiaan Barnard mentioned that it restored "potency to three of four men who'd received heart transplants."[23,24] And new research by Stanford physiologists has demonstrated impressive evidence that yohimbine can stimulate sexuality. Based on their study of rats, the scientists concluded that

> **These data suggest that yohimbine may be a true aphrodisiac, since it increases arousal in sexually experienced male rats, facilitates copulatory behavior (including ejaculation) in sexually naive males, and induces sexual activity in males that were previously sexually inactive . . .**
>
> **Although preliminary clinical data are suggestive of a libido-promoting effect in human males, caution should be exercised— especially concerning possible interactions between yohimbine and other medications . . . Further research could lead to developments in the pharmacologic treatment of sexual dysfunction.[25]**

Even though yohimbine is available in this country, most physicians have never heard of it; and even if they had, chances are they wouldn't know how to prescribe it or warn about side effects. That doesn't mean people should bypass their doctor and start self-medicating. The drug can cause anxiety, increase blood pressure, affect kidney function, increase heart rate, and cause tremor. It should not be taken by anyone with kidney disease.

Before people even consider yohimbine, they should have a long talk with a physician who has at least read the article written by Dr. Morales and his associates ("Nonhormonal Pharmacological Treatment of Organic Impotence," *Journal of Urology* vol. 128, pp. 45–47, July, 1982). Assuming no reasons can be found that would mean treatment is not advisable, the next hurdle is finding yohimbine. Most drugstores probably don't carry it, but a pharmacist can order this prescription product from Consolidated Midland Corporation under the brand name **Yocon.** Although this African herbal remedy won't help everyone, and larger studies are necessary before it receives Mother Hubbard's seal of approval, there is room for optimism.

And that's not all, folks. There's more good news. Not only are researchers starting to investigate drugs which reverse impotence, they are also are beginning to unlock the secrets of human sexuality. They now recognize that chemicals occurring naturally in the brain (neurotransmitters) seem to regulate both desire and ability.

> **The aphrodisiac effects of neurotransmitter manipulation were discovered in the 1960s when L-dopa [Dopar, Larodopa] began to be used extensively to treat parkinsonism. Doctors noticed that some patients exhibited heightened sexual interest after taking the drug.   Since then, the medical profession has generally downplayed this effect.**
>
> **Yet an analysis of the literature indicates a much broader pattern of aphrodisiac effects in L-dopa patients than that reported by some investigators. . . .**
>
> **In studies in which the subjects were questioned about their sexual habits, increased sexual interest and/or activity has been found in about 30% of cases.[26]**

Some physicians reject the L-dopa (levodopa) reports as mere fantasy or wishful thinking. Others assert that alleviating the symptoms of Parkinson's disease will naturally lead to increased activity of all sorts. Yet there have been too many accounts of increased sexuality in the medical literature to chalk this up to chance.[27–29]

Now before you rush out and demand a prescription for L-dopa, keep in mind that it is a potent medicine. The drug, used for the treatment of Parkinson's disease, works by increasing the levels of a naturally occurring brain chemical called dopamine. Side effects can include nausea and vomiting, difficulty in urinating, dizziness, depression, irregular heart beats, and—after long-term therapy—uncontrolled movements of the head, arms, and hands. As far as I'm concerned, those risks are too great to justify the use of levodopa in stimulating sexuality. But it does give us an important clue to the puzzle.

Another drug that also affects the dopamine system in the brain is called **Parlodel** (bromocriptine). Relatively new to this country, the substance has a fascinating history. Like L-dopa, **Parlodel** is useful in treating parkinsonism. But it does more, *much* more!

For one thing, it can help alleviate a bizarre syndrome called galactorrhea, which can affect both men and women and is characterized by breast enlargement and secretion of milk. In women it is often accompanied by lack of menstrual periods and infertility. The condition usually occurs when a person's hormonal system goes haywire and starts producing excessive amounts of a substance called prolactin.

The number of different drugs that can bring on galactorrhea include blood-pressure medications—like methyldopa (**Aldoclor, Aldomet, Aldoril**), and reserpine (**Ser-Ap-Es, Serpasil, Diupres, Hydropres, Regroton, Salutensin,** and the like)—and antipsychotics, such as chlorpromazine (**Thorazine**), thioridazine (**Mellaril**), trifluoperazine (**Stelazine**), prochlorperazine (**Compazine**) and haloperidol (**Haldol**). Women who go off birth control pills may also experience this problem, as may people suffering from tumors of the pituitary gland.

Interestingly, too much prolactin also leads to loss of libido and impotence. **Parlodel** can block prolactin, end milk production, and restore fertility. It can also have a profound affect on sexuality!

Take the case of Mr. G. B. in Montreal, Canada. At age 65 he was experiencing headaches and feeling tired most of the time. But what really had him upset was his total lack of interest in sex. At first he thought it was merely because he was getting older, but when his friends and colleagues of the same age related their sexual exploits, he began to get upset and decided it was time to consult a doctor.

> As far as sexual function was concerned the patient stated that he experienced a gradual decline in sexual interest over the last 5 years; for the last 2 years he claimed that he had no sexual desire at all. He also noticed a decrease in the frequency of erectile episodes during day or night and a prolongation in the time required to acquire an erection.[30]

The doctors discovered that Mr. G. B. had a pituitary tumor that was producing too much prolactin. They removed most of the tumor surgically and were pleased to see some improvement in prolactin levels, but the symptoms remained. Four months later they started Mr. G. B. on **Parlodel**.

> Three months later we received a phone call from his wife followed by a letter in which she described her husband as "rejuvenated." According to her he was now spending money on expensive clothing, had joined a fitness club, was developing narcissistic attitudes, and his interest in sex had increased

to such a degree that she could not cope with it. According to her, these events occurred after her husband had started bromocriptine [Parlodel] and she was primarily asking for cessation of therapy.

On coming for reevaluation the patient was accompanied by an attractive 42-year-old woman who he wished to marry. Upon questioning the future bride she stated that the behavior of the patient was normal and they had intercourse 3–5 times a week. The patient was able to maintain a full erection, [and] showed no premature ejaculation. . . . He compared his current sexual activity to that of when he was 24 years old. . . .

A month later we were requested to provide a medical report on his condition and treatment, to be used in divorce proceedings because his wife was claiming that "his brain was sick." He is presently happily remarried, and has full potency while on bromocriptine.[31]

Now, one case history is not enough to convince anyone from Missouri. But hold on to your bonnet there *are* other reports. Several years ago Italian endocrinologists discovered that **Parlodel** could restore potency to some men and even have an effect on women. Dr. Andrea Genazzini of the University of Siena tested **Parlodel** on women who had lost their menstrual cycles. Dr. Genazzini found that "in some women who never had erotic feelings in their entire lives, [**Parlodel**] restored sexual desire and led to normal sexual activity."[32–33] Not only does the drug restore regular cycles and fertility in women with excess levels of prolactin, it may also improve libido.

Other studies have found that **Parlodel** may be of some benefit to patients who suffer sexual problems associated with dialysis or diabetes.[34–37] It has also been reported to provide considerable help in reducing symptoms of premenstrual-tension syndrome.[38,39] The drug may even turn out to lower pressure within the eye and therefore be beneficial for glaucoma patients.[40] Interestingly, many of **Parlodel**'s effects on libido, potency, and infertility may have to do with its ability to stimulate LHRH.

As intriguing as this drug may appear, it, too, has side effects and should only be considered after a physician has carefully evaluated hormonal function to make sure there is indeed an elevation in prolactin levels. **Parlodel** can cause nausea, dizziness, headache, constipation, and fatigue.

Okay, okay, I hear you. You're getting impatient. I've painted a rainbow, but the pot of gold keeps disappearing just before we reach the end. What's the point of all this? Well, first, it's important to realize that human sexuality depends to a great extent on hormonal and chemical regulation. Our levels of dopamine, LHRH, and prolactin will profoundly influence our libido and potency. When these substances get out of whack, as in the case of good old Mr. G. B., life can be pretty miserable.

Now that's not to say that psychological factors aren't important. They are! Impotence and loss of libido can be caused by all sorts of things, including stress, fatigue, depression, physical ailments, alcohol, and other drugs. Love, consideration, and romance, plus a good dose of TLC (Tender Loving Care), are just as important as hormonal balance. But for far too long people have assumed that sexuality was purely "mental." It's now clear that hormones have a lot to do with it as well, and we are getting closer to figuring out how they work and what to do to correct imbalances.

Sex and the Fat Rat

When I read the headline, "DuPont Drug Keeps Rats Skinny And Gives Them a Great Love Life," I figured it was just another sensational teaser to get me to read the article. But the story wasn't in a supermarket tabloid—it was in *The Wall Street Journal*.

> When life in the laboratory gets boring, some rats pass the time by overeating. They often learn the hard way that pigging out has heavy consequences.
>
> But a drug developed by DuPont Co. and used in experiments at Temple University keeps gluttonous rats from getting fat. David Margules, founder of Temple's National Obesity Research Foundation, injected rodents with naloxone and put them on an all-they-could-eat diet of marshmallows and chocolate chips. He was confident the temptation would be too great. "Try controlling yourself when you're eating M & M's," he says.
>
> Naloxone apparently stimulated oxygen consumption, thus burning off the extra calories and preventing the animals from becoming obese.
>
> The drug also seems to stimulate something else: In another test group, Dr. Margules and a colleague at a laboratory in France noticed increased interest among genetically obese rats in copulating. Observes Dr. Margules: "You could say they became more amorous."[41]

Too much! Lose weight and improve your love life simultaneously. Ridiculous, right? That's what I thought until I started digging. What I discovered could be one of the most interesting drug developments of the 1980s.

Naloxone (**Narcan**) is a fascinating drug that's been available since 1971. It was originally developed to counteract the effects of narcotic overdose. No emergency room in the country can afford to be without this lifesaver. A junkie who is on the verge of checking out because of too much heroin can be miraculously brought back to life with a small injection of **Narcan**. One minute he's comatose, having difficulty breathing—and the next he's awake and breathing normally. Chicago paramedics report that the drug saves 50 to 100 lives a month.

> **You get to a scene and there's an overdose lying there, paramedic Joe McLeary said. And the crowd is yelling at you, cursing you, telling you to hurry up because there's a guy lying there, about dead. You inject Narcan. Bang, he's up jumping and yelling. The crowd stares at you like you are Lazarus. You turn from zero to hero in 30 seconds. To them, it's paramagic.**[42]

Narcan can also help reverse some of the depressant effects of anesthetics, barbiturates, and antianxiety agents like **Valium**. If morphine is administered during surgery, an anesthesiologist is likely to have a hypo filled with **Narcan** handy to bring the patient back in the event respiration slows too much.

In a word, naloxone almost instantly reverses the effects of opioid narcotics. But so far the drug has barely produced anything but a big yawn. Lets face it, there are few headlines when a junkie is pulled back from the brink of disaster. And since the drug can only be administered by injection, there is little possibility for widespread use.

Enter its chemical cousin naltrexone (**Trexan**)—an oral and longer-lasting version of naloxone. Presto! All of a sudden it's a whole new ballgame. For one thing, naltrexone offers tremendous hope for narcotic addicts who truly want to kick the habit. Used prophylactically, it completely blocks the effects of opiates. Anyone taking naltrexone or naloxone won't get high.[43–46]

Let me put it another way. Imagine someone who loves hot fudge sundaes (speaking from experience, I can honestly say that addiction to such a decadent dessert is not purely hypothetical). Now imagine a pill that would render hot fudge sundaes tasteless. Cruel and inhuman punishment, you might say, and I would have to agree. But if you were sincerely trying to wean yourself away from such depravity, so that you would lose weight, it might be the only way to accomplish the task. Well, that's what naloxone and naltrexone do for the addict—they take away any pleasurable experience associated with abuse of narcotics without producing any effect of their own. One **Trexan** user reports that he doesn't "even think about it any more because I know I can't feel it. If I was clean and I didn't have naltrexone in my system, I don't know what I would do. But with the naltrexone in my system it's like a suit of armor."[47]

Interesting, but what does that have to do with you and me? We aren't addicts, and these drugs don't seem to have much relevance to us. Or do they? After all, 80 million Americans are overweight. Go ahead, pinch those love handles. If you come up empty, you're one of the lucky ones. For the rest of us the battle of the bulge never stops. No one knows why some people get fat. Oh sure, we eat too much and exercise too little, according to the standard explanation—and it's true. But obesity is incredibly complicated, and there are lots of theories to explain why one person can eat like a horse and never gain weight while someone else seems to add pounds just by walking past the dessert tray.

One of the newest and most intriguing concepts in the study of obesity is the "set point." Investigators speculate that there is an internal regulator in the brain that sets its own "ideal" weight for the body and then tunes the appetite to maintain that weight. No matter how much we diet, we always seem to end up back where we started after a while. This "thermostat" is thought to be located in the hypothalamus—the so-called satiety or pleasure center of the brain.[48] Although scientists don't know how the set point gets established, it's clear that for many of us the end result is unrelated to our concept of ideal weight.

Opiates and the Brain

Two of the substances that stimulate appetite are natural opiates: endorphins and enkephalins.[49,50] The discovery of these morphinelike chemicals within the body is revolutionizing our understanding of the brain. Endorphins and enkephalins appear to play a crucial role in protecting the body against pain.[51,52] Acupuncture, for example, may work by triggering the release of these compounds.[53] And they may well be responsible for the commonly reported cases of soldiers wounded in battle who may not be aware they've been injured until the fighting is over. Athletes, too, may not realize they've been hurt until after the game. And the so-called runner's high appears to be a very real phenomenon, probably caused by stimulation of endorphin receptors within the brain.

Scientists now believe that not only are natural opiates important in controlling pain, but they may play an important role in mental illness (schizophrenia and manic depression), epilepsy, stress reactions, and even learning and memory.[54-55]

They may also explain why some people react to placebos (sugar pills). It matters little what the problem—arthritis, angina, high blood pressure, or the common cold—anywhere from 30 to 60 percent of those people who receive a placebo will experience relief. It may very well be that the mere act of swallowing a pill, any pill—even a sugar pill—stimulates the body to secrete endorphins. And some people are more susceptible than others.

Have you ever been in the embarrassing situation of having an almost unbearable toothache or other pain only to find that no sooner do you walk into the office and have the dentist or doctor ask where it hurts than the problem seems magically to disappear. There you are, stuck with a silly grin on your face trying to explain how poorly you were feeling, and now everything is fine. Of course, no sooner do you leave than the pain comes back with a vengeance. Again it may be your body's own natural opiates responding to the doctor's office or white coat or goodness knows what. Perhaps the best example of all is a mother's kiss. It can work almost like magic for a child who comes running with a cut or scratch. Endorphins and enkephalins? Quite possibly.

Research on these compounds is generating tremendous excitement because it could eventually lead to the development of potent pain relievers that would have little or no potential for addiction or abuse. Equally important, there would be no need to keep increasing the dose to maintain effective relief, which is a major problem with most modern-day analgesics.

If these natural opiates are responsible for stimulating appetite as well as providing pain relief, then drugs like naloxone or naltrexone, which block opiate action, should counteract most of the effects of the endorphins and enkephalins. Bingo! Naloxone pretreatment does indeed block the benefits of placebos as well as acupuncture.[56]

So far, all of these discoveries are of little more than academic interest—the kind of stuff that makes a pharmacologist's blood race but leaves the average person cold. But now consider the possibility that naltrexone may offer some very real practical benefits besides keeping junkies from getting high or overdosing. For one thing, the drug might provide a path to weight control.

Now don't get nervous. Old Joe has *not* sold out to the drug companies! I have been, and remain, one of the most vocal critics of diet pills and fad diets ever to come down the pike. Permanent weight loss requires a change in eating *behavior*. What I mean is this: most people who overeat do so not from hunger but for all kinds of other reasons, such as boredom, anxiety, stress, or habit. When they learn to deal with these issues in other ways, they can begin to eat more appropriately. And let's not forget exercise. It has even been suggested that regular exercise may influence endorphins to help reset your appetite thermostat downward.

But—and that is one humongous **BUT**, for many of us these solutions are hard as hell to stick with. Oh sure, we promise ourselves we'll exercise more, but something always seems to come up to interfere with

our good intentions. Or we go to dinner at a really nice restaurant and
. . . well, you know what happens. Or something stressful occurs in our
lives, and we start stuffing our faces to ease the tension. Ultimately food
can become an addiction, just like a drug. And that's where naloxone
and naltrexone just might help out.

Remember Dr. Margules and his fat rats? In that ingenious, almost
diabolical experiment, rats and mice were offered all the marshmallows
and chocolate chips they could eat. The result: obesity. One little devil
reached the mouse equivalent of an 800-pound person. But the rodents
that received naloxone did not get fat even when they overate.[57]

As Dr. Margules explains:

> My work with mice showed the first important support for the
> idea that the obese might have an addictive attachment to
> food through these endorphins. In 1978, I discovered that the
> endorphins occur in excess quantities in obese mice.
>
> The endorphins stimulate the urge to eat and they also slow
> down the metabolism so not much energy is burned.
>
> (Naloxone blocks the release of the endorphins.) It's helping
> weight control in two ways. It's inhibiting weight gain and
> increasing energy expenditures.[58,59]

Unlike previous diet pills, which act by stimulating the nervous system and suppressing appetite temporarily, naloxone actually seems to
help burn off calories more rapidly by increasing energy expenditure.
Even more intriguing, other researchers have shown that "stress-induced
eating" (my problem) also seems to have something to do with endorphins.
It turns out that you can get rats to eat by pinching their tails; naloxone
blocked this behavior.[60]

Add another piece to the puzzle, Watson. Some scientists believe they
see in such animal research signs to suggest that obesity may be partially
caused by addiction to the body's own opiates.[61] Every time that rat
takes a bite of a marshmallow or a chocolate chip, some endorphins
squirt out of a nerve center in the brain. Maybe that's why it's impossible to eat only one M&M.

Fascinating, but rats are rats, not people. How can a few pudgy
rodents provide any useful information about the way overweight humans might respond to this drug? Although research is still in the preliminary stage, there is evidence that the drug does indeed produce a "weight
loss and diminished appetite" in humans.[62,63] And Dr. Mark Gold, research director at Fair Oaks Hospital in Summit, N.J., reported that
naltrexone does show promise: "People lost weight even though food
intake was stable. Some people told us food had less interest to them.
That's information you can't get from rats."[64] Maybe, just maybe, nalox-

one and naltrexone will help us to understand some of the underlying factors behind obesity, and they may even open the door to successful treatment.

And what about the sexual side effects of naloxone? Dr. Margules noted that his tubby rats "became more amorous" after receiving the drug. There is ample evidence that naloxone and naltrexone increase levels of LHRH (our old aphrodisiac friend) and stimulate sexuality in rodents.[65,66] And one study noted much the same effect in humans: "Three subjects reported recurrent spontaneous penile erections 1–3 hours following naltrexone administration."[67]

Will these drugs really help to make you skinny and improve your love life? That remains to be proven. Candidly, I have to admit that I doubt it. But initial reports are certainly interesting. At the very least these experiments will go a long way toward unlocking the secrets to eating behavior and the hormonal regulation of sexuality. And that ain't half bad!

How long will it be before naltrexone (**Trexan**) becomes available? It's available right now—but only for narcotic addicts. The DuPont drug company is actively pursuing the weight loss concept, but it may take a while before the drug receives approval from the FDA for any other purpose. There are even some tantalizing preliminary hints that naloxone may be of some benefit to people who suffer from chronic, severe constipation, Alzheimer's disease, or shock due to blood poisoning.[68–70]

Lest you think all of this is pie in the sky, let me hasten to add that Hoffmann-LaRoche is also hot on the heels of a compound the drug company thinks will revolutionize weight control. Dr. Richard Faust, Director of Roche's Research, Planning, and Development program, confided that a drug already being tested in human subjects has shown remarkable promise. This preparation is completely different from all diet pills on the market and does not stimulate the nervous system. Instead, the mystery compound affects metabolism and food utilization so that "it's not deposited as fat." This drug also seems to reduce "the amount of food intake necessary to feel comfortable."[71]

Dr. Faust wouldn't tell me what the secret substance is, but one compound I know the Roche scientists to be studying is cholecystokinin (CCK). It is a natural chemical found in our bodies that is known to reduce appetite and curb eating behavior. Perhaps the researchers are trying to tinker with CCK and come up with a way to fool the body into thinking it has just finished a seven-course meal.

If all this sounds too good to be true, maybe it is; but then again, if you had told people 50 years ago that there would be a cure for VD, they would probably have looked at you in amazement. Who knows what the future holds in store—maybe even a baldness remedy?

B Is For Bashful, Baldness, and Balderdash

"Losing hair?" the ads ask. "Rejuvenate hair follicles, stimulate scalp circulation, and strengthen hair roots with our scientific discovery." "Balding?" queries another ad. "Now you have the opportunity to grow glorious hair back. If you're losing hair, can you afford *not* to try this new breakthrough?" A headline shouts, "MONEY BACK GUARANTEE!" and supplies fuzzy before-and-after photographs that are supposed to convince us that "SEEING IS BELIEVING."

We're told that "If your hair is only 'sleeping,' biotin solution will wake it up, and you'll be on your way to the most fabulous head of hair you can possibly have!" Finally, they hit us where it really hurts. In advertising copy for the Nexxus Hair Rejuvenating Program our masculinity is challenged.

> Ever since the Biblical legend of Samson has been known, a man's virility, strength—sex appeal—has been associated with an abundance of hair.

> The appearance of youth is also identified with plenty of hair. . . . When baldness approaches, beginning with the first evidence of thinning—the receding hairline, the telltale round spot of disappearing hair at the top of the head—panic sets in.

> BUT NOW THERE IS HOPE
> RESEARCH AND TECHNOLOGY
> HAVE COME TO THE RESCUE

> THANKS TO THIS RESEARCH THE AVERAGE BALD MAN
> NO LONGER NEEDS TO SUFFER THE TORMENT
> OF LOST HAIR

According to the FDA, such ads are nothing but balderdash. A panel of experts studied 18 ingredients found in hair products sold in barbershops and beauty parlors, along with those promoted directly to consumers in magazines and sold through the mail. The panel turned thumbs down on all 18 ingredients, including wheat-germ oil, estrogen, lanolin, and Vitamin C.[72] And for once the AMA agrees. Dr. Jason Gittmann wrote a letter to the *Journal of the American Medical Association* inquiring about some of these products.

> Several patients and friends have asked my opinion of apparently similar products marketed under different trade names (i.e., Bio-Genesis, Bio-Prima, and Bioscal) and heavily advertised in the lay press as being effective in 80% of users in stopping hair loss in male-pattern alopecia [baldness]. An air

of respectability is lent by claims that the product was developed by researchers in Finland, and endorsed by the medical examiner, Federal Republic of West Germany. . . . It is expensive (a 1-oz, two-week supply costs almost $25), and no mention is made of its active ingredients. Is there any scientific validity to the claims made for this product?[73]

The AMA's resident expert on such questions is Dr. Joseph Jerome, who offered a response. "We remain skeptical of all claims, testimonials, and endorsements of hair-restoring or hair-loss-preventing products."[74] Dr. Jerome pointed out that the Finnish studies were "preponderantly animal studies," and if hair does grow it tends to be so fine that it is "not noticeable at distances of approximately 2 m [six feet]."[75]

Each year Americans throw away approximately $3 million on this mail-order madness. And that doesn't even count the junk they buy in barbershops and the home remedies they try. It is hard to imagine the sorts of things people have applied to their bald heads in the hope of stimulating hair growth. The ancient Egyptians thought that fat would do the trick; they prepared a concoction of hippopotamus, crocodile, and snake fat. More recent remedies have included horse manure, crushed bees and wasps, and leeches. People have even used modified vacuum cleaners that were supposed to stimulate the scalp and make those lazy, good-for-nothing hair follicles go back to work.

Why, you ask, are so many fooled so often by so much silliness? People are suckers for such products because people are so desperate. One example culled from the hundreds of letters we have received on this subject from readers of our newspaper column shows what it's all about.

I'm 39 and I cringe every time I look in the mirror. My hairline is "receding" on a dead run, and it makes me look much older than I am. I know it sounds petty, but I feel I'm being passed over for promotions because of it.

My social life is also suffering. I'm afraid to approach any really attractive women my own age because I dread telling them how old I am.

I've got to do something, but the idea of wearing a toupee makes me puke. My dermatologist is willing to do a hair transplant, but I'm not eager to spend thousands on anything that's going to hurt or only be partly effective. Are any of the baldness remedies I see advertised in the newspaper or in men's magazines any good? I'll try anything!

You can see how susceptible these folks are to any promise of relief.

And naturally the quick-buck artists are always ready to prey upon this vulnerability with all sorts of bizarre remedies.

So where's the good news? I promised an up-beat chapter, not a downer. Well, throw away your hat, here comes word of a truly extraordinary breakthrough—no bull! One of the best-kept secrets at the Upjohn Company these days is the story behind the story of a blood-pressure medication called **Loniten** (minoxidil).

Loniten was first approved by the FDA in 1979 for patients with severe hypertension who had not responded to more traditional treatments. It worked, but there was a price to be paid. The drug caused water buildup (edema), increased heart rate, changes in the electrocardiogram, and occasionally pressure around the heart. Fortunately few patients experienced these dangerous side effects, but they did start reporting something else that had them quite upset.

Within three to six weeks after starting **Loniten** 80 percent of the people noticed that their fine body hairs—the ones that are usually invisible—started to thicken, darken, and grow. According to the drug company, "It is usually first noticed on the temples, between the eyebrows, or in the sideburn area of the upper lateral cheek, later extending to the back, arms, legs, and scalp."[76] Researchers have also noted bushy eyebrows and "increased hair growth in the nostrils and ears."[77]

Yucko! Unless you're planning on trying out for the lead in *Return of the Werewolf*, **Loniten** doesn't sound very appealing. And indeed, sales were lackluster; the folks at Upjohn certainly weren't rejoicing. But then an extraordinary thing happened—a light bulb went on inside someone's head. The realization dawned that the drug was actually growing hair, even on what had previously been bald heads.[78,79]

But there was a very big problem. No one could possibly justify giving this heavy-duty blood pressure medication to a bunch of baldies, just to see if it would grow hair. The risks were too great and the benefits too "insignificant." But what if these test subjects didn't swallow the medicine? What if the tablets were mashed, mixed with some goo to turn the stuff into a lotion or ointment, and then smeared on some hairless volunteers?

Guess what happened? The headline in *Skin and Allergy News* told it all: "Topically Applied Vasodilator Found to Promote Hair Growth." The story followed.

> **Minoxidil, a potent vasodilator used orally in the treatment of hypertension, appears to have "dramatic" hair-growing properties when applied topically to some patients with male pattern baldness or alopecia areata, Dr. Vera Price said at the annual meeting of the American Academy of Dermatology.**
>
> **Although the search for a treatment of male pattern baldness has been rivaled in duration and intensity only by that for the**

Holy Grail, Dr. Price strongly urged physicians to refrain from the temptation of using minoxidil on their bald patients until after Upjohn's controlled clinical trials are completed within the next year. . . .

"Physicians who use it now can easily get into the kind of trouble that will cause the drug to be taken away from us by a higher authority," warned Dr. Price.[80]

Needless to say, Upjohn didn't want to run into trouble with the FDA. After all, **Loniten** could become the goose that laid the golden egg, the pot of gold at the end of the rainbow, the biggest pharmaceutical bonanza of all time. In order to prevent repercussions from any "higher authority," Upjohn clamped a total news blackout on this story. But some executives are more than a little excited. Vice President Lawrence Hoff confessed to one reporter, "I think about minoxidil on Mondays and it gets me going the whole week."[81]

But little bits and pieces have been leaking out. At the time of this writing, over 20 physicians around the country are testing **Loniten** on baldies. And were the guinea pigs willing to sign up! One doctor reported being inundated with bald men almost "tearing down the doors" to get into the study. "More than 18,000 called or wrote trying to enroll; 96 were chosen."[82]

The studies are being underwritten and supervised by Upjohn in a carefully controlled, double-blind manner, and the results are still secret. But it's hard not to notice when someone starts to grow hair. The grapevine has it that the drug does indeed work for some people. The case of one subject in the experiment, a jogger, was so unusual that it was hard to keep quiet. He noticed (to his dismay) that hair had started sprouting on the tops of his ears. Apparently the **Loniten** that he had spread on his bald head had dripped down to his ears as he was running and sweating and had stimulated hair growth there. Fortunately there was a simple solution to his problem—a sweatband.

Dermatologists will be hard put to contain their excitement if **Loniten** works for male pattern baldness (the kind caused by our genes) as well as alopecia areata (the kind caused by our immune systems). In alopecia areata, the body seems to make antibodies to its own hair follicles, and hair is rejected just as if it were a foreign body. As a result some areas of hair seem to disappear from the body. This condition can affect women as well as men.

Dr. Virginia Weiss, associate professor of dermatology at the University of Illinois, found that 21 of 29 patients with alopecia areata responded to **Loniten**. In one case a thirteen-year-old girl who had been totally bald since the age of eight applied **Loniten** to her entire scalp. "Within 5 weeks, active regrowth of hair was found at treated sites."[83]

Nine months later the girl had "normal hair" over almost all areas of her scalp.

More scientific evidence is also accumulating. British dermatologists recently reported impressive results with **Loniten**.

> There have been many treatments suggested for alopecia areata. Most are unsatisfactory either because of side effects or because the hair regrowth is vellus [fine hard-to-see hair] only and therefore cosmetically unacceptable. . . .
>
> Our initial results show that topical minoxidil can induce regrowth of hair in a substantial proportion of patients suffering from alopecia areata. Out of 26 patients, 21 showed some response, though in only 16 was this cosmetically acceptable. Nevertheless, as compared with most other treatments, topical minoxidil appears to be relatively non-toxic, is easy to use, and is free from any local or systemic [whole body] side effects. In none of the patients treated was there any change in pulse rate or blood pressure or any cutaneous [skin] side effect.[84]

No one really knows how **Loniten** works to stimulate hair growth. One theory has it that the drug increases blood flow to the skin and that this improved circulation somehow stimulates the hair follicles to go back to work.[85,86] Whatever the mechanism, it does seem to work for some people (though others barely see improvement). So far there doesn't appear to be any reliable way to predict who will benefit and who won't; but at least to date, no bad side effects have been associated with the topical application of **Loniten**.[87]

Dr. Virginia Weiss's formula for making **Loniten** lotion has been published, but please, dear reader, don't take this cookbook formula as an endorsement of **Loniten**! It is a powerful drug, which *may* get into the body and cause side effects. Even though there should be less danger from applying it topically than from swallowing it orally, we won't know for sure until all tests are complete. And many questions remain about its effectiveness. Before the FDA gives its approval for the use of **Loniten** in the treatment of baldness, several more years will probably go by.

But according to the *Wall Street Journal*, a lot of balding people— and their dermatologists—aren't waiting.

> **"I'm using it and so are many of my colleagues," says Michael Reed, who practices in New York City. One of his patients, a middle-aged housewife, dabs a teaspoonful of the liquid on her balding scalp every evening, pulls on a yellow**

plastic swim cap and goes to sleep. "Not very sexy," she says, "but it works." After using minoxidil since last summer, she says she recently discarded the wig she wore for years.

Also not waiting for FDA approval is Cambridge Chemists, a drugstore on New York City's East Side. Pharmacists there make a liquid version of minoxidil for patients of about 20 area physicians, including Dr. Reed. The pharmacy crushes prescription tablets of Loniten (the form in which Upjohn sells the drug for severe high blood pressure), mixes them with an alcohol-based solution and sells them a one-month supply of two ounces for about $75.[88]

Now we don't suggest that you rush right out and start spending good money to smear this stuff on your scalp. Nevertheless, for the first time in centuries there is good news for the hopelessly hairless. Hooray!

Biotechnology and Blue Sky

Okay, I've offered new drug developments which might help you be shaggy, slim, and safely sexy. But let's face it, thrilling as those prospects are, they are hardly of life-and-death importance. Don't drug companies have anything on tap to combat the far more important problems of cancer, heart disease, arthritis, pain, depression, and hypertension? In fact, though the puzzles are far from solved, there is some very encouraging news on many of these fronts. The key that could lead to successful treatment of some of our worst ailments may be something amorphous called biotechnology.

First, a quick history lesson. Humanity's introduction to drug development probably came when Neanderthals started tasting leaves and roots. If they survived, the experiments were a success. Eventually the bolder "scientists" of the day found that some plants seemed helpful in relieving certain symptoms. Through this kind of trial and error medicinal herbs like willow bark, foxglove, ephedra, and cinchona were discovered. We learned how to purify the active ingredients—aspirin, digitalis, ephedrine, quinine—in these plants, and pharmacy was born.

Eventually medicinal chemists started tinkering with molecules and making compounds from scratch. But even today the science of creating new drugs is mostly hit or miss. Pharmacologists test thousands of chemicals to find a handful of safe and effective medications. And often the most interesting breakthroughs occur serendipitously—like the famous blood pressure pill, **Loniten,** that accidentally grows hair.

But the situation is changing. Today molecular biologists are starting to turn to the ultimate "organic" source of drugs—the human body. It turns out that we may make our own best medicine.

All physiological functions are regulated by chemicals the body itself manufactures. The problem is that these sometimes get out of whack. Biochemical imbalances can lead to depression and schizophrenia, high blood pressure, and heart attacks. And when the immune system fails to function properly, we become susceptible to a whole host of diseases, from allergy and asthma to rheumatoid arthritis, lupus, and cancer.

Until recently the only way to adjust the system was to dump in drugs. But that procedure was often a little like trying to repair a watch with a monkey wrench. A good case in point is cortisone, an important drug in the treatment of rheumatoid arthritis. While it can't cure the disease, it will relieve the symptoms of pain and inflammation. Unfortunately cortisone also affects the body in many other ways and can cause increased susceptibility to infection, fatigue, fluid retention, potassium depletion, diabetes, muscle cramps and weakness, osteoporosis, depression, cataracts, ulcers, insomnia, increased appetite, and weight gain. A drug of this kind blasts the whole body, not just the part we're trying to treat.

Biotechnology, on the other hand, is starting to provide revolutionary new tools that will allow us to fine-tune the system. Such techniques as recombinant DNA and monoclonal antibodies have enabled scientists to manufacture natural body chemicals in significant quantities for the first time. One of the initial products of this effort has been interferon.

Researchers have known about interferon since 1957. It was recognized early on that the body fights off, or "interferes" with, viral infections like the flu, herpes, and the common cold by making interferon. You can think of it as our Paul Revere, sending out biochemical messages that help to mobilize body resources to prevent virus reproduction. Interferon also seems to stimulate the immune system to make "natural killer cells" that seek out and destroy foreign cells, possibly even cancer cells.

Needless to say, everyone and his uncle wanted to get some interferon to test, and cancer researchers were the most anxious of all. And no wonder: traditional cancer treatment is hardly benign. It involves cutting (surgery), burning (with radiation), and poisoning (with chemotherapy). Anything that seemed less toxic and more natural, stimulating the body's own underactive immune system, was like a breath of fresh air. The media picked up on the excitement within the scientific community and were quick to proclaim that a cure for cancer was almost at hand.

But there was a huge problem: the body only makes minute amounts of interferon. In order to obtain enough for a few crude experiments, investigators had to painstakingly process huge quantities of blood. As a result interferon research was prohibitively expensive, and the substance that was finally extracted was usually less than 10 percent pure.

One early clinical test, for example, set its sights on preventing the common cold with what was undoubtedly the world's costliest nosespray, at $700 a squirt. It was also so impure that one of the investigators admitted that it was "99 percent rubbish." The scientists were unsure whether their good results were produced in spite of the impurities in the interferon or because of them. Cancer researchers fared even worse. To treat just one patient for a short time cost as much as $30,000. At that rate it would have taken decades and hundreds of millions of dollars to conduct any kind of decent experiments.

Enter genetic engineering or what is now called biotechnology. By the late 1970s scientists were beginning to master the techniques of gene splicing and cloning and were using a substance called recombinant DNA. What they did was take a tiny piece of genetic material from a human cell which contained the instructions to make a specific protein (interferon, for example). They then inserted it into a common bacterium called *E. coli*. A few of these bacteria were placed in special fermentation tanks, where they could reproduce like crazy, making almost unlimited quantities of the desired compound. Virtually overnight huge amounts of scarce human proteins like interferon could be harvested, purified, and made ready for clinical testing at affordable prices.

But soon after well-controlled experiments got under way, it became clear that interferon was not going to live up to its initial billing. The "wonder drug" of the 1980s did not instantly cure everything from cancer to the common cold. And it caused debilitating, flulike side effects, such as fatigue, fever, chills, muscle aches, and loss of appetite. Almost overnight the pendulum swung in the other direction. The press and the public were ready to write off interferon as just another false hope.

What a mistake! While it's certainly true that interferon is not a panacea, it does represent the first step in a biotechnology revolution that is changing the face of drug development. Dr. Anna Marie Skalka, Associate Director of Biological Research and Development at Hoffman-La Roche, expresses the kid-in-a-candy-store enthusiasm these breakthroughs in molecular biology have produced.

> **It is absolutely fantastic! We have tools we never dreamed we could have. We have a new and richer understanding of how a cell functions, and it is just a most exciting time to be in science.**[89]

What Dr. Skalka means is that by mastering the techniques of gene splicing, researchers are beginning to unlock the secrets of the cell. What they have learned already is incredible. What they will discover is hard to imagine, but the sky's the limit.

And don't write off interferon. We now know that the body makes at least 13 or 14 different interferons, and some definitely do have anticancer potential. Preliminary research suggests that cancer of the kidneys and skin cancer (malignant melanoma) may respond to one or more different kinds of interferon. And one type of leukemia (hairy cell) that is hard to treat has responded favorably as well. Ultimately other cancers may turn out to be sensitive to some sort of interferon, especially when therapy is started early.

There is even evidence that interferon may be useful in treating shingles, chicken pox, and pink eye, in removing stubborn warts, and in preventing the common cold. It may also have a place in the treatment of hepatitis B, herpes, and multiple sclerosis.[90-93]

Ultimately these biologically engineered "drugs" may work best in combination with other, more traditional treatments by restoring an immune response that is suppressed by chemotherapy. Interferon seems helpful, but another product of biotechnology may be even better. Scientists in the know believe that IL-2 (Interleukin-2) and similar chemicals "may reshape medicine as much as the development of antibiotics did three decades ago."[94]

There is a growing conviction that the secret to many of humanity's worst scourges lies with the immune system. If you were to spray influenza viruses equally throughout a room holding a hundred people, not everyone would come down with the flu; some people seem to have better immunity than others. If we could but help the body boost its own immune response, we could conceivably fight off infections, cancer, and many other diseases. AIDS (acquired immune deficiency syndrome) patients have an immune system that is shot all to hell. They come down with cancer (Kaposi's sarcoma) and other life-threatening infections because their bodies cannot fight back. Hopefully, biotechnology will help prime the pump and restore immunity.

And then there are monoclonal antibodies. They have been called "guided missiles, magic bullets, or smart biological bombs."[95] Our white blood cells normally produce millions of different antibodies in response to invasion by bacteria or viruses. They home in on their targets, lock on, and then help to destroy the foreign attacker. Each one is very specific, and they are harmless to normal cells.

Medicine has long taken advantage of the body's own ability to produce these extraordinary compounds through the process of immunization. Doctors inject a killed or weakened virus in a safe manner, so that the patient can produce his own antibodies. Thus we have flu vaccines, pneumonia vaccines, and polio vaccines, to name just a few.

But until recently scientists were unable to produce pure and specific antibodies of their own. Biotechnology has changed all that. Researchers have been able to create scores of antibodies, and these are already being used in medical practice to diagnose such diseases as rabies and gonorrhea, give an early, accurate result on pregnancy tests, and screen blood to make sure it is safe for transfusions.

Even more dramatic work is in progress. If, for example, you could take an antibody to a particular type of cancer cell and link it to one of the chemotherapeutic agents used against that cancer, you could target the poison. Instead of killing off normal healthy cells, leading to all sorts of horrible side effects, and leaving some of the cancer cells alone, these potent chemicals, carried by the right monoclonal antibody, could selectively destroy only the cancerous tissue. Although most of the development on such products remains to be done, one company has already started making specific antibodies against B-cell lymphoma, a cancer that kills 10,000 people each year.[96]

By now you've heard so many improbable promises that you may think this is all pie in the sky. Where's the proof that biotechnology will really live up to its billing? Well, the future is now! We will mention just a few of the biotech products on the market or nearing approval.

HGH (human growth hormone) should eliminate dwarfism forever. Until recently abnormally small children had to depend on scarce HGH obtained from human cadavers. Now an unlimited supply has become available through genetic engineering. Of course, this situation could open a can of worms, because extra HGH can help even normal-sized young people to grow. Parents who want seven-foot basketball players could conceivably give their kids HGH and watch them shoot up.

GRF (growth hormone-releasing factor) is another breakthrough for biotechnology. It spurs tissue growth and may speed the healing of wounds, help mend broken bones, and aid burn victims. GRF may have extraordinary economic consequences as well, since it could increase the growth rate and size of cattle as well as other animals.

Then there is TPA (tissue plasminogen activator). We have known for over 20 years that this natural body substance plays an important role in blood clotting. Apparently it helps to dissolve tiny clots that form in our bodies all the time. But the available amounts of TPA were so minute that testing was impossible. Then along came Genentech, one of the hottest of the biotech companies on the West Coast. The firm was able to genetically engineer TPA in large quantities. As a result this drug has the potential of halting heart attacks in minutes.

Most heart attacks occur when a blood clot lodges in a coronary artery and cuts off the flow of oxygen and essential nutrients to heart tissue. Soon that part of the heart begins to die, leading to potentially fatal irregular heart rhythms. But TPA homes in on the blood clot like a guided missile and within minutes dissolves it away, opening up the coronary artery so that blood can once again start circulating freely.

Dr. Burton Sobel, director of cardiology at Washington University in St. Louis, is one of the first TPA researchers. He is so impressed with his results that he foresees a day when high-risk patients carry a syringe of TPA with them at all times. If they begin developing signs of a coronary, they can actually inject themselves and reverse the heart attack before it starts.[97] Science fiction? Not at all. Patients have already been treated with TPA, and preliminary results are incredibly exciting. Here is one clear case where hundreds of thousands of lives could be saved each year.

Biotechnology is an area of seemingly unlimited potential. People with hemophilia, sickle-cell anemia, and diabetes will no doubt benefit from other drugs that result from genetic engineering. Scientists at Genentech have already developed a process for making Factor VIII, the missing substance hemophiliacs need to prevent hemorrhaging. This should provide almost unlimited quantities of a pure life-saving compound at an affordable price. The excitement within the scientific community is intense. Someday biotechnology may produce not only agents that are effective against cancer, but also antibodies and vaccines that will battle all kinds of bacterial, viral, fungal, and parasitic diseases. Within our lifetime we may yet see most of the worst plagues wiped off the face of the earth.

References

1. Corbin, A. "From Contraception to Cancer: A Review of the Therapeutic Applications of LHRH Analogues as Antitumor Agents." *Yale J. Biol. Med.* 55(1):27–47, 1982.

2. Labrie, F., et al. "Antifertility Effects of Luteinizing-Releasing Hormone (LHRH) Agonists." *Prog. Clin. Biol. Res.* 74:273–291, 1981.

3. Nillius, S. J. "Peptide Contraception—New Principles for Family Planning." *Lakartidningen* 78(34):2845–22848, 1981.

4. Maia, H. Jr., et al. "Mid-Cycle Contraception with LHRH in Women." *Reproduccion* 5(4):251–260, 1981.

5. Labrie, F., et al. "Contraception with LHRH Agonists, A New Physiological Approach." *Reproduccion* 5(4):229–241, 1981.

6. Sheehan, K. L., et al. "Luteal Phase Defects Induced by an Agonist of Luteinizing Hormone-Releasing Factor: A Model for Fertility Control." *Science* 215(4529): 170–172, 1982.

7. "Peptide Agents May Spark Contraception Revolution." *Medical World News* Sept. 17, 1979, pp. 4–6.

8. "Nasal Spray Contraceptive." *Gallagher Medical Report* 1(4):1, 1983.

9. Eckhouse, John. "Next: A Contraceptive that Fights Cancer, Too." San Francisco *Examiner,* June 13, 1982.

10. Fraser, H. M. "New Prospects for Luteinising Hormone Releasing Hormone as a Contraceptive and Therapeutic Agent." *Br. Med. J.* 285:990–991, 1982.

11. "Peptide Agents may Spark Contraception Revolution." *Medical World News,* Sept. 17, 1979, pp. 4–6.

12. Personal communication, Robert. L. Moss, 1982.

13. Winter, Ruth and McAuliffe. "Hooked on Love: Chemical Sex." *Omni* 6(8):78–82, 1984.

14. Benkert, O. "Pharmacotherapy of Sexual Impotence." *Mod. Probl. Pharmacopsych.* 15:158–173, 1980.

15. Benkert, O. "Studies on Pituitary Hormones and Releasing Hormones in Depression and Sexual Impotence." *Prog. Brain Res.* 42:25–36, 1975.

16. Benkert, O., et al. "Sexual Impotence: A Double-Blind Study of LHRH Nasal Spray Versus Placebo." *Neuropsychobiology* 1:203–210, 1975.

17. Corbin, A. Op. cit.

18. Klijn, J. G., and de Jong, F. J. "Treatment With a Luteinising-Hormone-Releasing-Hormone Analogue (Buserelin) in Premenopausal Patients with Metastatic Breast Cancer." *Lancet* 1(8283):1213–1216, 1982.

19. Editorial. "New Treatment for Prostatic Cancer." *Lancet* 2:438, 1983.

20. Walker, K. J., et al. "Therapeutic Potential of the LHRH Agonist, ICI 118630, in the Treatment of Advanced Prostatic Carcinoma." *Lancet* 2:413–415, 1983.

21. Morales, A., et al. "Nonhormonal Pharmacological Treatment of Organic Impotence." *J. Urol.* 128(1):45–47, 1982.

22. "Scorned African Aphrodisiac Scores Against Organic Impotence." *Medical World News* 23(2):115, 1982.

23. Margolis, R., et al. "Statistical Summary of 10,000 Male Cases Using Afrodex in Treatment of Impotence." *Curr. Ther. Res.* 13(9):616–622, 1971.

24. Macfarlane, C. A., et al. "Yohimbine—An Alternative Treatment for Erectile Dysfunction." *Weekly Urological Clinical Letter* 27(27):1–2, 1983.

25. Clark, John T., et al. "Enhancement of Sexual Motivation in Male Rats by Yohimbine." *Science* 225. 841–849, 1984.

26. Kent, Saul. "Drugs to Boost Sexual Potency." *Geriatrics* 36(7):158–166, 1981.

27. Bowers, M. B.; Woert, M. van; and Davis, L. "Sexual Behavior During L-dopa Treatment for Parkinsonism." *Am. J. Psychiat.* 12:127–129, 1971.

28. Calne, D. B., and Sandler, M. "L-Dopa and Parkinsonism." *Nature* 226:21–24, 1970.

29. Goodwin, F. K., et al. "Levodopa, Alterations in Behavior." *Clin. Pharmac. Ther.* 12:383–386, 1971.

30. Tolis, G.; Bertrand, G.; and Pinter, E. "Divorce and Remarriage in a 65-Year-Old Male Following Transphenoidal Surgery and Bromocriptine for Hyperprolactinemic Impotence: A Dilemma." *Psychosomatic Medicine* 41(8):657–659, 1979.

31. Ibid.

32. Gold, Michael. "In the Mood for Love." *Science 81* 2(1):76–77, 1981.

33. Continuum. "Aphrodisiac." *Omni,* vol 1, Oct., 1978, p. 46.

34. Pierini, A. A., and Nusimovich, B. "Male Diabetic Sexual Impotence: Effects of Dopaminergic Agents." *Arch. of Andrology* 6:347–350, 1981.

35. Campieri, C., et al. "Prolactin, Zinc and Sexual Activity in Dialysis Patients." *Proc. EDTA* 16:661–662, 1979.

36. Bommer, Jurgen, et al. "Improved Sexual Function in Male Haemodialysis Patients on Bromocriptine." *Lancet* 2:496–497, Sep. 8, 1979.

37. Gura, V., et al. "Hyperprolactinemia: A Possible Cause of Sexual Impotence in Male Patients Undergoing Chronic Hemodialysis." *Nephron* 26:53–54, 1980.

38. Anderson, A. N., et al. "Effect of Bromocriptine on the Premenstrual Syndrome: A Double Blind Clinical Trial." *Br. J. Obstet. Gynaecol.* 84:370–374, 1977.

39. Benedek-Jaszmann, L. J., and Hearn-Sturtevant, M.D. "Premenstrual Tension and Functional Infertility. Aetiology and Treatment." *Lancet* 1:1095–1098, 1976.

40. Mekki, Qais A., et al. "Bromocriptine Lowers Intraocular Pressure Without Affecting Blood Pressure." *Lancet* 1:1250–1251, 1983.

41. Allen, Frank. "DuPont Drug Keeps Rats Skinny and Gives Them a Great Love Life." *The Wall Street Journal*, May 28, 1982. p. 19.

42. Keegan, Anne. "Junkies Curse Drug that Saves Their Lives." Chicago *Tribune* July 20, 1983, Section 1, p. 2.

43. Archer, Sydney. "Historical Perspective on the Chemistry and Development of Naltrexone." *Naltrexone Research Monograph 28*, R.E. Willette and G. Barnett, eds. National Institute on Drug Abuse, 1980, pp. 3–9.

44. Renault, Pierre F. "Treatment of Heroin-Dependent Persons with Antagonists: Current Status." *Naltrexone Monograph 28*, R. E. Williams and G. Barnett, eds. National Institute of Drug Abuse, 1980, pp. 11–21.

45. Verebey, Karl. "The Clinical Pharmacology of Naltrexone: Pharmacology and Pharmacodynamics." *Naltrexone Research Monograph 28*, R. E. Willette and G. Barnett, eds. National Institute on Drug Abuse, 1980, pp. 147–158.

46. Bivens, Terry. "Drug-Treatment Breakthrough No 'High' For Addicts." Philadelphia *Inquirer* December 28, 1982, pp. 1–2.

47. Reynolds, Frank. "ABC World News Tonight", January 6, 1983.

48. Morley, J. E. "The Neuroendocrine Control of Appetite." *Life Sci.* 27:355–368, 1980.

49. Morley, J. E. "The Role of the Endogenous Opiates as Regulators of Appetite." *Am. J. of Clin. Nutr.* 35:757–761, 1982.

50. Margules, David L., et al. "B-Endorphin Is Associated with Overeating in Genetically Obese Mice (ob/ob) and Rats (fa/fa). *Science* 202:988–991, 1978.

51. "Pain—Diagnosis and Management." *Guidelines to the Neurosciences* 5(1):1–4, 1981.

52. Greenberg, Joel. "Psyching out Pain." *Science News* 115:332–333, 1979.

53. Kiser, R. Sanford, et al. "Acupuncture Relief of Chronic Pain Syndrome Correlates with Increased Plasma Met-Enkephalin Concentrations." *Lancet* 2:1394–1396, 1983.

54. Verebey, Karl, ed. "Opioids in Mental Illness: Theories, Clinical Observations, and Treatment Possibilities." *Annals of the New York Academy of Sciences* 398:1–512, 1982.

55. Faden, Alan I., and Holaday, Jonn W. "Opiate Antagonists: A Role in the Treatment of Hypovolemic Shock." *Science* 205:317–318, 1979.

56. Greenberg. Op. cit.

57. Mandenoll, A., et al. "Endogenous Opiates and Energy Balance." *Science* 215(4539):1536–1538, 1982.

58. Quoted in Herskowitz, Linda. "Battle of the Bulge, in Mice, for Starters." Philadelphia *Inquirer*, April 20, 1982.

59. Margules. Op. cit.

60. Morley, John, E., and Levine, Allen, S. "Stress-Induced Eating is Mediated Through Endogenous Opiates." *Science* 209:1259–1261, 1980.

61. Morley, John E. and Levine, Allen S. "The Central Control of Appetite." *Lancet* 1:398–401, 1983.

62. Sternbach, Harvey A., et al. "Anorexic Effects of Naltrexone in Man." *Lancet* 1 (8268) :388–389, 1982.

63. Personal communication, Dr. David Pohl, Associate Medical Director at DuPont, January 11, 1983.

64. Allen. Op. cit.

65. Myers, Brent M., and Baum, Michael J. "Facilitation by Opiate Antagonists of Sexual Performance in the Male Rat." *Pharmacol. Biochem. & Behav.* 10:615–618, 1979.

66. Myers, B. M., and Baum, M. J. "Facilitation of Copulatory Performance in Male Rats by Naloxone: Effects of Hypophysectomy, 17 alpha-Estradiol and Luteinizing Hormone Releasing Hormone." *Pharmacol. Biochem. & Behav.* 12:365–370, 1980.

67. Mendelson, Jack H., et al. "Effects of Naltrexone on Mood and Neuroendocrine Function in Normal Adult Males." *Psychoneuroendocrinology* 3:231–236, 1979.

68. Yeston, Neil S., et al. "Naloxone in Reversal of Hypotension in Septic Shock." *JAMA* 250:2287, 1983.

69. Reisberg, Barry, et al. "Effects of Naloxone in Senile Dementia: A Double-Blind Trial." *N. Engl. J. Med.* 308:721–722, 1983.

70. Kreek, M. J., et al. "Naloxone, a Specific Opioid Antagonist, Reverses Chronic Idiopathic Constipation." *Lancet* 1:262–262, 1983.

71. Personal communication, Dr. Richard Faust, Hoffman-La Roche.

72. Thompson, Richard S. "Balding is Forever, Experts Say." *FDA Consumer* February, 1981, pp. 10–12.

73. Gittmann, Jason E. "Hair Restoration: Old Claims in New Bottles." *JAMA* 244(11):1267, 1980.

74. Jerome, Joseph B. "Hair Restoration: Old Claims in New Bottles." *JAMA* 244(11):1267, 1980.

75. Ibid.

76. Huff, Barbara B., ed. *Physicians' Desk Reference*, 36th edition. Oradell, N. J., Medical Economics Co. 1982, p. 1955.

77. Hagstrom, Karl-Erik; Lundgren, Rolf; and Wieslander, Jan. "Clinical Experience of Long-Term Treatment with Minoxodil in Severe Arterial Hypertension." *Scand. J. Urol. Nephol.* 16:57–63, 1982.

78. Zappacosta, A. R. "Reversal of Baldness in Patient Receiving Minoxidil for Hypertension." *N. Engl. J. Med.* 303:1480–1481, 1980.

79. Burton, J. L., and Marshall, A. "Hypertrichosis Due to Minoxidil." *Br. J. Dermatol.* 101:593–595, 1979.

80. Jancin, Bruce. "Topically Applied Vasodilator Found to Promote Hair Growth." *Skin and Allergy News,* Jan. 1982, p. 1.

81. Waldholz, Michael. "Ray of Hope Shines on Balding Heads as Lotion Is Tested." *The Wall Street Journal*, March 1, 1984, p. 1.

82. Carey, Joseph. "Two New Studies Search for Hair-Raising Results." *USA Today*, June 14, 1983.

83. Weiss, Virginia C., et al. "Topical Minoxidil in Alopecia Areata." *J. Am. Acad. Dermatol.* 5(2):224–226, 1981.

84. Fenton, David A., and Wilkinson, John D. "Topical Minoxidil in the Treatment of Alopecia Areata." *Br. Med. J.* 287:1015–1017, 1983.

85. Ressmann, A. C., and Butterworth, T. "Localized Acquired Hypertrichosis." *Arch. Dermatol. Syph.* 65:458–463, 1952.

86. Rook, A. In Rook, A., et al., eds. *Textbook of Dermatology,* 2nd ed. Oxford, 1972, Blackwell Scientific Publications, vol. 2, p. 1580.

87. Weiss. Op. cit.

88. Waldholz. Op. cit.

89. Personal communication, Anna Marie Skalka, Assistant Vice President and Director of Biological Research & Development, Hoffmann-La Roche, Inc., February 6, 1984.

90. Merigan, Thomas C. "Human Interferon as a Therapeutic Agent—Current Status." *N. Engl. J. Med.* 308:1530–1531, 1983.

91. Merigan, Thomas C. "Interferon—The First Quarter Century." *JAMA* 248: 2513–2516, 1982.

92. Waldholz, Michael. "Ballyhoo has Faded, But Interferon Still has Boosters at High Levels." *The Wall Street Journal,* September 30, 1983, p. 1.

93. Hager, Tom. "The Interferon-Cancer Trials: Hardly Hopeless But Not Too Heartening." *JAMA* 250:1007–1010, 1983.

94. Waldholz, Michael. "New Drug Could Reshape Medicine as Much as Advent of Antibiotics." *The Wall Street Journal,* December 16, 1983, p. 33.

95. Hecht, Annabel. "Handmade Antibodies That Go Forth and Multiply." *FDA Consumer* January 1983, pp. 7–9.

96. "Damon Biotech Plans Cell-Growth Process Cancer Treatments." *The Wall Street Journal* October 20, 1983, p. 14.

97. "Tissue-Type Plasminogen Activator Lyses Coronary Thrombi in Minutes." *Medical World News* 25(2):17–18, 1984.

CHAPTER 4

Drug Advances of the Eighties

Winning the War Against Infection: New Drugs for Bacteria and Viruses ▪ *The* **Symmetrel** *Scandal and the* **Zovirax** *Zap* ▪ *Arthritis Patients Strike Gold:* **Ridaura** ▪ *New Anti-inflammatory Agents:* **Feldene** *and Lots More* ▪ *Oh My Aching Back* ▪ *Dissolving Disks with Papaya:* **Chymodiactin** ▪ *Defeating Depression:* **Wellbutrin** *and* **Tolvon** ▪ *A Revolution in Allergy and Asthma Treatment:* **Nasalide, Beconase, Vancenase,** *and* **Nasalcrom** ▪ *Where Do We Go from Here?*

Okay, I've whetted your appetite with tales of aphrodisiacs, baldness remedies, and heart-attack cures, not to mention chemicals to heal wounds, increase growth, and control weight. But those were just the appetizers; now it's time for the meat and potatoes. Over the last several years an extraordinary number of important new drugs have been approved by the FDA and are now stocked by pharmacies.

Some of the most impressive advances have been in our ability to fight infection. It seems almost inconceivable that before 1940 the world was terrorized by TB, VD, pneumonia, polio, cholera, influenza, and a host of other infections that killed and maimed millions of people every year. If you developed chest congestion and a bad cough, it was a very big deal. Everyone worried, because if your cold turned into pneumonia, you could be dead in a few days. Today you get barely any sympathy if you hack your fool head off. Even if it turns out that you have pneumonia, a little penicillin will usually clear it up fast.

Not long ago epidemics of polio created hysteria. When I was two years old, I became paralyzed. I still remember the hospital and the traction, the tears and the terror, and the children around me who were dying. I survived and regained the total use of my legs, but hundreds of thousands weren't so lucky. Today hardly anyone remembers the iron lung, or a time when parents worried about letting their children swim in the community pool. Between vaccines and antibiotics, we have virtually wiped out most of the dread infectious diseases.

And now the great-grandchildren of penicillin—the amazing new antibiotics of the eighties—are faster, more powerful, and far safer than anything we had before. There is almost no bacterial infection we know of that won't fall to one of these "third generation" cephalosporins or monobactams. Drugs with strange-sounding names, like **Claforan** (cefotaxime), **Moxam** (moxalactam), **Cefobid** (cefoperazone), **Cefizox** (cefizoxime). **Pipracil** (pipracillin), and **Fortaz** (ceftazidime), are taking over where the "-cillins" and "-cyclines" left off.

> **Dr. Larry Medders, an Athens, Ga., orthopedic surgeon, was worrying about the possible amputation of a patient's right leg. Especially stubborn bacteria had infected the leg and were resisting all treatment. Two Lederle salesmen visiting Athens General Hospital heard about the case and rushed in a supply of new Pipracil. In four days the infection cleared, and two weeks later Dr. Medders' patient walked home.[1]**

But as exciting as these important advances are, the real breakthroughs of the eighties are in antiviral therapies. Until recently the only weapons we had against viruses were vaccines. For a long time researchers were afraid they'd never be able to develop safe and effective antiviral agents, since anything that killed the virus might also be toxic to healthy human cells. After all, viruses are sneaky little devils that invade our own cells, take over, and wreak havoc. But the fears were unjustified. Not only are such drugs possible; several have already been developed and marketed, and lots more are in the pipeline.

The Symmetrel Scandal

Actually the first safe and effective antiviral agent has been available for almost twenty years. The trouble is that it hasn't been used. Scientists at DuPont started looking for drugs that would kill viruses right after the Second World War. After screening over 20,000 compounds, they finally came up with **Symmetrel** (amantadine), a chemical that seemed effective against type A influenza. It was rapidly approved by the FDA and went on the market in 1966.

But almost no one noticed, except the Russians. Quick to recognize the drug's potential, they have used it prophylactically against the flu since the "Hong Kong influenza pandemic of 1968 and 1969. Russia . . . purchased over 10 million doses from DuPont to use during the next flu season."[2] So the Russians are using amantadine by the truckload and have found it to be extremely effective in both preventing and treating the flu. If they have really had such success with an American drug, why are our own doctors so far behind?

For reasons that still amaze me, **Symmetrel** simply never took off in this country. A lot of doctors in high places were committed to vaccines. According to Dr. Arnold Chanin, a long-time booster of

Symmetrel, "To those who have made virology, immunology and vaccine development their life's work, chemotherapy and chemoprophylaxis [drug treatment] of influenza presents a radical and threatening concept."[3]

The year after the drug was introduced, Dr. Albert Sabin, developer of the oral polio vaccine, wrote a critical review in the *Journal of the American Medical Association* questioning **Symmetrel**'s usefulness.[4] One result of this editorial was to dampen physicians' interest in the new antiviral medicine. Dr. Chanin suggests that Sabin's comments had a long-lasting negative impact on **Symmetrel** and set back antiviral drug research for years.

> **The ultimate irony is that Dr. Sabin dealt the death blow to antiviral drug use and research in the U.S. with his scathing criticism of amantadine. . . . If this drug had been made available to the American public during the height of the A/Hong Kong/68 epidemic, we would have begun the era of antiviral chemoprophylaxis and chemotherapy against influenza A. We would be on a par with Russia in the use of antiviral drugs.[5]**

Doctors apparently doubted the usefulness of **Symmetrel** partly because they had been taught from day one in medical school that there just wasn't any effective treatment against viruses except immunization. Flu shots were, and still are, the way most physicians prepare their high-risk patients for a coming influenza season. But flu bugs are fickle and often tend to alter their chemistry enough to outsmart the virologists who must prepare the vaccines months in advance. As a result, flu shots are far from foolproof. Effectiveness may range from a high of 70 percent down to 50 percent or less.

Vaccines pose another problem: They may temporarily screw up the body's ability to metabolize other drugs. There is evidence that flu shots reduce the concentration of some vital enzymes in the liver. As a result other medications may begin to build up in the blood stream, leading to toxic levels and unexplained overdose reactions.[6,7]

People on certain medicines should be alert to side effects from flu shots. These drugs are a blood thinner called **Coumadin** (warfarin); antianxiety agents like **Valium** (diazepam), **Librium** (chlordiazepoxide), **Tranxene** (clorazepate), and **Seconal** (secobarbital); an anticonvulsant like **Dilantin** (phenytoin); such asthma drugs as theophylline (**Elixophyllin, Slo-Phyllin, Theo-Dur, Tedral,** and others); and arthritis medicines like **Butazolidin** (phenylbutazone). Before getting a vaccination, it would make sense to discuss this interaction problem with the doctor. If necessary, she can adjust the drug dose until the liver enzymes recover from the effect of the flu shot.

There are other reasons why physicians seem reluctant to prescribe **Symmetrel** to prevent or treat the flu. Dr. R. Gordon Douglas, Jr., chairman of the Department of Medicine at Cornell Medical College has described the situation.

> **During amantadine's first ten years [1966 to 1976], physicians were more or less aware that it had been licensed and yet was still not being used. This was widely misinterpreted to mean that amantadine did not work.**
>
> **In addition, amantadine was initially introduced at a time when physicians believed there were no antivirals. A generation of doctors were taught in the 1950s that antibiotics did not work and, in fact, were contraindicated for viral infections.[8]**

Many physicians seem to have generalized that information to include **Symmetrel**. It is ironic, however, that the prescribing of antibiotics skyrockets whenever there is a flu outbreak, while the sale of **Symmetrel** stays pretty steady.[9]

There was, however, another reason why most physicians ignored this fascinating medication. Policy-makers at the National Institutes of Health, regulators at the Food and Drug Administration, and even the drug company that developed **Symmetrel** were slow to recognize its potential. Although the FDA approved the drug for prevention of one particular strain of flu (Asian A-2) as far back as 1966, the agency did not actually give it the green light for treatment of all type A influenza infections until 1980, though early on there was evidence that the drug worked.

Endo Laboratories, a subsidiary of DuPont, was responsible for selling doctors on **Symmetrel**. Unfortunately the company was relatively small, and its promotional campaign left a lot to be desired. Dr. Jay Sanford, Dean of the Uniformed Health Services Medical School and a leading authority on **Symmetrel,** has speculated that the lack of enthusiasm may have been caused by insufficient advertising.

> **I frankly think it's marketing. The company has not invested in the opportunity to try to really market the compound. It's a sad commentary on physicians that an effective drug, if it isn't marketed well, doesn't get used. And another me-too compound, if it's marketed well, sells.[10]**

Then there's type A influenza itself. A lot of docs believe that the flu is such a minor ailment that you'd be better off toughing it out, without special treatment.[11] Traditional medical wisdom has it that you are supposed to rest in bed, drink plenty of fluids, and take aspirin. Well, I am here to tell you that advice is no damn good—and it never was any good.

First off, the flu *is* a big deal. It can make you feel like you've been hit by a Mack truck and are about to die. In fact, a lot of people *have* died as a result of complications from the flu. Few physicians practicing medicine in the 1970s and 1980s remember the incredible slaughter caused by the "Spanish influenza" epidemic between 1917 and 1919. Worldwide, over 20 million were killed. In the United States alone there were 25 million cases and more than 500,000 deaths.

Oh, but that was an especially virulent strain, you say; nothing like that has happened in recent years. True enough, but that doesn't mean the flu is anything to be sneezed at. According to the CDC (Centers for Disease Control) in Atlanta, between 1968 and 1982 more than "200,000 excess deaths are estimated to have occurred in association with influenza epidemics in the United States."[12] During the 1980–1981 flu season alone the body count reached as many as 60,000 to 70,000 deaths; this mortality rate shocked even epidemiologists, who normally take such statistics in stride.

We'll never know how many of these deaths could have been prevented had doctors prescribed **Symmetrel,** but be assured that a fair number of those people did not have to die. Dr. Chanin gives his opinion.

> **The CDC is still telling American physicians to use "bed rest, aspirin and fluids" to treat uncomplicated influenza. The media faithfully echo this refrain with every new flu outbreak. I wonder how many people needlessly die because they fail to seek medical attention solely because this wonderful advice is drummed into them annually![13]**

If you've really got the flu, bed rest, aspirin, and plenty of fluids won't do much to speed recovery or make you feel less miserable. A study carried out at the University of Rochester School of Medicine that compared aspirin with **Symmetrel** for relieving symptoms concluded that **Symmetrel** "proved to be superior in reducing symptoms. . . . Side effects were more severe in the aspirin-treated group, leading to the failure of more than one-third of this group to complete treatment."[14] And not incidentally, children with influenza (or chicken pox) should not receive aspirin (or **Pepto-Bismol,** which contains an aspirinlike salicylate) because of a potential link to Reye's syndrome.

Why, then, do most physicians still tell their patients to rely on the tried and untrue benefits of aspirin? Beats me; I guess old habits die hard. **Symmetrel,** on the other hand, can prevent the flu if it is taken prophylactically (ahead of time, as a preventive). And if you do catch the bug, this drug will help to speed recovery. Numerous studies support the effectiveness of **Symmetrel,**[15–18] but one of the most impressive was published in the *New England Journal of Medicine*. Researchers at the

University of Vermont found that this medication was 91 percent effective in warding off the flu.[19] An editorial in the same issue of the journal endorsed wider use of **Symmetrel** in preventing the flu and went a step further.

> **Perhaps the drug should also be used more widely for the treatment of influenza. Certainly, it is effective for the relief of symptoms and allows a more rapid return to school or employment. A specific diagnosis of influenza is not required for every patient before administering amantadine; epidemiologic diagnosis will suffice. Thus, in the winter months when the Centers for Disease Control or state or local health departments report influenza A activity in or near the region, a patient with acute onset of fever, chills, headache, and cough can be presumed to have influenza and treated accordingly.[20]**

I couldn't agree more. A reader of my newspaper column reported that she had come down with the flu and was feeling absolutely miserable.

> **I felt like hell. I had a high fever, a runny nose and my brain felt swollen. My eyes hurt, my head hurt and my body ached all over. I was so sick I couldn't even get out of bed to go to the drugstore to get the medicine.**
>
> **My friend brought the Symmetrel to me that afternoon. I took it convinced that nothing could do much good and that I would be dead the next day no matter what. To my amazement it worked like magic. I got up the following morning at 6:30 feeling great. Within twenty-four hours I was back on my feet and fully functional.**

Not everyone responds so dramatically. But if the drug is taken within the first 24 hours or so after coming down with flu symptoms, the majority of patients will be back on their feet within a day or two.

Unfortunately there is a price to pay for such benefit—**Symmetrel** does cause side effects. Approximately 7 to 13 percent of those taking this medicine develop symptoms of insomnia, jitteriness, light-headedness, and difficulty concentrating. Rarely people may experience depression, hallucinations, difficulty urinating, and low blood pressure.

Some doctors believe that reducing the dose may dramatically reduce the risk of adverse reactions without losing effectiveness.[21] Dr. Chanin suggests that "like the Russians, who have had vast experience with amantadine, I have found the drug to be effective at 100 mg daily, considerably less than the 200 mg daily dosage endorsed by the NIH

[National Institutes of Health] and therefore less likely to cause side effects."[22]

Interestingly, the Russians have all but abandoned amantadine for its chemical cousin rimantadine. They have been using this newer drug since the early 1970s because they found it just as effective and less likely to cause side effects. Research in this country tends to confirm the finding, but unfortunately rimantadine is not yet available. At the time of this writing DuPont is on the verge of submitting the drug to the FDA for approval; it will probably take another year or two before rimantadine makes it onto our pharmacy shelves. In the meantime, if you hear that the flu is loose in your community and you start to feel like you've been hit by a Mack truck, you might want to discuss the benefits of **Symmetrel** with your doctor.

One other interesting breakthrough on the flu front has to do with a new drug called **Virazole** (ribavirin).[23] It, too, seems effective in speeding recovery from influenza. Unlike **Symmetrel,** however, it cannot be taken orally. Instead, the drug only works in aerosol form, and therefore it has to be administered through a special machine. This circumstance will probably restrict its use to very sick folks who have to be hospitalized. Nevertheless, it's nice to know that we are adding to our antiviral armamentarium.

Help for Herpes Is Here

Just when people started to take the so-called sexual revolution for granted, herpes came along and screwed things up. Before 1940 fear of venereal disease had a dampening affect on casual encounters. Although there were lots of popular "cures" for the clap, until the advent of penicillin nothing really worked very well. But with the development of effective antibiotic therapy, fear of VD faded. Even if someone did catch something gross like gonorrhea, a real cure was only as far away as the nearest pharmacy. Then herpes hysteria hit.

We were suddenly told that there was a strange, incurable disease loose in the land, and it was spreading like wildfire. Horrible herpes was an epidemic of immense proportion. As many as 20 million Americans were reported to be infected with type-2 herpes (the below-the-waist variety), while another 40 million or so supposedly suffered with herpes simplex-1, which causes cold sores and fever blisters.

But it wasn't that simple. For one thing, the sexual acrobatics of the 1960s and the 1970s resulted in greater experimentation. This in turn spread herpes simplex-1 below the waist, and type-2 was found in the mouth. Everything was mixed up, but the one certainty was that herpes had snuck up on us and was raging out of control.

Reports appeared in the medical literature that the virus could survive for over four hours on toilet seats, plastic benches, towels, and even hot tubs.[24–26] People panicked. They had visions of some life-threatening disease that could never be cured. Many of their fears were unjustified: rarely does anyone contact the disease through casual contact, and often what people fear may be herpes is really something else instead.

But it's easy to understand why folks were scared. Herpes *can* be horrible. People who come down with an initial venereal infection suffer. First they develop blisters (lesions) on their genitals. They may have a low-grade fever accompanied by headache, general malaise, swollen lymph glands, difficult urination, and aches and pains. After one or two days the blisters break and are replaced by raw, red, painful ulcers. These crust over and eventually heal, but the whole process can last as long as three to six weeks and leave permanent emotional scars.

As if that weren't bad enough, there is always the fear of a recurrence. You see, herpes viruses are sneaky little varmints. Once they get done doing their dirty work, they migrate up a nerve and hide near the spinal cord in specialized cells called ganglia. There they can lie dormant for weeks, months, or years. Some people may never be bothered again (as long as their immune system remains vigilant), while others may have repeat attacks every month or two, year in and year out.

Although most people will suffer a recurrence within three to six months, subsequent attacks tend to diminish in severity and frequency. One theory has it that during the very first herpes episode the body absorbs a certain finite amount of virus, which gradually gets depleted with each recurrence. Eventually the virus seems to burn itself out, though if the immune system becomes weakened from cancer chemotherapy or the use of immune-suppressing steroid drugs, a repeat attack is almost guaranteed, and such a recurrence can be incredibly virulent.

As bad as all this sounds, some other complications are even worse. Although all the evidence is not yet in, there is a suspicion that the herpes virus predisposes women to cervical cancer. The risk seems relatively small, but periodic Pap smears are a must for anyone who has been infected.

Pregnancy poses another problem. A woman who has active herpes lesions around the time of delivery can infect her baby as it passes down the birth canal. Neonatal herpes infections have increased dramatically over the last two decades.[27] And to a baby herpes can be life-threatening.

So we're all agreed that herpes is horrible. But a lot of people don't give the disease much thought. After all, they don't go in for hanky-panky; nothing to worry about. Not so fast, my friend. It comes as a major surprise to most folks to learn that herpes infections can affect other parts of the body, and you don't have to fool around to come down with these serious ailments.

Herpes simplex virus can also invade the eye. Hundreds of thousands of people are affected by herpes keratitis, the leading infectious cause of blindness in this country.

Then there's potentially fatal herpes encephalitis. No one understands exactly how it happens, but occasionally the virus gets into the brain. Once there, it destroys gray matter and can cause severe brain damage or death.

But these are rare ailments and most people still don't think twice about catching such serious diseases. The vast majority of Americans still think of herpes as something that affects the other guy. They'd be wrong.

So far we've been discussing *simplex* viruses—the kind that most commonly cause cold sores and fever blisters (type-1) and genital lesions (generally type-2). But believe it or not, chicken pox is also caused by herpes. It's a different kind of herpes virus, called varicella zoster, and is clearly not a venereal disease. Most kids catch chicken pox at some time in their lives. Once infected, they are susceptible to another kind of herpes infection—shingles—which can develop much later in life, often as a result of weakened immunity. Shingles, by the way, can be incredibly painful, and in some rare cases it damages nerves and leaves people in almost unbearable pain even after the blisters themselves have disappeared.

Epstein-Barr, another herpes virus, is responsible for infectious mononucleosis. "Mono" is usually fairly mild, but it has been known to put some people out of action for months. The Epstein-Barr virus is also strongly associated with certain kinds of cancers, especially Burkitt's lymphoma. Another herpes villain is cytomegalovirus, or CMV. It has cropped up in association with AIDS (acquired immune deficiency syndrome).

Needless to say, with so many millions affected, doctors were willing to try just about anything . . . and often did. Patients were given everything from ether and beeswax to zinc and lysine. But nothing showed much promise. Drug companies, too, were anxious to discover some way of treating all these dreaded herpes viruses. Parke-Davis was one of the first out of the starting gate with a drug called **Vira-A** (vidarabine). Unfortunately this medication was only effective as an ointment for eye infections and intravenously against herpes encephalitis. **Vira-A** did not seem to work against genital herpes, and questions about its cancer-causing potential may have limited the drug's acceptability.

Solving the Mystery of Zovirax

But another company was involved in basic research on DNA biochemistry long before there was any word about a herpes epidemic. Over the years scientists at Burroughs Wellcome had been unlocking the secrets of cellular reproduction and had a long commitment to cancer chemotherapy and anti-infective agents. By the early 1970s a number of investigators at Burroughs were involved in developing an antiviral agent that might be effective against herpes keratitis of the eye. Microbiologist Dr. Dannie King and Gertrude (Trudy) Elion, head of the experimental therapy division, rolled up their sleeves and went to work on a drug called **Viroptic** (trifluridine).

But they had to fight for **Viroptic**. Although there was a serious medical need for such a drug, the market potential was never great. The people who held the purse strings either did not see the looming herpes epidemic or didn't appreciate the foundation **Viroptic** would play in the development of broader antiherpes medications. According to Dr. King

> **Time and time again I found myself having to defend the project to the R&D [Research and Development] and the marketing people as being something we should keep alive and keep progressing with. There is always the tendency in tight times to drop out of sight those projects that might not have the tendency to make a lot of money. And I would say on four or five occasions [the project] came very close to being canned.[28]**

Viroptic ultimately proved very effective in treating herpes infections in the eye and was approved by the FDA in 1980 for use in eyedrops. Though the drug was too toxic to be useful internally to combat other herpes infections, it did lay the framework for the main event—**Zovirax** (acyclovir).

Trudy Elion is a visionary in pharmaceutical research. If you met this short, red-haired, freckled lady with the wonderful Bronx accent and a twinkle in her eye, you would swear she was the perfect grandmother. Instead of bouncing grandchildren on her knee and baking cookies, though, Trudy creates magic in the laboratory. Her babies are drugs. She played a key role in developing many extraordinary therapeutic agents including **Zyloprim** (allopurinol) for gout and **Imuran** (azathioprine), which is used to treat severe rheumatoid arthritis and to prevent tissue rejection in kidney transplants. She also helped create several important anticancer compounds.

But Trudy's crowning glory came when she helped unlock the secrets of one of the most fascinating antiviral drugs ever developed. BW 248U was one of numerous compounds created at Burroughs Wellcome's North Carolina research facility. Since the plant had no virology lab, the chemicals were shipped to England for testing. When the telegram from Wellcome Research Labs in Beckenham, Kent, arrived announcing that BW 248U had extraordinary activity against herpes viruses, Trudy knew they had hit pay dirt.

One of the first things she did was to test the substance on healthy cells. To her amazement, nothing at all happened. It was the strangest thing she'd ever seen. "How could it be so active against the virus and so totally nontoxic to normal cells?" she asked herself. Trudy mobilized her lab for action, and after lots of hard work—Eureka! In one of the most elegant research efforts I've ever heard of, she and a handful of colleagues untangled the mechanism by which this incredible drug works to kill herpes viruses.

Zovirax by itself is a do-nothing drug. If you don't have herpes, the medicine won't affect you. But it's a whole other story if you're infected. The drug is activated only by a herpes virus enzyme (thymidine kinase, or TK) which converts the drug into an antiviral poison. The virus is fooled into incorporating the chemical into its structure, and in this way it self-destructs. Because of this unique mechanism of action, **Zovirax** does not affect healthy cells and thus appears amazingly safe.

If all that sounds a little too complicated, think of **Zovirax** as if it were a gun that isn't cocked. The only way to activate this particular pistol is to bring it into contact with a herpes virus containing the magic enzyme thymidine kinase. Once this enzyme cocks the gun, it's ready to fire— but it can only be pointed at herpes-infected cells; normal cells are immune. Essentially, once the gun is ready to fire, the herpes virus pulls the trigger and commits suicide.

As Trudy's team began to unravel this scenario, the excitement at Burroughs Wellcome was almost infectious. It was like finding water in the middle of the desert to discover a potent antiherpes agent while the country was in the grip of a growing epidemic. But to keep other companies from discovering the secret, Trudy Elion and Dannie King did their best to keep their enthusiasm under cover. At one point Dannie, Trudy, and the head of the toxicology department were on their way to a meeting in Boston. Dannie turned to speak to Trudy.

> **"Look, the only people who know about this product are on this damn airplane."** . . . **Trudy said, "Should I get off the airplane?" And I said, "One or the other; we'll flip a coin."**
>
> **She and I had squirreled the files on this product away in our offices. Almost none of the information had appeared in formal reports. Very little of it had been highlighted in the minutes of meetings. It was very, very clandestine, because we knew we were on a hot item.[29]**

Soon, though, it became apparent to everyone who came into contact with the drug that **Zovirax** was an extremely important compound. The research moved unbelievably quickly, and at each step the findings seemed almost too good to be true. There was virtually no toxicity, and the carcinogenicity screens turned up negative. Most important of all, this medication worked like a bandit against most herpes viruses.

After the initial clinical data started trickling in, there was no doubt that **Zovirax** could dramatically reduce viral reproduction and speed the healing of an initial herpes attack. [30–34] Results were even more impressive when the drug was given to immunocompromised patients—people who had developed severe herpes infections after their immune systems had been zapped either by cancer chemotherapy or after organ transplants. For such people a simple cold sore can become almost life-threatening; they have no resistance, and the virus may eat into the lip and face and then move down the throat, trachea, and esophagus. Ultimately the herpes infection can invade the liver, lungs, or brain and lead to death.

Intravenous administration of **Zovirax** either prevented the herpes lesions from gaining a foothold or, once they were started, provided striking relief. [35–37] One group consisted of patients who had received bone-marrow transplants as part of their therapy for cancers such as leukemia and lymphoma. Because their immune systems had been wiped out, they developed terribly painful herpes outbreaks (shingles and cold sores that had spread around the eyes and mouth). Then **Zovirax** was administered.

> **All patients experienced pain relief within 24 h[ours] of starting treatment. No new skin lesions occurred after 24 h. . . . The best results were achieved when treatment was started within 4 days of the onset of local zoster. In all such early cases, progression of the rash was arrested and scarring was very slight.**

> **This clinical study of twenty-three patients receiving acyclovir suggests that the drug will prove to be safe, non-toxic, easily administered, and efficacious in the treatment of herpes virus infections in immunosuppressed patients.** [38]

By now it was obvious that **Zovirax** was living up to expectations. The drug worked magnificently for those people whose immune systems were so weakened that they could not fight off herpes infections. It also worked for normal folks with garden-variety herpes. The FDA was excited and put the new antiviral medication on the fast track.

Company officials elected to move forward as quickly as possible with a topical (ointment) formulation and an intravenous preparation. The plan seemed a good one at the time. After all, some people were literally dying from herpes infections, and if the intravenous form could be put on the market quickly, lives would be saved. **Zovirax** ointment seemed a safe bet, too, since it could clear FDA hurdles faster than an oral version.

On March 30, 1982—only eight months after Burroughs Wellcome submitted it to the FDA—**Zovirax** ointment was approved for herpes. The company stood back and waited with great expectation. Some were sure the drug would be a license to print money. They were sorely disappointed. This great breakthrough medicine was not the overnight miracle everyone anticipated.

The problems had less to do with the drug than with people's misunderstanding of the herpes virus. Everyone was looking for a cure for herpes. They figured that you should be able to use the medicine a couple of times and that would be it—horrible herpes would be gone forever, just the way antibiotics eliminated VD.

Wrong. Remember that after an attack this nasty bugger migrates up nerves and hides in the ganglia, where it lies dormant and invulnerable. Though **Zovirax** worked to speed healing, it did nothing to prevent recurrences. That was the first disappointment.

The second problem had to do with the ointment itself. Patients had to apply it to their lesions up to six times a day. Messy and yucky. People wanted to forget about their herpes blisters, not rub goo all over them every couple of hours.

Then there was the issue of treating repeat attacks. Although the first herpes infection is bad—lasting from three to six weeks—recurrences are usually much less severe. Most people heal within a week or less. Although **Zovirax** ointment shortened the duration of the more severe first attack, it didn't have the same impact on the shorter, secondary attacks. Once the blisters have formed, it takes several days for them to heal no matter what you do.

There were reports that if people used the ointment at the earliest possible moment, before a blister actually appeared, they might be able to prevent cold sores from forming.[39] But such a regimen required constant vigilance; at the first sign of tingling or numbness they had to start using the ointment. Some patients may have been sufficiently motivated, but few doctors were sharp enough to mention the proper use.

And that brings up the last, and perhaps most important, problem for **Zovirax**—doctors didn't trust the drug. Much as they were reluctant to prescribe **Symmetrel** for the flu, they were skeptical of **Zovirax** for herpes. When asked what went wrong, a marketing man at Burroughs Wellcome replied.

> **Our pre-launch market research information showed us that physicians were very uncomfortable with antivirals. They don't know them. They had no experience with them. It's not like anything else.[40]**

To sum up, then, **Zovirax** ointment was a bust. It didn't cure herpes, it had only a minimal impact on repeat attacks, and doctors were suspicious of all antiviral medicines. The wonder drug looked like a loser.

Enter **Zovirax** oral capsules.* Unfortunately this drug had to overcome the cloudy reputation created by its topical predecessor. But unquestionably here was a winner. Study after study proved that oral **Zovirax** worked very well for both an initial herpes infection and recurrences. Norwegian dermatologists reporting in the *Lancet* provided some results.

> **In patients with initial genital herpes . . . acyclovir significantly reduced the duration of virus shedding, itching, and pain, the time to crusting and complete healing, and new lesion formation compared with controls. . . .**
>
> **New lesion formation was completely prevented after the start of treatment in all patients receiving acyclovir. In comparison 29% of female and 57% of male patients receiving a placebo developed new lesions. . . .**
>
> **Currently, oral acyclovir provides the best specific outpatient treatment of initial genital herpes. The duration of symptoms and lesions may be expected to be reduced by 50 percent or more providing treatment is started early enough.**[41]

Dr. Yvonne Bryson, an authority on herpes and its treatment, has studied the effects of oral **Zovirax** in patients at UCLA's Infectious Disease Clinic for several years. She, too, found the drug extremely effective in reducing virus shedding and the formation of new lesions as well as in speeding healing.[42] But Dr. Bryson's most extraordinary discovery surfaced well after the initial phase of the study was over.

Over the next several years she monitored the patients who had received ten days' medication with **Zovirax** for their initial herpes attack but no medicine after that. She then compared the number of recurrences in the treated group with those in a control group that had received placebo therapy for the first herpes outbreak. During the first six months after the initial infection there was no difference—both groups averaged about two repeat attacks.

But after that, a dramatic difference began to emerge. The placebo group averaged around three attacks over the next year, while the **Zovirax** group only averaged one-sixth as many outbreaks. It was as if the drug reduced the amount of virus (viral load) that migrated up the nerve and hid in the ganglia. While not a cure, therefore, the drug did appear to dramatically change the natural course of the disease if it was used during that very first herpes infection.[43]

But what about the 20 million people who are long past their first herpes experience? Will the drug do anything for them? Dr. Richard Reichman at the University of Vermont School of Medicine has demonstrated that when oral **Zovirax** is used promptly (less than 48 hours after

*Oral **Zovirax** should shortly have full FDA approval.

symptoms appear) to treat recurrences, it can reduce virus shedding and lesion formation and can speed healing.[44,45] When patients started using the oral medicine at the very first sign of a repeat attack—during the "prodromal" phase when the skin starts to itch, tingle, or become a little numb—the benefits were even more dramatic.[46]

But the really hot news these days is that prophylactic treatment with oral **Zovirax** can prevent herpes outbreaks in the majority of patients.[47–49] Studies demonstrate that for most people, two to five capsules a day can keep herpes at bay. The normally staid editors of the *Journal of the American Medical Association* have waxed enthusiastic.

> **The antiviral agent acyclovir offers a genuine ray of hope to patients with herpes—both as an effective treatment and as potential prophylaxis . . .**
>
> **The potential market for prophylactic acyclovir is awesome . . . assuming just one in five persons elect oral prophylaxis, a projected 1 million persons with a history of recurrent HSV infection would be taking acyclovir daily. This would make acyclovir the second most commonly prescribed daily prophylactic medication, next to oral contraceptives.**
>
> **It is encouraging that clinicians will now have a therapy to offer those patients suffering from recurrent genital herpes infections.[50]**

Nevertheless, investigators insist that this is not a cure; it is maintenance therapy, and it isn't for everyone. People who have no more than a mild recurrence once or twice a year would be foolish to take two or more capsules daily, day in and day out, to prevent that rare herpes attack. However, this kind of treatment could be a godsend for folks who are unfortunate enough to get hit every month or two. And so far virtually no side effects have been associated with short-term therapy.

Nevertheless, some drawbacks are evident in prolonged treatment. Once **Zovirax** is stopped, most people will find that their herpes returns, just like before. It's definitely not a cure. And you can bet it will be expensive. Lastly, we don't know what, if any, long-term problems may show up if lots of folks start taking this drug daily.

What's the bottom line on this medicine? Here are some suggestions for successful treatment.

First, if you think you may be coming down with an initial herpes attack, get yourself into a doctor's office for an accurate diagnosis, fast! According to Dr. Yvonne Bryson, there's a good chance it won't be herpes at all. One-third of the patients who come to her UCLA Infectious Disease Clinic thinking that they have herpes have something else instead.

But if it really is a first herpes attack, you may want to hop on it hard. Not only should a course of oral **Zovirax** reduce symptoms and speed healing, it may make you less contagious. Or of far greater significance, prompt early treatment could dramatically reduce the number of subsequent attacks.

If you already have herpes, you will have a tough decision. If the outbreaks are infrequent (less than three a year) and relatively mild, you may choose to do absolutely nothing and let them go away by themselves. Gradually the virus should burn itself out. But if you are bothered by frequent, painful attacks (more than six a year), you may seriously want to consider treating each attack fast, even before the blisters appear. There is mounting evidence that if people use **Zovirax** during the prodromal period of tingling and numbness, they can either avert an attack or reduce its severity.

Finally, some individuals may want to consider prophylactic treatment. Again, this should probably be reserved for those who really suffer from severe chronic herpes attacks that never seem to want to burn themselves out.

The best thing about oral **Zovirax** is that it gives the patient control over the disease. Imagine the situation where a woman is starting to date again after a period of abstinence. She definitely does not want to have herpes rear its ugly head. Well, she could feel reasonably secure taking the drug prophylactically for awhile to keep the virus under control. Or imagine the middle-aged man who is happily married but in a moment of passion foolishly dallies and contracts herpes. To avoid giving the disease to his wife and creating a terribly traumatic breakup, he may opt to use the drug to prevent another outbreak.

Obviously any decision to use **Zovirax** (either orally or in ointment form) for cold sores or genital herpes will require careful consultation with a physician. The drug is still new, and there is much we need to learn about both it and herpes. There is growing evidence the drug will be effective for treating shingles, chicken pox, and possibly even mononucleosis. If we're really lucky, it may even help to reduce some of the herpes-associated cancers. **Zovirax** may turn out to be one of the truly great developments of the 1980s. Only time will tell.

And what's amazing is that **Zovirax** is merely the first in a long series of antiherpes drugs being developed. Burroughs Wellcome has another compound it's excited about, and a drug called foscarnet is being used in Sweden with impressive results. Then there are a whole host of experimental compounds that are impossible to pronounce. There's bromovinyldeoxyuridine (BVDU), 2-deoxy-D-Glucose, phosphonoacetic acid, arildone, cyclaradine, thiosemicarbazone, and lots of chemicals identified most easily by such abbreviations as ABPP, BIOLF-62, Win 412583-3, FIAC, VDU, IDC, IVDU, and araC. Finally, a major effort is under way to develop a herpes vaccine.

No one knows where antiviral research is headed. But it's clear that we are just beginning to unlock the secrets of successful treatment for some of humanity's last remaining infectious plagues. The future looks bright indeed.

Arthritis Patients Strike Gold

One plague we have not done well with in recent years has been arthritis. We are in the middle of what could almost be called an arthritis epidemic. Over thirty million people suffer from this painfully debilitating condition, and almost seven million of those have the severe and potentially crippling form of the disease—RA (rheumatoid arthritis).

Getting at the cause of arthritis has been a nightmare. About the best researchers can say is that it's the result of a complex inflammatory process. So what else is new? Although our knowledge of this disease advances slowly, more and more people fall victim. It's no wonder that drugs like **Oraflex** are welcomed so eagerly and uncritically by a public desperate for relief.

Unlike the more common osteoarthritis, which is associated with aging, rheumatoid arthritis causes a lot more than swollen, tender joints. Patients often develop anemia, lose their appetite, feel exhausted, experience aching muscles, and generally have a devil of a time just getting around. And RA shows no mercy, striking people of all ages, even young children.

"Portrait of Eric" tells a poignant story by a photographer doing a documentary on a twelve-year-old patient.

> **The first time I photographed Eric I worried about angles and apertures and adequate film speed. The pictures were lousy because they failed to dig beneath the surface. I had made the camera a barrier.**

> **The next time I photographed Eric was in a tiny room where he was doing physical therapy . . . in that tiny room, I was forced to enter Eric's world. The therapist cupped Eric's hand and bent his fingers toward his palm. Eric winced, the tears welled in his eyes. He fought off the tears and stared straight into my camera lens.**

> **I couldn't keep my hands still. I wanted to weep and I did. The photographs blurred from shake and fuzzed because I couldn't focus through my tears.**

> **Eric stared through the lens deep inside me, sharing his pain and hiding it, challenging me to face up to my own feelings about pain. He dared me to look him in the eye.[51]**

My friend Kate was 32 when she first noticed that a few joints in her fingers were stiff. At first she didn't think anything of it, but the pain and inflammation continued to worsen, and pretty soon all her joints started to ache. Within a few months just getting out of bed in the morning was torture.

Kate is a beautiful woman who had a promising career in clinical psychology. But rheumatoid arthritis has completely turned her life upside down. The pain is always with her. Something as simple as shaking hands can bring almost unbearable suffering. Yet she always tries her best not to let her patients or friends know how much their firm handshakes hurt.

Kate has tried almost everything medical science has to offer. The first line was lots of aspirin until her ears were ringing and her stomach screamed in protest. Then her doctors prescribed NSAIDs (nonsteroidal anti-inflammatory drugs)—**Motrin** (ibuprofen), **Naprosyn** (naproxen), **Clinoril** (sulindac), **Tolectin** (tolmetin), and **Indocin** (indomethacin), but most of these drugs were barely better than aspirin and they too hurt her stomach. The **Indocin** helped for a while, but it gave her horrible headaches and an ulcer.

Next came **Aralen** (chloroquine), an antimalarial drug that occasionally helps RA patients. But in Kate's case it was only partially effective. Her rheumatologist was just about to consider cortisone or **Cuprimine** (penicillamine), a heavy-duty arthritis drug with serious side effects, when he was able to get Kate into an experimental gold treatment program. It worked wonders! For Kate, the old expression "good as gold" took on new meaning.

What's that you say? Gold isn't a drug? I beg to differ. Water-soluble gold shots have been around for over 50 years as a last resort for the victims of rheumatoid arthritis. Doctors usually hold out until the bitter end before starting gold therapy, because the patient has to come in for weekly injections for as long as 20 weeks, after which a maintenance dose is administered monthly.

Besides the expense and inconvenience of going in for shots, patients have had to contend with serious side effects: 30 percent or more drop out because of an itchy skin rash or mouth ulcers that can become insufferable. Worse, gold shots can cause serious damage to the kidneys. Urine tests have to be run every couple of weeks to monitor kidney function, because if the damage is allowed to progress, it can become permanent and possibly lead to kidney cancer. Blood tests are also necessary, because a small number of patients experience problems with bone marrow and liver function.

Way back in the early days of gold therapy large doses were given, and as a result, some patients died. Needless to say, gold developed a very bad reputation, and you can understand why doctors saved it as a last resort.

But that's a shame, because gold can be extremely effective; 60 to 70 percent of RA patients experience some benefit, and many recover so dramatically that almost all pain and inflammation disappear. The real kicker is that gold therapy works best if it is started early in the disease, before irreversible damage is done to joints. Talk about your Catch-22—here is a really helpful treatment for a devastating disease, most effective if used early; but because of serious side effects, it is often saved until it's too late to do much good.

That situation may soon change. The SmithKline drug company has developed an *oral* gold preparation called **Ridaura** (auranofin) which may represent an important advance in the treatment of rheumatoid arthritis.*
Not only is **Ridaura** far more convenient than gold shots, it may be less toxic.

The gurus at what was then the Smith, Kline & French pharmaceutical company decided back in the late 1960s to overhaul some of their research programs. Here, straight from the horse's mouth, is the story on the development of **Ridaura**. It started with a mandate:

> **Come up with something that will have an impact on the disease—the course of the disease. Do not give us another anti-inflammatory drug.**
>
> **So Dr. Don Walz, who looks like your classic mad scientist, [and our chemists] came up with an oral gold molecule. . . . It does seem to affect the course of the disease by what are called the objective parameters—not just does the patient feel good, but the chemical tests that would indicate the presence of rheumatoid arthritis seem to regress somewhat. It seems capable, if used early enough, of preventing the kind of damage that occurs in the worst of rheumatoid arthritis patients. . . . The X-ray findings, the chemical findings and just how patients feel seem to indicate that it is highly effective.[52]**

Oral gold proved to be almost as beneficial as injectable gold.[53] "It was also found through radiographic examinations that **Ridaura** might possibly prevent progression of the bone destruction in the joints."[54] Even some patients who hadn't been helped by gold shots benefited from **Ridaura**.[55] Patience is necessary, however. It takes about three months for benefits to start showing up, and the maximum improvement may not manifest itself for six months or a year.

But what about side effects? To everyone's amazement, they appear to be less serious than expected. Kidney damage does not seem to be nearly as

---

*At the time of this writing **Ridaura** has not been approved by the FDA, but approval is expected soon.

common with **Ridaura**.[56,57] But it's not perfect by any means. Diarrhea is one of the most frequent problems with this drug. In one study about 40 percent of the patients reported digestive tract upsets, defined as two to four loose stools per day.[58] Over time this problem may lessen, though. A skin rash can also be bothersome (up to 18 percent will suffer), but in most cases it is nowhere near as bad as that experienced with gold shots. In early clinical studies such side effects weren't severe enough to discourage most patients.[59,60] The dropout rate with **Ridaura** has been roughly one-fourth that with gold shots (6 percent as against 27 percent).[61]

For the first time in a long while, then, a drug may soon become available that may halt or even slightly reverse the ravages of rheumatoid arthritis. Though it is *not* a cure, **Ridaura** appears to be able to ease swollen and painful joints; reduce morning stiffness, fatigue and weakness; reverse anemia and loss of appetite; and increase grip strength in a significant number of patients.[62]

It also seems to be safer than previous gold therapy. The drug can therefore be given to RA patients earlier, before irreversible damage is done to joints. Although researchers are not yet sure how gold works, they believe that it may actually correct some underlying defect in the immune system.[63]

Terrific, you say. But this is gold, and gold is expensive. Won't I go broke paying for the stuff? No. While it's true that there's gold in **Ridaura,** there is so little that it's not as if you were tapping into Fort Knox. The cost of a month's supply will be roughly comparable to a month's worth of other anti-inflammatory drugs like **Tolectin, Motrin, Naprosyn,** or **Clinoril**. Which isn't to say that it will be cheap. These drugs can cost around $25 to $30 a month, and if you double that by adding **Ridaura,** the yearly bill for arthritis drugs could easily exceed $500.

That's a heck of a lot more than good old aspirin, which usually costs less than $60 a year. But aspirin won't do the job for everyone, and it too, can cause serious side effects in large doses. **Ridaura** is no miracle medicine, but it could be the most interesting advance in the treatment of rheumatoid arthritis that we've seen in quite some time.

Not Another NSAID

But what about osteoarthirits—have there been any breakthroughs for the 25 million Americans who suffer from this most common form of arthritis? Unfortunately the answer is no. Oh sure, nonsteroidal anti-inflammatory drugs continue to propagate almost faster than rabbits. At last count almost 30 new compounds were either in the pipeline or being reviewed by the FDA.

I have even heard of one with the brand name **ANSAID,** which, someone told me, stands for "Another Non-Steroidal Anti-inflammatory Drug."
I only wish they had had a sense of humor and called it *NANSAID*—or
"Not Another NSAID." Unfortunately differences between brands are
usually minimal and to date none has been shown to be significantly
more effective than large doses of aspirin.

One of the most recent additions to the NSAID sweepstakes is **Feldene**
(piroxicam). Like its ill-fated competitor **Oraflex** (benoxaprofen), **Feldene**
is only taken once a day, making it more convenient than drugs like
Motrin and **Rufen** (ibuprofen), **Butazolidin** (phenylbutazone), **Tolectin**
(tolmetin), **Indocin** (indomethacin), **Meclomen** (meclofenamate), **Anaprox**
(naproxen sodium), **Clinoril** (sulindac), **Nalfon** (fenoprofen), and
Naprosyn (naproxen).

Once-a-day therapy with **Feldene** offers the advantage of long-lasting
relief, especially for night-time pain and next-morning stiffness.[64] Does
this convenience make **Feldene** better than existing drugs? For most
people probably not, though someone who has to take lots of other
medicines may appreciate the drug's simplicity.

Feldene appears to be about as effective as most other NSAIDs. One
article published in *JAMA* reports that after several months of treatment
the drug lowers something called rheumatoid factor by 62 percent.[65] This
factor is a protein found in the blood of most patients who suffer from
rheumatoid arthritis. Reducing it could well be of benefit.

What about side effects? Well, keep in mind one indisputable fact—
all NSAIDs produce a relatively high incidence of adverse reactions.
Digestive-tract upsets (heartburn, stomach pain, nausea, diarrhea, and
the like) can affect between 10 to 40 percent of patients taking drugs of
this class.[66] Skin rash, ringing in the ears, headache, fluid retention,
and allergic reactions are also not uncommon.

More serious reactions to NSAIDs—such as stomach ulcers, blood
disorders (including aplastic anemia and agranulocytosis), visual disturbances, kidney and liver damage—are rare, but they are very serious and
in some cases life-threatening.

One recent report from the United Kingdom compared nine of their
most frequently prescribed arthritis drugs, including **Feldene**. The good
news is that overall **Feldene** had one of the lowest rates of adverse
reactions. It seemed somewhat less likely to cause liver and kidney
problems and blood disorders than many of its peers. But **Feldene** was
slightly higher than some others with regard to stomach ulcers and gastrointestinal hemorrhage.

It is probably still too early to really tell how **Feldene** will compare.
Only after long-term experience will we know whether this drug is more
or less likely to cause serious problems. One immediate drawback we do
know about is price. Believe it or not, one 20 mg capsule can cost you
$1.11;[68] a six-month supply could run almost $200. Contrast that with a

six-months' supply of aspirin at $20 to $30, and you can see just how much convenience costs. But lest you get the wrong impression, let me hasten to add that all the NSAIDs are expensive, and **Feldene** is competitive if you evaluate the cost on a monthly basis.

Even though it's expensive, **Feldene** has been incredibly successful. One drug-industry expert, Sheldon Silverberg, offered an insight on the 1982 introduction of **Feldene**:

> **"I think Feldene will certainly be the top product launched in 1982 and could prove to be the top product launched so far." He predicted that if the one-a-day nonsteroidal anti-inflammatory averages an increase of 40,000 new Rxs a months through December, Feldene (piroxicam) could reap sales of $20 million per month by the end of the year . . . "the fact is that that product is a $200 million a year product in 1983," the Prescription Data Service Executive declared.[69]**

As of this writing, two million people in the United States have taken **Feldene,** and the numbers are climbing fast. But popularity alone doesn't make it a better mousetrap. As my mother always says, just because everyone else is doing it doesn't mean you should. People are easily disenchanted with almost any anti-inflammatory drug. When a new one comes along, they are ready to try it until the next one and then the next after that.

If, you, too, are dissatisfied with your arthritis medicine, **Feldene** may be worth a try; but don't expect a miracle. No matter what arthritis drug you take—whether it be **Motrin** or **Clinoril**, **Naprosyn**, or **Indocin**—make sure you get regular blood and kidney-function tests. Liver, kidney, and blood diseases are rare but potentially life-threatening complications that can be caught with proper monitoring. People taking one of the NSAIDs should contact the doctor immediately if they notice water retention (edema), a change in the color of the urine, greater frequency of urination, or back pain, since any of these can be a sign of kidney damage.

Several reports, incidentally, claim that **Clinoril** may be much easier on the kidneys than many other NSAIDs and thus more appropriate for anyone with reduced kidney function.[70,71] I also have one caution to offer. There is a suspicion that a potassium-sparing diuretic called triamterene (found in the very commonly prescribed **Dyazide** as well as in **Dyrenium** and **Maxzide**) may substantially increase the risk of kidney damage for patients taking NSAID arthritis drugs like **Indocin**.[72,73] If you or anyone you know is on **Dyazide** and is also taking an arthritis drug, ask your doctor to review this potentially dangerous drug interaction and make sure to ask for a creatinine clearance test to check the condition of the kidneys.

No doubt an ever-increasing number of NSAIDs will emerge over the next several years. Because such drugs represent a billion-dollar bonanza to pharmaceutical manufacturers, lots and lots of me-too compounds will be competing for your dollars. But remember one thing: so far none of these drugs has truly distinguished itself as really superior to aspirin in anti-inflammatory action or pain control. And lest we be seduced by the theory that new is better, we must never forget the legacy of **Oraflex**.

Dissolving Away Bad Backs With Meat Tenderizer

Unless you've suffered from lower back pain, you are not allowed to read the next few pages. Only a fellow victim can appreciate and sympathize with the pain, the helplessness, the frustration that comes with being immobilized with a bad back. My first contact with LBP (lower back pain) was when I was eight and my Dad ended up flat on his back on the floor for two weeks. It hit him while he was casually tying a shoe lace, and I knew from his tone of voice that the pain was almost unbearable.

My firsthand experience started as a teenager. One Saturday morning after basketball practice I was lifting a box into a closet, and bam, I knew I was in big trouble. Since that fateful day I have had periodic attacks, sometimes as the result of doing something as simple as stooping to change a diaper, other times after a long car ride or a quick game of soccer. No matter what triggers an attack, the pain can be excruciating. If you've been there, you know there is no way to get comfortable or concentrate on anything else while your back hurts.

According to the experts, "at least 70 percent of us will experience LBP at some time in our lives. Acute LBP is a self-limited illness. Approximately 40% of patients remit in 1 week, 60–80 percent in 3 weeks, and 90 percent or more within 2 months."[74] They make it seem simple, almost uneventful; "self-limited" sounds so benign. Believe me, when you're in the middle of an attack, there is very little consolation in the knowledge that the pain will ultimately go away. I guess I am one of the lucky ones, though; one to two weeks of rest is about all it usually takes for me to be back on my feet. But for some the pain doesn't go away by itself.

No matter what doctors may say, lower back pain is more often than not a medical mystery. There are lots of things that can go wrong, and diagnosis can be an art as much as a science.

Let's take a crash course in back anatomy. Your spine is made up of 33 little bones, or vertebrae, stacked up like blocks. Your spinal cord runs down the center of these blocks, carrying vital messages back and forth from your brain to your body. There are also ligaments that attach one bone to another and tendons that attach muscles to bones. In most minor back cases what goes wrong is that a muscle is "pulled" or those ligaments or tendons get stretched or strained. Some rest and maybe a little aspirin usually puts Humpty Dumpty back together again. Another option is TENS (transcutaneous electrical nerve stimulation). See page (328) for this new approach to pain control.

The real trouble starts when we look at the spongy shock absorbers between the blocks. These cushions or discs are Mother Nature's way of protecting the vertebrae. They are filled with a jellylike substance (mucoprotein, called the nucleus pulposus) and help to prevent the bones from grinding against each other. Some doctors use the analogy of a jelly-filled doughnut to describe a disc.

But discs are sensitive little buggers. Lifting a heavy suitcase can put over 500 pounds of pressure on the lower back. When a disc becomes damaged and ruptures, the jellylike material leaks out and presses on exquisitely sensitive spinal nerves. The "slipped disc" hasn't really slipped at all; it's the pressure of that leaking gelatinous nucleus pulposus that produces the agonizing pain radiating through the buttocks and down the leg. As back muscles tighten up in a futile effort to protect the nerves, you end up hunched over.

If you suffered a herniated disc before 1963, your options were limited. When bed rest, heat, and pain relievers didn't help, the surgeons were called in. First iodine was injected between the vertebrae and an X-ray (myelogram) was taken to make sure the disc was indeed ruptured. Then the damaged cartilage was removed and a piece of bone from the hip or shin was inserted (fused) to immobilize the affected vertebrae. Make no mistake, a laminectomy was major surgery, with the risk of infection or hemorrhage. The procedure was also expensive.

But Dr. Lyman Smith had a better idea. Although he was an orthopedic surgeon who had done more than his share of laminectomies, Dr. Smith had one of those flashes of inspiration that are so few and far between. Instead of cutting and grafting, why not dissolve the bad disc chemically? He turned to the lowly papaya for his experiments.

People have known for centuries that papain, an enzyme from this fruit, will dissolve tough meat. (Just look on the label of most commercial meat tenderizers, and you'll find that the active ingredient is still papain; this enzyme is also used in such things as contact-lens cleaner, digestive aids, tooth powder, and even beer.) Dr. Smith isolated one particular enzyme—chymopapain—and tested it on animals. His research convinced him that the enzyme would dissolve both damaged disc material and the nucleus pulposus and eliminate the cause of the pain without harming nerve tissue or vertebrae.

Dr. Smith's initial studies on patients were impressive, and as the word spread, physicians were quick to try the procedure, called chemonucleolysis. Between 1963 and 1975 about 15,000 people were treated experimentally, and at least 70 percent got relief. More than 1,600 doctors learned the delicate art of injecting chymopapain into the area around a ruptured disc. The technique appeared to be at least as good as surgery with far less risk, cost, and inconvenience. Here, in his own words, is Doctor Smith's evaluation.

> The relief from pain was frequently dramatic. Often, immediately after a patient woke up, he would report that his leg pain was gone. With well-motivated patients—those who truly want to go back to work, such as airline pilots, farmers, and doctors—I was 90 percent successful.[75]

By the early 1980s the cost of a laminectomy could range anywhere from $6,000 to over $10,000, depending on the surgeon and the kind of hospital selected. The average hospital stay was six to ten days. In contrast, it was estimated that a chymopapain injection would have cost less than $5,000 and required two, or at most three, days in the hospital.[76] With such data, you'd figure that everyone would be jumping for joy— physicians, patients, health-insurance companies, and federal officials. The only hurdle left for marketing chymopapain was FDA approval, which seemed a mere formality.

The formality became a stumbling block—or, more accurately, a brick wall. FDA officials sometimes seem to act like dinosaurs wearing blinders. They move forward ever so slowly and in only one direction, with little capacity for creative thinking. Before the feds would give chymopapain a green light, they wanted a double-blind controlled study.

Normally I am absolutely 100 percent behind the idea of carefully controlling research in this way. Such trials by fire are essential if you want to eliminate psychological anticipation or bias on the part of either investigators or subjects. Usually half the patients receive the actual drug and half are given a placebo or inactive substance. Neither physician nor patient knows who is getting the placebo and who the real thing.

But chymopapain is different. There are always unavoidable risks in spinal injections. Many doctors had serious ethical doubts about a double-blind study for chymopapain, since half the people would take a risk for which they could theoretically get no improvement. Dr. Smith had some comments about the FDA and about Baxter, the drug company that was spearheading the testing of his brainchild.

> Before I ever heard of the f---ing FDA, I took the Hippocratic oath to do the best for my patients. . . .
>
> I told the board chairman of Baxter that I thought the new study was immoral and unethical in view of the risk to patients who might get no benefits. What kind of flaky SOBs

are you going to get for a study if you tell people they have only a 50-percent chance of getting the real thing? Would *you* submit to that?[77]

When the controversial 1975 study was evaluated everyone was flabbergasted. To universal amazement, both the treated and placebo groups benefited equally. Soon after, Baxter, the manufacturer of chymopapain, withdrew its application for approval. Meanwhile the same company actively marketed the drug in Canada, where it had long since received approval, and many United States patients traveled north to be treated.

Why did the placebo turn out to be almost as effective as the real thing? That mystery is still hotly debated. Many experts feel that the original 1975 study was flawed for many reasons, not the least of which was that the placebo really wasn't a placebo. Instead of injecting plain salt water, the researchers apparently used an active compound that was itself capable of dissolving discs. This error created a seven-year medical war over the effectiveness of chymopapain. Orthopedic specialists argued among themselves and with the FDA over the merits of injection therapy versus more traditional surgery.

Meanwhile the drug was being used in Canada and Europe with apparent success. Dr. Lyman Smith was even invited to Russia by the Central Institute for Orthopedics and Trauma to attend a symposium on chymopapain. Dr. Smith reported on his reception.

For gosh sakes, I was treated like a great benefactor of the Soviet people, the Russians are so happy with chymopapain. I was toasted at a banquet presided over by the Soviet Minister of Health. They even named the Soviet procedure after me: Lymanectomy.[78]

There was no such recognition in the United States. Once again we are reminded that a prophet in his own land often goes unhonored and unrewarded. But eventually the weight of the evidence became overwhelming. Follow-up studies done on patients treated earlier, and new studies on over 20,000 patients in other countries, especially Canada, proved that chymopapain really is effective; 70 to 90 percent of the ruptured-disc patients benefited from the drug. Many patients were free of pain within hours of being injected. Paper after paper in medical journals reported impressive rates of success.[79,80]

Finally, 19 years after Dr. Smith began his work, chymopapain, under the brand name **Chymodiactin**, was approved by the FDA. It's not without risk. One of the factors that held up approval was concern about life-threatening allergic reactions; about 1 percent of the people who receive a chymopapain injection suffer anaphylactic shock. But the mortality rate of the procedure is very low—0.01 percent.

That doesn't mean chymopapain is for everyone. In fact, it isn't for most folks. Like surgery, it should be a treatment of last resort. Back problems can have at least 30 different causes. If you treat a bad back with "tincture of time," it will heal all by itself in most cases. Before patients can even be considered as candidates for **Chymodiactin,** or **Discase**, another brand of chymopapain, they have had to spend at least two weeks in bed and an additional four to six weeks resting. They will also have had to have either a CAT scan or a myelogram (a dye test) to prove beyond a shadow of a doubt that the disc is indeed ruptured. Additional criteria include sciatic pain in the leg, pain when the leg is raised, decreased reflexes, and muscle weakness.

And even then some people should not be treated. Anyone who is allergic to the papaya enzyme cannot be considered, nor can anyone whose back pain could be caused by something other than a herniated disc, such as a misaligned spine or a bony spur.

But if after two months a person is still in agony from a slipped disc and meets all the other criteria, a **Chymodiactin** injection is worth discussing with an orthopedic surgeon. It is *not* a simple procedure, however, and patients *must* select a doctor with the same care the doctor selects his patients. What I mean is that once all the criteria are met, the success of the procedure depends in large measure on the skill of the physician. Someone who has performed 50 chymopapain injections clearly has a leg up on the guy who has only done three or four.

Anyone who is considering chemonucleolysis should ask the doctor nicely how many he has performed in the last six months and what his success rate has been. The professional education department of Smith Laboratories, makers of **Chymodiactin**, can also provide information about which doctors in a particular area have had experience with the procedure. The phone number is (800) 356-2225.

Even with all my enthusiasm for chymopapain (anytime you can avoid major surgery, you're ahead of the game), I don't want to give the impression that **Chymodiactin** injections are a breeze. You won't be able to hop out of bed and start doing the tango as soon as the anesthesia wears off. While approximately 50 percent get very good results and have little, if any, pain, the other 50 percent will experience stiffness and soreness, and 30 percent will develop muscle spasms for two to three days after the injection. Most of the pain and stiffness should disappear after several weeks, however.

One final caveat—not everyone will benefit; 10 to 15 percent of those who receive chymopapain will still have disc problems. That figure, by the way, is not much different from the number of people who don't respond to surgery. And anyone who does not obtain relief from chemonucleolysis may benefit nicely from a follow-up laminectomy. At least six weeks should be allowed to go by between procedures, however, since it takes at least that long to be sure the injection has indeed been a failure.

Chymodiactin is not an instant cure for a bad back. Any procedure that involves the spinal column carries a risk of infection or nerve damage and paralysis. Nevertheless, for those people who experience excruciating pain from a slipped disc that won't go away by itself, **Chymodiactin** is a welcome alternative to an expensive and debilitating operation that has risks of its own. A group of researchers summarize their experiences with the drug.

> **Chymopapain proved highly effective in eliminating the need for further surgery, which is more traumatic, more costly, and requires a longer convalescence than chemonucleolysis.**[81]

Breaking the Back of the Blues

Depression is a black hole. It's an infinitely large darkness into which millions of people fall every year. The vast majority come out again—some because of the help they receive, others in spite of it. A few are swallowed by the darkness, finding suicide the only solution to their despair. But advances on a number of research fronts have a lot of people believing that the day may be approaching when no one need be lost to the darkness of depression ever again.

For those who have never suffered depression, the true meaning and force of the illness is almost unfathomable and inexplicable, but I'll try to explain nonetheless. Those who have been there need no reminder. Those who haven't, need some sense of the dimensions in order to understand a disease that is quite likely to strike them or someone they know.

Depression is a problem so common and pervasive that it has been called "the common cold of psychiatry."[82] A survey by the National Institute of Mental Health found about 5 percent of the population suffering from depression, and that's probably a gross understatement.[83] Even if it's accurate, the figure translates into more than 10 million people who are depressed at any one time. And each year at least 25,000 feel so trapped that they take their own lives.

Supposedly misery loves company—but that's no consolation if you're the one who's suffering. The statistics tell us that as many as 1 out of every 5 Americans will have at least one bout with this dreadful disorder in his or her lifetime.[84]

The dictionary description of depression is "despondency; melancholy; dejection." That's not even close; it's a little like defining nuclear war as "an explosion." Depression (unlike nuclear war) comes in degrees, from the occasional blah feeling experienced by all of us when life seems to be ganging up, to unrelenting despair, which may have no relation to life events. One person described depression as a state of terminal sadness.

How do you know when you've crossed the line from "normal" depression—in response, perhaps, to a loss—to the truly debilitating, seemingly irreversible state of severe depression? Some clues to watch for: if you start to have trouble sleeping or eating, if nothing seems to matter and life loses its luster, if you seem to be moving in slow motion, and if you find it too difficult to get up the energy to see old friends, you need help. If thoughts of suicide run through your mind, you need help NOW!

While most people who haven't been depressed can understand, at least intellectually, the idea of feeling a bit down, most don't have a clue about the depths of sadness and helplessness a victim goes through, and they aren't prepared for it to last very long. "Why don't you cheer up?" helpful friends will ask, implying that the person could effect a miraculous cure with just a bit of effort. And when the expected rebound doesn't appear on schedule, those same friends may become disgusted and frustrated. If their depressed friend won't even try to buck up, then the hell with him, they conclude.

But depression can rarely be overcome by will power and "cheering up." Research is beginning to show the biochemical bases behind this disorder. Since it is now clear that people have no more control over the imbalance of brain chemicals that triggers depression than they have over their heart rate, it's little wonder that psychological pep rallies don't help very much. However, as science learns more and more about this phenomenon, the possibility of correcting the imbalance, or at least reestablishing some measure of equilibrium with drugs, gets closer all the time.

Depression is a mental prison with chemical bars, and escape isn't easy. What scientists have been trying to do is find the key to unlock those chemical gates. A number of neurotransmitters (chemical messengers that transmit nerve impulses)—including norepinephrine, serotonin, and acetylcholine—are known to affect people's moods.

No one really knows what makes brain chemistry go haywire. There's evidence that some people have a genetic predisposition to depression.[85,86] But it seems that in many other cases some combination of events and body systems simply conspires to create chemical mayhem. We know for certain that depression isn't anyone's fault; but the most pressing question for millions of depressed people is not necessarily what causes the condition but what can be done to get rid of it.

Many depressed people can be helped by medication, but the side effects of conventional drugs can be discouraging. Until recently only two classes of medication could provide relief from these symptoms.

The first group of antidepressants, the MAO (monoamine oxidase) inhibitors, includes **Nardil** (phenelzine), **Marplan** (isocarboxazid), and **Parnate** (tranylcypromine). These can work very well for many people, but some patients do experience disturbing side effects, including dizziness, agitation, dryness of the mouth, blurred vision, weight gain, constipation, insomnia, and inability to achieve orgasm.

A more critical drawback is their incompatibility with many common drugs (cold and allergy remedies, diet pills, asthma medicines, narcotics such as **Demerol**, and amphetamine-type compounds like **Ritalin**). Certain foods can also cause serious problems for people taking these antidepressants. Watch out for aged cheese (Camembert, cheddar, Brie, Emmentaler, and Gruyere), avocados, ripe bananas, bologna, chicken livers, salami, pickled herring, beer, and red wine. Interactions can lead to a sudden dangerous rise in blood pressure.

Far more commonly prescribed antidepressants are the so-called tricyclics. These include **Elavil, Amitril, Endep, Etrafon, Limbitrol,** and **Triavil**, all of which contain amitriptyline; **Tofranil, Imavate, Jamimine,** and **Presamine,** which contain imipramine; **Aventyl** and **Pamelor** (nortriptyline); **Vivactil** (protriptyline); and **Adapin** and **Sinequan** (doxepin).

In many ways the tricyclics were a breakthrough in treating depression, and they became the drugs of first choice during the 1960s and 1970s. They offered unprecedented hope to those who had been treatable until then only with psychotherapy and waiting it out. Just imagine what it means to someone mired in depression to be given a pill that can begin to lift the overwhelming cloud.

But like the MAO inhibitors, these drugs are far from perfect. They are very slow to get about their business, and for the severely depressed person the several weeks it can take for a tricyclic to start doing its job can seem like years. Some other major problems include low blood pressure when a person stands up suddenly, dry mouth, blurred vision, sedation, constipation, sexual problems (reduced desire and orgasmic ability), urinary retention, and irregular heart rhythms.

An adverse reaction that is rarely mentioned to patients is weight gain, which is quite common and may be one of the most insidious and serious drawbacks to this therapy. Imagine a depressed person, struggling to overcome all kinds of negative feelings, gradually discovering that he or she has been gaining weight constantly, even with rigorous dieting. Scientists are not certain whether this problem is due to increased appetite, altered metabolism, or a combination of the two, but one thing is for sure: this complication can add to the sense of hopelessness and helplessness that is part of depression. For some, all these side effects are serious enough to interfere with treatment. Worse yet, when taken in excessive doses, tricyclics can be fatal.

It should be clear by now that the old standby antidepressants leave a lot to be desired. Though these drugs do help to relieve depression when they are used in high enough doses, they cause unpleasant side effects often enough to turn treatment into torture. According to one report, half of those who start with these drugs eventually throw in the towel because of adverse reactions.[87]

New Antidepressants for the 1980s

Drug companies, recognizing that there is a tremendous need for better mousetraps, are scurrying to come up with alternatives. In recent years several new compounds have been introduced. There was a big buildup for **Ludiomil** (maprotilene) and **Desyrel** (trazodone), but both have been somewhat disappointing. **Ludiomil** can cause drowsiness, dizziness, dry mouth, and constipation, which makes it quite similar to its predecessors. It has also been reported to produce a slightly higher incidence of seizures than other tricyclic antidepressants.

Desyrel goes to work quickly and is less likely to induce dry mouth, constipation, blurred vision, or urinary difficulties, and it seems much safer for the heart. But it can cause unpleasant drowsiness, dizziness, and fatigue. Some people on **Desyrel** report feeling light-headed and slightly confused. Family members have mentioned that patients may act befuddled and not think clearly while taking this drug. Another side effect, fortunately quite rare, is priapism—a prolonged, painful erection which may lead to impotence if not treated promptly.

So where's the good news? Neither **Desyrel** nor **Ludiomil** sounds like *the* answer to depression. Correct, my dear Watson—but waiting in the wings are lots of truly new and exciting compounds that seem to have far fewer side effects than traditional treatments.

One of the most impressive newcomers is **Wellbutrin** (bupropion).* Unlike many other antidepressants, it does not make people feel sleepy or lethargic, and it doesn't interact dangerously with alcohol. Many patients feel their mood lifting without the discomfort they usually associate with drug therapy. Best of all, people not only don't add pounds, they tend to lose what they gained on tricyclics.

There has also been the report that sexual side effects don't seem to be a problem with **Wellbutrin**. In fact, one preliminary study demonstrated that of 28 men who had experienced lowered libido and impotence while on tricyclics, 24 recovered sexual function when they were switched to **Wellbutrin**.[88]

Other benefits of this medication seem to be its rapid therapeutic effect and its safety for patients with heart disease. And in the event of

*At the time of this writing, **Wellbutrin** is awaiting imminent approval by the FDA.

an overdose, the drug seems much less dangerous than traditional tricyclics. Psychiatrists from New York University who reviewed a number of the newer antidepressants concluded that **Wellbutrin** "is virtually devoid of adverse effects."[89]

That doesn't mean the drug doesn't cause some side effects in some people. Insomnia, agitation, tremor, nausea, and dizziness have been reported, and susceptible individuals may run a risk of epilepticlike seizures. But overall, **Wellbutrin** appears to be a relatively safe and promising new antidepressant.[90]

Another drug that looks good is **Tolvon** (mianserin). This medication got its start in life for the treatment of allergies, but early on, researchers found that it gave the test subjects a mood boost. The drug has been effective for about 85 percent of those using it, including some who had no success with other antidepressants.

More than 100,000 people have received **Tolvon** in Europe, where it is considered safe and effective.[91] About the only side effects that are mentioned are occasional drowsiness, fatigue, and muscle weakness. There is also a concern that some patients will relapse after long-term treatment, but further research will be necessary to confirm this suspicion.

Wellbutrin and **Tolvon** are just a few of the new generation of antidepressants coming on line in the 1980s. Over the next several years there will be a growing list of drugs that are more easily tolerated and more effective. Millions of depressed people looking for relief have a lot to be cheerful about—the future does indeed look brighter.

Allergy Advances Help Stifle Those Sneezes

At long last allergy and hay-fever victims can put away their Kleenex. A quiet revolution in allergy treatment can sidestep the sneezes, runny noses, and itchy eyes that turn hay-fever season into misery. As a sufferer myself, I can vouch for the fact that using up a dozen handkerchiefs is definitely not a nice way to spend a balmy spring day.

Time was, the only simple remedies an allergic person could find were antihistamines and decongestants. The gremlin responsible for most of our problems—swollen sinuses, sneezing, dripping, and itching—is histamine. To feel better, it makes sense to stop histamine in its tracks, and that's just what antihistamines are supposed to do. But while they ward off the sniffles, they often leave the sneezer feeling spacey or sleepy. As a result, millions of people—surgeons, lumberjacks, pilots, linemen, and just about anyone who needs to drive to work—can't use them. **Actifed**, **Allerest**, **Benadryl**, **Chlor-Trimeton**, **Contac**, **Coricidin**, **Co-Tylenol**, **Dristan**, **Excedrin P.M.**, **PBZ**, **Phenergan**, **Sine-Off**, **Sudafed Plus**, **Teldrin**, **Triaminic**, and many others all come with warnings about not operating machinery or driving a vehicle. Even if they promise to keep you going, you may wonder what good it is if you feel as if you were walking under water. Antihistamines can also cause dry mouth, difficulty with urination, and occasionally impotence. They must never be taken with other sedating drugs like alcohol, because the sedative effect can be magnified.

Even if they don't put you to sleep, you may not be a good candidate for allergy remedies. Most contain decongestants along with the antihistamines. That means that millions of people with high blood pressure, heart disease, glaucoma, thyroid disease, diabetes, and prostate problems should steer clear of them.

The other popular alternative is nasal sprays containing decongestants. These reduce congestion effectively, but they can quickly cause more harm than good. People who rely on them for more than a few days at a time run the risk of becoming addicted to the nose spray. Since allergies clearly last longer than three days, the value of nasal decongestants is questionable at best.

Fortunately the quest for better allergy medications has produced some important new advances in recent years. A new antihistamine named terfenadine provides relief comparable to that which older antihistamines offer, but rarely makes people drowsy. It is also much less likely to increase the sedating effect of drugs such as **Valium** or alcohol, and will probably be the first of the new generation of antihistamines to be approved by the FDA.

Steroid nose sprays, the earliest breakthrough for allergy treatment, use a different approach from antihistamines. Until these topical compounds were developed, cortisone-type drugs, or steroids, were given only by mouth and only for severe allergic disorders that did not respond to traditional treatment. There is no question that such steroids as **Cortisone**, **Cortef**, **Cortone**, **Decadron**, **Dexone**, **Haldrone**, **Kenacort**, **Medrol**, **Meticorten**, and **Prednisone** are effective in relieving allergic and asthmatic symptoms, but they circulate in the body from the nose to the toes and can cause a host of serious side effects. These can include cataracts, ulcers, susceptibility to infections, menstrual problems, acne, mood changes, muscle weakness and cramps, weakness, weight gain, fluid retention, and potassium depletion. No matter how miserable hay fever can make you feel, these side effects are rarely worth risking for the symptomatic relief you receive.

But over the last several years steroid nasal sprays have been developed that virtually eliminate the usual problems of cortisone-type drugs. These new products deliver the steroids directly to the nasal passages, where they are needed, and little, if any, of the active medicine is absorbed into the body. It's a little like throwing a dart and hitting the bull's-eye compared to the old way of shooting the target with a shotgun and blowing the whole thing to smithereens.

Nasalide (flunisolide), **Beconase**, and **Vancenase** (beclomethasone) provide the symptomatic relief of steroids without the usual side effects. Several squirts a day can provide impressive respite from congestion, runny nose, sneezing, and itching for up to 70 percent of those who suffer. Some people complain of temporary sneezing and stinging after spritzing with these products but compared to the sluggishness antihistamines produce, that seems a relatively small price to pay. Newer products will probably be even more effective and less irritating.

While the steroid nasal sprays are good news for hay-fever victims, the latest advance in the allergy battle is equally exciting. Another prescription medicine called **Nasalcrom** (cromolyn) was recently approved by the FDA to ease allergic symptoms. It has been available in Europe for over a decade to soothe stuffy noses, and the same chemical, marketed under the name **Intal**, has been used for years in this country by asthma patients to prevent wheezing attacks.

Nasalcrom, which is not a steroid, works prophylactically to prevent histamine from being released in the nose. Antihistamines work by blocking the effects of histamine after it has already been released, which can be a little like trying to close the barn door once the horse is gone. If too much histamine gets out, it can be hard to stop. **Nasalcrom** closes the door first by stabilizing the cells and keeping them from liberating histamine in the first place. Breathe in that ragweed pollen, and nothing bad happens. Like the new steroid sprays, **Nasalcrom** isn't taken orally but comes as a spray that is used up to six times a day. It, too, has minor side effects—temporary stinging, sneezing, and irritation. And some people report an unpleasant aftertaste and headaches. Despite these annoyances, the benefits of long-lasting relief should have a lot of hay-fever victims smiling instead of sniffling when the pollen counts starts to soar.

Where Do We Go From Here?

We have only scratched the surface of the important new drugs that have become available in the 1980s. There are many other exciting advances in the chapters ahead. For example, you will learn about the breakthrough ulcer medicines **Tagamet, Carafate**, and **Zantac.** You will discover some exciting heart drugs—**Cardizem, Procardia, Calan**, and **Isoptin**—that are revolutionizing treatment of angina and high blood pressure.

In Chapter 10, a new drugs table will provide you with nuts-and-bolts information about improvements in asthma therapy that have made it possible for most asthmatics to lead normal lives without dangerous drug reactions. Medications like **Ventolin** and **Proventil** (albuterol), steroid aerosols such as **Beclovent** and **Vanceril** (beclomethasone) and long-acting theophylline products like **Theo-dur** and **Slo-phyllin** are better tolerated, more effective, and more convenient than earlier formulations.

You will also discover information about an amazing acne drug called **Accutane,** antifungal agents that are dynamite against athlete's foot and nail infections, a drug to dissolve gallstones (**Chenix**), chewing gum to help you stop smoking (**Nicorette**), a heart medication that just might help control ringing in the ears (**Tonocard**), and much, much more.

In the previous two chapters we have smelled the roses. Drug advances in the 1980s offer safer contraceptives, herpes treatments, hair restorers, better diet pills, stronger pain killers, heart-attack reversers, flu cures, more effective arthritis treatments, better antidepressants, and more impressive control of allergy, asthma, acne, angina, and goodness knows what else.

The future is incredibly bright. In the pipeline there are even better allergy and asthma medicines, safer anti-inflammatory agents, improved heart drugs, and more effective ulcer medications. If we were to look further down the road, it is not inconceivable that we would see a "smart pill" in the not too distant future, and perhaps even a drug for senility.

Biotechnology may lead to far better treatment of a whole host of viral ailments such as the common cold, measles, and hepatitis. In the process of developing such impressive new medications scientists are unlocking the secrets of the cell, which in turn may give us important clues to the process of growth. Investigators believe that some day we will have chemicals capable of healing wounds rapidly and perhaps even controlling, if not curing, cancer. Ultimately we may be able to retard the aging process itself.

Science fiction? Perhaps. But remember, many of the medicines we take for granted today would have seemed inconceivable 50 years ago. And many of the drugs that have become available in just the last several years are breakthroughs in their own right. But before we drown in euphoria, let us not forget that the only safe way to take any medication— new or old—is to become informed. The next chapters will try to bring you up to date on the medicines you put in or on your body. Information is your only protection!

References

1. Waldholz, Michael. "Potential of Costly New Superdrugs Leaves Doctors Excited but Wary." *The Wall Street Journal* March 11, 1982, p. 27.

2. Chanin, Arnold. "The Swine Influenza Controversy." *Western J. Med.* 125:81–82, July, 1976.

3. Chanin, Arnold. "A Boost for Amantadine." *Med. Trib.* 20(37): 1, November 21, 1979.

4. Sabin, Albert, B. "Amantadine Hydrochloride." *JAMA* 200:135–142, 1967.

5. Chanin, Arnold. "Letters." *Medical World News*, November 14, 1977.

6. Kramer, P., and McClain, C. J. "Depression of Aminopyrine Metabolism by Influenza Vaccination." *N. Engl. J. Med.* 305:1262–1264, 1981.

7. Renton, K. W., et al. "Decreased Elimination of Theophylline After Influenza Vaccination." *Can. Med. Assoc. J.* 123:288–290, 1980.

8. Zoler, Mitchel L. "Amantadine's Rocky Road to Acceptance." *JAMA* 249:991, 1983.

9. "Flu Outbreaks in Many Areas Lift the Slump for Druggists." *The Wall Street Journal*, February 3, 1983, p. 1.

10. Personal communication, Jay Sanford, 1981.

11. "The Choice of Antimicrobial Drugs." *Medical Letter* 22:5–12, 1980.

12. "Influenza Vaccines, 1983–1984." *Morbidity and Mortality Weekly Report* 32(26):333–337, 1983.

13. Chanin, Arnold. *Western J. of Med.* Op. cit.

14. Younkin, Scott W., et al. "Reductions in Fever and Symptoms in Young Adults with Influenza A/Brazil/78 H1N1 Infection After Treatment with Aspirin or Amantadine." *Antimic. Agents and Chemo.* 23:577–582, 1983.

15. Togo, Y., et al. "Studies on Induced Influenza in Man. I. Double-blind Studies Designed to Assess Prophylactic Efficacy of Amantadine Hydrochloride Against A2/Rockville/165 Strain." *JAMA* 203:1089–1094, 1968.

16. Smorodintsev, A. A., et al. "Evaluation of Amantadine in Artificially Induced A2 and B Influenza." *JAMA* 213:1448–1454, 1970.

17. Wendel, H. A., et al. "Trial of Amantadine in Epidemic Influenza." *Clin. Pharmacol. Ther.* 7:38–43, 1965.

18. Oker-Blom, N., et al. "Protection of Man from Natural Infection with Influenza A2 Hong Kong Virus by Amantadine: A Controlled Field Trial." *Br. Med. J.* 3:676–678, 1970.

19. Dolin, Raphael, et al. "A Controlled Trial of Amantadine and Rimantadine in the Prophylaxis of Influenza A Infection." *N. Engl. J. Med.* 307:580–584, 1982.

20. Douglas, R. Gordon. "Amantadine as an intiviral Agent in Influenza." *N. Engl. J. Med.* 307:617–618, 1982.

21. Zoler, Mitchel L. "Chemotherapeutic Agents Against RNA Viruses: Ranks Swelling." *JAMA* 249:989–992, 1983.

22. Chanin, Arnold. *Medical Tribune*, Op. cit.

23. Breese, Caroline, et al. "Ribavirin Treatment of Experimental Respiratory Synbctial Viral Infection." *JAMA* 249:2666–2670, 1983.

24. Larson, T., and Bryson, Y. "Fomites and Herpes Simplex Virus: The Toilet Seat Revisited, Abstracted." *Pediatr. Res.* 16:244, 1982.

25. Turner, R., et al. "Shedding and Survival of Herpes Simplex Virus from 'Fever Blisters.'" *Pediatrics* 70:547–549, 1982.

26. Nerukar, Lata S. "Survival of Herpes Simplex Virus in Water Specimens Collected from Hot Tubs in Spa Facilities and On Plastic Surfaces." *JAMA* 250:3081–3083, 1983.

27. Sullivan-Bolyai, John., et al. "Neonatal Herpes Simplex Virus Infection in King County, Washington." *JAMA* 250:3059–3062, 1983.

28. Personal communication, Dannie King, May 12, 1982.

29. Ibid.

30. "Proceedings of a Symposium on Acyclovir." *Am. J. Med.,* July 20, 1982, pp. 1–392.

31. Pagano, Joseph. "Acyclovir Comes of Age." *Am. Acad. Dermatol.* 6:396–397, 1982.

32. Corey, Lawrence. "The Diagnosis and Treatment of Genital Herpes." *JAMA* 248:1041–1049, 1982.

33. Corey, Lawrence, et al. "A Trial of Topical Acyclovir in Genital Herpes Simplex Virus Infections." *N. Engl. J. Med.* 306:1313–1319, 1982.

34. Corey, L. J., et al. "Treatment of First-episode Genital Herpes Simplex Virus Infections with Acyclovir: Results of Topical, Intravenous and Oral Therapy." *J. Antimicrob. Chemother.* 12(Suppl. B):79–88, 1983.

35. Saral, Rein, et al. "Acyclovir Prophylaxis of Herpes-Simplex-Virus Infections: A Randomized, Double-Blind, Controlled Trial in Bone-Marrow-Transplant Recipients." *N. Engl. J. Med.* 305:63–67, 1981.

36. Mitchell, Charles D., et al. "Acyclovir Therapy for Mucocutaneous Herpes Simplex Infections in Immunocompromised Patients." *Lancet* 2:1389–1392, 1981.

37. Chou, Sunwen, et al. "Controlled Clinical Trial of Intravenous Acyclovir in Heart-Transplant Patients with Mucocutaneous Herpes Simplex Infections." *Lancet* 2:1392–1394, 1981.

38. Selby, P. J., et al. "Parenteral Acyclovir Therapy for Herpes Virus Infections in Man." *Lancet* 2:1267–1270, 1979.

39. Fiddian, A. P., and Ivanyi, Ludmila. "Topical Acyclovir in the Management of Recurrent Herpes Labialis." *Br. J. Derm.* 109:321–326, 1983.

40. Personal communication, Paul Dryer, July 7, 1983.

41. Nilsen, Arvid E., et al. "Efficacy of Oral Acyclovir in the Treatment of Initial and Recurrent Genital Herpes." *Lancet* 2:571–573, 1982.

42. Bryson, Yvonne J., et al. "Treatment of First Episode of Genital Herpes Simplex Virus Infection with Oral Acyclovir." *N. Engl. J. Med.* 308:916–921, 1983.

43. Bryson, Yvonne. "Oral Acyclovir in Genital Herpes." Presentation at Burroughs Wellcome, February 20, 1984.

44. Reichman, Richard C., et al. "Controlled Trial of Oral Acyclovir in the

Therapy of Recurrent Herpes Simplex Genitalis." *Am. J. Med.*, Acyclovir Symposium, July 20, 1982, pp. 338–341.

45. Reichman, R. C., et al. "Patient-Initiated Therapy of Recurrent Herpes Simplex Genitalis with Orally Administered Acyclovir." *Clin. Res.* 31(2):373A, 1983.

46. Reichman, R. C., et al. "Treatment of Recurrent Genital Herpes Simplex Infections with Oral Acyclovir: A Controlled Trial." *JAMA* 251: 2103–2107, 1984.

47. Bryson, Yvonne. "Oral Acyclovir in Genital Herpes." Op. cit.

48. Straus, Stephen E., et al. "Supression of Frequently Recurring Genital Herpes: A Placebo-Controlled Double-Blind Trial of Acyclovir." *N. Engl. J. Med.* 310: 1545–1550, 1984.

49. Douglas, John, M., et al. "A Double-Blind Study of Oral Acyclovir for Suppression of Recurrences of Genital Herpes Simplex Virus Infection." *N. Engl. J. Med.* 310: 1551–1556, 1984.

50. Whittington, William L., and Cates, Willard J., Jr. "Acyclovir Therapy for Genital Herpes: Enthusiasm and Caution in Equal Doses." Editorial, *JAMA* 251: 2116–2117, 1984.

51. Keller, Robert. "Portrait of Eric." *The National Arthritis News* 2(2):6–7, 1981.

52. Personal communication, Marcia Amsterdam, October 15, 1981.

53. Furst, Daniel E. "Mechanism of Action, Pharmacology, Clinical Efficacy and Side Effects of Auranofin." *Pharmacotherapy* 3:284–298, 1983.

54. Homma, M., et al. "Interim Results of a Multicenter Open Study with Auranofin in Japan." *J. Rheumatol.* 9(Suppl 8):160–168, 1982.

55. Gunby, Phil. "Searching for Oral Gold—For Some Arthritis Patients." *JAMA* 244:2022–2077, 1980.

56. Bernhard, G. C. "Auranofin Therapy in Rheumatoid Arthritis." *J. Lab. Clin. Med.* 100(2):167–177, 1982.

57. Weisman, Michael, et al. "Analysis of Auranofin as a Rheumatoid Remitting Agent." *J. Rheumatol.* 9(Suppl 8):132–136, 1982.

58. Bandilla, Klaus, et al. "Oral Gold Therapy with Auranofin (SK&F 39162) A Multicenter Open Study in Patients with Rheumatoid Arthritis." *J. Rheumatol.* 9(Suppl 8): 154–159, 1982.

59. Schattenkirchner, Manfred, et al. "Auranofin and Sodium Aurothiomalate in the Treatment of Rheumatoid Arthritis." *J. Rheumatol.* 9(Suppl 8):184–189, 1982.

60. Katz, Warren A., et al. "The Efficacy and Safety of Auranofin Compared to Placebo in Rheumatoid Arthritis." *J. Rheumatol.* 9(Suppl 8): 173–178, 1982.

61. Thomas, Patricia. "Oral Gold's Milder Side Effects Called Advance." *Medical Tribune* June 6, 1984, p. 8.

62. Berglof, Frans-Erik, et al. "Auranofin: An Oral Chrysotherapeutic Agent for the Treatment of Rheumatoid Arthritis." *J. Rheumatol.* 5:68–74, 1978.

63. Finkelstein, A. E., et al. "New Oral Gold Compound for Treatment of Rheumatoid Arthritis." *Am Rheum. Dis.* 35:251–257, 1976.

64. Wiseman, Edward H., and Boyle, James A. "Piroxicam (Feldene)." *Clin. Rheum. Dis.* 6:585–613, 1980.

65. Goodwin, James S., et al. "Administration of Nonsteroidal Anti-inflammatory Agents in Patients with Rheumatoid Arthritis." *JAMA* 250:2485–2488, 1983.

66. Coles, L. Stephen. "From Experiment to Experience: Side Effects of Nonsteroidal Anti-Inflammatory Drugs." *Am. J. Med.* 74:820–828, 1983.

67. Weber, J. C. P. "Epidemiology of Adverse Reactions to Nonsteroidal Anti-inflammatory Drugs." In *Advances in Inflammation Research*, K. D. Rainford and G. P. Velo, eds., Raven Press, N.Y., 1984, pp. 1–7.

68. "Benoxaprofen (Oraflex) and Piroxicam (Feldene): Two new Drugs for Arthritis." *Medical Letter* 24:63–66, 1982.

69. "Feldene's 1982 U.S. Sales Should be in $80 Mil. Range; $200 Mil. in 1983—PDS' Silverberg." *F-D-C Reports* 44(39):3–4, Sept. 27, 1983.

70. Ciabattoni, Giovanni, et al. "Effects of Sulindac and Ibuprofen in Patients with Chronic Glomerular Disease." *N. Engl. J. Med.* 310: 279–283, 1984.

71. Sedor, John R., et al. "Effects of Sulindac and Indomethacin on Renal Prostaglandin Synthesis." *Clin. Pharmacol. Ther.* 36: 85–91, 1984.

72. Bunning, Robert D., and Barth, Werner F. "Sulindac: A Potentially Renal-Sparing Nonsteroidal Anti-inflammatory Drug." *JAMA* 248:2864–2867, 1982.

73. Favre, L., et al. "Reversible Acute Renal Failure from Combined Triamterene and Indomethacin." *Ann. Intern. Med.* 96:317–320, 1982.

74. Quinet, Robert J., and Hadler, Nortin M. "Diagnosis and Treatment of Backache." *Seminars in Arthritis and Rheumatism* 8(4):261–287, 1979.

75. In Star, Jack. "Bad Times for the Bad-Back Drug." *Chicago* November 1978, pp. 168–174.

76. "Chymopapain for Slipped Discs." *Internal Medicine Alert* and Press Release, FDA, Washington, D.C. Nov. 10, 1982.

77. Star. Op. cit.

78. Ibid.

79. Sorbie, Charles. "Chemonucleolysis in the Treatment of Lumbar Disc Protrusion." *Can. Med. Assoc. J.* 124:840–846, 1981.

80. Javid, Manucher J. "Safety and Efficacy of Chymopapain (Chymodiactin) in Herniated Nucleus Pulposus With Sciatica." *JAMA* 249:2489–2494, 1983.

81. Op. cit.

82. Roberts, R. E., and Vernon, S. W. "Depression in the Community: Prevalence and Treatment." *Arch. Gen. Psych.* 39:1407, 1982.

83. "Sampling America's Emotional Health." *Science News*, 124(19), November 5, 1983.

84. Molnar, George. "Pharmacotherapy of Depressions." *N.Y. State J. of Med.* 82:1717–1720, 1982.

85. Weitkamp, Lowell R., et al. "Depressive Disorders and HLA: A Gene on Chromosome 6 That Can Affect Behavior." *N. Engl. J. Med.* 305:1301–1306, 1981.

86. Maugh, Thomas H. "Is There A Gene for Depression?" *Science* 214:1330–1331, 1981.

87. Blackwell, Barry. "Antidepressant Drugs. Side Effect and Compliance." *J. Clin. Psych.* 43(11) sec. 2:14–18, 1982.

88. Personal communication, Warren, Stern, August 31, 1983.

89. Shopsin, B., Cassano, G.B. and Conti. L. "An Overview of New 'Second Generation' Antidepressant Compounds: Research and Treatment Implications." In *Antidepressants: Neurochemical, Behavioral, and Clinical Perspectives*, S. J. Enna et al., eds., New York, Raven Press, 1981, pp. 219–251.

90. Feighner, John P. "The New Generation of Antidepressants." *J. Clin. Psych.* 44(5) sec. 2:49–55, 1983.

91. Ibid.

CHAPTER 5

Breakthroughs For Bellyaches

Taming **Tagamet**: *A License to Print Money* ▪
Adverse Reactions and Interactions ▪ **Tagamet**
and the Cancer Controversy ▪ *Vitamin C to the*
Rescue ▪ *The Great Ulcer War:* **Zantac** *Arrives*
▪ *The* **Carafate** *Challenge* ▪ *The Ulcer Diet Gets*
Rougher: Puncturing the Myths and Living with
Your Ulcer.

The most spectacular new drug of the 1970s—perhaps of the century—
arrived without fanfare. Until **Tagamet** (cimetidine), most major drug
companies didn't take tummy troubles terribly seriously. Oh sure, Americans gorped down antacids almost like candy, but most pharmaceutical
big wigs probably wrote that off to our penchant for eating junk food on
the run. Ulcers just didn't seem like such a widespread problem—certainly
not of the magnitude of arthritis or high blood pressure. Even **Tagamet**'s
manufacturer, Smith Kline & French, didn't realize what a gold mine the
company had in this pale-green pill.

SK&F was an unlikely candidate for producing the most profitable
drug in the history of the industry. According to one report,

> [T]he SmithKline Corporation fit the profile of a company
> going nowhere: It lagged in developing the new products nec-
> essary for success in the research-intensive drug industry. . . .
> The development of Tagamet came at a time when SmithKline's
> research department had nothing much else to show for itself.
> "They were at or near the bottom of the pharmaceutical
> group," said one industry analyst.[1]

Mary Walton, a reporter for the Philadelphia *Inquirer*, documents the
incredible history behind this local firm.

> The company had been born in 1830 as a drugstore on North
> Second Street. Over the years the drugstore evolved into a
> wholesaler of medications and began manufacturing a line of
> tonics, hangover cures, infant formulas and the like.[2]

The company was little different from the patent-medicine peddlers of
that era in that it made extraordinary claims for some rather dubious
products. There was **Red Raven Water**, "a surefire cure for hangover!"

and **Lows Magnetic Liniment** which, when used externally *and* internally, promised speedy relief from "rheumatism, neuralgia, headache, toothache, pain in the face, side, or back, bruises, burns, cuts, sprains, diarrhea, colic, cramps, coughs, colds and nervous diseases."[3] Given that the "liniment" had an alcochol content of 138 proof, it's hardly any wonder people forgot what ailed them, whether a toothache, cold, or nervous disease.

Treatment of "nervous diseases" was to become an important cornerstone of the Smith & Kline product line. Toward the end of the nineteenth century **Hydro Bromate Caffeine** was promoted to an eager public.

> **This elegant preparation is an almost certain remedy for nervous exhaustion due from any cause, either from excitement of any kind, Indigestion, Sedentary Occupation, Alcoholic Excess, the Suprasensitiveness of Chloral, Morphia, and Opium habitues; and with Ladies the headaches so peculiar to their sex; the Physician, Lawyer, Teacher, Clergyman, Merchant, and all others following occupations requiring a brain or nerve stimulant of a refreshing and harmless character in regard to its after effects, will thoroughly appreciate its action.[4]**

Another successful tonic was **Eskay's Neuro Phosphates**, a strychnine-and-alcohol-based formula supposed to be good for the "convalescent, the overworked, the constitutionally delicate, the neurasthenic, the chronically fatigued, the anorectic, and the aged."[5] Though scientists today would question the safety and effectiveness of such stimulants, in that period they sold well. Yet it wasn't until the 1930s that the company got its first really big break with "speed."

Benzedrine, known generically as amphetamine, was first sold for colds and hay fever. People were delighted to discover that the little inhaler opened up their nasal passages almost like magic. There followed **Benzedrine Solution, Benzedrine Elixir**, and **Benzedrine Tablets**. In the 1940s Smith Kline & French introduced a stronger cousin called **Dexedrine** (dextroamphetamine), which was sold as a diet pill and a mood elevator. You better believe profits were elevated, too! In those days the FDA was pretty lax, and abuse of such stimulants was not an issue.

In the decade that followed, housewives all across the nation discovered amphetamine highs. They were delighted to suppress their appetite, and as an added bonus they got a little "boost" in the middle of the day. What no one told them was that the effect on appetite faded within a few weeks, but if they stopped the medicine, psychological depression could result. As a consequence some people just kept taking them. I had an elderly aunt who was one of the most prim and proper ladies you would ever hope to meet, and yet even in her eighties she continued to depend on her little heart-shaped "energy pills" to help her make it through the day.

The company's success with these "uppers" was followed in the 1950s with the ultimate "downer." French researchers had discovered a compound that they weren't quite sure what to do with. It produced an "artificial hibernation" and increased the potency of anesthetics. The drug was offered to several American pharmaceutical manufacturers, but because its promise seemed limited, they rejected the deal of the decade.

Then Smith Kline & French got its shot. Soon after acquiring the license, the company found that this extraordinary compound could calm mental patients. Chlorpromazine (**Thorazine**) became the nation's first really practical antipsychotic medicine. Instead of being handled with padded cells, wet sheets, and straight jackets, agitated schizophrenic patients were given **Thorazine**. SK&F then cornered the market with two related compounds—**Compazine** (prochlorperazine)˙and **Stelazine** (trifluoperazine). These drugs soon became the principal form of treatment for mental illness.

And patients often took their medicine whether they liked it or not. The company came up with lots of dosage forms and used advertising that encouraged doctors to administer the medicine even over patients' objections.

> **Drug evasion can be a disturbing problem in treating paranoid patients. Their suspicions can lead them to cheek their tablets and dispose of them later.**
>
> **Stelazine Concentrate can easily solve this problem.**
>
> **By disguising the concentrate in liquids or semisolid foods, you are assured that suspicious patients get the full benefit of the potent antipsychotic effect of "Stelazine."**
>
> **When you see—or suspect—drug evasion in your "Stelazine" patients, specify the concentrate form.**[6]

Many patients disliked their medicine for reasons other than paranoia. These heavy-duty tranquilizers space people out, and in large doses they can turn them into something close to zombies. Even worse, if they are used long enough, the drugs can produce something called tardive dyskinesia—uncontrollable movements and muscle spasms that include neck twitching, lip chewing, and tongue biting. All too often these side effects are irreversible, even after the drugs are discontinued. A parkinsonian tremor is also common.

During the 1960s I worked in a neuropharmacology lab at a psychiatric research facility where it was common to see patients shuffling about the grounds jerking and twitching as they walked. Many also experienced other symptoms of these medications, including stuffy nose, constipation, dizziness, blurred vision, difficult urination, and impaired sexuality. It was hardly any wonder that sometimes they tried to avoid their medicine.

Between the uppers and the downers (which together made up 70 percent of sales), the company flourished throughout the 1950s and early 1960s, but toward the end of that decade the success was going flat. **Thorazine** was coming off patent, opening the door to cheaper generic competition. Other companies were introducing successful antipsychotic medications of their own, so that Smith Kline & French lost its edge. Because diet pills were also falling into medical disrepute, **Benzedrine** and **Dexedrine** were no longer the winners they had once been.

It looked as if the company had shot its bolt. No promising new drugs loomed on the horizon. According to one insider, the research and development "went dry in the mid-60's. We had nothing substantial to introduce to the marketplace."[7] Without its over-the-counter cold remedy **Contac** and the development of an unexpectedly successful diuretic called **Dyrenium** (a forerunner of **Dyazide**), SK&F would have been in trouble. As it was, company coffers were hurting, and by 1969 almost 200 employees had been fired and management was looking to cut unproductive research. As a result, **Tagamet** almost didn't see the light of day. The research program responsible for developing the drug came "within a hair" of being terminated, according to Robert F. Dee, Chairman of the Board of the SmithKline Corporation.[8]

Taming Tagamet

Dr. James Black hardly appears to be a hired gun. Although he has been knighted for his accomplishments in pharmaceutical research, he is a very modest person, dedicated to scientific investigation, "the sort of person whom his peers describe as 'a real scientist,' a practitioner of 'elegant' research."[9] It is ironic that someone who has helped to develop the two most successful drugs in history has little concern or interest in the money his discoveries have generated but instead has gone from company to company, wherever he had a chance to do the research he was interested in. As he confessed to Mary Walton, "People in my business are almost like prostitutes. We go where people will support us."[10]

In 1964 the support came from the British subsidiary of SmithKline. While at ICI Pharmaceuticals, Ltd., James Black had already notched his gun with the beta-blocker **Inderal** (propranolol), a heart and blood-pressure medication that would go on to become the most prescribed pill

of the early 1980s.* He moved on to SK&F with a new target; he had set
his sights on histamine, and if he could make his idea work, it would
revolutionize the treatment of ulcers.

Histamine must rank as one of the cruelest chemicals our bodies make.
It has caused more than its share of suffering, since it stimulates the
secretion of stomach acid that makes ulcers ache, as well as producing
the all too familiar symptoms of hay fever and hives. I can speak with
feeling on this subject, since my personal all-time record is 37 sneezes,
nonstop. The cat that provoked this allergic attack split after the second
sneeze but left me with red, itchy eyes and a stuffy, runny nose.

Such symptoms can be partially controlled with histamine-blocking
compounds called, cleverly enough, antihistamines. Thousands of brands
of cold and allergy remedies contain antihistamines like chlorpheniramine (**Allerest, Chlor-Trimeton, Contac,** and others), pyrilamine
(**Excedrin P.M.**), tripelennamine (**PBZ**), and triprolidine (**Actifed**). Although they often make people feel drowsy or "dopey," these medications can stifle sneezes and suppress sniffles.†

But they don't do a darn thing for stomach acid. Since ulcer patients
don't benefit from classic antihistamines, most researchers never really
considered the potential of histamine antagonists for blocking acid secretion.
Instead they went along with the bland-diet-and-antacid approach. But
James Black is the kind of scientist who thinks creatively. In a stroke of
genius, which he modestly disclaims, he and his colleagues hypothesized
that histamine might follow different rules in the stomach than it does
elsewhere in the body. What if they could create a special, new kind of
antihistamine that would work in the stomach rather than in the nose?

The concept was brilliant, but could they pull it off? The SmithKline
researchers in England spent more than ten years and created over one
thousand compounds before they struck pay dirt at last. Theirs was a
precarious struggle. Halfway through the quest their program was almost
axed. Remember, there was a cash crisis back in Philadelphia; corporate
managers were cutting back. And at the time, as Black points out, the
scientific consensus was that "control of acid secretion was no place for
histamine. . . . The intellectual climate was against the idea."[11]

From headquarters, the histamine research looked vulnerable as hell.
Chairman Robert Dee described Black's work: "He sank a lot of dry
holes. We were within an ace of calling it quits in 1969. We then
decided to go one more year."[12] Throughout the crunch the researchers
plugged away. As Sir James puts it, "I was absolutely certain I would find
the antagonist . . . I just didn't doubt that we would finish it."[13] Fortunately for SmithKline, the brass held out just long enough to allow Black
and his team to come up with proof that they were on the right track.

*For a more complete discussion of beta-blockers, see page 182.
†For further information on antihistamines, see the discussion on pages 125–27.

In 1972 their breakthrough was announced to the world. They had finally found a way to block the action of histamine in the gut.[14] Out of this effort **Tagamet** was born.

It worked far better than anyone ever dreamed, except perhaps James Black. Just as he had hoped, this histamine antagonist stopped acid secretion right in its tracks. Numerous studies demonstrated that a few days after patients started on **Tagamet**, their pain disappeared. Even better, within weeks 70 to 80 percent experienced healing of their ulcers.

The effect was so dramatic that SmithKline could hardly wait to get it on the market, and for once the FDA went along. Although the drug didn't seem to be any more effective than intensive antacid therapy, it was much more convenient. Instead of swallowing quarts and quarts of chalky glop, patients could casually pop a pill four times a day. Relief was spelled SK&F. The feds gave **Tagamet** priority treatment, putting it on the so-called fast track. The drug sailed through the approval process in record time. And then the fun began.

SmithKline executives were hoping that **Tagamet** would be a winner. They had every reason to be optimistic; in 1977, when the drug was first introduced in the United States, the worldwide market for ulcer medicine amounted to approximately $400 million. Had they ultimately captured half that, they would have been ecstatic. As Sir James remarks, even during the investigational phase, "It was pretty obvious that Smith Kline & French had no idea. . . . They were greatly underestimating how much money they would make."[15] Little did they know that **Tagamet** would become the hottest drug in the history of the pharmaceutical industry. Within one year sales had hit almost $200 million, and by 1979 they had reached $450 million.[16] In 1981 *The Wall Street Journal* summed up the drug's success.

> SmithKline's **Tagamet** brand of cimetidine, which can heal peptic ulcers, is the most successful prescription drug ever marketed. World sales hit $620 million last year, industry sources estimate, and may rise this year to nearly $800 million.[17]

By 1983 over 30 million people had taken the drug and worldwide sales (in 123 countries) had far exceeded $800 million.[18] As you read these words it is quite likely that **Tagamet** will be the first billion-dollar baby of the drug industry. To put all this into perspective, consider **Valium**. For years it was the most widely prescribed drug in this country, but it didn't reach its lofty status overnight. And even at its peak in the mid-1970s, sales "only" reached $500 million annually. Compared to **Valium**, **Tagamet** has been a shooting star—a gold mine which, incredibly, accounted for half of SmithKline's 1982 earnings.[19]

How did **Tagamet** do it? Where did all those ulcers come from? That is the billion-dollar question. According to the National Institutes of Health, each year approximately four million Americans experience duodoneal ulcers (ulcers in the upper part of the small intestine). Another 600,000 develop gastric (stomach) ulcers.[20] Even assuming that hundreds of thousands of people go undiagnosed and uncounted, far fewer than five million ulcer sufferers probably seek medical treatment annually.[21,22] Yet in 1982 retail pharmacies filled over 20 million prescriptions for **Tagamet**.[23] And hospitals dispensed countless millions more. Given that a month's supply can cost the consumer over $35, it is easy to see why SmithKline executives are smiling all the way to the bank. Their new drug almost amounts to a license to print money.

Even if every single ulcer patient received a prescription for **Tagamet**— and even a couple of refills—that still wouldn't account for the incredible number of pale-green pills swallowed every day in this country. Dr. John Kurata, an epidemiologist for CURE (Center for Ulcer Research and Education) in Los Angeles, told a reporter, "There aren't that many patients with ulcers to account for that volume" of **Tagamet** sales.[24] So what's going on?

It doesn't take a genius to figure out that **Tagamet** is being prescribed for a lot more than ulcers. Dr. Craig Rothman, in a letter to the editor of the *New England Journal of Medicine*, complained about the overuse of this medication.

> **Cimetidine is heavily prescribed at all levels of medical practice, often without proper indication. For example, in the community it is commonly used to treat indigestion or any symptoms even remotely related to "acid."[25]**

His suspicions were confirmed in a survey of almost 2,000 patients taking **Tagamet**. Dr. Arthur Cocco discovered that over half had never actually had a definite diagnosis of ulcers; many had received the drug because of something as amorphous as "abdominal pain."[26] Other physicians have also reported "indiscriminate and inappropriate" use of the drug in hospitalized patients.[27,28] One study found that 38 percent of the patients receiving **Tagamet** had no condition that would justify its use,[29] while another group of doctors who examined the question "were amazed at the variety of disorders for which cimetidine was given."[30] "A Second Look at Cimetidine", published in the *Journal of Clinical Gastroenterology*, summarizes the criticisms.

> **The problem of cimetidine therapy starts when it is used for almost any gastrointestinal condition in a knee jerk fashion. Cimetidine is not any better than antacids. It gained rapid acceptance in the treatment of ulcer disease only because of its ease of administration and lack of side effects, like diar-**

rhea . . . cimetidine is not a cure-all and is over utilized . . . I
will be heartbroken if some serious side effect comes into light
after 15–20 years of its use. . . .

It is mind-boggling to imagine the number of patients now
using this medication.[31]

From all indications it would appear that the drug was being used as a
superantacid. Instead of **Tums**, **Rolaids**, or **Maalox** many folks were
popping **Tagamet** at the first sign of acid indigestion.

But there is another, more insidious, reason why so much **Tagamet** is
being used by so many people. Once you get started, it's hard to stop—
like being caught in a vicious cycle. As long as you keep taking the
drug, ulcers are kept at bay. But within three months of stopping, as
many as 70 percent of patients experience a relapse, and in one year that
number can rise as high as 90 percent.[32–39] It's hardly any wonder that
people keep popping those little green pills. If they want to keep the pain
of an ulcer away, they may have to keep swallowing **Tagamet** indefinitely.
Or, as Mary Walton puts it, "Lo and behold, **Tagamet** junkies."[40]

Adverse Reactions

But what about side effects? In the beginning physicians and patients
were so enamored by the apparent effectiveness and convenience of
Tagamet that side effects simply weren't an issue. And SmithKline has
done its best to create an aura of confidence. Extremely beautiful color
photographs of people looking self-assured and active grace medical
journals. The message is, in the words of Dr. Stanley Crooke, Vice
President of Research and Development for SmithKline, "**Tagamet** is
extraordinarily safe."[41] Corporate executives believe that the drug is so
safe, in fact, that they foresee a day when it could become available over
the counter.[42]

But is it *really* so safe? Yes and no. If you think I'm waffling, you're
right. On the one hand, the drug does have a surprisingly good track
record. Careful review of the medical literature turns up a relatively low
incidence of adverse reactions, probably less than 5 percent.[43,44] Paradoxically, digestive-tract upset is the most common complaint, with side
effects ranging from diarrhea and gas to nausea and vomiting. But GI
(gastrointestinal) symptoms occur in only about 2 percent of the people
who take **Tagamet**. If you compare that number to the approximately 20
percent who experience diarrhea while on heavy antacid therapy, **Tagamet**
comes out the clear-cut winner.

Of far greater concern is the effect of the drug on mental functioning.
Side effects can include confusion, dizziness, restlessness, drowsiness,

slurred speech, headache, lethargy, twitching, delirium, and visual hallucinations. Such adverse reactions are quite uncommon in young, healthy adults (probably 1 percent or less); older people, on the other hand, are much more susceptible. If they aren't forewarned about the possibility of mental confusion, they may think that they are losing their minds or going senile.

Sexual side effects have also been reported. They include reduced libido, impotence, and enlarged tender breasts in men.[45-48] Fortunately such reactions are extremely rare and generally only occur if the drug is given in very high doses. Equally uncommon are reports of dizziness, rash, headache, and joint pain. Based on all this information, then, I would have to agree that the drug appears relatively safe when taken by itself.

The Trouble With Tagamet: Drug Interactions

Ah, but there's the rub: **Tagamet** is often taken along with other medications. People who get ulcers don't live in a vacuum; they may also suffer from high blood pressure, anxiety, heart disease, asthma, or goodness knows what. The gastroenterologist who prescribes **Tagamet** may forget to warn his ulcer patient to watch out for drugs prescribed by the internist, cardiologist, or psychiatrist. But taking **Tagamet** with other common medicines can spell disaster.

This compound slows down the metabolism of many other drugs, and as a result they can build up in your body to toxic levels. A reader of our newspaper column described what can happen.

> **I've been under a lot of pressure lately in my job, so my doctor prescribed Librium a few months ago to help me deal with the stress. Last week he discovered a peptic ulcer, and prescribed Tagamet.**
>
> **Now I feel like a zombie—so slow and dopey I have trouble staying on top of things at work. Walking is difficult and driving is impossible.**
>
> **My doctor says that this couldn't be due to the Tagamet, and that I'm taking too little Librium to produce this effect. I'm afraid to stop taking either medicine, but I can't function like this.**

The doctor was wrong. **Tagamet** could have caused this reaction by itself, but it is more likely that it was the interaction that caused the reader's problems. By itself **Librium** wasn't enough to produce drowsiness, but **Tagamet** may well have allowed the drug to accumulate and produce an overdose reaction.[49]

Other medications that could interact with **Tagamet** include anti-anxiety agents like **Valium** (diazepam) and **Tranxene** (clorazepate), antidepressants like **Tofranil** (imipramine), beta-blocking high blood pressure medications such as **Inderal** (propranolol), and **Lopressor** (metoprolol), heart drugs such as **Procardia** (nifedipine), and asthma medicine containing theophylline (**Bronkotabs, Elixophyllin, Marax, Quibron, Slo-Phyllin, Tedral, Theo-Dur, Theolair,** and so on).[50-55] The anticoagulant **Coumadin** (warfarin), the seizure medicine **Dilantin** (phenytoin) and the heart drug **Pronestyl** (procainamide) may be particularly dangerous when combined with **Tagamet**.[56-58]

These are just *some* of the medications that can be more dangerous when taken with **Tagamet**. The possibility exists that many other drugs could also be affected, among them caffeine, alcohol (if you drink, Tagamet may make you drunker), phenobarbital, digitoxin, morphine, chemotherapeutic agents used to fight cancer, lidocaine (**Xylocaine**), meperidine (**Demerol**), quinidine (**Cardioquin, Quinaglute, Quinidex, Quinora**), and desipramine (**Norpramin, Pertofrane**).[59,60] The accompanying chart describes the possible problems of such interactions. A final word of caution: just because a drug is not listed on the chart, does not make it safe in combination with **Tagamet**. There is much we don't know about these unique and potentially hazardous drug interactions.

Drug Interactions With Tagamet (cimetidine)

Anyone who receives a prescription for **Tagamet** *must* notify his physician and pharmacist of any other medications (prescription or over the counter) being taken. **Tagamet** may increase the toxicity of many other drugs. If there is no way to avoid such combinations, a recalculation of the dosage could be essential.

If a person who is prescribed **Tagamet**

ALSO TAKES:	THIS COULD RESULT:

ANTACIDS
  Aluminum & Magnesium
    Maalox
    Mylanta II
    Gelusil
 	
  Aluminum hydroxide
    Amphojel
    Alternagel
 	
LAXATIVES
  Magnesium hydroxide
    Milk of Magnesia
	Whoops! After everything we just said about **Tagamet** making other drugs more dangerous, we have to immediately contradict ourselves on this one. Antacids and magnesium-containing laxatives can prevent absorption of **Tagamet**. That means you don't get the maximum benefit and end up wasting money! This problem can be diminished if you take antacids at least one hour before or one hour after **Tagamet**.[61] While not a dangerous interaction, this is one that few physicians warn about even though it is probably extremely common.

(continues next page)

If a person who is prescribed **Tagamet**

ALSO TAKES:	THIS COULD RESULT:
ANTIANXIETY AGENTS Valium Librium Tranxene Azene Centrax	Sedatives, tranquilizers, antianxiety agents—no matter what you call them—**Tagamet** may make these drugs more dangerous. Blood levels go up by about one-third, and unless the doses of these drugs are recalculated, you could end up spaced out and oversedated.
ANTICOAGULANTS Warfarin **Coumadin**	Watch out! This could be nasty. Blood thinners are tricky all by themselves. Add **Tagamet** to **Coumadin**, and you could be in for a toxic reaction—spell that hemorrhage. If there is absolutely, positively no way to avoid taking the two drugs together, frequent blood tests are essential, and it is likely that your MD will have to recalculate the dose of **Coumadin**. This could be a biggie![62]
ANTICONVULSANTS Phenytoin **Dilantin**	This seizure medicine can be increased by almost one-third if taken with **Tagamet**. Side effects may be more likely, and there is concern that serious blood disorders could result. Frequent tests are a must!
ASTHMA MEDICINES Theophylline **Bronitin** **Bronkaid** **Bronkotabs** **Elixophyllin** **Marax** **Phedral** **Primatene M** **Quadrinal** **Quibron** **Slo-Phyllin** **Tedral** **Theobid** **Theo-Dur** **Theolair** **Verquad** etc.	As you can see from this partial list of asthma medications, theophylline is everywhere, including in many over-the-counter products. Paradoxically, some of the most common side effects of this drug include stomach pain and nausea. These may well be caused by stimulation of stomach acid, and some doctors have suggested that **Tagamet** could be helpful for patients who have ulcers and must take theophylline. That could be a big mistake. **Tagamet** slows the elimination of this asthma medicine by as much as 60 percent and can lead to serious toxic reactions. Once again, a careful adjustment of dose is crucial if these two drugs are taken together.[63–65]

If a person who is prescribed **Tagamet**

ALSO TAKES:	THIS COULD RESULT:

CAFFEINE
Coffee
Tea
OTC drugs
  Anorexin
  Appedrine
  Apress
  Aqua-Ban
  Ayd's Extra Strength
  Caffedrine
  Cenadex
  Dex-A-Diet II
  Dexatrim
  Gold Medal Diet Caps
  Nodoz
  Odrinex
  Prolamine
  Quick-Pep
  Spantrol
  Summit
  Tirend
  Vivarin
  Wakoz
  etc.
	This interaction is a question mark. There is evidence that **Tagamet** can slow the metabolism of caffeine and as a result prolong its effects in the body. Although it is not yet proven, "the possibility exists that, with repeated caffeine administration (i.e. ingestion of several cups of coffee per day), cardiovascular or nervous system toxicity still may result."[66] What that means is that you could have increased blood pressure, irregular heart beats, jitteriness, and insomnia.[67–69] Since coffee and caffeine can stimulate secretion of stomach acid, anyone with an ulcer should probably steer clear of these things anyway. And if you are taking **Tagamet**, why not play it safe? Avoid all caffeine-containing products.
	
	And, oh yes, cigarettes should go too! Turns out that smoking will undo the acid-lowering benefits of **Tagamet**.

HEART MEDICINE Beta-Blocker **Inderal**	This could well be *the* most important drug interaction with **Tagamet**. By slowing metabolism and elimination of **Inderal**, blood levels are raised and side effects become more likely. Watch out for reductions in heart rate.[70, 71] Although **Inderal** has this effect all by itself, **Tagamet** could make it worse. If you absolutely MUST take a beta-blocker, ask your doctor about **Tenormin** or **Corgard**. They may be less likely to be affected by **Tagamet**.
Lidocaine **Xylocaine**	These drugs are used to treat problems of irregular heart beats. Serious toxicity could result if they are taken simultaneously with **Tagamet**. A report in JAMA suggests that "There are many thousands on these two commonly prescribed drugs [lidocaine and **Tagamet**], and their interaction is probably responsible for much of the unexplained mental confusion and episodes of unexplained arrhythmias (irregular heart beats) seen in CCUs [Coronary Care Units]."[72] They may even be responsible for a number of unexplained deaths. Danger signs include drowsiness, tremor, and disorientation.

(continues next page)

If a person who is prescribed **Tagamet**

ALSO TAKES:	THIS COULD RESULT:
Procainamide **Procan** **Pronestyl**	Procainamide can also be adversely affected by **Tagamet**. Symptoms of overdose include loss of appetite, nausea, lethargy, confusion, low blood pressure, and irregular heart beats. Careful monitoring and dosage adjustment is essential![73]
IRON SUPPLEMENTS **Feosol** **Fergon** **Fer-In-Sol** **Geritol** **Iberer** **Niferex** **Nu-Iron** etc.	Here's an interaction I'll bet few docs ever warn about, but it's one that can be quite important. First, iron supplements are often irritating to the stomach, causing heartburn, nausea, pain, and diarrhea. It would be easy to imagine a physician prescribing **Tagamet** for such symptoms. But if he does, it could prevent the iron from being absorbed into your system.[74] This is a classic double bind. But if you want to get the most out of your iron pills, you will probably have to forego the **Tagamet**.

Tagamet and the Cancer Controversy

One subject, more than any other, is sure to strike fear into the hearts of SmithKline executives. Mention the word *cancer* in connection with **Tagamet** and they become disagreeable, if not downright nasty. It's hardly surprising: they're sitting on the biggest pot of gold ever found at the end of a rainbow. They've got a drug doctors and patients love because it works extremely well, is convenient, and causes blessedly few side effects on its own. Best of all, it brings millions of people back for more, day in and day out. Anything that could conceivably queer the deal of the century gets no applause at SmithKline.

So when the *Sunday Times* of London ran the headline, **"Doctors raise cancer fears over 'wonder drug' used by millions,"** corporate execs were hardly thrilled. The paper had gotten wind of Peter Reed's research on **Tagamet.** One of Britain's leading gastroenterologists and a senior lecturer in medicine at the Royal Postgraduate Medical School, Reed discovered a cloud on the **Tagamet** horizon that could wipe out the rainbow and its pot of gold. What Peter Reed found was that **Tagamet** may work too well: it is so good at shutting down the secretion of acid that it seems to allow a change in the stomach's natural environment.

Think about it for a minute. Normally your stomach is almost sterile; nothing survives long in a hydrochloric acid bath at a pH (measure of acidity) around 2. A few drops of such acid would burn a hole in metal. So all the little beasties that live in your mouth or lower down in your digestive tract are killed pretty damn fast if they somehow manage to arrive in your tum.

But **Tagamet** is extremely efficient at reducing stomach acid, even at night. Researchers have expressed concern that if acid flow is significantly diminished, bacteria that would normally be wiped out might continue to live inside your stomach.[75–79] Several groups of British researchers have found that patients taking **Tagamet** do develop bacterial colonies within their stomachs.[80–82]

Why is this such a big deal? A few bugs here or there shouldn't make any difference. Germs are all over the place—in our mouths and in the small intestine, and for sure they are lower down in the digestive tract. In case you had any doubts about that, just ask yourself where gas comes from. Yup, right the first time. It's all those little critters working away on undigested food that makes for flatulence. But except for unpleasant smells and nasty looks from anyone close enough to be offended, there appears to be little danger from the presence of bacteria at the bottom end of the digestive process.

It's a whole other matter at the upper end. Scientists fear that if bacteria set up housekeeping in your stomach, they can go to work converting nitrate to nitrite. Who to what? Nitrate is a chemical which can come from food, water or even saliva; by itself it probably does little harm. But if nitrate is turned into nitrite by bacteria, all hell can break loose, because the end product can be something very bad indeed—nitrosamines. Nitrosamines are among the most potent cancer-causing chemicals known to man. Guess what Peter Reed found in the stomachs of patients taking **Tagamet**? Right again! He found nitrosamines.

> In our study cimetidine [Tagamet] treatment was associated with significantly raised N-nitrosamine concentrations—in some cases up to a hundred times normal. . . .
>
> The effects of continued mucosal exposure to high N-nitrosamine concentrations is considered by some to be a cancer hazard.[83,84]

Needless to say, Reed's findings did not go over well at SmithKline. Dr. Roger Brimblecombe, Vice President of Research and Development for SK's British subsidiary, fired off a letter to *Lancet* criticizing Reed's research techniques and his conclusions.[85] And indeed, the company's scientists have done studies of their own work which, they assert, show that **Tagamet** does not raise levels of those nasty nitrosamines.[86,87]

If these findings sound terribly contradictory and confusing to you, you're right. Reed himself would admit that his research raises more questions than it answers. But, as he points out, "I don't think it is entirely inconceivable that it would be in the drug firm's interest to naturally denigrate and dismiss any comments that one would make about this compound."[88] Even the developer of **Tagamet,** Sir James Black, offers some words of caution.

> Whether or not this drug produces cancer, the cancer-forming situation could occur by *any* device that stops acid secretions. [We must remember that] drugs can never be good for you. They are merely less bad for you than the condition you're seeking to alleviate. I don't want drugs to be given the Good Housekeeping Seal of Approval. I want all doctors to become knowledgeable and discriminating.[89]

I, too, wish that all physicians were knowledgeable and discriminating about the drugs they prescribe. Unfortunately I fear that such a day will be long in coming. Many aren't even aware that a controversy surrounds their favorite ulcer medicine.

There is as yet no convincing evidence that **Tagamet** actually causes cancer in humans. Although several suggestive reports have surfaced in the British medical literature, there has been no controlled scientific study that would confirm or disprove such an association.[90–95]

And that, dear reader, is the crux of the problem. It is shocking that there should be even a question about a drug which is taken so often by so many. Peter Reed would be the first to breathe a sigh of relief if the theoretical problem he posed turned out to be groundless. But it would be a tragedy if even a tiny fraction of the millions of patients now taking **Tagamet** were exposed to the risk of cancer, especially since some investigators feel that the danger could be averted.

Vitamin C to the Rescue

By now you probably have the idea that I am down on **Tagamet** and wouldn't touch it with a ten-foot pole or recommend it to my worst enemy. On the contrary! I think it is a revolutionary drug which has improved the life of millions of ulcer patients. And fear of cancer need not scare people away. Even if **Tagamet** does promote the formation of nitrosamines, that doesn't mean you have to put up with carcinogenic chemicals bouncing around in your stomach. The solution to this apparent paradox is good old Vitamin C. Scientists have known for quite some time that ascorbic acid has antioxidant properties and is extremely efficient at blocking nitrosation.[96–103]

In fact, some food manufacturers include Vitamin C in their products along with preservatives for this very reason. Several years ago there was concern that the nitrates and nitrites used in hot dogs, bacon, bologna, salami, ham, dried salted fish, and other such meats could be converted to nitrosamines either in the frying pan or in your tummy.[104–106] And researchers have suggested that nitrosamine formation may be responsible for a higher incidence of stomach cancer in certain populations.[107]

Now while I am pretty careful about what I eat, I confess to an occasional craving for a good hot dog, especially if it is smothered in onions, mustard, and relish. To make matters worse, in my part of the country a new delicacy has been created—the Bagel Dog. The purveyor of this extravaganza wraps a delicious hot dog in bagel dough and cooks it in such a manner as to produce a taste treat beyond description. What to do? Should I worry about those nitrites turning into nitrosamines, or (God forbid) give up on hot dogs altogether?

Fortunately the nitrosamine researchers of this world came to my rescue. They discovered that Vitamin C could dramatically reduce, if not prevent, nitrosamines from forming. So now, whenever I get the urge for a salami sandwich or a Bagel Dog, I pop some Vitamin C at the same time and enjoy.

It is quite possible that the same principle could hold true for the interaction of **Tagamet** and ascorbic acid.[108] One of the world's leading authorities on nitrosamines offers the following commentary on the Vitamin C connection.

> **I sort of feel the SmithKline people have been somewhat cynical in their approach and have been forced, like the lion tamer forces the tiger, back into the corner. I don't think they've been very forthcoming in looking for ways of dealing with the adverse situation they create in the stomach.**
>
> **Why haven't they changed their package insert information to advise, for example, taking ascorbic acid? . . . It's just well known that if you can get some ascorbic acid there . . . it's going to have a positive effect.[109]**

Even Peter Reed, the man who discovered the nitrosamine link in the first place, believes that Vitamin C could make an important difference for **Tagamet** users. His preliminary studies have demonstrated a significant reduction in nitrosamine concentrations after dosing with ascorbic acid.[110]

But how much Vitamin C is enough to provide protection? Ah, now that's a toughie. Dr. Reed recommends 4 grams (4,000 mg) a day in divided doses. That means approximately 1,000 milligrams at each meal and a final dose before bedtime.

Dr. Steven Tannenbaum, Professor of Toxicology and Food Chemistry at the Massachusetts Institute of Technology and a nitrosamine expert, thinks that figure may be a little high; he uses around 2 grams (500 mg doses spread out through the day, with 1000 mg at bedtime).[111] He also suggests that 400 mg of Vitamin E might help, for although it isn't as powerful as Vitamin C, it too has antioxidant properties. Another study has shown that together they may help keep nitrosamines from forming.[112]

Okay, let's circle the wagons and regroup. **Tagamet** truly is a remarkable breakthrough. But as of this writing, there is uncertainty about what it does to the environment in your stomach. Does reduced acidity increase the presence of bacteria, nitrite, and nitrosamines? Is there an increased risk of gastric cancer? There are still more questions than answers. The cloud on the **Tagamet** horizon has neither grown larger nor has it disappeared. There is no guarantee that ascorbic acid will provide perfect protection, but if I had an ulcer and was prescribed **Tagamet**, I would certainly consider taking out a little vitamin insurance, just to be on the safe side.

The Great Ulcer War

Tagamet's incredible success did not go unnoticed by other drug companies. Once they realized how lucrative bellyaches could be, they started lining up to battle for their share of what had once been the **Maalox** market. Glaxo's contender, **Zantac**, sounds like the leader of an invading intergalactic strike force, but in fact it's the trade name for ranitidine, another histamine antagonist.

Soon after they learned of Sir James Black's breakthrough, Glaxo's chemists started scurrying around the laboratory trying to come up with a better mousetrap. They may have succeeded. Although **Zantac** doesn't seem to be any better than **Tagamet** at healing ulcers, it is more potent.[113–115] That means that ulcer patients only need two pills a day instead of four, and it's possible one may be almost as good.

So big deal; a little more convenience is nice, but it's hardly a major victory. True enough, but **Zantac** may have found a chink in **Tagamet**'s armor. Do you remember that problem of drug interactions we mentioned a while back? Many commonly prescribed medications (**Inderal**, **Valium**, **Librium**, and so on) may become more toxic if they are combined with **Tagamet**. Since a lot of people who develop ulcers are also anxious or suffer from high blood pressure, this is a real weak point in SmithKline's wonder drug.

Zantac, on the other hand, appears to have little, if any, interaction potential.[116–119] Though there are reports that **Zantac** may increase the effects of the anticoagulant **Coumadin** and prolong a high-blood-pressure drug called **Lopressor**,[120] most research indicates that it is far less likely than **Tagamet** to muck up the metabolism.[121,122] Therefore patients won't have to worry so much about overdose reactions from their other medications—a big plus.

Other side effects may also be less common with **Zantac**. For one thing, the hormonal problems don't seem to crop up. Impotence, reduced sperm counts, and enlarged breasts are rare in men taking **Tagamet,** but they seem to be even less likely for patients on **Zantac**.[123,124] Further,

Tagamet can produce mental confusion in older people; preliminary reports on **Zantac** suggest that this adverse reaction may also be less common.[125,126]

About the only side effect that has been mentioned with any frequency is headaches, and they occur in only about 1 percent of those taking the drug. Tiredness, dizziness, diarrhea, constipation, nausea, and skin rashes have also been reported, but they are extremely rare and may not even be associated with the drug, since patients taking placebos also experienced a similar incidence of these side effects. All in all, the drug has remarkably little toxicity.

By now you may be getting the idea that the **Zantac** invasion could really give **Tagamet** a tough time. And indeed, in Great Britain Glaxo has grabbed 30 percent of the ulcer market with its newcomer.[127] The really big bucks, however, are in the United States, and here is where the major battle will be fought.

On the surface it looks like an uneven match. SmithKline has had a five-year head start, has a sales force of more than 900 detailmen, and operates with full coffers.[128] What's more the company is spoiling for a fight. One SmithKline marketing executive "speaks of waging 'a holy war' in defense of this lucrative turf."[129] Glaxo is big in Britain but an underdog in the United States, with only about one-third as many sales reps. However, in an unprecedented flanking maneuver Glaxo has allied itself with the giant Hoffmann-La Roche company, which has a force 800 strong and lots of experience in the marketing trenches.[130]

No one knows who will ultimately win the billion-dollar battle, but you can bet that Glaxo and SmithKline will not be the only contenders. Merck Sharp & Dohme is busy testing a stomach histamine blocker more potent than either **Tagamet** or **Zantac**. And Bristol-Myers and Boehringer -Ingelheim are itching to join the fray with their own new drugs.

No matter what the final outcome, it is important to remember that all these drugs work pretty much the same way—that is, they block the secretion of stomach acid. Until there are some solid answers to Peter Reed's question concerning nitrosamine formation and its relation to stomach cancer, a cloud will hang over all such compounds.[131]

The Carafate Challenge

While the big boys have been battling, a little-known competitor, Marion Laboratories, has been plodding along with a new ulcer drug of its own called **Carafate** (sucralfate). Though it hasn't captured headlines like **Tagamet** or **Zantac** and physicians have been slow to prescribe it, **Carafate** may be the most exciting drug of the lot.

Introduced in 1981 with little fanfare, this ulcer medicine works in a manner that is unique. Unlike histamine antagonists or antacids, it doesn't block or neutralize acid and therefore does not change stomach pH. Bacteria are therefore less likely to flourish and nitrosamine formation shouldn't be a problem. Chalk up a big one for **Carafate**.

The drug heals ulcers by forming a protective layer over the injured tissue. It homes in on the ulcer crater and creates a barrier that keeps acid and all the other nasty chemicals your stomach uses to digest food from doing further damage. **Carafate** may also stimulate growth of new cells and increase production of mucus within the stomach.[132,133] It is, after all, the natural production of mucus that helps to prevent acid from eating a hole in your stomach lining. Although it works in a completely different way than does **Tagamet**, **Carafate** appears to be just as effective.[134–136]

Another plus is its lack of side effects. Since the drug is hardly absorbed into the body at all, it has virtually no toxicity. Constipation is the most common problem, but that only occurs in about 2 percent of the people taking the drug. Dry mouth, nausea, diarrhea, and skin rash have been reported, but these reactions are also infrequent, occurring in 1 percent or less.

Carafate also comes out a winner in the matter of drug interactions. Unlike **Tagamet**, there is no evidence that it makes other drugs more toxic. Antacids, however, will wipe out this drug's effectiveness and must not be used simultaneously.[137] **Carafate** may also reduce the effectiveness of **Dilantin** or tetracycline when these drugs are taken at the same time; if they are spaced at least one hour apart, that problem seems to be eliminated.[138] The biggest disadvantage to **Carafate** is that the pill tends to dissolve in the mouth, so you have to swallow quickly. And because it must be taken four times a day on an empty stomach (one hour before each meal and at bedtime), the drug is a little less convenient than **Zantac**—but what the hey.

There is one last little detail about **Carafate** that your doctor probably isn't aware of but which may stand you in good stead at your next cocktail party. If you like a couple of drinks at the end of a hard day, beware of **Tagamet** and **Zantac**. These drugs may make your tummy feel fine, but they could lull you into a sense of false confidence. Preliminary research in animals suggests that the histamine antagonists could actually make the stomach lining far more susceptible to the ravages of alcohol.[139] **Carafate**, on the other hand, seems to protect the tum from the terrible things booze does to it.[140]

By now you are probably wondering why, if **Carafate** is so safe and effective, nobody ever heard of it, while **Tagamet** is almost a household word. A big part of the answer is marketing. Remember that SmithKline spends a bundle on slick advertising and has over 900 sales reps. The Glaxo/Roche army is more than 1,200 strong. In comparison, Marion is strictly small potatoes, with only 350 detailmen and a relatively small advertising budget. Given that doctors prescribe where the promotion is, it's hardly any wonder that **Carafate** has barely captured 5 percent of the ulcer market.[141]

The Ulcer Diet Gets Rougher

For over a century conventional ulcer therapy has relied on antacids, a bland diet, and a blander life style to reduce stress. The only innovation for decades was the addition of fruit or mint flavoring to chalky antacids to make them more palatable. The problem with this regimen was that in the humongous doses doctors recommended, antacids often caused diarrhea (up to 40 percent of patients got the runs). Not only that, after a week or two of seven doses daily most people dreaded the taste and the traditional bland ulcer diet provided no relief for those tortured taste buds.

To add insult to injury, researchers have recently discovered that ulcers are not the result of psychological stress, and worse, that the recommended ulcer diet doesn't really help.[142,143] Drinking lots of milk may even have caused more harm than good. One of our column readers discovered this the hard way.

> My ulcer is ruining my life. The pain is bad enough but the diet and antacid my doctor has prescribed are even more of a torture.
>
> I'm a good cook and love to eat but this diet he has me on is no fun at all. What's more, everyone insists that milk will help my ulcer—my doctor, my wife, my boss. But it doesn't!
>
> My stomach hurts as much an hour after a glass of milk as after a glass of beer, which is on my verboten list.

It's hardly surprising that this patient was suffering. Three researchers at the University of California at San Diego tested nine different beverages to see how they affected the secretion of stomach acid. To everyone's amazement, milk and beer were bad news—even worse than tea, coffee, Sanka, Coke, Tab, and 7-Up, all of which stimulated excess acid production.[144–146]

This isn't to say that you should ignore what you eat or drink. Clearly smoking, booze, coffee, and many arthritis medications, including aspirin, can wreak havoc with sensitive stomachs. And if you know that pizza and pickles make you suffer, it would be foolish to pig out on them. But there's no point in depriving yourself of favorite foods if they won't cause you added distress.

If nothing else, the flurry of new ulcer research has shown that a surprising number of ulcers generally heal by themselves, with the aid of nothing more powerful than a placebo. In study after study it has been demonstrated that anywhere from one-quarter to almost three-fourths of ulcer patients treated with inactive "sham" pills will recover within three months or so.[147-150] It's hardly any wonder that the traditional dietary recommendations seemed to help a lot of people.

Even as a bland diet is no longer considered necessary, some doctors think the opposite approach might be helpful. Nowhere have physicians flip-flopped more completely than about fiber. Just a few years ago their unequivocal admonition was NO roughage! It didn't matter whether you had a sensitive stomach or suffered from diverticular disease, you were supposed to eliminate lettuce, celery, peas, tomatoes, oranges, and lots of other fruits and vegetables, because fibrous foods would irritate the digestive tract. There was no room for compromise.

Now, without batting an eye, they do a complete 180 degree turn around and embrace fiber as if it were a long-lost friend. Articles in medical journals recommend fiber for prevention or treatment of diverticulosis, irritable bowel syndrome, constipation, colon cancer, hemorrhoids, diabetes, atherosclerosis, and gallstones.[151,152] And wouldn't you know it—now duodenal ulcers have been added to the list.[153] This is a tall order, and I don't know whether fiber can fulfill the promise.

But on the other hand, why not go for it? Everyone agrees that fibrous foods are healthy in their own right. High-fiber foods you might try include All Bran, blackberries, Corn Bran, Bran Chex, broccoli, Grapenuts Flakes, dried figs, lentils, turnip greens, winter squash, strawberries, Bran Buds, Shredded Wheat, artichokes, lima beans, peas, peanut butter, eggplant, carrots, brussels sprouts, pears, and raisins. Of course if you want to get really serious, you can always buy pure bran and add it to milk or juice. A word of caution, however. Not everyone can tolerate a heavy-duty bran diet. Bloating, cramps, diarrhea, and flatulence would be a clear indication to back off.

If bran doesn't strike your fancy, there's another dietary approach that may hold greater promise and be far easier to swallow. Some hotshot gastroenterologists at the University of California at Irvine and the Veterans Administration Medical Center in Long Beach, California, have been experimenting with essential fatty acids (EFAs), found in unsaturated vegetable oils. These scientists are particularly enthusiastic about arachidonic acid (found in peanuts and peanut oil) and linoleic acid, which is high in safflower, sunflower, corn, and soybean oils.

In animal experimentation they have found that these compounds can protect the stomach lining against alcohol damage.[154] They responded to an inquiry about the significance of this research.

**In the animal model it works extremely well; it does protect
the stomach against alcohol injury or aspirin or bioacids, so**

it's conceivable that it would be very important eventually as a dietary preventive measure or as a therapeutic measure.[155]

Their claim is simple.

The pharmaceutical companies may not like this, but if you will change your dietary habits and will eat more of these essential fatty acids, you can have the best medication with natural foods.[156]

Now it's important to get one thing straight. These physicians are definitely not flaky food faddists. They are solid establishment types doing elegant work that may be in the forefront of ulcer therapy. This state-of-the-art research centers on protecting the stomach cells with a class of naturally occuring compounds called prostaglandins, or PGs for short. These chemicals, which are found throughout your body, play a critical role in almost every life process including reproduction, respiration, and circulation. One of the most exciting discoveries of late centers around the role of PGs in both preventing and healing ulcers.[157,158]

Incidentally, scientists now believe that one reason that such arthritis drugs as aspirin, **Motrin** (ibuprofen), **Naprosyn** (naproxen), **Indocin** (indomethacin), **Butazolidin** (phenylbutazone), **Clinoril** (sulindac), and **Feldene** (piroxicam) cause indigestion, stomach irritation, and ulcers is because they turn off the body's natural ability to manufacture protective prostaglandins.

One of the goals in ulcer research, therefore, is to figure out ways to create PGs and either administer them in a pill or get the body to make its own. As drug companies are scrambling to test such compounds, one made by Upjohn called **Arbacet** (arbaprostil) looks quite promising.

Perhaps equally exciting is the work of the California gastroenterologists who are trying to get the body to make its own protective prostaglandins. They hope that foods high in linoleic and arachidonic acid may do the trick by encouraging the body to make PGs which, in turn, will protect us from stomach problems.

It's incredible that only a few years ago the only ammunition we had in the fight against ulcers was a heavy dose of antacid. Almost overnight there has been a revolution so profound that it has completely changed the way we think about and treat digestive disease. Between **Tagamet, Zantac, Carafate,** unsaturated vegetable oils, prostaglandins, and a host of new and different compounds under development, the clear winners of the great ulcer war are patients, who now have a wide range of therapeutic agents to choose from.

References

1. Baris, Scott A. "Smith Kline's Revival But New Drug Triggers a Controversy." *NY Times* 128(3):4 Sep. 16, 1979.

2. Walton, Mary. "The House That Ulcers Built." *Today: The Inquirer Magazine* February 21, 1982, pp. 11–14.

3. Marion, John Francis. *The Fine Old House*, Philadelphia: SmithKline Corporation, 1980, p. 42.

4. Ibid. pp. 44.

5. Ibid. pp. 77.

6. Ad for Stelazine in *Am. J. Psychiatry* 121(7):XIX, 1964.

7. Baris. Op. cit. p. 5.

8. Walton. Op. cit.

9. Ibid.

10. Ibid.

11. Personal communication, James Black, April 20, 1983.

12. Baris. Op. cit.

13. Personal communication, James Black. op cit.

14. Black, J. W., et al. "Definition and Antagonism of Histamine H_2-receptors." *Nature* 236:385–390, 1972.

15. Personal communication, James Black, Op. cit.

16. "Annual Prescription Survey." *Drug Topics* March 14, 1980, p. 48.

17. Bishop, Jerry E. "Ulcer-Drug Battles Loom as Competitors Take Aim at Tagamet." *The Wall Street Journal*, Oct. 8, 1981, p. 1.

18. Allen, Frank. "SmithKline's Tagamet is Cleared by FDA for Short-Term Care of Gastric Ulcers." *The Wall Street Journal*, January 6, 1983, p. 36.

19. Ibid.

20. 1975 National Health Survey. National Institutes of Health.

21. McHardy, Gordon. "Peptic Ulcer Increase in Women." *Female Patient* 7:41–46, Apr, 1982.

22. Eisenberg, M. Michael. *Ulcers*. New York: Random House, 1978, p. 5.

23. 1982 Prescription sales data compiled by Pharmaceutical Data Services.

24. D'Emilio, Frances. "Tagamet's Popularity Could Cause Problems." Associated Press, published in Durham *Sun*, Dec. 9, 1982, p. 4-c.

25. Rothman, Craig, M. "Cimetidine Used Indiscriminately." *New Engl. J. Med.* 303:47, 1980.

26. Cocco, Arthur E., and Cocco, Dorothy V. "A Survey of Cimetidine Prescribing." *New Engl. J. Med.* 302:1281, 1981.

27. Schade, Robert R., and Donaldson, Robert M. "How Physicians Use Cimetidine: A Survey of Hospitalized Patients and Published Cases." *New. Engl. J. Med.* 304: 1281–1284. 1981.

28. Brater, D. Craig, and Toney, Flora. "Misuse of Cimetidine." *New Engl. J. Med.* 303:701, 1980.

29. Wald, A., et al. "Inappropriate Use of Cimetidine in Hospitalized Patients." *So. Med. J.* 76:701–705, 1983.

30. Brownlee, H. James, et al. "Abuse of Cimetidine in Outpatient Practice." *N. Engl. J. Med.*, May, 1983, p. 1226.

31. Mangla, Jagdish C. "A Second Look at Cimetidine." *J. Clin. Gastroenterol.* 3:341–345, 1981.

32. Bodemar, G., and Walan, A. "Maintenance Treatment of Recurrent Peptic Ulcer by Cimetidine." *Lancet* 1:403–407, 1978.

33. Dronfield, M. W., et al. "Controlled Trial of Maintenance Cimetidine Treatment in Healed Duodenal Ulcer: Short and Long-term effects. *Gut* 20:526–530, 1979.

34. Gray, G. R., et al. "Long Term Cimetidine in the Management of Severe Duodenal Ulcer Dyspepsia." *Gastroenterology* 74:397–401, 1978.

35. Hetzel, D. F., et al. "Prevention of Duodenal Ulcer Relapse by Cimetidine: A One Year Double Blind Trial." *Med J. Aust.* 1:529–531, 1979.

36. Hansky, J., and Korman, M. G. "Long-Term Cimetidine in Duodenal Ulcer Disease." *Dig. Dis. Sci.* 24:465–467, 1979.

37. Korman, Melvyn F., et al. "Relapse Rate of Duodenal Ulcer After Cessation of Long-Term Cimetidine Treatment: A Double-Blind Controlled Study." *Dig. Dis. Sci.* 25:88–91, 1980.

38. Winship, D. H. "Cimetidine in the Treatment of Duodenal Ulcer. Review and Commentary." *Gastroenterology* 74:402–406, 1978.

39. Martin, Derrick F., et al. "Difference in Relapse Rates of Duodenal Ulcer After Healing with Cimetidine or Tripotassium Dicitrato Bismuthate." *Lancet* 1:7–10, 1981.

40. Walton. Op. cit.

41. Personal communication, Stanley T. Crooke, October 15, 1982.

42. "Tagamet Rx-to-OTC?" *F-D-C Reports* 44(47):T&G–10, 1982.

43. Freston, James W. "Drugs Five Years Later: Cimetidine: II. Adverse Reactions and Patterns of Use." *Ann. Int. Med.* 97:728–734, 1982.

44. Gifford, L. M., et al. "Cimetidine Postmarket Outpatient Surveillance Program: Interim Report on Phase 1. *JAMA* 243:1532–1535, 1980.

45. Medical News. "Antiandrogen Effects of Ulcer Drug Averted with Experimental Agent." *JAMA* 248:621–622, 1982.

46. Spence, R. W., and Celestin, L. R. "Gynaecomastia Associated with Cimetidine." *Gut* 20:154–157, 1979.

47. Biron, Pierre. "Diminished Libido with Cimetidine Therapy." *Can. Med. Assoc. J.* 121:404–405, 1979.

48. Short reports. "Male Sexual Dysfunction During Treatment with Cimetidine." *Br. Med. J.* 1:659–660, 1979.

49. Desmond, Paul V., et al. "Cimetidine Impairs Elimination of Chlordiazepoxide (Librium) in Man." *Ann. Int. Med.* 93:266–268, 1980.

50. Freston. Op. cit.

51. Feely, John, et al. "Reduction of Liver Blood Flow and Propranolol Metabolism by Cimetidine." *New Engl. J. Med.* 304:692–695, 1981.

52. Klotz, Ulrich, and Reimann, Ingrid. "Delayed Clearance of Diazepam Due to Cimetidine." *New Engl. J. Med.* 302:1012–1014, 1980.

53. Donovan, M. A., et al. "Cimetidine and Bioavailability of Propranolol." *Lancet* 1:164, 1981.

54. Jackson, J. E., et al. "Cimetidine Decreases Theophylline Clearance." A Presentation to the American Society for Pharmacology and Experimental Therapeutics, August 20, 1980, Rochester, Minnesota.

55. Bauman, J. H., and Kimelblatt, B. J. "Cimetidine as an Inhibitor of Drug Metabolism: Therapeutic Implications and Review of the Literature." *Drug. Intell. Clin. Pharm.* 16:380–386, 1982.

56. Serlin, M. J., et al. "Cimetidine: Interaction with Oral Anticoagulants in Man." *Lancet* 2:317–319, 1979.

57. Somogyi, Andrew, and Heinzow, Birger. "Cimetidine Reduces Procainamide Elimination." *New Engl. J. Med.* 307:1080, 1982.

58. Medical News. "Lidocaine-Cimetidine Interaction Can Be Toxic." *JAMA* 247:3174–3175, 1982.

59. Desmond, P. V., et al. "Effect of Cimetidine and Other Antihistamines on the Elimination of Aminopyrine, Phenacetin and Caffeine." *Life Sci.* 26:1261–1268, 1980.

60. Powell, J. Robert. "Influence of Cimetidine on Drug Elimination." Lecture Notes for the University of North Carolina School of Pharmacy.

61. Steinberg, William, et al. "Antacids Inhibit Absorption of Cimetidine." *New Engl. J. Med.* 307:400–403, 1982.

62. Serlin. Op cit.

63. Jackson, J. E., et al. "Cimetidine-Theophylline Interaction." *Pharmacologist* 22:231, 1980.

64. Jackson, J. E., et al. "Cimetidine Decreases Theophylline clearance." *Am. Rev. Respir. Dis.* 123:615–617, 1981.

65. Reitberg, D. P., et al. "Alterations of Theophylline Clearance and Half-Life by Cimetidine in Normal Volunteers." *Ann. Intern. Med.* 95:582–585, 1981.

66. Sorkin, Eugene M., and Darvey, Diane L. "Review of Cimetidine Drug Interactions." *Drug Intel. Clin. Pharm.* 17:110–120, 1983.

67. Broughton, L. J., and Rogers, H. J. "Decreased Systemic Clearance of Caffeine Due to Cimetidine." *Br. J. Pharmacol.* 12:155–159, 1981.

68. May, D. C., et al. "Effects of Cimetidine on Caffeine Disposition in Smokers and Nonsmokers." *Clin. Pharmacol. Ther.* 31:656–661, 1982.

69. Desmond. Op. cit.

70. Feely, J., et al. "Reduction of Liver Blood Flow and Propranolol Metabolism." *New Engl. J. Med.* 304:692–695, 1981.

71. Bauman, J. H. "Influence of Cimetidine on Pharmacokinetics of Propranolol." *Br. Med. J.* 283:232, 1981.

72. Medical News. "Lidocaine-Cimetidine Interaction Can be Toxic." *JAMA* 247:3174–3175, 1982.

73. Somogyi. Op. cit.

74. Esposito, R. "Cimetidine and Iron Deficiency Anemia." *Lancet* 1:444–445, 1979.

75. Ruddell, W. S., et al. "Gastric Juice Nitrite. A Risk for Cancer in the Hypochlorhydric Stomach?" *Lancet* 2:1037–1039, 1976.

76. Reed, P. I., et al. "Gastric Juice N-Nitrosamines in Health and Gastroduodenal disease." *Lancet* 2:550–552, 1981.

77. Reed, P. I., et al. "Effect of Cimetidine on Gastric Juice N-Nitrosamine Concentration." *Lancet* 2:553–556, 1981.

78. Reed, P. I., et al. "Cimetidine, Nitrosation, and Carcinogenicity." *Lancet* 2:1281–1282, 1981.

79. Muscroft, T. J., et al. "The Microflora of the Postoperative Stomach." *Br. J. Surg.* 68:560–564, 1981.

80. Ruddell, W. S., et al. "Effect of Cimetidine on the Gastric Bacterial Flora." *Lancet* 1:672–674, 1980.

81. Reed. "Effect of Cimetidine." Op. cit.

82. Muscroft, T. J., et al. "Cimetidine and the Potential Risk of Post-operative Sepsis." *Br. J. Surg.* 68:557–559, 1981.

83. Reed. "Effect of Cimetidine." op. cit.

84. Correa, P., et al. "A Model for Gastric Cancer Epidemiology." *Lancet* 2:58–60, 1975.

85. Brimblecombe, Roger. "Cimetidine, Nitrosation, and Carcinogenicity." *Lancet* 2:686–687, 1981.

86. Personal communication, Roger Brimblecombe, October 27, 1978.

87. Milton-Thompson, G. J., et al. "Intragastric Acidity, Bacteria, Nitrite, and N-Nitroso Compounds Before, During, and After Cimetidine Treatment." *Lancet* 1:1091–1095, 1982.

88. Personal communication, Peter Reed, May 15, 1983.

89. In Walton. Op. cit.

90. Elder, J. B., et al. "Cimetidine and Gastric Cancer." *Lancet* 1:1005–1006, 1979.

91. Ruddell, W. S. "Gastric Cancer in Patients who Have Taken Cimetidine." *Lancet* 1:1234, 1979.

92. Reed, P. I., et al. "Gastric Cancer in Patients who Have Taken Cimetidine." *Lancet* 1:1234–1235, 1979.

93. Hawker, P. C., et al. "Gastric Cancer after Cimetidine in Patient with Two Negative Pre-Treatment Biopsies." *Lancet* 1:709–710, 1980.

94. Mortensen, N. J. McC., and Eltringham, W. K. "Cimetidine, Nitrosation, and Cancer." *Lancet* 1:984, 1981.

95. Colin-Jones, D. C., et al. "Cimetidine and Gastric Cancer: Preliminary Report From Post-Marketing Surveillance Study." *British Medical Journal* 285:1311–1313, 1982.

96. Mirvish, Sidney, et al. "Ascorbate-Nitrite Reaction: Possible Means of Blocking the Formation of Carcinogenic N-Nitroso Compounds." *Science* 177:65–67, 1972.

97. Raineri, R., and Weisburger, J. H. "Reduction of Gastric Carcinogens with Ascorbic Acid." *Ann N.Y. Acad. Sci.* 258:181–189, 1975.

98. Weisburger, J. H., et al. "Inhibition of Carcinogenesis: Vitamin C and the Prevention of Gastric Cancer." *Prev. Med.* 9:352–361, 1980.

99. Ames, B. N. "Carcinogens and Anti-carcinogens." *Prog. Clin. Biol. Res.* 109:3–19, 1982.

100. Schmahl, D., and Eisenbrand, G. "Influence of Ascorbic Acid on the Endogenous (Intragastral) Formation of N-nitroso Compounds." *Int. J. Vitamin. Nutr. Res.* 23:91–102, 1982.

101. Tannenbaum, Steven, R. "N-Nitroso Compounds: A Perspective on Human Exposure." *Lancet* 1:629–631, 1983.

102. Kalus, W. H., and Filby, W. G. "Inhibition of Nitrosamine Formation by Ascorbic Acid: Participation of Free Radicals in its Anaerobic Reaction with Nitrite." *Experientia* 36:147–149, 1980.

103. Mergens, W. J., et al. "The Influence of Ascorbic Acid and DL-alpha-tocopherol on the Formation of Nitrosamines in an In Vitro Gastrointestinal Model System." *IARC Sci. Publ.* 31:259–269, 1980.

104. Marquardt, H., et al. "Mutagenic Activity of Nitrite-Treated Foods: Human Stomach Cancer May Be Related to Dietary Factors." *Science* 196:1000–1001, 1977.

105. Weisburger, J. H., and Raneri, R. "Dietary Factors and the Etiology of Gastric Cancer." *Cancer Res.* 35:3469–3474, 1975.

106. Hartman, P. E. "Review: Putative Mutagens and Carcinogens in Foods. I.

Nitrate/Nitrite Ingestion and Gastric Cancer Mortality." *Environ. Mutagen.* 5:111–121, 1983.

107. Kolonel, L. N., et al. "Association of Diet and Place of Birth with Stomach Cancer Incidence in Hawaii Japanese and Caucasians." *Am. J. Clin. Nutr.* 34:2478–2485, 1981.

108. Weisburger, J. H. "Cimetidine, Nitroso Compounds, and Gastric Cancer." *Lancet* 1:1323, 1981.

109. Personal communication, Steven Tannenbaum, July 6, 1983.

110. Personal communication, Peter Reed, May 15, 1983.

111. Personal communication, Steven Tannenbaum. Op. cit.

112. Oshima, H., and Bartsch, H. "Quantitative Estimation of Endogenous Nitrosation in Humans by Monitoring N-Nitrosoproline Excreted in the Urine." *Cancer Res.* 41:3658, 1981.

113. Walt, R. P., et al. "Comparison of the Effects of Ranitidine, Cimetidine and Placebo on the 24 Hour Intragastric Acidity and Nocturnal Acid Secretion in Patients with Duodenal Ulcer." *Gut* 22:49–54, 1981.

114. Brater, D. C., et al. "Clinical Comparison of Cimetidine and Ranitidine." *Clin. Pharmacol. Ther.* 12:484–489, 1982.

115. Barr, G. D., et al. "Comparison of Ranitidine and Cimetidine in Duodenal Ulcer Healing." *Med. J. Aust.* 2:83–85, 1982.

116. Heagerty, A. M., et al "Failure of Ranitidine to Interact with Propranolol." *Br. Med. J.* 284:1304, 1982.

117. Klotz, U., et al. "Effect of Ranitidine on the Steady State Pharmacokinetics of Diazepam." *Eur. J. Pharmacol.* 24:357–360, 1983.

118. Speeg, K. V., et al. "Inhibition of Microsomal Drug Metabolism by Histamine H_2-Receptor Antagonists Studied In Vivo and In Vitro in Rodents." *Gastroenterology* 82:89–96, 1982.

119. Henry, D. A., et al. "Cimetidine and Ranitidine: Comparison of Effects on Hepatic Drug Metabolism." *Br. Med. J.* 281:775–777, 1980.

120. Spahn, H., et al. "Influence of Ranitidine on Plasma Metoprolol and Atenolol Concentrations." *British Medical Journal* 286:1546–1547, 1983.

121. Powell, J. R., and Donn, K. H. "The Pharmacokinetic Basis for H_2-Antagonist Drug Interactions: Concepts and Implications." In press.

122. Breen, K. J., et al. "Effects of Cimetidine and Ranitidine on Hepatic Drug Metabolism." *Clin. Pharmacol. Ther.* 31:297–300, 1982.

123. "Drugs That Cause Sexual Dysfunction." *The Medical Letter* 25:73–76, 1983.

124. Jensen, Robert T., et al. "Cimetidine-Induced Impotence and Breast Changes in Patients with Gastric Hypersecretory States." *New Engl. J. Med.* 308:883–887, 1983.

125. Editorial. "Cimetidine and Ranitidine." *Lancet* 1:601, 1982.

126. Pedrazzoli, Sergio, et al. "Ranitidine Reverses Cimetidine-Induced Mental Confusion in a Patient with Zollinger-Ellison Syndrome." *Arch. Surg* 118:256, 1983.

127. Heard on the Street. "Glaxo's Drug Zantac Makes Strong Showing Against Tagamet but Market Reaction is Mixed." *The Wall Street Journal*, July 26, 1983.

128. "Glaxo Unit to Promote Its Zantac Ulcer Drug in U.S. with Hoffman." *The Wall Street Journal*, November 9, 1982.

129. Dreyfuss, Joel. "SmithKline's Ulcer Medicine 'Holy War.' " *Fortune*, September 19, 1983, pp. 129–136.

130. Waldholz, Michael, and Koenig, Richard. "New Ulcer Drug Near Approval, Setting Up A Big Fight With SmithKline's Top Seller." *The Wall Street Journal* November 12, 1982, p. 27.

131. Editorial *Lancet*. Op. cit.

132. Tarnawski, A., et al. "Effect of Sucralfate on Normal Gastric Mucosa. Histologic Ultrastructural and Functional Assessment." Presentation Delivered at Digestive Disease Week, Washington, D.C., May 25, 1983.

133. Hollander, Daniel, et al. "Sucralfate Protection of Gastric Mucosa Against Alcohol Induced Necrosis: A Prostaglandin Mediated Process? Presentation Delivered at Digestive Disease Week, Washington, D.C., May 24, 1983.

134. Marks, I. N., et al. "Comparison of Sucralfate with Cimetidine in the Short-Term Treatment of Chronic Peptic Ulcers." *S. Afr. Med. J.* 57:567–573, 1980.

135. Marks, I. N., et al. "Ulcer Healing and Relapse After Initial Treatment with Cimetidine or Sucralfate." *J. Cllin. Gastroenterol.* 3(suppl 2):163–165, 1981.

136. Martin, François, et al. "Comparison of the Healing Capacities of Sucralfate and Cimetidine in the Short-Term Treatment of Duodenal Ulcer: A Double-Blind Randomized Trial." *Gastroenterol.* 82:401–405, 1982.

137. White, John P. "What Patients Need to Know About Ulcers." *Drug Topics* 127(18):79, 1983.

138. Editorial. "Sucralfate." *Ann. Int. Med.* 97:269–273, 1982.

139. Tarnawski, A., et al. "Comparison of Antacid, Sucralfate, Cimetidine and Ranitidine in Protection of Gastric Mucosa Against Ethanol Injury." Presentation Delivered at Digestive Disease Week, Washington, D.C., May 23, 1983.

140. Ibid.

141. Personal communication, Ann Grinham, May 21, 1983.

142. White. Op. cit., p. 74.

143. Frye, Janet P. "Bland Diet Not Best For Ulcers." *The Leader*, May 12–19, 1983, p. 11.

144. MacArthur, K. D., et al. "Relative Stimulatory Effects of Commonly Ingested Beverages on Gastric Acid Secretion in Humans." *Gastroenterol.* 83(1, pt 2):199–203, 1982.

145. Barclay, G. V., et al. "Effects of Graded Amounts of Intragastric Calcium on Acid Secretion, Gastrin Release and Gastric Emptying in Normal and Duodenal Ulcer." *Dig. Dis. Sci.* 28:385–391, 1983.

146. Isenberg, Jon I., et al. "Healing of Benign Gastric Ulcer with Low-Dose Antacid or Cimetidine: A Double-Blind, Randomized, Placebo-Controlled Trial." *N. Engl. J. Med.* 308:1319–1324, 1983.

147. Colin-Jones, D. G. "Ranitidine in the Treatment of Peptic Ulceration." In: Riley, A. J., and Salmon, P. R. (eds.), *Ranitidine Proceedings of an International Symposium Held in the Context of the Seventh World Congress of Gastroenterology.* Excerpta Medica, 1982, pp. 16–29.

148. Hollander, Daniel. "Efficacy of Sucralfate for Duodenal Ulcers: A Multicenter, Double-Blind Trial." *J. Clin. Gastroenterol.* 3(suppl 2):153–157, 1981.

149. Moshal, Michael G., et al. "Short- and Long-Term Studies of Duodenal Ulcer with Sucralfate." *J. Clin. Gastroenterol.* 3(suppl 2):159–161, 1981.

150. Tollison, Joseph W., and Griffin, Joseph, W. Jr. "High-Fiber Diet and Colorectal Disease." *Am. Fam. Phys.* 22(1):121–125, 1980.

151. Kay, Ruth McPherson. "Dietary Fiber." *J. Lipid Res.* 23:221–242, 1982.

152. Baron, J. H. "High Fibre Good or Low Fibre Bad for Duodenal Ulcers?" *Lancet* 2:980, 1982.

153. Tarnawski, A., et al. "Are Nutrient Essential Fatty Acids (Prostaglandin Precursors) Cytoprotective?" Poster presentation at Digestive Disease Week, Washington, D. C., May 23, 1983.

154. Personal communication, Daniel Hollander, May 24, 1983.

155. Personal communication, A. Tarnawski, May 23, 1983.

156. Robert, Andre. "Cytoprotection by Prostaglandins." *Gastroenterol.* 77:761–767, 1979.

157. Konturek, Stanislaw J. "Gastric Cytoprotection." *Mount Sinai J. Med.* 49:355–369, 1982.

158. Vantrappen, G., et al. "Effect of 15(R)-15-Methyl Prostaglandin E_2 (Arbaprostil) on the Healing of Duodenal Ulcer." *Gastroenterol.* 83:357–363, 1982.

CHAPTER 6

Help For Your Heart

Good News About Heart Attacks ▪ *The Mystifying MRFIT: A Big Boondoggle?* ▪ *Saving Your Heart with Aspirin* ▪ *Surviving a Heart Attack* ▪ *Dissolving Away Coronaries with* **Streptase** ▪ *Eight Life-Saving Steps* ▪ *Joining the Survivor's Club:* **Persantine** *and* **Anturane** ▪ *Living Longer But Enjoying It Less: The Beta Blocker Blahs* ▪ *The Calcium Channel Blocker Challenge* ▪ *Tying up the Loose Ends* ▪ *Drug Table*

The numbers tell it all: each year 1.5 million Americans suffer heart attacks.[1] Of that number 350,000 die before they even make it to a hospital, and another 200,000 will pass away during the high-risk period that follows.[2] Now throw in another 200,000 deaths from strokes and hypertensive disease. Then there are the millions of walking wounded who survive their coronary but are left with painful angina or irregular heart beats and the fearful feeling of living on borrowed time. There are few of us who haven't been touched in some way, directly or indirectly, by cardiovascular disease.

The statistics are grim but hardly news. What has researchers intrigued is the dramatic drop in deaths from strokes and heart disease during the past several decades.[3–5] In the last ten years alone the number of people dying from heart attacks and other cardiovascular complications in the United States has declined by an extraordinary 28 percent.[6] Even more impressive is the 45 percent reduction in coronary mortality since 1963 for people between 35 and 44 years of age.[7]

How come? What are we doing right? Everyone has an explanation for this unexpected good news. If you're a jogger, you're convinced that running will protect your heart and blood vessels. If you're into health food and vitamins, there is no doubt in your mind that it's fresh fruits, vegetables, and Vitamin C or E that are saving your life. Reformed smokers believe that kicking the nicotine habit is the answer, while dieters are convinced of the value of weight loss, lowered cholesterol intake, and elimination of salt. Psychologists support stress reduction and changes in the type-A personality. Doctors tend to buy into high-tech solutions, praising coronary-care units, surgery, and defibrillators. Pharamaceutical manufacturers would like to believe that it's their drugs which are the key to success. The list goes on and on.

So what *is* the answer? Not surprisingly, no one answer explains it all.

And there are some bizarre contradictions. On the one hand, dietary changes seem important, especially when it comes to fat. But in Japan, where there has been an incredible 200 percent increase in saturated fat consumption in recent years, deaths from heart-disease have actually gone down.[8] Swedes are jogging more, eating less fat, and receiving excellent medical care; yet instead of reducing coronary problems, heart disease is claiming more victims there each year.[9]

Now try this one on for size. Everyone is after us to lose weight. Shedding pounds is supposed to be good for our hearts and arteries. But the incredible plunge in deaths from heart attack that has been seen over the last 20 years was actually associated with an overall weight gain.[10]

If that's got you puzzled, pay attention to the next contradiction. There is no doubt that cutting back on cigarettes has to be good for you—and indeed, there are numerous studies that suggest smokers are at far greater risk of heart attacks than nonsmokers. But even here the case is not open and shut. An editorial in the British journal *Lancet* remarks, "In the UK the decline in smoking among men has yet to be succeeded by a decline in mortality."[11]

And what about that terrible type-A personality? Several years ago we heard that the workaholic who was constantly under the gun, highly competitive, and couldn't stand to wait in line was on a fast track to a heart attack. Executives who fit the stereotype were made to feel guilty if they couldn't relax and take life easier. Once again, though, the theory isn't holding up well.

> **The popular notion that desk-pounders and clock-racers are likely to develop heart disease has run into a big challenge. A prospective study of men has found no link between type-A behavior and either heart attacks or death from coronary artery disease.**
>
> **Among 1,550 middle-aged men followed for an average of seven years, those showing impatience, competitiveness, hostility, and other type-A traits wound up with no more of these cardiac events than controls who were either classic type-Bs or nearly as placid.[12]**

The Mystifying Mr.Fit

If you're confused by all these findings, you're in good company. The latest high-powered large-scale research project has bamboozled even the scientists whose bread and butter is studying heart attacks, mortality curves, and lifestyles. The problem is MRFIT.

MRFIT (Multiple Risk Factor Intervention Trial), a study started back in the early 1970s, was an attempt to prove once and for all that you could reduce your risk of suffering a heart attack if you watched your diet, quit smoking, and controlled high blood pressure. It was the most ambitious research program of its kind ever undertaken. The National Heart, Lung, and Blood Institute recruited 12,866 men from around the country between the ages of 35 and 57—all people who were generally healthy but at increased risk of heart attack because of high blood pressure, elevated cholesterol levels, or smoking habits. The study, carried out at 22 medical centers around the country, cost over $100 million and took ten years to complete. The investigators involved (250 in all) were heavy hitters, and everyone—dieticians, drug company executives, and heart specialists—was looking forward to the good news.

What the researchers did was randomly divide the volunteers into two approximately equal groups. One group of 6,438 volunteers, the so-called usual-care contingent, got no special attention or treatment. They were on their own. Help, if needed, would have to come from their "usual source of medical care."

The other 6,428 men, the "special intervention" group, got the full treatment. If they were smokers, they were given individual counseling by physicians to help them quit. In addition, ten weekly rap sessions for small groups focused on problems of smoking, dietary change, and high blood pressure. Each participant was counseled as well by an "intervention team" that included nutritionists, nurses, physicians, and scientists who were skilled in modifying behavior. Last, but by no means least, everyone with a diastolic blood pressure of over 90 was treated with medication. Specific goals were established for each person (for smoking, cholesterol, and blood pressure), and frequent follow-up meetings were scheduled to help insure that everyone was making progress. Most men were followed for at least six years with many hanging in for the full seven that were devoted to research.

By now you've got the picture. This was a very big deal. MRFIT should have been a piece of cake, and the results should have been unequivocal. If all had gone according to Hoyle, the guys in the special intervention group would have far outdistanced the unfortunate fellows who were left on their own. Such intensive care and supervision was naturally expected to promote overall better health, but most especially to reduce heart attacks and deaths. To everyone's shock and dismay, the study bombed.

Oh, there was a dramatic drop in heart attacks and deaths all right— but it couldn't be attributed to MRFIT. Once the scientists got done sifting the data and analyzing the statistics—a task that took several years to complete—they discovered that there was no significant difference in the death rate between the two groups.[13] Incredible, bizarre, outrageous! The experts were flabbergasted. How could this be? After all that time and over $100 million, there should have been something to show for the effort.

Before the dust had settled, researchers started scrambling desperately for answers. But they had been hit by a double whammy. Not only did their carefully planned program not make a difference, they discovered to their astonishment that people with high blood pressure who received medication seemed to be dying faster than those who did not receive drugs.

> **The patients with entry diastolic blood pressures between 90 and 94 . . . who received antihypertensive therapy had higher mortality and morbidity than those who were treated less vigorously. Furthermore, cardiovascular mortality was higher in those hypertensive men with abnormal electrocardiographic findings who were more intensively treated with drugs. We are left then with an apparent paradox: More intensive therapy may cause more cardiovascular mortality.[14]**

Could it have been that in their eagerness to get patients' blood pressure down the doctors were winning the battle but losing the war? The drug results were so shocking that an editorial in the *Journal of the American Medical Association* warned, "The implications of these surprising findings are so major as to demand caution, since the results fly in the face of current medical dogma and practice."[15]

You better believe that a lot of physicians were nervous about the unexpected MRFIT findings. There was no doubt that the pills brought blood pressure down; but patients died anyway—maybe even faster. All of a sudden there was a tiny cloud on the horizon that might challenge the incessant reminder to "take your medicine." Important reputations had been made supporting drugs to control hypertension. The grand old man of high-blood-pressure treatment, Dr. Edward D. Freis, offered his candid response: "I think this result is weird. I'd like to see it confirmed."[16]

Needless to say, lots of doctors were ready to offer explanations why MRFIT was such a mess. First they blamed the unusual and puzzling results on the "usual care" fellows—the guys who were recruited to do nothing. They made up the so-called control group, left out there all alone without special encouragement or counseling.

The problem was that these men didn't die fast enough. Researchers had anticipated that at least 442 of the 6,438 in this high-risk delegation would have kicked the bucket by the end of the sixth year; to their dismay, less than half that number had bitten the dust. Only 219 had died—screwing up the statistics. By reducing their heart attacks and staying alive, these guys were doing just as well as the men who got all that special stop-smoking encouragement, dietary advice, and high-blood-pressure medication.

So how did these men do it? In order to explain this one, the experts needed to pull a rabbit out of the hat. What they came up with was another famous about-face. Usually doctors bemoan the fact that they can't get their patients to stop smoking or change their rotten diets. Now, all of a sudden they tried to solve the MRFIT mystery by telling us that the unsupervised group of men were so health-conscious and made such important changes in lifestyle all by themselves that they were able to reduce their heart attacks just as much as could the precious special-intervention group.

Unfortunately the facts don't back up these claims. Oh, it's true that our loners did improve themselves a little. They cut back on cigarettes, reduced their cholesterol level slightly (from 241 to 233), and got their diastolic blood pressure down from 91 to 83.6. But the MRFIT fellows did significantly better; the men who got counseling and supervision beat the controls by 100 percent in smoking reduction; after six years, 32 percent of the MRFITs smoked, whereas 46 percent of the unsupervised men still smoked. The special-intervention group had a 44 percent greater reduction in blood pressure and beat out the usual-care guys by 38 percent when it came to lowering serum cholesterol.[17]

Unfortunately such success didn't translate into fewer deaths from heart attacks. When it came down to what really counts—living or dying—there was no real difference between the two groups. So the moral of this amazing tale is: there is no moral. After ten years, $115 million, and 12,866 human guinea pigs, we are no closer than we were before to understanding why Americans are winning the coronary crusade. There may even be more questions today than there were ten years ago. The dramatic drop in strokes and heart attacks could conceivably be attributed to wine consumption, aspirin intake, or Vitamin C.[18–22]

No matter what the reason, we *are* winning this fight, make no mistake about that. So what to do? Where does all this leave us? Should we just stop worrying about cigarettes, cholesterol, and blood pressure? Of course not. I am a redundancy freak. I want to reduce my risks every which way I can. That means no ciggies, less fat (both saturated *and* unsaturated), less coffee, less salt, less stress, more fruits and vegetables, extra fiber, lots of Vitamin C and E, and as much exercise as possible. These are all good common-sense healthful suggestions. I don't care if some are less important than others; as far as I'm concerned, it's part of a package deal, and the more bells and whistles the better.

We may never be able to prove beyond a shadow of a doubt that exercise is helpful[23] or that fat is a villain, but if we mistakenly err on the side of prudence, the worst that could happen is that we might lose a little extra weight and look and feel better. If we err on the side of slothfulness, we could end up prematurely dead. Most important, do not feel guilty! Even if you can't do it all, don't despair. Nobody's perfect!

I've been known to indulge in extra rich chocolate cake on occasion myself, with hardly a second thought. Just do what you can and read on—we have some life-saving tips coming right up.

Saving Your Heart with Aspirin

The most dramatic breakthrough in the prevention of heart attacks probably won't come from bypass surgery or the latest beta blocker. More likely than not it will come from the lowly aspirin tablet, a drug we all take pretty much for granted. The newest research hot off the presses of the *New England Journal of Medicine* is so astounding that it should revolutionize the way doctors treat high-risk heart-attack patients.[24]

Dr. Daniel Lewis and his colleagues at 12 Veterans Administration medical centers undertook an ambitious project to test if low doses of aspirin could protect people from a first heart attack. There has been considerable controversy over the years as to whether or not aspirin is beneficial in preventing *repeat* heart attacks in people who had already survived at least one. Although the results from quite a few studies strongly suggested that aspirin is protective, several were inconclusive, and most doctors have been reluctant to recommend routine aspirin use.[25–31]

The VA researchers recruited men who were suffering from something called unstable angina. During the previous month these patients had developed a new onset or sudden worsening of their chest pain (defined as "one or more episodes per day, duration of longer than 15 minutes, or occurrences at rest or during minimal activity").[32] Anyone who experiences this kind of unstable angina is in big trouble, because the risk of subsequent heart attack and death is significant.[33] Lewis and his associates divided their 1,266 high-risk patients into two groups; one delegation would get aspirin and the other a placebo. In order to carry out this work in the standard double blind and controlled manner, the investigators needed to come up with a way to provide the "medicine" in such a way that neither group could tell what they were getting.

Figuring that most people would probably be curious enough to taste the tablets in order to figure out which group they were in, the docs decided to disguise the drugs by using unmarked **Alka-Seltzer** tablets (containing 324 mg of aspirin). Every day for three months the men in one group dissolved their aspirin in water and glugged while the others plopped and fizzed with nonaspirin **Alka-Seltzer** as a placebo. I want to emphasize that the physicians used **Alka-Seltzer** not because they believed it was better than regular aspirin, but because it was a convenient way of camouflaging which group of patients was actually getting the real drug and because it was less likely to cause stomach problems than regular aspirin.

Enough suspense—what happened? The results weren't just good, they were great! The men who were getting one aspirin a day halved their heart attack rate compared to the controls. Now believe me, that is an incredible victory all by itself. Any time you can prevent a heart attack, it's good news for sure. But far more important, they scored big in the game that really counts—there were 51 percent fewer *deaths* among the aspirin takers. Not only was the aspirin dramatically decreasing heart attacks, it was also saving lots of lives. And the benefit lasted after the aspirin had been discontinued. Researchers found that even after one year "the mean mortality rate in the aspirin group was 43 percent less than that in the placebo group."[34]

Aspirin has been shown to have a parallel benefit in the brain. Canadian and French teams have demonstrated approximately the same degree of reduction in strokes and deaths for men who had suffered something called TIA (transient ischemic attack).[35,36] These TIAs, caused by reduced blood flow to the brain, are believed to be early warning signs of an impending stroke, much as unstable angina warns of increased risk of heart attack. That aspirin has been shown to work both in the brain and the heart makes a very strong case for the drug's protective role against fatal cardiovascular attacks.

Why were Dr. Lewis and his colleagues successful in demonstrating such impressive benefit from aspirin when others failed? Perhaps it's partly because they kept the horse in the barn. Giving aspirin after a heart attack does seem to do some good, but it may be a little like closing the door after the horse has already escaped. Once you've had a coronary, some damage usually remains, and aspirin is not always able to overcome it.

But the real key to their success may have been in picking the right dose. Because no one knew exactly how much aspirin would work, in the past the "more is better" principle was often employed; but in reality less may be best. Too much aspirin may even be counterproductive. British researchers have suggested that as little as 40 mg (one-eighth of an adult tablet, or half a child's aspirin) every other day may be enough to provide protection.[37]

It seems almost inconceivable that such a tiny chunk of aspirin can do any good. Using one-eighth of an aspirin tablet to treat a headache, for example, would be like trying to kill a fly with a feather. True enough, but aspirin turns out to be a far more complicated drug than most people ever imagined.

To understand how aspirin can protect against heart attacks, you have to know what a heart attack really is. Should be a snap, right? After all, with so many millions of people popping off with MIs (that's doctor talk for myocardial infarctions—another name for heart attacks), you would think they'd have it knocked. Wrong! Researchers are still fighting over what really brings on a heart attack; is it spasm (like squeezing a garden hose), or is it blood clots? The prevailing view is that the atherosclerosis that junks up our coronary arteries somehow predisposes us to develop blood clots, which in turn shut off blood flow and oxygen to the heart muscle. This process leads to tissue death and can ultimately make the heart beat irregularly or stop altogether.

So the trigger behind this whole event seems in most cases to be the formation of a blood clot. If you could prevent clots by putting a safety catch on the trigger, you might be able to save your heart. And that, my dear reader, seems to be exactly what aspirin does best—but only in tiny doses. Larger doses (say more than one tablet) could undo the benefits.

Please indulge me for a moment while I explain this fascinating process. Your body makes two chemicals that appear to play a critical role both in blood clotting and in regulating the diameter of blood vessels. What's so bizarre is that they work at cross-purposes.

On the one hand there is thromboxane. It's a baddie, since it helps make blood stickier and promotes clot formation. Thromboxane also helps to constrict blood vessels—just about the last thing anyone with heart disease needs. Let's dub it T for Terrible Thromboxane.

Opposing T is prostacyclin—a substance that dilates blood vessels and helps to prevent blood clots. This is the good guy, so we'll call our hero P for Powerful Prostacyclin. Wouldn't it be nice if our coronary arteries contained only P, with no T lurking around to start funny business? Damn straight! Unfortunately, aspirin is indiscriminate; it has a shotgun effect. Given in doses of one tablet or more, it will shoot down the manufacture of both thromboxane and prostacyclin almost completely.[38] So we nail the bad guy, but we also zap our hero. Don't feel bad if you're a little confused by this. Even physicians have been puzzled, like the New York doctor who wrote to the *Journal of the American Medical Association*, "Recent information seems to indicate that 80 mg of aspirin a day is near the optimal dosage . . . would one 325 mg tablet every three days be satisfactory or is it necessary to take 80 mg every day?"[39]

The answer from the AMA's expert consultant, Dr. William McGivney: 325 mg. of aspirin every three days is probably counterproductive, because it shuts powerful P down so much for so long. A much smaller daily dose, somewhere between 25 or 30 mg. and 80 mg, is probably effective at shutting down Terrible T while leaving Powerful P more or less alone.[40,41]

Sooo, the moral of *this* story seems to be that "Less is Best." Investigators are eagerly trying to find out how low they can go and still achieve a therapeutic benefit. I am afraid it will still be some time before we can know the optimum dose. Even if they told us tomorrow, though, there is no good way to divvy up such a small amount of aspirin. In fact, trying to come up with one-quarter or one-eighth of a regular tablet is in itself almost impossible.

Well, where does all this aspirin stuff leave us? Is it just esoteric nonsense, or can we take it to the bank? I am not ready to tell everyone who is at risk of a heart attack or stroke (probably 30 to 40 million Americans) to start smashing up aspirin and popping down one minuscule chunk every other day. For one thing, some people are allergic to aspirin, even in such infinitesimal doses. They break out in a rash or start to wheeze. For another, I would probably get nailed by doctors who still think that the whole aspirin story is pretty flaky. Finally, I don't want people believing that they can go back to their old slothful ways just by taking out a little aspirin insurance. Stopping smoking, reducing dietary fat, and increasing exercise are still numero uno in my book.

Before you make up your mind on the aspirin question, however, you might be interested in one additional piece of information. Trying to resolve any lingering doubts once and for all, Harvard researchers have mailed out letters to 200,000 physicians in the hope of recruiting 20,000 docs willing to participate in a humongous five-year study.[42] These medical guinea pigs will take one 325 mg. aspirin tablet (a large dose, perhaps too large) every other day. Oh, and by the way, they will also be taking a 30 mg. beta-carotene capsule (**Solatene**) every other day. Beta-carotene is a precursor of Vitamin A, and some reports suggest that it may protect cells and help to prevent cancer.

As for me, I figure what's good for the goose is good for the gander. If these docs are popping down beta-carotene and aspirin, I'll eat two to three carrots a day (lots of natural yummy-tasting beta-carotene there) and yes, I must confess, I do swallow an itsy-bitsy teeny-weeny piece of aspirin every other day—just in case.

P.S. I am also very big on onions, garlic, and cloud ears (also known as mo-er and Chinese black tree fungus). These foods have all been shown to contain ingredients that possess powerful anticlotting properties which differ somewhat from aspirin. Hey folks, I'm not talking flaky food faddism! Believe me, this is serious business, published in such eminent journals as *Lancet*, the *New England Journal of Medicine,* and *The American Journal of Clinical Nutrition*.[43–47] Best of all, I happen to think that onions, garlic, and mo-er taste terrific. The only stumbling block might be convincing everyone one else around you that you only reek for therapeutic reasons.

Surviving a Heart Attack

Even if you watch your diet, exercise, stop smoking, and take aspirin, there's still no guarantee that you will escape a heart attack. Though you will have cut your risks substantially, you can't always beat the genes or the roll of the dice. After all, with over a million MIs a year, heart disease is still our number-one killer.

Having a heart attack, however, does not mean that you have to cash in your chips permanently. There are approximately seven million people in this country who have made it through at least one MI. A great many go on to live long and productive lives. If you can get over that initial heart attack hump, your chances are pretty darn good. The good news is that the gains being made in helping people to survive a heart attack are almost as impressive as those in prevention. But you've got to act fast if you want to take advantage of the latest advances.

What should you do, then, if you suspect you are having the big one? To answer that question, I decided to ask my friend Ralph what he would do if *he* were having a heart attack. After all, Ralph is a hotshot cardiologist. Let me tell you a little bit about Ralph. At 43 he looks barely 35. He takes good care of himself. He runs five miles a day, is in superb shape, and eats sensibly without being fanatical. Ralph is a special kind of doctor. Besides having a great bedside manner and a wonderful sense of humor, he is delightfully modest and an all-around nice guy. Most important of all, he's one of the smartest doctors I know and really stays on top of all the new developments in his profession.

When I confronted him with the question of what he would do in the unlikely event he thought he was having an MI, Ralph allowed as how the first and most important hurdle would be to admit to himself that something was wrong. Most people wait far too long (an average of three hours) from the time the symptoms start until they seek medical help.

Doctors themselves are terrible patients and often wait even longer. I know about one physician who felt symptoms in the morning but continued to work in the hospital all day long, teaching medical students and seeing patients. When he come home that evening, his wife took one look at his ghastly gray face and insisted that they return to the hospital for an electrocardiogram. After protesting bitterly, the nut finally agreed. Of course he had been having a serious heart attack most of the day but was doing his best to deny it. He was lucky to survive. According to the American Heart Association, "Most heart attack victims die within the first two hours after the signals begin."[48] It's hardly any wonder, then, that 350,000 don't even make it to the hospital.

Ralph's first recommendation is: *Don't delay!* Every minute is crucial. If you experience "uncomfortable pressure, fullness, squeezing, or pain in the center of your chest, lasting two minutes or more," call an ambulance and have your butt hauled to the nearest emergency room pronto! Other symptoms that sometimes accompany a heart attack include pain that spreads to your shoulders, neck, jaw, arms, or back, sweating, weakness, dizziness, fainting, nausea, or shortness of breath.[49]

Even if you think you are just having a bad attack of indigestion that somehow seems only a little more worrisome than usual, head for the ER (emergency room). So what if it turns out to be a false alarm? You can always turn around and come home again, and all you've lost is a little time. If you miss the real thing, you could lose your life. But *never, ever* drive yourself. The worst thing that can happen to a heart-attack victim is to go into fibrillation while driving a car. The heart stops beating regularly and instead looks like a bag of worms. Because no blood is being pumped to the brain, you faint—not good form in the middle of the freeway.

Ideally you want a skilled emergency medical team, equipped with a defibrillator, to escort you to the hospital. Remember, it's the heart fibrillation that kills. Modern technology can literally shock you back from the grave with impressive speed. But getting an ambulance to your house or business isn't always fast or simple. You are therefore in a real bind—do you wait and wait for professional help, or do you get some-one to drive you to the hospital? Clearly it's a judgment call that depends on a lot of variables. If you are only five or ten minutes from the hospital, you will probably be able to get there faster than it would take for an ambulance to get to your house. But if you live out of town, it may be best to wait for the cavalry to arrive.

Here is a case where advance planning is crucial. Call your local ambulance company and find out, first, if all their vehicles carry defibrilla-tors and, second, about how long it would normally take to reach you and get you to the hospital. If they don't come equipped with defibrilla-tors or if it seems that they will take too long, it may be worth making a run for it—but only with someone else at the wheel.

Ralph suggests that you tell the ambulance people that you are on your way and carefully describe your route. If your driver leaves his emer-gency flashers going, turns on his headlights, and honks when he sees the ambulance, you can stop and make a switch along the way. And if you beat the ambulance to the hospital, so be it. The point is, get there as quickly and safely as possible!

Time is critical, because there is now hope that doctors can reduce the damage of an MI if they act fast enough and you have a little luck on your side. Inside your heart a blood clot has probably lodged in a coronary artery and is slowly cutting off the supply of oxygen and other nutrients to one part of your heart. The death of this tissue can lead to a kind of electrical short circuit or instability, which in turn may produce life-threatening irregular heart rhythms.

As soon as you arrive at the ER, they will hook you up to an electrocar-diograph and get some lidocaine ready to pump into a vein in case you start showing signs of an abnormal heart rhythm. Oxygen is ready in the event breathing becomes a problem. If you are in serious pain—it may feel like an elephant sitting on your chest—the medical team will inject morphine to make you more comfortable.

But all those procedures are old hat. They are nothing more than a holding action and will not prevent or halt the damage being done to the heart muscle. The old watch-and-wait is not enough for Ralph.

He would not be satisfied to lie back and let the blood clot wreak its havoc. Ralph has a very succinct way of putting it: "No matter what they do, if more than 40 percent of your heart is damaged, school is out—permanently!" If it were his heart, Ralph would want someone to move as quickly as possible to unblock the clot and get blood and oxygen flowing to the starving heart muscle again. Ralph would want an injection of streptokinase (**Streptase, Kabikinase**) at the earliest possible moment—either at home, in the ambulance on the way to the hospital, or as soon as he arrived in the emergency room.

Strepto who? What in the world is this streptokinase and why is it so exciting? To get a perspective on this hot new treatment, we have to go back just a few years to a hospital in Göttingen, Germany, as two physicians, Drs. Peter Rentrop and Karl Karsch, made medical history. A patient in the heart catheterization laboratory was being checked out for arteriosclerosis. Suddenly, right in the middle of the procedure, he began to have a heart attack.

A physician had already threaded a catheter into the man's artery and had injected a radio-opaque dye so that the artery would show up in x-rays. Suddenly, the artery became completely blocked. Rentrop was called in to help and, out of desperation, he poked a thin wire through the obstruction to restore blood flow. Within 2 minutes, the patient's electrocardiogram began looking normal and his heart attack, apparently, ceased.

This experience made Rentrop and Karsch realize that it is possible, and perhaps even desirable, to insert a catheter into a blocked artery during a heart attack. They then decided to try injecting streptokinase through the catheter rather than breaking up clots mechanically with a wire.[50]

What an incredible story! It sounds amazingly crude—a little like the Roto-Rooter man unplugging a drain. But this discovery started the world's top cardiologists racing each other to see who would be the first to prove what, if any, benefit could be achieved with the new "liquid plumber."

As exciting as all this is, the streptokinase story is hardly new. In fact, much of the late-blooming enthusiasm just now hitting the medical journals could almost be described as a rediscovery of the wheel. Streptokinase actually got its start through a chance discovery back in 1933. A bacteriologist named Dr. William Tillett, working in a laboratory at Johns Hopkins University, had tried an unsuccessful experiment with streptococcal germs (the same kind of bugs that cause your "strep" throat).

"Somewhat later, before discarding the test tubes, Tillett happened to look at them again. Surprisingly, the tube to which the culture had been added was now liquid, although it had previously been clotted."[51]

Dr. Tillett immediately recognized the significance of his discovery, but 13 years passed before anyone was able to test its practical potential. For one thing, purification of the active substance was tough, and for another, Tillett was more of a basic scientist than a clinical investigator. The compound lay dormant until 1946, when Tillett and an eager young medical resident, Sol Sherry, really started looking into the human potential of SK (streptokinase). Over the next three decades Sherry and various other researchers demonstrated the clear value of SK for dissolving blood clots.[52-54] As early as 1958 they had proven that the drug was feasible for clots in legs and lungs, and most important of all, for the treatment of heart-attack victims.[55]

You would think that with these discoveries, streptokinase would have been embraced with open arms by the medical community. Instead, the drug was sandbagged. The docs apparently had their heads in the muck when it came to evaluating these studies. Dr. Sherry puts it more diplomatically. "Many of these evaluations claimed a significant reduction in deaths among treated patients as compared to untreated subjects, but the cardiology community in the United States never took them seriously or expressed only a passing interest."[56]

In part the problem was ideological. The loudest shouters in the "cardiology community" apparently believed that blood clots had little to do with heart attacks. Therefore anything that dissolved blood clots was by definition irrelevant. It took more than 20 years for the power brokers in the medical establishment to get ready to hop on the bandwagon and examine the potential benefits of streptokinase.

One of the prime movers and shakers, Dr. William Ganz, galvanized an American Heart Association audience in 1981 by making a heart attack disappear right before their eyes with an injection of streptokinase.

> The audience emitted a collective gasp. On a movie screen in front of them, a nasty clot was high-tailing it through a coronary artery. Within about 30 seconds, the clot had dissolved.
>
> The man who had caused the clot lysis—William Ganz, MD, professor of medicine at UCLA and senior research scientist, Cedars-Sinai Medical Center, Los Angeles—modestly denied "planning" the event that his extraordinary film footage captured so that it would occur at that precise moment.[57]

Ganz did more than dazzle his audience with pretty pictures. He reported that his group of cardiologists had been able to dissolve away blood clots and reopen coronary arteries for 20 out of 21 patients who were experiencing heart attacks.[58] In a follow-up study he reported that 41 of 47 patients experienced complete unblocking when streptokinase was squirted directly into their coronary arteries.[58] Ganz wasn't the only one to report such success; other investigators around the country have found that they, too, can reopen clogged coronary arteries in about 80 percent of MI patients.[59-64]

The key to success, however, seems to be timing. The longer it took to get the patients to the hospital, get them hooked up to the EKG, wheel them to the cath lab and insert a catheter into the coronary artery in preparation for the juice, the less the likelihood of benefit. Remember that every minute the heart muscle goes without oxygen increases the possibility of irreversible tissue death.

One of the latest studies shows that if the streptokinase can be started within four hours after the beginning of chest pain, there is an 80 percent chance of opening the coronary arteries; in turn this seems to dramatically reduce pain, improve the electrocardiogram, diminish damage to the heart, and most important, dramatically improve survival.[65,66] If you have to wait more than five and a half hours for the streptokinase, it appears to be far less effective.[67,68]

Okay, now it's all clear and simple. At the first sign of a heart attack call the ambulance, get to the hospital, and bingo, your troubles should be over. Not so fast, my friend. There are some major hurdles along the way. Even if you get into the emergency room posthaste, there is a better than even chance that your hospital won't have a cath lab. That means they won't be able to pass a cathether from your arm to the coronary artery in your heart and thereby inject streptokinase. Stop, go to jail, do not collect $200.

But even if your hospital does have all the fancy technology, it takes a long time to go through all the preliminary rigmarole. A good hour can pass by before the medical team is ready to start squirting—and *that*, added to the time spent in getting to the hospital, is valuable time lost.

What to do? Let's find out what Ralph advises. If you go back a few pages you will discover that Ralph would want an injection of streptokinase at the earliest possible moment, perhaps even before they put him into the ambulance. He wouldn't want to wait several hours until they could get a fancy heart catheter into his coronary artery. New research in Germany and the United States shows that intravenous injections are definitely practical.[69-72] It's a lot easier and faster to inject streptokinase into a vein than into a coronary artery, and the results seem to be almost as good.

The one physician who has had more experience with streptokinase than anyone else, Dr. Sol Sherry, now Chairman of the Department of Medicine at Temple University School of Medicine, has worked with the compound for 37 years. He agrees with Ralph.

> We're working very heavily here on IV streptokinase. We've
> treated 43 cases with good results—not as striking as with the
> intracoronary thrombolysis—but its application and availabil-
> ity to many many more patients will probably make this the
> way to go. . . . It can be given quite safely. That, we think, is
> the wave of the future.[73]

This is an exciting advance in heart attack treatment, but let me offer
some warnings. It is a tricky drug, and it requires an experienced medical team to administer it. There are no guarantees that it will work for
everyone or even prolong life. And there are side effects. The drug can
cause severe allergic reactions, produce a fever, lower blood pressure,
and induce hemorrhaging. Fortunately such adverse reactions are relatively rare. And the benefits seem to outweigh the risks for a great many
heart-attack victims.

Better still is what the future holds in store. As exciting as streptokinase may be, new gene-splicing technology promises compounds which
may be safer and even more effective at dissolving clots. One, called TPA
(tissue-type plasminogen activator), goes after blood clots like a heat-
seeking missile. When administered intravenously it circulates through
the body without doing anything. But if it encounters a blood clot it
immediately goes to work setting off a chemical chain reaction which
dissolves the clot. And since it is a substance made by the human body
itself, it is not likely to produce the side effects some people suffer with
streptokinase. Doctors are very excited about the possibility that intravenous injections of TPA, which could be administered by ambulance
attendants, may destroy blood clots and open blocked blood vessels
far more quickly and safely than any other method known so far.[74,75]
If we can't prevent the darned things in the first place, at least we're
learning how to reduce or reverse the damage they do once they get
started.

But beating a heart attack will require planning. Do not wait until the
fateful moment to start rushing around madly trying to remember what to
do. **First**, assume that it *could* happen to you. You think that's about as
likely as a helicopter blade falling on your head? Well, my friend, it's
time for a good honest look in the mirror. I'm not talking about that roll
around your middle—though it probably won't improve your chances.
But look at your *ears*. This is going to sound bizarre, but if there is a
crease running diagonally across your ear lobe, you may be somewhat
more likely to have gummed-up coronary arteries and run the risk of a
heart attack.[76,77] No one really understands why there should be a connection between ear lobe creases and clogged arteries, but there's a surprising amount written on this subject in the medical literature and the
association has held up for at least a decade.

Check a patient's ear to detect heart disease? Some cardiologists sneer at the idea. Others say there's something to it.

After surveying the surprisingly substantial body of evidence that has accumulated since the connection was proposed in 1973, and doing a study of his own involving 1,000 patients, Dr. William J. Elliott of the Washington University School of Medicine concludes that a glance at the earlobe can indeed give you a clue to the presence of coronary artery disease. But, he notes, it must be used with the appropriate dash of caution. What you look for is a crease running diagonally across the ear lobe . . .

"It's the sort of thing that I use as an initial screening factor. It's very easily evaluated . . . But . . . I certainly wouldn't recommend an angiogram for a 65-year-old person who is being seen for another condition merely because he has an earlobe crease . . ."

Finding it in an individual, Dr. Elliott cautions, means he is at risk for the diagnosis of coronary artery disease, but it is not necessarily true that this patient *has* coronary artery disease.[78]

Now please don't panic if you find a slight pucker across those lovely lobes. The last thing I would want is to have you rushing off for triple bypass surgery. But it probably wouldn't hurt to check in with a cardiologist who can run some tests and assess your other risk factors. Is that a pack of cigarettes in your pocket? Did Grandma, Uncle Harry, or dear old Dad ever have a heart attack? If you smoke or have a family history of heart problems, it's past time to start getting your health act together. Get serious about quitting smoking, cut your dietary fat and cholesterol to a minimum, exercise daily, shed those extra pounds, and find ways to reduce or deal effectively with stress. This should minimize your chances of a heart attack, but if disaster strikes, prepare now to survive.

Second, make sure that you have all critical telephone numbers (ambulance, doctor) readily available by your telephone. **Third,** call the ambulance company in advance to find out if the vans have defibrillators and how long it would reasonably take to get to your house in an emergency. **Fourth,** write out clear instructions on how to find your home. Relatives and friends tend to panic during emergencies. Time will be saved if they can read the instructions to the ambulance company. **Fifth,** make sure everyone in your household knows how to perform CPR (cardiopulmonary resuscitation)—it saves lives! **Sixth,** ask your doctor about hospital procedures. If there is more than one medical facility in your community, find out which is closest or best able to handle heart-attack patients.

Seventh, talk over the streptokinase question; your physician may be as excited as Ralph about the potential for intravenous administration.

Finally, if and when the time comes, don't be a hero! And don't panic. Let someone else take charge. If you are like most people you will deny, Deny, **DENY!** "Who, me? Have a heart attack? Never!" But if you've been having chest pain and a spouse or friend looks at you and tells you that you look terrible, let them take executive action and call the ambulance. Otherwise you will still be protesting long after the streptokinase could be doing good things for your heart.

Joining the Survivors' Club

All right, you made it. Congratulations! Now that you've gotten over the heart-attack hump, you'd think it would be all downhill pedaling from here. Not hardly; there is always the chance you could have another one. Approximately 100,000 heart attack victims die from a second MI within the year.

Gruesome! I know we're not supposed to discuss such things. People don't need a sword of Damocles hanging over their heads, especially not heart patients. It's bad enough overcoming the physical and psychological trauma of the first one without worrying about the possibility that another may be right around the corner. But I have never been big on BS, so let's be straight about this and look as realistically as possible at the options.

Before you let the stats sink in so far that they get you depressed, keep in mind that at least 85 percent of the folks who make it through a heart attack will *not* have a repeat during the next twelve months. By the way, those first three months are the toughest hurdle to get over; if you make it past six, your odds start looking better and better all the time. And after a year they are better still.

Now you have two options. You can sit back, relax, and try to put the whole thing out of your mind. You may even be able to convince yourself that it was all a mistake and could never happen again. Denial is a powerful coping mechanism for a lot of people before, during, and after a heart attack. But what would Ralph do?

First, he would want to know whether he's at a high or low risk of having another heart attack. In recent years cardiologists have come up with some incredibly sophisticated techniques for figuring out who's most vulnerable.[79] If the heart attack was "minor" and your heart is still in pretty good shape and you come through the tests with flying colors, you don't want to take handfuls of unnecessary pills for the rest of your life. Some of them have a host of unpleasant side effects that might make you wonder whether you're really living longer or if it just feels that way. Put another way, quite a few of these drugs can slow you down or space you out so that you may begin to question whether the quantity of life you gain is worth the quality you lose.

Even so, for folks in the high-risk category, it's probably worth some inconvenience to overcome the odds. There are a surprising number of medications that appear to lower your chances of having another heart attack. If you weren't taking aspirin before, there is a good possibility that your doctor may consider it now. An analysis of six major studies suggests that aspirin can reduce the incidence of second MIs by 21 percent.[80,81] Once again, the issue of dose is unresolved. Ask your doctor for his or her recommendation, but recognize that the final word on this subject still isn't in.

In addition to aspirin, your physician may prescribe either **Persantine** (dipyridamole) or **Anturane** (sulfinpyrazone). Both are theoretically supposed to make one component of blood, called platelets, less "sticky" and therefore less likely to clot and jam up a coronary artery. Do they work? I wish I had a nice simple answer to that question.

Several major studies have produced equivocal results. Dr. Sidney Wolfe, Director of Health Research Group, includes **Persantine** in his book *Pills That Don't Work*. Its value in treating angina (its only official use) is controversial, and at this time I would have to say that there is still some question whether a combination of **Persantine** and aspirin is significantly better at saving lives than is aspirin alone.[82,83] A heavy-duty study of coronary-bypass patients at the Mayo Clinic showed that the combination unquestionably helps to keep clots from blocking these repaired blood vessels to the heart.[84] And some doctors, including famed Texas heart surgeon Denton Cooley, believe that "these drugs should be used prophylactically since they have very few side effects."[85]

Persantine can produce adverse reactions, though. Because it acts a lot like nitroglycerin to dilate arteries, it can cause symptoms of headache, dizziness, light-headedness, weakness, flushing, nausea, stomach cramping, vomiting, and skin rash. Fortunately such adverse reactions are really quite rare in the lower doses used to prevent blood clots. But if some of these unpleasant reactions do occur, it will be up to patient and doctor to weigh the theoretical benefit of **Persantine** against the real discomforts of any actual side effects.

The value of **Anturane** has also been questioned. This drug has been around since 1959 to treat gout, but it never stimulated great interest or captured headlines. Then, in 1980, a major study published in the *New England Journal of Medicine* grabbed everyone's attention.

During the critical six to seven months following a heart attack, when people are at the highest risk, **Anturane** seemed to work a miracle—it reduced the number of sudden deaths by a whopping 74 percent![86] And the effect seemed to last; two years later there were 43 percent fewer deaths among those who had taken the drug. Some of the country's leading cardiologists called **Anturane** a great lifesaver. Newspapers announced that thousands and thousands of lives would be saved and quoted the researchers as stating that "there were no reports of serious side effects." About the only problem that occurs with any frequency is stomach upset, and this can be minimized if the drug is taken with meals. Anemias and skin rashes have also been reported, but such reactions are rare.

Everything looked fantabulous until the FDA put the data under a magnifying glass. The feds complained that the study wasn't analyzed correctly and that "the cause-of-death classification and all conclusions based on it are unreliable."[87] The upshot was that the FDA refused to grant a Good Housekeeping Seal of Approval for **Anturane's** use after heart attacks.

But the issue has not gone away. Some cardiologists who have reanalyzed the data still insist that the drug did indeed save lives.[88] And a recent Italian study suggests that **Anturane** can definitely reduce the risk of repeat heart attacks.[89]

So where does this leave us? The value of **Persantine** or **Anturane** for MI victims is still up in the air. Whether doctors prescribe one or the other probably depends more on how familiar and comfortable they feel with it rather than any significant superiority of one compound over the other. But remember, we are all operating in a gray zone here. Neither drug has received an official FDA blessing for such use. Nevertheless, as I said earlier, I am all for redundancy when it comes to heart-attack prevention, as long as the benefits outweigh the risks. The final decision is between you and your doctor.

Living Longer But Enjoying It Less?
Watch Out for Those Beta-Blocker Blahs!

If **Valium** and other minor tranquilizers were *the* drugs of the 1970s, then **Inderal** and other beta blockers are The drugs of the 1980s. It boggles the mind how the beta-blocker bandwagon has gathered momentum over the last few years—almost 60 million prescriptions were filled for these drugs in 1983.[90]

Inderal (propranolol), the first and most popular beta blocker, has climbed steadily until it reached the number-one position on the doctors' hit parade of most prescribed drugs in 1982.[91] And it has remained at or near the top of the charts for years, putting **Inderal** right up with **Tagamet** as one of the all-time big best-sellers in the pharmaceutical industry. In 1983 over 30 million **Inderal** prescriptions were filled in this country alone. That's right, mate, 30 million, shooting it way past that old leader of the pack, **Valium.** Every day 10 million Americans swallow a little hexagonal pill with a big letter *I* stamped on the back. That's nearly 1 out of every 20 people.

Despite its incredible commercial success (each year sales in the United States amount to over a quarter of a billion dollars), the drug has had a relatively low profile. Ask the man on the street if he has ever heard of **Valium** or **Tagamet**, and chances are good you will get a nod. He might even whip some out of a pocket and hand you one. Mention **Inderal**, and you would probably get a blank stare. The drug certainly hasn't been a shooting star.

It got off to a rather slow start back in 1967, when the FDA first approved it for the treatment of irregular heart beats (arrhythmias)—a relatively small market. **Inderal** got a big boost in 1973, when the FDA gave it the green light for angina. But the real milestone wasn't passed until 1976, when the drug got a seal of approval for high blood pressure. All of a sudden millions of people were eligible for this hot "new" beta blocker. As if that wasn't enough, the FDA approved **Inderal** for treating migraine headaches in 1979. Unofficially, the drug is also occasionally prescribed for actors and musicians who suffer incapacitating stage fright and for people who experience severe stressful physical symptoms when they have to give a speech.

How, you may ask, can one drug be good for so many different things—heart irregularities, high blood pressure, angina, and migraine? The simple answer is that it blocks beta receptors. But that leaves the question of what in the world a beta is and why it should be blocked.

Okay, hang in with me for a momentary digression. This is the sort of stuff pharmacologists live for; we like to go nosing around asking how drugs really work. Why do some medications produce diarrhea while others cause constipation? Why does **Inderal** slow the heart while adrenaline makes its beat faster and stronger?

The answer to such mysteries lies in something called receptors. For years we had to take them pretty much on faith, since it was impossible to actually see receptor molecules sitting on our cells. We now know that they do indeed exist in huge quantities (often thousands to the cell) and that they help to regulate almost all bodily functions.

The analogy that has been used over and over is that of the key and lock, with the lock representing the receptor and the key a natural body chemical or a drug. In order for you to lift your finger to turn this page, your brain must send a chemical message to your finger where a chemical "key" called acetylcholine is squirted out of a nerve ending. These molecules fit into special receptor "locks" and trigger the contraction of muscles in your finger.

Now, take beta receptors. They are all over the place—in your heart, in your lungs, and all around the little muscles that surround blood vessels. Here's how they work. Say you're in a big hurry because you're late for an important appointment. You don't see a stop sign and go barreling through the intersection, barely missing a police car that just happened to be going by. The result is that a zillion adrenaline molecules pour into your blood stream and make a beeline for all your beta receptors. As these "locks" fill with adrenaline "keys," they unlock all sorts of body reactions. Your heart starts pounding a mile a minute; your lungs open up, and you may find yourself panting; your hands are probably starting to shake, especially as you hear the siren coming closer and closer. The whole shebang is caused by stimulation of beta receptors.

A beta blocker, logically enough, blocks beta receptors. It can modulate or even prevent much of this kind of reaction. Think of a drug such as **Inderal** as a little like a wad of bubble gum that gets stuck in a lock. With the gum blocking the hole, the key (in this case adrenaline) won't fit. And if adrenaline can't fit into beta receptors, it can't stimulate heart rate. To put it another way, it would be as if you stuck a block under the gas pedal. No matter how hard you pressed on the accelerator, you couldn't make the car go any faster. **Inderal** slows down and stabilizes the heart's normal rhythm, reduces the work output of the heart, decreases the need for oxygen, and reduces blood pressure.

The discovery that the drug was also beneficial for migraine sufferers was purely serendipitous. People with a history of severe headaches who were taking **Inderal** for angina or high blood pressure noticed that their migraine attacks came much less frequently while they were on this medicine. Follow-up studies confirmed that *some* people do indeed benefit when the drug is used prophylactically—it won't abort an attack in progress, however. About one-third of these patients report fewer migraines when they use **Inderal**, but another third complain that they have as many or more headaches after they start using the drug. Unfortunately there's no way to predict in advance who will benefit and who won't, which means that trial and error is the name of that tune.

So far **Inderal** sounds like a pretty amazing drug, but the latest chapter in the beta-blocker saga is, if anything, even more incredible. At the end of 1981 headlines bannered a hot news story all across the country: **"Revolutionary Beta Blockers Prevent Second Heart Attacks"— "Experts Say Drug to Save Thousands of Heart Victims"—"New Drugs Revolutionize Medicine."** If you think the headlines sounded great, wait until you read some of the actual stories.

> **Last month, federal investigators suddenly cut short a major test of a heart drug—not because of bad side effects, but because the drug was so effective that advisers said it was unethical to withhold it from patients in the control group.[92]**

> **Few drugs have had as great an impact on medicine as the beta blockers . . . recent studies have shown that the beta blockers can help lower significantly the incidence of fatal**

and nonfatal heart attacks among people who have already had one.

It is now clear the beta blockers are one of those infrequent advances that revolutionize the practice of medicine.[93]

And **Inderal** was at the head of the parade. *The Wall Street Journal* wasn't content merely to announce the good news. The editors took the opportunity to take a potshot at the FDA. The headline above the editorial in this normally staid paper could have competed with anything you might find on the front page of one of the supermarket tabloids.

100,000 Killed

A federal agency's announcement last week that its tests show a drug called propranolol [Inderal] can save 6,500 lives annually by warding off second heart attacks may have given some readers the impression a new wonder drug had been found. In truth, propranolol is not so much a success story as a scandal. Doctors could have been saving those lives years ago had the Food and Drug Administration not obstructed the use of propranolol. . . .

If you use last week's estimates . . . propranolol could have prolonged more than 100,000 lives in the U.S. over the last 16 years. . . .

The propranolol history raises a question, unthinkable a few years ago, about whether we should even have an FDA.[94]

Shocking! Scandalous! And pure BS! The editorial tries to create controversy where none exists. I have little doubt that the editors of *The Wall Street Journal* would love nothing better than to see the Food and Drug Administration disappear and let the pharmaceutical industry police itself, but they blew it when they picked **Inderal** to banner such a cause. After all, the FDA approved this drug as far back as 1967. Any doctor who wished could have started prescribing **Inderal** for heart-attack patients at that time. But it has only been since 1981 that cardiologists had solid proof that **Inderal** and several other beta blockers could help to prevent second heart attacks.

In that year the results of three major studies of beta blockers were announced. A Norwegian group reported that when the drug **Blocadren** (timolol) was given to patients after a heart attack, their death rate could be reduced by 39 percent.[95] A large United States study known as BHAT (B-Blocker Heart Attack Trial) showed that **Inderal** could cut mortality rates by 39 percent the first year and after two years by about 26 percent.[96] The third investigation was carried out in Sweden with the drug **Lopressor** (metoprolol). It found that the death toll could be lowered by 36 percent.[97]

Whoopee! So much good news makes you want to start taking one of these drugs even if you're healthy. A lot of docs think that **Inderal** and its beta-blocker brothers are the greatest thing since sliced bread. The bandwagon is gathering speed. Some cardiologists believe that everyone who has a heart attack should immediately be given one of these drugs as a matter of course.

For people with angina, irregular heart rhythms, high blood pressure, abnormal electrocardiograms, or other serious risk factors such a policy makes eminent sense. But I have several reservations about blindly prescribing such drugs to one and all, year in and year out, especially if the risk of a repeat heart attack is low.

First, for every person who really has his life prolonged by taking a beta blocker, 20 to 50 will probably end up taking it needlessly.[98] That's because we still don't have a perfect formula for predicting who is actually at risk of having another heart attack and who isn't. The vast majority of MI victims—80 to 90 percent—are *not* high risk patients. So what, you're probably muttering to yourself. All else being equal, why not pull out all the stops and try to improve your odds even if you're in a low-risk category?

The problem is that all else is not equal. If beta blockers were benign drugs with few, if any, side effects, I'd be delighted to hop on the bandwagon with everyone else. But there *are* side effects, many of them downright disagreeable.

First there's fatigue. A lot of folks really do get the blahs. They feel tired, weak, and lethargic. Some people describe a lightheaded or cloudy feeling, as if they were not quite dealing from a full deck. Then there's depression—common enough for one medical wag to dub the syndrome the "Beta-Blocker Blues." A case report published in the *American Journal of Psychiatry* describes a patient who had no history of psychiatric problems before she started on **Inderal**.

> **Ms. A was a 33-year-old housewife without psychiatric history who was prescribed propranolol [Inderal] for control of ventricular arrhythmia . . . Mrs. A noted symptoms of fatigue, mental sluggishness, and the desire to sleep throughout the day. Because her arrhythmia was incompletely controlled, the dose was increased to 120 mg/day. Two weeks later Ms. A experienced more severe psychiatric symptoms. She had difficulty falling asleep and began to lose interest in hobbies and housework. She found herself hesitant to be around others or even to leave the house. She began to have crying spells and to have profound insomnia. She then lost interest in sex and felt guilty and worthless. She felt she would be better off**

dead and sought to purchase life insurance for herself. She planned to commit suicide by shooting herself with a pistol in a manner that might appear as an accident. . . . Although Ms. A did not admit her suicidal intent at this point, the nurse suggested to her physicians that propranolol should be discontinued.

Ms. A initially had felt the medication was responsible for her depression, but as the syndrome worsened and her symptoms increased she had not considered stopping her medication. Her husband, on the other hand, felt her change in mood was related to the propranolol. . . .

In a double-blind protocol, Ms. A was switched from propranolol to placebo: 8 days later she felt much improved.[99]

Such psychological side effects can be insidious because doctors rarely mention them and patients hardly ever suspect that something as basic as a heart pill might be dragging them down. No one has a good handle on how common this problem really is, but it may be more frequent than is generally recognized. Forgetfulness is another potential downside to drugs like **Inderal**.[100] An older person might chalk up absent-mindedness to early senility when in fact the medication may be responsible.

Sexual side effects have also been reported. Decreased libido may occur in both men and women, and impotence can also be a problem.[101] Although extremely rare, Peyronie's disease has been associated with both **Inderal** and **Lopressor**.[102,103] In this condition the penis develops fibrous material that leads to a strange angularity or curvature during erection. Sexual intercourse can become painfully difficult, if not impossible.

Other side effects that can be more than just bothersome include breathing difficulties (anyone with asthma should avoid **Inderal** like the plague), low blood pressure, tingling in the extremities, cold fingers and toes (a Raynaud's-type syndrome), nausea, stomach pain and diarrhea. A slow pulse is to be expected, but if the heart rate slows too much, it can be real cause for concern. Some people may even start losing their hair after they have been on **Inderal** for a while. As in depression, this is one side effect few people would associate with their medicine. Fortunately it is usually reversible once the drug is discontinued.

Diabetics must be especially careful if they use insulin and also receive a prescription for a beta blocker. When blood-sugar levels fall too fast, hypoglycemia can result, leading to sweating and a rapid pulse. Usually such symptoms are a tip that something is wrong, and a diabetic can correct the problem by eating something that will boost glucose levels. But drugs like **Inderal** may mask these symptoms. With their early warning system short-circuited, diabetics can conceivably get into serious hypoglycemic trouble.

There is one other side effect of drugs like **Inderal** that has some doctors quite concerned. Many beta blockers do bad things to blood fats. In one study they raised triglyceride levels by 24 percent and lowered something called HDLs (high-density lipoproteins) by 13 percent.[104,105] Now HDLs are good guys, because they seem to help in ridding the body of nasty cholesterol. Most physicians would like to see HDL levels go up, not down. No one knows the long-term impact of such changes, but some doctors have expressed concern that short-term benefits may later be superseded by increased risk of arteriosclerosis and heart disease.[106]

By now you are probably beginning to wonder what in hell is going on here. If **Inderal** is the greatest thing since sliced bread, maybe we better start passing the tortillas. Well, it's not as bad as it seems. Most people don't experience these unpleasant side effects. Dizziness and lethargy may fade away after several weeks of treatment, and a careful adjustment of dose can often help make beta blockers easier to tolerate.

But if life's pleasures begin to fade, you may begin to wonder whether you have traded away quality of life for an indeterminate increase in quantity. If insomnia, nightmares, loss of appetite, loss of hair, loss of interest in sex, impotence, depression, cold fingers, or fatigue start getting you down, it's time to have a heart-to-heart talk with your cardiologist. There are now many different beta blockers on the market these days—including **Lopressor** (metoprolol), **Corgard** (nadolol), **Tenormin** (atenolol), **Blocadren** (timolol), **Visken** (pindolol), **Trandate** and **Normodyne** (labetalol)—and more are on the way. Some seem less likely to produce side effects than others, so it may require a little trial and error to match the most favorable drug to each patient.

The medications which seem to enter the brain most easily, causing lethargy, nightmares, and other psychological side effects, include **Inderal**, and to a lesser extent, **Lopressor**, **Visken**, **Trandate**, **Normodyne**, and **Blocadren**. **Tenormin** and **Corgard** seem least likely to get into the nervous system and cause this type of difficulty. At the end of this chapter you will find a quick overview of these various beta blockers.

One word of caution. *Do not* ever discontinue any beta blocker suddenly on your own accord. And I mean *NEVER!* The following warning appears with the **Inderal** package insert provided to physicians and pharmacists. Unfortunately these health professionals don't always pass it on to their patients. But here it is for everyone to read.

IN PATIENTS WITH ANGINA PECTORIS, there have been reports of exacerbation of angina and, in some cases, myocardial infarction [heart attack], following *abrupt* discontinuation of INDERAL (propranolol) therapy. Therefore, when discontinuance of INDERAL is planned the dosage should be

gradually reduced and the patient carefully monitored. In addition, when INDERAL is prescribed for angina pectoris, the patient should be cautioned against interruption or cessation of therapy without the physician's advice. If INDERAL therapy is interrupted and exacerbation of angina occurs, it usually is advisable to reinstitute INDERAL therapy and take other measures appropriate for the management of unstable angina pectoris.[107]

The bottom line here is that beta blockers do relieve angina, do lower blood pressure, and *do* save lives. But picking the right patient, selecting the right brand, calculating the right dose, and deciding when to phase out the drugs are issues physicians must weigh carefully. We don't all need to have our beta receptors plugged with **Inderal, Lopressor, Corgard, Tenormin,** or **Blocadren**. If side effects begin to make life unbearable, maybe it's time to consider some other alternatives.

The Calcium Channel Blocker Challenge

The hottest heart drugs of the 1980s may ultimately not be beta blockers after all, but rather something called calcium channel blockers. Such drugs as **Calan** and **Isoptin** (verapamil), **Procardia** (nifedipine), and **Cardizem** (diltiazem) are catching on like wildfire. Cardiologists are excited, and many patients appear delighted with these newcomers. Not only do they seem to do just about everything the beta blockers do, in some cases they do it better and with fewer side effects.

One British cardiologist who has had considerable experience with these different drugs contrasted them.

Most patients don't tolerate beta-blockers exceedingly well because although the angina is relieved they become walking zombies . . . That is why we think that calcium blockers hold such an advantage over beta-blockers—because they will control stable angina as well.[108]

A Stanford physician was even more blunt. "When you take patients off the beta-blockers and put them on a calcium blocker, they feel as if they've been let out of prison."[109]

Now, most people think of calcium as pretty important stuff. From the time we're little squirts, and even after we're grown, everyone tells us that calcium is crucial for strong bones and healthy teeth—which it is. But calcium does much, much more. Its movement across cell membranes activates special proteins responsible for muscular contraction throughout the body. In practical terms that means that calcium plays a key role in keeping your heart beating, your lungs breathing, your biceps flexing, and your digestive tract functioning. In fact, the proper workings of almost everything in the body depend on the regulation of calcium.

If calcium is so darn important, then, why would anyone want to do anything so foolish as to block it? Not to worry. Medications like **Calan, Procardia,** and **Cardizem** don't actually cut off or block calcium; instead, they act more like traffic cops to regulate its proper flow. The clinical significance of such action is almost revolutionary in its scope.

Improved circulation, especially to the coronary arteries, has given people who suffer severe, debilitating angina a new lease on life. Dr. James Muller, a Harvard cardiologist, described a 43-year-old patient who had terrible attacks of chest pain almost every hour. "He had been on every medication available and nothing worked. When we tried nifedipine [**Procardia**] it completely stopped the pain just like a miracle drug."[110]

The calcium channel blockers have likely helped thousands of people to resume activities they had given up because of angina, and they did not develop the fatigue and depression associated with beta blockers. Some have gone back to work, others have rediscovered favorite sports like golf, swimming, and tennis. These medications have been a special godsend for people with asthma. Most people with breathing problems can't tolerate beta blockers since **Inderal, Corgard,** and others can seriously aggravate lung disease. Calcium antagonists, on the other hand, may actually prevent constriction of air passages, especially after exercise. Some investigators have even gone so far as to suggest that **Isoptin, Calan,** and **Procardia** may be beneficial in preventing exercise-induced asthma.[111–114]

But that is just the beginning of the good news. In some cases candidates for coronary bypasses have been spared surgery by the advent of this class of drugs. And when all else fails, the careful combination of a beta blocker and a calcium antagonist may be more effective than either drug alone. Although this regimen is still quite experimental (and not yet approved by the FDA), one British cardiologist is enthusiastic.

> In fact, we seem to have taken a lot of people with severe two- and three-vessel disease off the waiting list for surgery. Quite a few of our patients have been rejected for surgery because in England the waiting list is so long . . . these are people for whom you can't do anything so you put them on the drug combination. We had a waiting list of 18 months for surgery in our hopsital. Now, literally, the surgeons have come to us asking if we had any patients. They're getting a bit concerned. It's such a difference, really.[115]

Angina isn't the only symptom that responds to calcium blockers.

Calan and **Isoptin** have demonstrated an impressive ability to calm certain types of irregular heart rhythms. Nasty-sounding arrhythmias like paroxysmal supraventricular tachycardia often disappear almost magically after such medications. No other drug works as fast, efficiently, or safely for this abnormal heart condition.

Another benefit of **Procardia, Cardizem, Calan,** and **Isoptin** appears to be a reduction in high blood pressure.[116–121] Because of their ability to dilate arteries throughout the body, these agents can produce a dramatic improvement in hypertension, especially for people who have been resistant to other treatments or who experience potentially life-threatening hypertensive crisis. In preliminary studies the calcium blockers seem to be as good or better than beta blockers for some patients.

So far so good—but what about heart attack treatment and prevention? Here, too, there is hope that calcium channel blockers may have a role. Although it is yet too soon to tell whether such drugs can actually diminish the damage of an acute heart attack, reduce the risk of fatal fibrillation, or help prevent recurrences, investigators are extremely excited about animal research and are hopeful that major trials in human subjects will prove equally encouraging.[122–129] One preliminary study has indeed demonstrated a dramatic drop in heart attacks and sudden deaths among patients taking **Cardizem.**[130]

Nice, very nice. Theoretical, experimental, and far from proven, but it would be a big bonus if the calcium channel blockers turn out to be helpful against heart attacks. As long as we're speculating, try this on for size. Several researchers have tested the ability of calcium antagonists to prevent the development of atherosclerosis in animals.[131–133] The results are tantalizing. If these drugs could do the same thing in humans, we could be on our way to slowing or perhaps even stopping coronary-artery disease.[134]

But some clinicians claim that calcium channel blockers aren't the only route to that goal. For years I have listened to evangelists of EDTA (edetate disodium) therapy claim to do exactly that with their so-called Roto Rooter of the cardiovascular system. They claim that EDTA chelates (grabs on to) calcium and plaque in clogged blood vessels and removes them from the system. This is supposed to help relieve angina, reduce high blood pressure, improve stamina, stave off senility, and prevent "hardening of the arteries."[135] Patients are injected intravenously with EDTA as many as 20 or 30 times over the course of several months. At a cost of $50 to $100 per injection, the bill can quickly add up to thousands of dollars.

To say the medical establishment has been critical of EDTA would be an understatement. The publication *Physician's Drug Alert* dubbed this therapy the "Snake oil of the 1980's." I, too, have been highly critical, since solid scientific evidence to support EDTA's clinical effectiveness has been lacking. The claims just sounded too good, and for my money the whole thing smacked of scam.

But now, with the possibility that calcium antagonists may have a beneficial effect against atherosclerosis, we may have to reevaluate EDTA. All these drugs seem to have some similarity, since they act to regulate calcium within cells. Nevertheless, we still need a good double-blind controlled study with solid results before anyone can truly evaluate EDTA chelation. Stay tuned for future developments. Until further word I have moved from negative to neutral.

So far we *can* say that calcium channel blockers have developed an impressive track record in a very short time. Not only do they work wonders against angina, but some seem valuable against irregular heart beats and high blood pressure. They may even be helpful in cases of asthma and heart attacks.

But that's not all. A surprising number of other potential benefits have been reported in the medical literature. A team of Canadian investigators has reported that its preliminary research suggests that a low dose of **Cardizem** may help to prevent severe migraine headaches.[136] And a group of French physicians has found that **Procardia** reduces both the frequency and severity of migraines in a small study of patients who also suffered something called Raynaud's phenomenon.[137]

Speaking of Raynaud's, guess what? Yup, calcium channel blockers seem to be helpful for this painful and occasionally debilitating ailment, too. People who have Raynaud's experience numbness, tingling, or burning in their hands and feet when exposed to cold temperatures or emotional stress. This condition seems to be caused by constricting spasms in the arteries that supply the extremities.

Doctors usually tell people who suffer from Raynaud's to avoid cold temperatures—something that is easier said than done for many folks. Barbiturates have been prescribed, along with blood pressure medicines like **Serpasil** (reserpine), **Aldomet** (methyldopa), or **Minipress** (prazosin). But these medications are only partially effective, and reserpine and methyldopa in particular can produce unpleasant side effects.

Calcium channel blockers to the rescue. Remember that these drugs seem to be effective in relieving blood-vessel spasms all over the body—heart, brain, lungs, or skin. A number of well-controlled studies now show that **Procardia** can reduce both the frequency and severity of such attacks.[138-141]

I should probably stop here and not mention some of the more unusual and as yet unproven uses of calcium channel blockers, but what the heck. Just remember that what you are about to read is still very experimental, though tantalizing.

Researchers have reason to believe that such drugs as **Procardia** may be helpful in relieving the pain of severe menstrual cramps and in treating premature labor.[142-145] There are even whispers that some of these agents may reduce brain damage during certain kinds of strokes.[146] Physicians providing emergency services are excited about the possibility that calcium blockers may be useful in some spinal-cord injuries and may extend brain survival in patients who have stopped breathing and are considered "clinically dead."[147] There are also reports that such drugs could prevent kidney failure associated with severe blood loss.[148] And I have even heard that cancer researchers are looking into the possibility these drugs may be helpful in improving current cancer treatments.[149]

By now you are probably getting the impression that calcium channel blockers are the greatest. *Stop!* There are two very important caveats. First, enthusiasm is easy when there's no solid data to refute early claims. In the cold hard light of well-controlled research, initial excitement often fades fast. Will the calcium antagonists deliver on all the potential promises? Of course not—no drug could. Are they useful for angina, irregular heart beats, high blood pressure, and Raynaud's phenomenon? You bet! Will they prevent arteriosclerosis and heart attacks, relieve migraines, ease asthma, and all the rest? Only time will tell. But even if they don't pan out for everything, you can't take away the primary benefits.

Second, these drugs *do* have side effects. Remember, we always have to pay the piper. Overall, with the information available to date, they seem well tolerated, and the number of people who develop adverse reactions is quite low. Because of important differences among these medications, it is not good to generalize, but the most common problems include constipation (primarily with **Calan** and **Isoptin**), light-headedness, headache, flushing, nausea, nervousness, and leg edema. For a more detailed analysis of the currently known side effects associated with beta blockers and calcium channel blockers, turn to the table at the end of this chapter.

Tying Up the Loose Ends

Well, my friend, we have come a long way in this chapter: from the mystery of MRFIT to the magic of aspirin; from the surprises of streptokinase for heart attacks to the benefits of beta blockers. And let's not forget the exciting challenge of the calcium channel blockers. There is no doubt that we are smack-dab in the middle of a revolution—a revolution in the treatment of our number-one killer, heart disease. But despite these important advances, never forget one thing: prevention is still the best medicine!

To keep those coronary arteries from getting clogged in the first place, it's only good common sense to try to lower your risks as much as possible. But like saving for a rainy day, it's a lot easier to think about than to do. If you're like me, you've been promising yourself to eat more sensibly for a long time. For months I've been dreaming about losing weight and getting more exercise—as soon as I finish this book. Probably we should all rearrange our priorities, so that we won't put off "living right" until it's too late. But unfortunately none of the risk-reducing strategies come complete with money-back guarantees.

After years of controversy, cholesterol is once again back on center stage. A major study by the National Heart, Lung, and Blood Institute found that reducing blood cholesterol does seem to diminish the likelihood of heart attacks.[150] To get those high-risk cholesterol levels down, researchers used a double-pronged attack of diet and drug. Like any medication, **Questran** (cholestyramine) has side effects (constipation, gas, and other digestive upset) and can be very expensive. Cutting back on the fat in your diet, however, can save you money and surely can only help.

Exercise, too, has long been a standby in any heart-attack prevention program. It comes as a great surprise to most people to learn that scientists are having trouble proving that it is really protective.[151] But even without indisputable proof, there does seem to be some evidence that it helps. More importantly, people who are physically fit feel better about themselves, and that is more than half the battle.

If you're not used to exercising though, don't go out and overdo. And for goodness' sake, *do* cool down slowly! The latest research indicates that people who stop suddenly and stand around shooting the breeze seem more at risk of heart problems.[152]

I could go on and on boring you with lectures about how to stop smoking (for information about how **Nicorette** chewing gum can help reduce withdrawal symptoms, see page 369) and improve your lifestyle. But by now I know you've heard it all before. None of these precautions is surefire, but it's like insurance: would you consider not having your home insured? Would you drive a car without coverage? For most of us, the premiums are "wasted" because calamities are really quite rare. And yet we would never dream of not preparing for emergencies.

The odds are far higher that you could suffer a heart attack than that your house will burn down. Don't you owe it to yourself and your family to treat your body at least as well as you treat your car and your house?

TABLE OF HEART DRUGS

This table will provide some practical information about side effects, precautions, and dangerous drug interactions. It is not possible to list every adverse reaction nor all potential drug interactions. Those side effects that may be serious are preceded by an asterisk (*). Contact your physician *immediately* if any occur. Other side effects should not be ignored. They, too, should be brought to the doctor's attention without undue delay.

The information is merely intended to provide some overall guidelines for effective drug use and is not meant to substitute for good communications between you and your physician and pharmacist.

THE BETA BLOCKERS

The beta blockers have come to dominate the treatment of heart disease and high blood pressure. **Inderal** is the most widely prescribed drug in the United States, and other beta blockers like **Lopressor**, **Tenormin**, and **Corgard** are hot on its heels. In general these drugs decrease heart rate and reduce blood pressure. By slowing the pulse, they allow the heart to take it a little easier, use less oxygen and thereby prevent (or reduce) the pain of angina.

Although all the beta blockers are effective in lowering blood pressure by themselves, they are most often prescribed together with a mild diuretic. The combination seems to reduce blood pressure more effectively than either drug alone. Most of the currently available beta blockers work in a very similar fashion, though some important differences do exist and are summarized under each drug in the table below.

Blocadren *(timolol 5 mg, 10 mg, and 20 mg tablets)*
Timoptic *(timolol 0.25% and 0.50% opthalmic solution)*

MFR: Merck Sharp & Dohme

FDA APPROVED USES: Hypertension and prevention of recurrent heart attacks. Timolol, also marketed as **Timoptic**, is used in drop form for glaucoma.

USUAL DOSE:
- Hypertension: 10mg to 20mg (occasionally up to 30mg) twice daily.
- Prevention of recurrent heart attacks: 10mg twice daily.
- Glaucoma: 1 drop of 0.25% or 1 drop of 0.50% opthalmic solution in affected eye(s) twice daily.

Blocadren was the first beta blocker to be officially approved for use in preventing repeat heart attacks (though others, such as **Inderal** and **Lopressor**, are just as likely to help). Timolol is also the only beta blocker that comes in eyedrop form for use in glaucoma (brand name **Timoptic**). If you asked me what real advantages **Blocadren** has over other any of the other beta blockers, I would be hard put to give you an answer. One slight advantage is convenience. Instead of taking a pill three or four times a day (as with **Inderal**), you only need two **Blocadrens**.

(continues next page)

Blocadren, Timoptic *(continued)*

PRECAUTIONS (oral tablets):
- May mask the signs and symptoms of dangerously low blood sugar in diabetics.
- May decrease your tolerance for strenuous exercise.
- If you have high blood pressure, do not take OTC decongestants, diet aids, or asthma medications without first consulting your doctor; they may aggravate hypertension.
- Do not abruptly stop taking this drug. Doing so many aggravate heart conditions and, rarely, may precipitate a heart attack.
- Do not take if you are asthmatic or have breathing problems.

PRECAUTIONS (ophthalmic solution):
- May transiently blur vision.
- When applying drops, press the corner of the eye, near the bridge of the nose, for at least one minute. This may prevent some of the medication from being absorbed through the tear ducts.
- Do not touch the tip of the dropper to your eye or any other surface.

PREGNANCY AND BREAST-FEEDING.
- Use in pregnancy has not been proven safe. Possible adverse effects to the baby from timolol are unclear.
- Timolol is found in breast milk, at least in animal studies. Whether it also appears in human breast milk is unknown. Breast-feeding should probably be stopped if **Blocadren** therapy is necessary.

COMMON SIDE EFFECTS (oral tablets):
- Drowsiness.
- Fatigue, decreased tolerance of exercise.
- Dry skin, eyes, mouth.
- Slow heart rate (contact your doctor if it is less than 50 beats per minute).
- Nausea, diarrhea (relatively common).
- Tingling sensation in fingers, toes.
*▪ Excessive faintness or dizziness from low blood pressure.

COMMON SIDE EFFECTS (ophthalmic solution):
- Slight reduction in heart rate.
- Blurred vision after instillation of eye drops.
*▪ Mild eye irritation.

UNCOMMON SIDE EFFECTS (oral tablets):
- Upset stomach.
- Nightmares, vivid dreams, hallucinations.
- Anxiety, insomnia, nervousness.

* *These side effects may be serious. Contact your physician immediately if they occur.*

Blocadren, Timoptic *(continued)*

- Constipation.
- Headache.
*- Mental depression, excess drowsiness, confusion (more common with higher doses and in the elderly).
*- Breathing difficulty (much more common in persons with asthma or other respiratory condition).
*- Unusually cold hands, toes, fingers.
*- Rash (allergic reaction; rare).
*- Unexplained sore throat with fever (rare).
*- Unexplained bleeding or bruising (rare).

UNCOMMON SIDE EFFECTS (ophthalmic solution):
*- Visual disturbances (infrequent).
*- Numbness of eye (rare).
*- Drooping eyelids (rare).

NOTE: Many of the side effects seen with the oral dosages have also been reported in persons using timolol eyedrops. In theory, any of the listed adverse reactions associated with **Blocadren** is also possible for **Timoptic**. In practice, most of them occur only very rarely.

SEXUAL SIDE EFFECTS:
- Not enough data to ascertain, but theoretically more than with atenolol or nadolol.

DRUG INTERACTIONS (oral tablets):
- The effects of a dose of insulin are increased by timolol. Of more concern is the ability of timolol to block most of the characteristic symptoms of dangerously low blood sugar. Diabetics, beware!
- The beneficial effects of **Theo-Dur**, **Bronkodyl**, **Respbid**, and dozens more (all theophylline), **Choledyl** (oxtriphylline), **Aminodur**, **Somophyllin**, and others (all aminophylline), and **Neothylline** and others (dyphylline) are decreased by timolol. An increased dose of the above drugs may be necessary to maintain desirable asthma control. Also note that timolol may exacerbate asthma and other respiratory conditions. Using **Blocadren** in these patients is not recommended.
- **Minipress** (prazosin) effects may be markedly increased by timolol. Adding **Minipress** to a blood-pressure treatment regimen already containing timolol may cause acutely low blood pressure.

DRUG INTERACTIONS (ophthalmic solution):
- Oral beta blockers: **Timoptic** can be absorbed to some extent through the tear ducts and can have additive effects with other orally taken beta blockers; such an interaction is unlikely to be of real concern, however.

* *These side effects may be serious. Contact your physician immediately if they occur.*

Corgard *(nadolol 40 mg, 80 mg, 120 mg, and 160 mg tablets)*

MFR: Squibb & Sons, Inc.

FDA APPROVED USES: Hypertension and angina.

USUAL DOSE:
- Hypertension: 80 mg to 320 mg once daily. Rarely, higher doses may be needed.
- Angina: 80 mg to 240 mg once daily.

Corgard is the only beta blocker which, given as a single daily dose, is approved for use in both hypertension and angina. Its two big advantages over **Inderal** are its once-daily dosing and its relative lack of side effects related to the central nervous system (drowsiness, depression, sexual dysfunction, etc.).

PRECAUTIONS:
- May mask the signs and symptoms of dangerously low blood sugar in diabetics.
- May decrease your tolerance for strenuous exercise.
- If you have high blood pressure, do not take OTC decongestants, diet aids, or asthma medications without first consulting your doctor; they may aggravate hypertension.
- Do not abruptly stop taking this drug. Doing so may aggravate heart conditions or, rarely, precipitate a heart attack.
- Do not take if you are asthmatic or have respiratory difficulty.

PREGNANCY AND BREAST-FEEDING:
- Use in pregnancy has not been proven safe. Do not use while pregnant unless absolutely necessary.
- Nadolol is found in breast milk, at least in animal studies. Studies have not been done to determine whether nadolol is present in human breast milk. It is probably prudent not to breast-feed while taking this drug.

COMMON SIDE EFFECTS:
- Decreased tolerance of exercise.
- Dry skin, eyes, mouth.
- Slow heart rate (contact your doctor if it is less than 50 beats per minute).
- Nausea and diarrhea (relatively common).
- Tingling sensation in fingers, toes.
- *∎ Excessive faintness or dizziness from low blood pressure.

UNCOMMON SIDE EFFECTS:
- Drowsiness, fatigue (probably occurs less frequently than with propranolol and metoprolol).

* *These side effects may be serious. Contact your physician immediately if they occur.*

Corgard, *(continued)*

- Upset stomach.
- Nightmares, vivid dreams, hallucinations (probably occur much less frequently than with propranolol and metoprolol).
- Anxiety, insomnia, nervousness (probably occur less frequently than with propranolol and metoprolol).
- Constipation.
- Headache.
*∎ Mental depression, excess drowsiness, confusion (probably occur less frequently than with propranolol and metoprolol).
*∎ Rash (allergic reaction; rare).
*∎ Unexplained sore throat with fever (rare).
*∎ Unexplained bleeding, bruising (rare).
*∎ Breathing difficulty (much more common in persons with asthma or other respiratory condition).
*∎ Unusually cold hands, toes, fingers.

SEXUAL SIDE EFFECTS:
*∎ Probably less likely. May be a good therapeutic substitute for **Inderal** and **Lopressor** if they cause sexual problems.

DRUG INTERACTIONS:
*∎ The effects of a dose of insulin are increased by nadolol. Of more concern is the ability of nadolol to block most of the characteristic symptoms of dangerously low blood sugar. Diabetics, beware!
*∎ The beneficial effects of **Theo-Dur**, **Bronkodyl**, **Respbid**, and dozens more (all theophylline), **Choledyl** (oxtriphylline), **Aminodur**, **Somophyllin**, and others (all aminophylline), and **Neothylline** and others (dyphylline) are decreased by nadolol. An increased dose of the above drugs may be necessary to maintain desirable asthma control. Also note that nadolol may exacerbate asthma and other respiratory conditions. Using **Corgard** in these patients is not recommended.
- **Minipress** (prazosin) effects may be markedly increased by nadolol. Adding **Minipress** to a blood-pressure treatment regimen already containing nadolol may cause acutely low blood pressure.

Inderal *(propranolol 10 mg, 20 mg, 40 mg, 80 mg, and 90 mg tablets)*
Inderal LA *(propranolol sustained release formula 80 mg, 120 mg, and 160 mg capsules)*

MFR: Ayerst Laboratories

(continues next page)

* *These side effects may be serious. Contact your physician immediately if they occur.*

Inderal, Inderal LA *(continued)*

FDA APPROVED USES: Hypertension; angina, abnormal heart rhythms, prevention of migraine headaches, repeat heart attacks, and several other rare disease states. Although not officially sanctioned for such, **Inderal** may help to alleviate the panic-induced symptoms of stage fright.

USUAL DOSE: (Doses vary widely according to individual needs and according to the illness being treated).

- Hypertension: usual doses are between 40 mg twice daily and 320 mg twice daily (or the equivalent of the sustained-release formula given once daily). Doses above or below these limits are not uncommon.
- Angina: 10 mg to 20 mg three or four times daily, up to 320 mg per day (or, if symptoms permit, the equivalent of the sustained-release formula given once daily). Higher doses are not much more effective.
- Abnormal heart rhythms: 10 mg to 30 mg, three or four times daily (the sustained-release formula is not approved for use in these conditions).
- Migraine prevention: 20 mg four times daily up to 240 mg per day (or the equivalent of the sustained-release formula given once daily).

Inderal, the granddaddy of the beta blockers, is still the most frequently prescribed of the lot. Although its utility and effectiveness are unquestioned, some of the newer beta blockers have distinct advantages over propranolol. **Inderal** is a "nonselective" beta blocker in that it affects not only the heart, but blood vessels and lung tissue as well. This leads to trouble for asthmatics and others with breathing problems, and in fact, propranolol should not be used by these people. **Inderal** also aggravates hypoglycemia (dangerously low blood sugar) in diabetics and should probably be prescribed very carefully, if at all, for these persons.

In recent years some physicians have become concerned that **Inderal** and several other beta blockers may raise triglyceride levels in the blood (**Corgard** is an exception which actually lowers triglycerides). They have voiced the fear that this elevation in blood fat (and a concomitant reduction in a protective substance called HDL (high density lipoprotein cholesterol) may increase the risk of atherosclerosis and coronary artery disease after many years of continuous use. The benefits of lowered blood pressure could conceivably be partly reversed by this negative effect. As of this writing, however, this problem is of more theoretical than practical concern.

Another unfortunate property of propranolol, which has been overcome by some of the newer beta blockers, is its ability to enter the

Inderal, Inderal LA (continued)

central nervous system (brain) and cause drowsiness, depression, memory loss, lethargy, nightmares, and sexual problems. **Inderal** is, in general, also susceptible to more drug interactions than some of the others. It should be noted, however, that **Inderal** is the only beta blocker that is indicated for use in certain cardiac arrythmias (disturbances of heart rhythm). **Inderal** isn't a bad drug, and I wouldn't go out of my way to suggest that people who are comfortably taking it suddenly switch to another beta blocker. However, **Tenormin** (atenolol; see below) has many positive features that **Inderal** doesn't and is one of my favorite beta blockers for use in hypertension these days.

PRECAUTIONS:
- Taking **Inderal** with food allows for better absorption into the blood stream.
- May mask the signs and symptoms of dangerously low blood sugar in diabetics.
- May decrease your tolerance for strenuous exercise.
- If you have high blood pressure, do not take OTC decongestants, diet aids, or asthma medications without first consulting your doctor; they may aggravate hypertension.
- Do not abruptly stop taking this drug. Doing so may aggravate heart conditions or may, rarely, precipitate a heart attack.
- Do not take if you are asthmatic or have respiratory difficulty.

PREGNANCY AND BREAST-FEEDING:
- Use in pregnancy has not been proven safe. Possible adverse effects to the baby from propranolol are unclear.
- Propranolol is found in small amounts in breast milk. Although no problems have yet been reported, breast-feeding should probably be stopped if **Inderal** therapy is necessary.

COMMON SIDE EFFECTS:
- Drowsiness (fairly common, especially at higher doses).
- Fatigue and decreased tolerance of exercise.
- Dry skin, eyes, mouth.
- Slow heart rate (contact your doctor if it is less than 50 beats per minute).
- Nausea and diarrhea (relatively common).
- Tingling sensation in fingers, toes.
*- Excessive faintness or dizziness from low blood pressure.

UNCOMMON SIDE EFFECTS:
- Upset stomach.

(continues next page)

*** These side effects may be serious. Contact your physician immediately if they occur.**

Inderal, Inderal LA *(continued)*

- Nightmares, vivid dreams, hallucinations.
- Anxiety, insomnia, nervousness.
- Constipation.
- Headache.
- Hair loss.
*• Mental depression, disorientation, excess drowsiness, memory loss, confusion (occurs more commonly with higher doses and in the elderly).
*• Breathing difficulty (much more common in persons with asthma or other respiratory condition).
*• Unusually cold hands, toes, and fingers.
*• Rash (allergic reaction; rare).
*• Unexplained sore throat with fever (rare).
*• Unexplained bleeding or bruising (rare).

SEXUAL SIDE EFFECTS:
- Impotence (not uncommon).
- Decreased libido (not uncommon).
- Peyronie's disease (painful, curved penile erections—rare).

DRUG INTERACTIONS:
- **Amytal** (amobarbital), **Butisol** (butabarbital), **Gemonil** (metharbital), **Lotusate** (talbutal), **Luminal** (phenobarbital), **Mebaral** (mephobarbital), **Mysoline** (primidone), **Nembutal** (pentobarbital), **Seconal** (secobarbital), **Tuinal** (amobarbital and secobarbital), and others (all barbiturates) decrease the effectiveness of propranolol by increasing its metabolism.
- **Thorazine** (chlorpromazine) increases the levels of propranolol in the blood, and possibly vice-versa.
- The effects of a dose of insulin are increased by propranolol. Of more concern is the ability of propranolol to block most of the characteristic symptoms of dangerously low blood sugar. Diabetics, beware!
- The beneficial effects of **Theo-Dur**, **Bronkodyl**, **Respbid** and dozens more (all theophylline), **Choledyl** (oxtriphylline), **Aminodur, Somophyllin,** and others (all aminophylline), and **Neothylline** and others (dyphylline) are decreased by propranolol. An increased dose of the above drugs may be necessary to maintain desirable asthma control. Also note that propranolol may exacerbate asthma and other respiratory conditions. Using **Inderal** in these patients is not recommended.
- **Minipress** (prazosin) effects may be markedly increased by propranolol.

* These side effects may be serious. Contact your physician immediately if they occur.

Inderal, Inderal LA *(continued)*

Adding **Minipress** to a blood pressure treatment regimen already containing propranolol may cause acutely low blood pressure.

- **Tagamet** (cimetidine) can markedly enhance the levels of propranolol in the blood. Excessively slow heart rate and blood pressure may result. (Note: **Tagamet** and **Inderal** are both *very* commonly prescribed.)
- Birth-control pills can increase the blood levels of propranolol.
- **Rimactane** (rifampin) decreases the amount of propranolol that is absorbed into the blood stream.
- Smoking can decrease the effectiveness of propranolol by increasing its metabolism.

Lopressor *(metoprolol 50 mg and 100 mg tablets)*

MFR: Ciba-Geigy

FDA APPROVED USES: Hypertension, prevention of repeat heart attacks. Metoprolol seems effective in angina as well.

USUAL DOSE:
- Hypertension: 100 mg once daily up to 450 mg daily as a single dose or in divided doses. Once-daily dosage is most common and is one of the advantages of metoprolol; but lower doses given every twelve hours controls blood pressure more effectively than one daily dose.

Lopressor is regarded as a "cardioselective" beta blocker and, as such, has some advantages over the "nonselective" **Inderal**. This selectivity means that at lower doses other organs, such as the lungs and blood vessels, are not as affected as the heart. Although selectivity disappears as the doses are increased, asthmatics and diabetics may find this a potential alternative to propranolol. Like **Inderal**, **Lopressor** can enter the brain relatively easily and therefore may share similar side effects, such as drowsiness, depression, confusion, memory loss, and sexual problems.

PRECAUTIONS:
- Taking **Lopressor** with food allows for better absorption into the blood stream.
- May mask the signs and symptoms of dangerously low blood sugar in diabetics.

(continues next page)

Lopressor, *(continued)*

- May decrease your tolerance for strenuous exercise.
- If you have high blood pressure, do not take OTC decongestants, diet aids, or asthma medications without first consulting your doctor; they may aggravate hypertension.
- Do not abruptly stop taking this drug. Doing so may aggravate heart conditions or may, rarely, precipitate a heart attack.
- Beta blockers may cause bronchial constriction and therefore cause or aggravate asthmatic attacks. **Lopressor** is less likely than the others (except **Tenormin**) to have this effect, but only when used in moderate doses (200 mg daily or less).

PREGNANCY AND BREAST-FEEDING:
- Use in pregnancy has not been proven safe. Do not use while pregnant unless absolutely necessary.
- No studies have been done to detect metoprolol in breast milk; therefore its safety while breast-feeding is unknown. It is probably prudent not to breast-feed while taking this drug.

COMMON SIDE EFFECTS:
- Drowsiness (fairly common, especially at higher doses).
- Fatigue and decreased tolerance of exercise.
- Dry skin, eyes, mouth.
- Slow heart rate (contact your doctor if it is less than 50 beats per minute).
- Nausea and diarrhea (relatively common).
- Tingling sensation in fingers or toes.
*- Excessive faintness or dizziness from low blood pressure.

UNCOMMON SIDE EFFECTS:
- Upset stomach.
- Nightmares, vivid dreams, hallucinations.
- Anxiety, insomnia, nervousness.
- Constipation.
- Headache.
- Hair loss.
*- Mental depression, excess drowsiness, memory loss, confusion (occurs more commonly with higher doses and in the elderly).
*- Rash (allergic reaction; rare).
*- Unexplained sore throat with fever (rare).
*- Unexplained bleeding or bruising (rare).

---

* These side effects may be serious. Contact your physician immediately if they occur.

Lopressor, *(continued)*

SEXUAL SIDE EFFECTS:
- Impotence and decreased libido (incidence unknown, but probably similar to **Inderal's**).
- Peyronie's disease (painful, curved penile erections—rare).

DRUG INTERACTIONS:
- **Alurate** (aprobarbital), **Amytal** (amobarbital), **Butisol** (butabarbital), **Gemonil** (metharbital), **Lotusate** (talbutal). **Luminal** (phenobarbital), **Mebaral** (mephobarbital), **Mysoline** (primidone), **Nembutal** (pentobarbital), **Seconal** (secobarbital), **Tuinal** (amobarbital and secobarbital), and others (all barbiturates) decrease the effectiveness of metoprolol by increasing its metabolism.
- **Thorazine** (chlorpromazine) increases the levels of metoprolol in the blood, and possibly vice-versa.
- The beneficial effects of **Theo-Dur**, **Bronkodyl**, **Respbid**, and dozens more (all theophylline), **Choledyl** (oxytriphylline), **Aminodur**, **Somophyllin**, and others (all aminophylline), and **Neothylline** and others (dyphylline) are decreased by metoprolol. An increased dose of the above drugs may be necessary to maintain desirable asthma control.
- **Minipress** (prazosin) effects may be markedly increased by metoprolol. Adding **Minipress** to a blood-pressure treatment regimen already containing metoprolol may cause acutely low blood pressure.
- **Tagamet** (cimetidine) can markedly enhance the levels of metoprolol in the blood. Excessively slow heart rate and blood pressure may result.
- Birth-control pills can increase the blood levels of metoprolol.
- **Rimactane** (rifampin) may decrease the amount of beta blocker absorbed into the blood stream.

Tenormin *(atenolol 50 mg and 100 mg tablets)*

MFR: Stuart Pharmaceuticals

FDA APPROVED USES: Hypertension. Although not yet approved for such, atenolol may be effective in the treatment of angina.

USUAL DOSE:
- Hypertension: 50 mg to 100 mg once daily.

Tenormin, like **Lopressor**, is "cardioselective," and the same caveats apply. Both of these drugs are less likely (at least at lower doses)

(continues next page)

Tenormin, *(continued)*

than the other beta blockers to cause bronchoconstriction (tightening of the airways in the lung) and therefore to worsen asthma and other respiratory problems. Some beta blockers are more likely to enter the brain and cause drowsiness and depression; these reactions are more pronounced in the elderly. **Tenormin** and **Corgard** are probably less likely to produce these side effects. Because **Tenormin** is the only beta blocker that is both cardioselective and does not easily penetrate the central nervous system, it is probably the best therapeutic choice among the beta blockers for use in hypertension. Another advantage is that it needs to be taken only once daily.

PRECAUTIONS:
- May mask the signs and symptoms of dangerously low blood sugar in diabetics.
- May decrease your tolerance for strenuous exercise and fatigue.
- If you have high blood pressure, do not take OTC decongestants, diet aids, or asthma medications without first consulting your doctor; they may aggravate hypertension.
- Do not abruptly stop taking this drug. Doing so may aggravate heart conditions or, rarely, may precipitate a heart attack.
- Asthma patients must be cautious with any beta blocker, even one that is theoretically safer than the others. At the first signs of breathing difficulty contact your physician!

PREGNANCY AND BREAST-FEEDING:
- Use in pregnancy has not been proven safe. Do not use while pregnant unless absolutely necessary.
- No studies have been done to detect atenolol in breast milk; therefore its safety while breast-feeding is unknown. It is probably prudent not to breast-feed while taking this drug.

COMMON SIDE EFFECTS:
- Decreased tolerance of exercise.
- Dry skin, eyes, mouth.
- Slow heart rate (contact your doctor if it is less than 50 beats per minute).
- Nausea and diarrhea (relatively common).
- Tingling sensation in fingers or toes.
*- Excessive faintness or dizziness from low blood pressure.

UNCOMMON SIDE EFFECTS:
- Drowsiness (probably much less frequent than with **Inderal** and **Lopressor**).

These side effects may be serious. Contact your physician immediately if they occur.

Tenormin, *(continued)*

- Upset stomach.
- Nightmares, vivid dreams, hallucinations (probably much less frequent than with **Inderal** and **Lopressor**).
- Anxiety, insomnia, nervousness (probably much less frequent than with **Inderal** and **Lopressor**).
- Constipation.
- Headache.
*- Mental depression, excess drowsiness, or confusion (probably occur much less frequently than with **Inderal** and **Lopressor**).
*- Rash (allergic reaction; rare).
*- Unexplained sore throat with fever (rare).
*- Unexplained bleeding or bruising (rare).

SEXUAL SIDE EFFECTS:
- May be much less likely than with other beta blockers. May be a good therapeutic substitute for **Inderal** or **Lopressor** if they should cause sexual problems.

DRUG INTERACTIONS:
- **Tenormin** is less likely to give asthma patients problems; nevertheless, anyone with breathing trouble will have to be cautious about taking this medicine and combining it with theophylline or any other asthma medicine. Check this out carefully with your physician!
- **Minipress** (prazosin) effects may be markedly increased by beta blockers. Adding **Minipress** to a blood-pressure treatment regimen already containing a beta blocker may cause acutely low blood pressure.

Trandate and Normodyne *(labetalol 200 and 300 mg tablets)*

MFR: **Trandate**: Glaxo
   Normodyne: Schering

FDA APPROVED USES: Hypertension.

USUAL DOSE: Starting dose is 100 mg twice daily: to be adjusted according to patient's response. Older people and those with reduced liver function may require lower doses.

And here we have the latest in the beta blocker sweepstakes. This drug is a little different from many of its predecessors because it also blocks

(continues next page)

* *These side effects may be serious. Contact your physician immediately if they occur.*

Trandate and Normodyne, *(continued)*

alpha receptors. I know, I know, what's an alpha? Never mind . . . you don't really want to know. Suffice it to say that this little extra pharmacological action doesn't dramatically change the nature of this drug. Labetalol may be less likely to cause cold hands and feet or slow heart rate, but it is not a dramatic advance over traditional therapy.

PRECAUTIONS:
- Patients with severe heart disease ("sick sinus syndrome" or very slow heart rate) should not receive labetalol.
- May mask the signs and symptoms of dangerously low blood sugar in diabetics.
- Taking labetalol with food allows for better absorption.
- If you have high blood pressure, do not take OTC decongestants, diet aids, or asthma medications without first consulting your doctor; they may aggravate hypertension.
- Labetalol may make asthma worse.
- Do not abruptly stop taking this drug. Doing so may aggravate heart conditions, or may, rarely, precipitate a heart attack.
- Caution should be used when labetalol is taken by people with reduced liver function. If jaundice develops, notify your doctor immediately so drug can be withdrawn.

PREGNANCY AND BREAST-FEEDING:
- Use in pregnancy has not been proven safe; however at the time of this writing, no fetal malformations have been reported.
- Preliminary data suggests this drug may be helpful in pregnancy-associated hypertension, but benefit must be carefully weighed against potential risk to fetus.
- Labetalol is found in small amounts in breast milk. Although no problems have yet been reported, breast-feeding should probably be stopped if labetalol therapy is necessary.

COMMON SIDE EFFECTS:
- *■ Dizziness, lightheadedness (occurs in 9-20% of people taking the drug).
- ■ Nausea, vomiting, constipation, indigestion (from 8-15% incidence).
- ■ Fatigue, lethargy, muscle cramps (5-33% incidence).
- ■ Tingling of scalp (incidence from 4-12%; Common initially, but tends to go away. Heat makes this effect worse.)
- ■ Headache, visual disturbances (from 2–9% incidence).
- *■ Skin rash (up to 6%).

* *These side effects may be serious. Contact your physician immediately if they occur.*

Trandate and Normodyne, *(continued)*

UNCOMMON SIDE EFFECTS:
- Nasal stuffiness (may affect as many as 4%).
- Diarrhea.
- Drowsiness.
*■ Mental depression, short-term memory loss, disorientation, nightmares.
*■ Collagen disorders (lupus).
- Dry eyes.
- Reversible hair loss.
*■ Difficult urination.
- Tingling sensation in fingers, toes (less common than with other beta blockers).
*■ Breathing difficulty (much more common in persons with asthma or other respiratory problems).

SEXUAL SIDE EFFECTS:
- Failure to ejaculate.
- Impotence.
- Peyronie's disease (painful, curved penile erections—rare).

DRUG INTERACTIONS:
At the time of this writing, labetalol is so new that few drug interactions have been reported. Doubtless many interactions not listed below will eventually be documented.
- **Tagamet** increases the effect of labetalol.
- Tricyclic antidepressants such as **Elavil**, **Triavil**, **Norpramin**, **Tofranil** and many others may cause tremor when taken with labetalol.
- Labetalol may cause dangerously low blood pressure in combination with the surgical anesthetic halothane.
- The beneficial effects of **Theo-Dur**, **Bronkodyl**, **Respbid**, and dozens more (all theophylline), **Choledyl** (oxtriphylline), **Aminodur**, **Somophyllin**, and others (all aminophylline), and **Neophylline** and others (dyphylline) are decreased by labetalol.
- Nitroglycerin together wtih labetalol may cause blood pressure to drop lower than expected.

Visken *(pindolol 5 mg and 10 mg tablets)*

MFR: Sandoz Pharmaceuticals

FDA APPROVED USES: Hypertension. Although not currently approved for use in angina, it is probably effective.

(continues next page)

* *These side effects may be serious. Contact your physician immediately if they occur.*

Visken, *(continued)*

USUAL DOSE:
- Hypertension: 20 mg to 60 mg daily, usually divided into two or three daily doses. Many people respond well to 5 mg three times a day.

Visken is unique in that it can both block and stimulate certain beta receptors. What this means in practical terms is yet to be fully determined, but it appears that the pulse is slowed to a lesser degree with **Visken** than with other beta blockers. This may be of advantage to some persons.

PRECAUTIONS:
- May mask the signs and symptoms of dangerously low blood sugar in diabetics.
- May decrease your tolerance for strenuous exercise.
- If you have high blood pressure, do not take OTC decongestants, diet aids, or asthma medications without first consulting your doctor; they may aggravate hypertension.
- Do not abruptly stop taking this drug. Doing so may aggravate heart conditions or, rarely, may precipitate a heart attack.
- Do not take if you are asthmatic or have respiratory difficulty.

PREGNANCY AND BREAST-FEEDING:
- Safety for use during pregnancy has not been proven. Do not use while pregnant unless absolutely necessary.
- Pindolol is found in human breast milk. Do not breast-feed if you must take this medicine.

COMMON SIDE EFFECTS:
- Weight gain (averaging about three pounds).
- Drowsiness.
- Fatigue and decreased tolerance of exercise.
- Dry skin, eyes, mouth.
- Nausea and diarrhea (relatively common).
- Tingling sensation in fingers, toes.
- *■ Excessive faintness or dizziness from low blood pressure.

UNCOMMON SIDE EFFECTS:
- Slow heart rate (less than the other beta blockers).
- Upset stomach.
- Insomnia, nightmares, vivid dreams, hallucinations.
- Anxiety, insomnia, nervousness.
- Constipation.
- Headache.

* *These side effects may be serious. Contact your physician immediately if they occur.*

Visken, *(continued)*

*▪ Mental depression, excess drowsiness, or confusion (occurs more commonly with higher doses and in the elderly).
*▪ Breathing difficulty (much more common in persons with asthma or other respiratory condition; *may* be less than with propranolol, nadolol, and timolol).
*▪ Unusually cold hands, toes, and fingers (*may* be less than with propranolol, nadolol, and timolol).
*▪ Rash (allergic, reaction; rare).
*▪ Unexplained sore throat with fever (rare).
*▪ Unexplained bleeding or bruising (rare).

SEXUAL SIDE EFFECTS:
▪ Not enough data to tell at this time.

DRUG INTERACTIONS:
▪ The effects of a dose of insulin are increased by pindolol. Of more concern is the ability of pindolol to block most of the characteristic symptoms of dangerously low blood sugar. Diabetics, beware!
▪ The beneficial effects of **Theo-Dur**, **Bronkodyl**, **Respbid**, and dozens more (all theophylline), **Choledyl** (oxtriphylline), **Aminodur**, **Somophyllin**, and others (all aminophylline), and **Neothylline** and others (dyphylline) are decreased by pindolol. An increased dose of the above drugs may be necessary to maintain desirable asthma control. Also note that pindolol may make asthma and other respiratory conditions worse (there is some debate on this and the final word is not yet in). Using **Visken** in these patients is not recommended.
▪ **Minipress** (prazosin) effects may be markedly increased by pindolol. Adding **Minipress** to a blood-pressure treatment regimen already containing pindolol may cause acutely low blood pressure.

THE CALCIUM BLOCKERS

The calcium blockers (also known as calcium antagonists, slow-channel blockers, and calcium entry blockers) are fascinating drugs. They act to dilate blood vessels, moderate heart contractions, and stabilize electrical activity within the heart by slowing the entry of calcium (necessary for muscle cell contraction) into cells. The net result is that the heart doesn't have to work so hard to provide blood to its own tissues, thereby lessening the symptoms of angina. One of the calcium channel blockers, verapamil (**Isoptin**, **Calan**), is also useful in correcting certain abnormal heart rhythms.

Even though all four commercially available calcium channel blockers

* *These side effects may be serious. Contact your physician immediately if they occur.*

act by slowing the entry of calcium, there are important differences
between these compounds. Some are better for treating arrhythmias,
while others may be more effective for high blood pressure or angina.
They vary considerably in their side effects and, unlike the beta blockers,
are individually very different in their chemical structures. If one calcium channel blocker doesn't work, another may. **Cardizem** (diltiazem)
is the newest calcium channel blocker to be marketed and although
experience with this compound is rather limited, it appears that it's
associated with far fewer side effects than the other two. All other things
being equal, this could become the first choice if your doctor feels that a
calcium channel blocker is indicated.

Calan and Isoptin *(verapamil 80 mg and 120 mg tablets)*

MFR: **Calan:** G. D. Searle & Co.
　　Isoptin: Knoll Pharmaceutical Co.

FDA APPROVED USES: Angina and abnormal heart rhythms (used intravenously for the latter condition).

USUAL DOSE:
 ▪ Angina: 80 mg three or four times daily to start. Most people are
   maintained on 320 mg to 480 mg total daily dose.

Verapamil is associated with quite a few side effects, some of which
may be serious. Adverse reactions are seen mostly during dosage increases and are, in general, related to the dose being used. Because
constipation is one of the most common complaints, try to increase the
bulk in your diet and avoid highly constipating foods. You should know
how to take your own pulse and should call your doctor if the heart rate
is below 50 beats per minute. Since dizziness and faintness are relatively
common, be careful not to stand up too suddenly.

PRECAUTIONS:
 ▪ Side effects are common with verapamil.
 ▪ Take on an empty stomach; one hour before meals or two hours after
   meals.

PREGNANCY AND BREAST-FEEDING:
 ▪ Verapamil has been shown in animal tests to cause birth defects.
   Although no such data exists for humans, this drug should not be
   taken by pregnant women unless absolutely necessary.
 ▪ It is unknown whether verapamil is found in human breast milk. It
   would be prudent to stop breast-feeding if the use of this medicine is
   necessary.

Calan and Isoptin *(continued)*

COMMON SIDE EFFECTS:
- Constipation (occurs in anywhere from 6% to 30% of people taking this drug).
- Nausea (about 2% incidence).
- Headache (about 2% incidence).
- Fatigue (about 1% incidence).
*- Dizziness (about 4% to 6% incidence).
*- Slow heart rate (less than 50 beats per minute; about 1% incidence).
*- Edema (swollen feet and ankles because of water retention; about 2% incidence).
*- Difficulty in breathing (about 1% incidence).

UNCOMMON SIDE EFFECTS:
*- Liver damage (may be detected by blood test; rare).

SEXUAL SIDE EFFECTS:
- Impotence has been reported; incidence is unknown.

DRUG INTERACTIONS:
- **Lanoxin** (digoxin) levels in the blood may be increased by as much as 70% in persons taking verapamil. This may lead to serious toxicity (See table, page 303, for the signs and symptoms of digitalis toxicity.)
- Since verapamil can decrease blood pressure, use with caution when combined with any antihypertensive medication.
- Because of additive effects on the heart, do not use verapamil and **Norpace** (disopyramide) together (unconfirmed interaction).

Cardizem *(diltiazem 30 mg and 60 mg tablets)*

MFR: Marion Laboratories, Inc.

FDA APPROVED USES: Angina.

USUAL DOSE: 30 mg three or four times daily, up to 240 mg total daily dose.

At the time of this writing, **Cardizem** is the most recent calcium channel blocker on the market. Although the FDA has approved it only for angina, it also appears effective in lowering blood pressure, and may be useful for several other conditions such as migraine and Raynaud's

(continues next page)

* *These side effects may be serious. Contact your physician immediately if they occur.*

Cardizem *(continued)*

phenomenon. The incidence of serious side effects reported to date is low, and the occurrence of side effects in general seems roughly comparable to that seen with placebo (an inert sugar pill) treatment.

So far, **Cardizem** would have to be considered my favored calcium blocker, as it seems to be better tolerated than the others.

PRECAUTIONS:
- Take on an empty stomach, one hour before or two hours after meals.

PREGNANCY AND BREAST-FEEDING:
- Diltiazem has caused birth defects and toxicity in animal studies. It is not known whether a similar danger exists with humans. Do not take diltiazem while pregnant if at all possible.
- It is not known whether diltiazem is found in the breast milk of nursing mothers. It would be prudent to stop breast-feeding if diltiazem treatment is necessary.

COMMON SIDE EFFECTS:
- Headache (occurs in about 2% of persons taking this drug).
- Fatigue (about 1% incidence).
- Nausea (about 3% incidence).
- * Skin rash (allergic reaction; about 2% incidence).
- * Edema (swollen feet and ankles due to water retention; about 2% incidence).
- * Abnormal heart rhythms (about 2% incidence).

UNCOMMON SIDE EFFECTS:
- Stomach upset, vomiting, diarrhea, constipation (less than 1% incidence).
- Sensitivity to sunlight (rare).
- * Slow heart rate (less than 50 beats per minute; rare).
- * Palpitations (less than 1% incidence).
- * Extreme dizziness and faintness from excessively low blood pressure (less than 1% incidence).

SEXUAL SIDE EFFECTS:
- Insufficient data at this time.

DRUG INTERACTIONS:
- Insufficient data at this time.

---

* These side effects may be serious. Contact your physician immediately if they occur.

Procardia *(nifedipine 10 mg capsules)*

MFR: Pfizer Inc.

FDA APPROVED USES: Angina. Although not approved for use in hypertension, it has been used with success for this condition. For the person with both angina and high blood pressure, it might kill two birds with one stone.

USUAL DOSE:
- Angina: The average effective dose is between 10 mg and 20 mg, given three times a day. Occasional patients need higher doses or more frequent dosing.

People taking **Procardia** quite commonly suffer from one or more nagging side effects; these are rarely serious enough, however, to warrant stopping the drug. Peripheral edema (swelling of the ankles and feet as a result of water retention) is very common but is easily managed by diuretics. It is imperative for the physician to rule out congestive heart failure, as this disease commonly produces the same symptoms. Since most of **Procardia's** adverse reactions are due to its ability to dilate blood vessels and thereby decrease blood pressure, try to avoid strenuous exercise and alcohol, as both may aggravate the condition.

PRECAUTIONS:
- Take on an empty stomach, one hour before or two hours after meals.

PREGNANCY AND BREAST-FEEDING:
- Nifedipine has been shown in animal tests to cause birth defects. Although no such data exist for humans, this drug should not be taken by pregnant women unless absolutely necessary.
- It is not known whether nifedipine is found in the breast milk of nursing mothers. It would be prudent to stop breast-feeding if nifedipine treatment is necessary.

COMMON SIDE EFFECTS:
- Low blood pressure (quite common).
- Dizziness and faintness (occurs in about 10% of persons taking this drug).
- Headache (about 10% incidence).
- Flushing and a sensation of warmth (very common).
- Nausea (about 10% incidence).
- Fatigue or weakness (about 10% incidence).
- Palpitations (about 2% incidence).
- * Edema (see above; about 10% incidence).

(continues next page)

* *These side effects may be serious. Contact your physician immediately if they occur.*

Procardia, *(continued)*

UNCOMMON SIDE EFFECTS:
- ▪ Stuffy nose and chest congestion.
- ▪ Giddiness, tremor, nervousness, changes in mood, insomnia.
- ▪ Constipation, diarrhea, stomach cramps, gas.
- ▪ Joint pain, inflammation, muscle cramps.
- *▪ Rash, hives, fever (allergic reactions; rare).
- *▪ Difficulty in breathing.
- *▪ Unusually fast heart rate.
- *▪ Increase in chest pain (rare).
- *▪ Fainting (less than 1% incidence).

SEXUAL SIDE EFFECTS:
- • "Sexual difficulties" (less than 2% incidence).

DRUG INTERACTIONS:
- ▪ **Lanoxin** (digoxin) levels in the blood *may* be increased by as much as 45% in persons taking nifedipine. (This finding is based on only one study; another study contradicts this evidence.) Because of the potential severity of this drug interaction, use these two drugs cautiously in combination until further data are available. (See table page 303 for the signs and symptoms of digitalis toxicity.)
- ▪ **Procardia** commonly causes low blood pressure and can cause dizziness and lightheadedness. This adverse effect may be accentuated by alcohol or any antihypertensive medication.

* *These side effects may be serious. Contact your physician immediately if they occur.*

References

1. American Heart Association, *Heart Facts 1983*, Dallas, 1983, pp. 2–3.

2. Ibid.

3. Editorial. "Why the American Decline in Coronary Heart-Disease? *Lancet* 1:183–184, 1980.

4. Garraway, W. Michael, et al. "The Declining Incidence of Stroke." *N. Engl. J. Med.* 300:449–452, 1979.

5. Editorial. "Why has Stroke Mortality Declined?" *Lancet* 1:1195–1196, 1983.

6. Personal communication, Susan Farley, American Heart Association, September 7, 1983.

7. Walker, Weldon J. "Changing U.S. Life Style and Declining Vascular Mortality—A Retrospective." *N. Engl. J. Med.* 308:649–651, 1983.

8. Editorial, *Lancet*, 1980. Op. cit.

9. Welin, L., et al. "Why is the Incidence of Ischaemic Heart Disease in Sweden Increasing?: Study of Men Born in 1913 and 1923." *Lancet* 1:1087–1983.

10. Walker. Op. cit.

11. Editorial, *Lancet*, 1980. Op cit.

12. "Type-A Behavior Found Not Linked to Heart Disease." *Medical World News* 24(6):23–24, 1983.

13. "Multiple Risk Factor Intervention Trial." *JAMA* 248:1465–1477, 1982.

14. Ram, C., and Venkata, S. "Should Mild Hypertension Be Treated." *Annals of Internal Medicine* 99:403–405, 1983.

15. Lundberg, George D. "MRFIT and the Goals of the Journal." *JAMA* 248:1501, 1982.

16. "CAD Risk Factor Study: Changing Life Style Does Help." *Medical World News*, October 11, 1982, pp. 8–13.

17. Seltzer, Carl C. "The Multiple Risk Factor Intervention Trial." *JAMA* 249:1435–1436, 1983.

18. Klatsky, Arthur L. "Ten-Year Study of Alcoholic Beverages and Cardiovascular Mortality." *Proceedings: Wine, Health & Society* Nov. 13–14, 1981, Oakland, GRT Book Printing. pp. 39–49.

19. Kane, John, P. "Alcoholic Beverages and High Density Lipoproteins." *Proceedings: Wine, health & Society* Nov. 13–14, 1981, Oakland, GRT Book Printing. pp. 29–38.

20. Lewis. H. Daniel, et al. "Protective Effects of Aspirin Against Acute Myocardial Infarction and Death in Men with Unstable Angina." *N. Engl. J. Med.* 309:396–403, 1983.

21. Editorial, *Lancet*, 1983. Op. cit.

22. Acheson, Roy M., and Williams, D. R. R. "Does Consumption of Fruit and Vegetables Protect Against Strokes." *Lancet* 1:1191–1193, 1983.

23. Eichner, Edward R. "Exercise and Heart Disease: Epidemiology of the 'Exercise Hypothesis.' " *Am. J. Med.* 75:1008–1023, 1983.

24. Lewis, H. Daniel. "Protective Effects of Aspirin Against Acute Myocardial Infarction and Death in Men with Unstable Angina." *N. Engl. J. Med.* 309:396–403, 1983.

25. Elwood, P. C. "A Randomized Controlled Trial of Acetylsalicylic Acid in the Secondary Prevention of Mortality from Myocardial Infarction." *Br. Med. J.* 1:436–440, 1940.

26. Boston Collaborative Drug Surveillance Group. "Regular Aspirin Intake and Acute Myocardial Infarction." *Br. Med. J.* 1:440–443, 1974.

27. Jick, H., and Miettinen, O. S. "Regular Aspirin Use and Myocardial Infarction." *Br. Med. J.* 1:1057, 1976.

28. Coronary Drug Project Research Group. "Aspirin in Coronary Heart Disease." *J. Clin. Dis.* 29:625–642, 1976.

29. Elwood, P. C., et al. "Aspirin and Secondary Mortality After Myocardial Infarction." *Lancet* 2:1313–1315, 1979.

30. Persantine-Aspirin Reinfarction Study Research Group. "Persantine and Aspirin in Coronary Heart Disease." *Circulation* 62:449–461, 1980.

31. Aspirin Myocardial Infarction Study Research Group. "A Randomized, Controlled Trial of Aspirin in Persons Recovered From Myocardial Infarction." *JAMA* 243:661–669, 1980.

32. Lewis. Op. cit.

33. Gazes, P. C., et al. "Preinfarction (Unstable) Angina—A Prospective Study—Ten Year Follow-Up." *Circulation* 48:331–337, 1973.

34. Lewis. Op. cit.

35. The Canadian Cooperative Study Group. *N. Engl. J. Med.* 299:53–59, 1978.

36. Bousser, M. G., et al. " 'AICLA' Controlled Trial of Aspirin and Dipyridamole in the Secondary Prevention of Athero-thrombotic Cerebral Ischemia." *Stroke* 14:5–14, 1983.

37. Hanley, S. P., et al. "A Regimen for Low-Dose Aspirin?" *Br. Med. J.* 285:1299–1302, 1982.

38. Weksler, Babette B., et al. "Differential Inhibition by Aspirin of Vascular and Platelet Prostaglandin Synthesis in Atherosclerotic Patients." *N. Engl. J. Med.* 308:800–805, 1983.

39. Katz, Ephraim. "Optimal Aspirin Dosage for Prevention of Heart Disease and Strokes?" *JAMA* 251:89, 1984.

40 McGivney, William T. "Optimal Aspirin Dosage for Prevention of Heart Disease and Strokes." *JAMA* 251:89–90, 1984.

41. Weksler. Op. cit.

42. AMA News Release. "MDs Sought in Nationwide Study to Assess Benefits of two Common Substances in Reducing Risk of Heart Attack, Stroke, and Cancer." American Medical Association News Release, March 12, 1982, pp. 1–3.

43. Makheja, Amar N., and Bailey, J. Martyn. "Identification of the Antiplatelet Substance in Chinese Black Tree Fungus." *N. Engl. J. Med.* 304:175, 1981.

44. Ariga, Toyohiko, et al. "Platelet Aggregation Inhibition in Garlic." *Lancet* 1:150–151, 1981.

45. Makheja, Amar N., et al. "Effects of Onion (Allium Cepa) Extract on Platelet Aggregation and Thromboxane Synthesis." *Prostaglandins and Medicine* 2:413–424, 1979.

46. Jain, R. C. "Effect of Garlic on Serum Lipids, Coagulability and Fibrinolytic Activity of Blood." *Am. J. Clin. Nutr.* 30:1380–1381, 1977.

47. Science Watch. "Anticlot Agent in Fungus." *New York Times,* February 17, 1981.

48. American Heart Association. Op cit.

49. Ibid.

50. Kolata, Gina. "New Heart Attack Treatment Discussed." *Science* 214:1229–1230, 1981.

51. Sherry, Sol. "Personal Reflections on the Development of Thrombolytic Therapy and Its Application to Acute Coronary Thrombosis." *Am. Heart J.* 102(6-2):1134–1139, 1981.

52. Johnson, A. L., and McCarty, W. R. "The Lysis of Artificially Induced Intravascular Clots in Man by Intravenous Infusions of Streptokinase." *J. Clin. Invest.* 39:426, 1959.

53. Fletcher, A. P., et al. "The Maintenance of a Sustained Thrombolytic State in Man. II. Clinical Observations on Patients with Myocardial Infarction and Other Thromboembolic Disorders." *J. Clin. Invest.* 38:1111, 1959.

54. Nydick, I., et al. "Salvage of Heart Muscle by Fibrinolytic Therapy After Experimental Coronary Occlusion." *Am. Heart J.* 61:93, 1961.

55. Fletcher, A. P., et al. "The Treatment of Patients Suffering From Early Myocardial Infarction with Massive and Prolonged Streptokinase Therapy." *Trans. Assoc. Am. Physicians* 71:287, 1958.

56. Sherry. Op. cit.

57. Gonzalez, Elizabeth R. "Intracoronary Thrombolysis to Abort Heart Attacks: Wave of the Future?" *JAMA* 245:11–13, 1981.

58. Ibid.

59. Ganz, William. "Intracoronary Thrombolysis in Acute Myocardial Infarction." *Am. J. Cardiol.* 52:92A–95A, 1983.

60. Rentrop, P., et al. "Selective Intracoronary Thrombolysis in Acute Myocardial Infarction and Unstable Angina Pectoris." *Circulation* 63:307–317, 1981.

61. Mathey, D. G., et al. "Nonsurgical Coronary Artery Recanalization in Acute Transmural Myocardial Infarction." *Circulation* 63:489–499, 1981.

62. Reduto, L. A., et al. "Intracoronary Infusion of Streptokinase in Patients with Acute Myocardial Infarction: Effects of Reperfusion on Left Ventricular Performance." *Am. J. Cardiol.* 48:403–409, 1981.

63. Markis, J. E., et al. "Myocardial Salvage After Intracoronary Thrombolysis with Streptokinase in Acute Myocardial Infarction: Assessment by Intracoronary Thallium-201." *N. Engl. J. Med.* 305:777–782, 1981.

64. Anderson, Jeffrey L., et al. "A Randomized Trial of Intracoronary Streptokinase in the Treatment of Acute Myocardial Infarction." *N. Engl. J. Med.* 308:1312–1318, 1983.

65. Swan, H. J. C. "Thrombolysis in Acute Evolving Myocardial Infarction." *N. Engl. J. Med.* 308:1354–1355, 1983.

66. Kennedy, J. Ward, et al. "Western Washington Randomized Trial of Intracoronary Streptokinase in Acute Myocardial Infarction." *N. Engl. J. Med.* 309:1477–1482, 1983.

67. Khaja, F., et al. "Intracoronary Fibrinolytic Therapy in Acute Myocardial Infarction: Report of a Prospective Randomized Trial." *N. Engl. J. Med.* 308:1305–1311, 1983.

68. Swan. Op. cit.

69. Schroder, Rolf, et al. "Intravenous Short-Term Infusion of Streptokinase in Acute Myocardial Infarction." *Circulation* 67:536–548, 1983.

70. "Streptokinase Still Lysing Coronary Clots." *JAMA* 250:2744–2745, 1983.

71. Rogers, W. J., et al. "Prospective Randomized Trial of Intravenous and Intracoronary Streptokinase in Acute Myocardial Infarction." *Circ.* 68:1051–1061, 1983.

72. Spann, James F. "Changing Concepts of Pathophysiology, Prognosis and Therapy in Acute Myocardial Infarction." *Am. J. Med.* 74:877–886, 1983.

73. Personal communication, Sol Sherry, September 28, 1983.

74. "Tissue-Type Plasminogen Activator Lyses Coronary Thrombi in Minutes." *Medical World News* 25(2):17–18, 1984.

75. Bishop, Jerry, E. "Genentech Seeks Human Tests of Drug to Dissolve Clots During Heart Attacks." *The Wall Street Journal*, November 16, 1983, p. 60.

76. Elliott, William J. "Ear Lobe Crease and Coronary Artery Disease: 1000 Patients and Review of the Literature." *Am. J. Med.* 75:1024–1032, 1983.

77. Kristensen, Bent O. "Ear-Lobe Crease and Vascular Complications in Essential Hypertension." *Lancet* 1:265, 1980.

78. "Coronary Earmark Confirmed." *Acute Care Med.* April 1984, pp. 45–46.

79. The Multicenter Postinfarction Research Group. "Risk Stratification and Survival After Myocardial Infarction." *N. Engl. J. Med.* 309:331–336, 1983.

80. Mustard, James F., and Kinlough-Rathbone, Raelene L. "Aspirin in the Treatment of Cardiovascular Disease: A Review." *Am. J. Med.*, Proceeding of a Symposium: New Perspectives on Aspirin Therapy. June 14, 1983, pp. 43–49.

81. Editorial. "Aspirin After Myocardial Infarction." *Lancet* 1:1172–1173, 1980.

82. Persantine-Aspirin Reinfarction Study Research Group. Op. cit.

83. Mustard. Op. cit.

84. Chesebro, James H., et al. "Effect of Dipyridamole and Aspirin on Late Vein-Graft Patency After Coronary Bypass Operations." *N. Engl. J. Med.* 310:209–214, 1984.

85. Fast Track. "Dr. Denton A. Cooley on Bypass: What Family Physicians Need to Know About Referral, Risk, and Rehab." *Modern Medicine*, March, 1982, pp. 82–94.

86. The Anturane Reinfarction Trial Research Group. "Sulfinpyrazone in the Prevention of Sudden Death after Myocardial Infarction." *N. Engl. J. Med.* 302:250–256, 1980.

87. Temple, Robert, and Pledger, Gordon W. "Special Report: The FDA's Critique of the Anturane Reinfarction Trial." *N. Engl. J. Med.* 303:1488–1492, 1980.

88. "Acute Myocardial Infarction and Its Consequences." *Cardiology* William C. Roberts, ed., Yorke Medical Books,1983, pp. 147–149.

89. Anturan Reinfarction Italian Study Group. "Sulphinpyrazone in Post-Myocardial Infarction. Report From the Anturan Reinfarction Italian Study." *Lancet* 1:237–242, 1982.

90. Personal communication, Sondra K. Gorney, Director of Communication, Ayerst Laboratories, October 20, 1983.

91. "The Top 200 Prescription Drugs of 1982." *American Druggist* February, 1982.

92. Edelson, Edward. "The New Heart Drugs." *Daily News* December 14, 1981, pp. 27.

93. Altman, Lawrence. "Therapy for Heart Disease." *New York Times*, February 2, 1982, p. C1.

94. Review & Outlook. "100,000 Killed." *The Wall Street Journal*, November 2, 1981, p. 26.

95. Norwegian Multicenter Study Group. "Timolol-Induced Reduction in Mortality and Reinfarction in Patients Surviving Acute Myocardial Infarction." *N. Engl. J. Med.* 304:801–807, 1981.

96. B-Blocker Heart Attack Trial Research Group. "A Randomized Trial of Propranolol in Patients with Acute Myocardial Infarction: 1. Mortality Results." *JAMA* 247:1707–1714, 1982.

97. Hjalmarson, A., et al. "Effect on Mortality of Metoprolol in Acute Myocardial Infarction." *Lancet* 2:823–827, 1981.

98. Zoltan, G. Turi, and Braunwald, Eugene. "The use of B-Blockers After Myocardial Infarction." *JAMA* 249:2512–2516, 1983.

99. Petrie, William, M., et al. "Propranolol and Depression." *Am. J. Psychiatry* 139:92–94, 1982.

100. Medigrams. "Methyldopa and Propranolol may Cause Memory Loss." *Am. Fam. Physician* 23(1):209, 1981.

101. "Drugs that Cause Sexual Dysfunction." *Medical Letter* 25:73–76, 1983.

102. Osborne, D. R. "Propranolol and Peyronie's Disease." *Lancet* 1:1111, 1977.

103. Wallis, A.A., et al. "Propranolol and Peyronie's Disease." *Lancet* 2:980, 1977.

104. Leren, P, et al. "Effect of Propranolol and Prazosin on Blood Lipids: The Oslo Study." *Lancet* 2:4–6, 1980.

105. Editorial. "Antihypertensive Drugs, Plasma Lipids, and Coronary Disease." *Lancet* 2:19–20, 1980.

106. Oliver, Michael F. "Risks of Correcting the Risks of Coronary Disease and Stroke with Drugs." *N. Engl. J. Med.* 306:297–298, 1982.

107. *Physicians' Desk Reference.* 37th edition, 1983. Medical Economics, Oradell, N.J. pp. 630.

108. Medical News. "Calcium Blockers for Heart Disease: Two Approved, More to Come." *JAMA* 247:1911–1917, 1982.

109. Waldholz, Michael. "Drug Makers Rush to Secure Market for New Class of Heart Medicines." *The Wall Street Journal*, April 19, 1981.

110. Personal communication, James Muller, January, 1982.

111. Patel, K. R. "Calcium Antagonists in Exercise-Induced Asthma." *Br. Med. J.* 282:932–933, 1981.

112. Triggle, D. J. "Airways Smooth Muscle and Calcium Transport." *Immunol. Aller. Pract.* 5(1):39–43.

113. Patel, K. R. "The Effect of Calcium Antagonist, Nifedipine, in Exercise-Induced Asthma." *Clin. Aller.* 11:429–432, 1981.

114. Henderson, Allan F., et al. "Effects of Nifedipine on Antigen-Induced Bronchoconstriction." *Am. Rev. Respir. Dis.* 127:549–553, 1983.

115. Medical News. "Calcium Blockers for Heart Disease: Two Approved, More to Come." *JAMA* 247:1911–1917, 1982.

116. "Calcium Blockade for Hypertension, Too?" *Medical World News* 23(6):57–58, 1982.

117. "Nifedipine for Hypertensive Crisis." *Medical World News* 24(5):124, 1983.

118. Gould, Brian A., et al. "The 24-Hour Ambulatory Blood Pressure Profile with Verapamil." *Circulation* 65:22–27, 1982.

119. Olivari, Maria T., et al. "Treatment of Hypertension with Nifedipine, A Calcium Antagonistic Agent." *Circulation* 59:1056–1062, 1979.

120. Kuwajima, Iwao, et al. "A Study on the Effects of Nifedipine in Hypertensive Crises and Severe Hypertension." *Jap. Heart J.* 19:455–467, 1978.

121. Klein, W., et al. "Role of Calcium Antagonists in the Treatment of Essential Hypertension." *Circ. Res.* (suppl. 1)52:174–181, 1983.

122. Hamm, Christian W., and Opie, Lionel H. "Protection of Infarcting Myocardium by Slow Channel Inhibitors (Calcium Antagonists)." *Am. J. Cardiol.* (Abstract) 49:942, 1982.

123. Temesy-Armos, Peter, et al. "Effect of Verapamil on Arrhythmias During Myocardial Ischemia." *Am. J. Cardiol.* (Abstract) 49:997, 1982.

124. Clusin, William T., et al. "Anti-Fibrillatory Action of Diltiazem During Global Left Ventricular Ischemia." *Am J. Cardiol.* (Abstract) 49:913, 1982.

125. Fujimoto, Toshifumi, et al. "Effects of Diltiazem on Conduction of Premature Impulses During Acute Myocardial Ischemia and Reperfusion." *Am. J. Cardiol.* 48:851–857, 1981.

126. Karlsberg, Ronald, and Aronow, Wilbert S. "Calcium Channel Blockers: Indications and Limitations." *Postgrad. Med.* 72(5):97–123, 1982.

127. Gazes, Peter C. "Treating Angina: When Can You Use Calcium Blockers?" *Modern Medicine* 51(3):64–80, 1983.

128. Braunwald, Eugene. "Mechanism of Action of Calcium-Channel-Blocking Agents." *N. Engl. J. Med.* 307:1618–1627, 1982.

129. News From the University of Rochester. "Major Heart Research Study Announced by the University of Rochester." Office of Communications, April 11, 1983.

130. Schroeder, John S., et al. "Prevention of Cardiovascular Events in Variant Angina by Long-Term Diltiazem Therapy." *J. Am. Coll. Cardiol.* 1(6):1507–1511, 1983.

131. Kramsch, D. M., et al. "Suppression of Experimental Atherosclerosis by the CA + +-antagonist Lanthanum." *J. Clin. Invst.* 65:967–981, 1980.

132. Rouleau, J. L., et al. *J. Am Coll. Cardiol.* 1:1453, 1983.

133. Gubner, Richard S. "Magnesium as a Physiologic Calcium Antagonist: A Unifying View of Calcium Blockers." *Medical Tribune*, October 12, 1983.

134. Vanhoutte, Paul M., and Cohen, Richard A. "Calcium-Entry Blockers and Cardiovascular Disease." *Am. J. Cardiol.* 52:99A–103A, 1983.

135. Walker, Morton. *The Chelation Answer,* New York: M. Evans, 1982.

136. Horwitz, Nathan. "Diltiazem Eases Migraine Attacks." *Med. Tribute* October, 1982.

137. Kahan, A., et al. "Nifedipine in the Treatment of Migraine in Patients with Raynaud's Phenomenon." *N. Engl. J. Med.* 308:1102–1103, 1983.

138. Kahan, A., et al. "Nifedipine for Raynaud's Phenomenon." *Lancet* 1:131, 1983.

139. Kahan, A., et al. "Nifedipine and Raynaud's Phenomenon." *Ann. Intern. Med.* 94:546, 1981.

140. Smith, C. D. and McKendry, R. J. R. "Controlled Trial of Nifedipine in the Treatment of Raynaud's Phenomenon." *Lancet* 2:1299–1301.

141. Rodeheffer, Richard J., et al. "Controlled Double-Blind Trial of Nifedipine in the Treatment of Raynaud's Phenomenon." *N. Engl. J. Med.* 308:880–883, 1983.

142. Mondero, Nancy A. "Nifedipine in the Treatment of Dysmenorrhea." *J. of A.O.A.* 82:704–708, 1983.

143. Sandahl, B., et al. "Trial of the Calcium Antagonist Nifedipine in the Treatment of Primary Dysmenorrhoea." *Arch. Gynecol.* 227:147–151, 1979.

144. Ulmsten, U., et al. "Treatment of Premature Labor with the Calcium Antagonist Nifedipine." *Arch. Gynecol.* 229:1–5, 1980.

145. Rush, R. W. "The Management of Preterm Labor with Intact Membranes." *S.Afr. Med. J.* 58:687–689, 1980.

146. "Calcium Channel Blockers to Prevent Arterial Spasm After Subarachnoid Hemorrhage." *Intern. Med. Alert* 5(6):21, 1983.

147. "Calcium Blockers Given After CPR May Save Brains Denied Blood Up to an Hour." *Med. World News,* January 18, 1982, pp. 11–24.

148. Associated Press. "Heart Drugs May Help Prevent Kidney Failure." Durham *Sun*, March 1, 1983, p. 10A.

149. Markell, Mary. "Calcium Drugs Get Duke Test." Durham *Sun*, December 22, 1982.

150. Bishop, Jerry E. "Clearer Diagnosis: Heart Research Is Firming Cholesterol Connection." *The Wall Street Journal*, January 10, 1984.

151. Dimsdale, Joel E., et al. "Postexercise Peril: Plasma Catecholamines and Exercise." *JAMA* 251:630–632, 1984.

152. Ibid.

CHAPTER 7

Hacking Away at High Blood Pressure

The Blood Pressure Bogeyman ▪ Doctors Bobble Blood-Pressure Readings: Miscuffing, Inaccurate Equipment and Misreading All Lead to Errors ▪ Is Your Doctor Giving You High Blood Pressure? ▪ Do-It-Yourself Blood-Pressure Readings: Electronic Wizardry Makes It Easy! ▪ Mild Hypertension: The Gray Zone Gets Grayer ▪ Hurting More than Helping?: MRFIT Raises Doubts ▪ Depletion & Disruption with Diuretics ▪ Replacing Potassium—the Plot Thickens ▪ The Sodium Controversy: Stickier than You Thought ▪ Cashing Out on Caffeine ▪ Simple Nondrug Steps to Success ▪ Gone Fishin': Learning to Relax ▪ Evaluation of Home Blood Pressure Devices ▪ Table: Blood Pressure Medicines.

High blood pressure has become the bogeyman of modern medicine. We are constantly reminded that the "silent killer" stalks millions of unsuspecting victims each year. The American Heart Association tells us that 37 million adult Americans (1 out of 5) suffer from hypertension, and we, too, could be victims without even knowing it.[1,2]

You can hardly visit a doctor's office these days without going through a ritual cuffing and pumping. And if your blood pressure climbs much above that mystical "normal" value of 120/80, chances are good that out will come the prescription pad and you will be encouraged, entreated, and otherwise exhorted to **TAKE YOUR MEDICINE!** It's not enough that the physician, nurse, and pharmacist repeat this message over and over; you will also be reminded by radio, television, newspapers, and magazines. Almost everyone, it seems, wants you to pop your pressure pills.

And why not? Hypertension *can* cause damage to eyes and kidneys. Left untreated, high blood pressure will increase your chances of a heart attack or stroke. It seems only logical, reasonable, and prudent, therefore, to knuckle down and take your medication faithfully. But wait a minute—things are not quite as simple as they seem.

First off, do you *really* have hypertension? Almost everyone assumes, incorrectly, that diagnosing high blood pressure is about as easy as taking your temperature. After all, you just stick your arm inside the cuff while the doctor pumps and then listens. As in golf, the lower the numbers, the healthier you are. Par is 120/80; anything over 140/90 makes a lot of docs itchy to start the drugs.

Baloney! A glass thermometer is a simple, accurate instrument that almost anyone can use correctly. That's a lot more than you can say for many blood-pressure devices, which are hard to use and often unreliable to boot. If your doctor has one of the old-fashioned kind, with mercury inside a glass tube, there is less likely to be a problem. But the circular dial gauges (aneroid manometers), which are portable and have become quite popular in recent years, are not nearly so reliable. One group of researchers showed that almost 30 percent of the aneroid instruments they tested in doctors' offices were off by up to 5 points.[3] Another study found that "Almost half the sphygmomanometers in a teaching hospital group had defects in the control valve which interfered with accurate blood-pressure reading."[4]

Doctors Bobble Blood-Pressure Readings

Then there is something called observer error. Listening with a stethoscope and recording blood pressure is not nearly as easy as you might think. The process requires interpreting subtle changes in soft sounds which can sometimes be hard to distinguish. The heart is a pump pushing blood through the system of pipes we call blood vessels; but the pressure is by no means steady. It is greatest when the heart contracts, and least when it relaxes between beats.

In order to measure these two different levels, you need to block off blood flow in the arm with a tourniquetlike device called a cuff. As air is slowly let out of the cuff to allow blood to start flowing again, it's possible to hear a sound that corresponds to the systolic—or maximum—pressure. That's relatively easy. The diastolic—or lower—pressure is tougher to detect because you have to listen to the sound as it slowly fades. This subtlety often leads to judgment calls—read that variability—a nice way of saying that people make mistakes.

If you were to stick five nurses and doctors in a room and ask each to measure the same patient, chances are good that you would get five different blood-pressure readings. That seems hard to believe, but how many times have you watched a sports event on television—football, baseball, basketball, tennis—and seen a bad call by the referee or umpire? It happens all the time. A ball that's really in is called out. A fumble is incorrectly declared an incompleted pass. A foul is ignored or missed. Whenever a decision depends on interpretation, there is room for error.

Numerous studies have shown that the same thing occurs when nurses and doctors try to read blood pressure.[5-9] The differences can be quite large, and interestingly, doctors' readings tend to be significantly higher than those of nurses.[10] A nurse I know theorized that the discrepancy might be due to differences in age. Doctors are often significantly older than nurses, and their hearing may not be as good. They may not always catch the very last blood-pressure sounds and as a result may falsely elevate diastolic blood pressure a few points.

Inaccurate gauges and observer error are not the only problems you may encounter when someone takes your blood pressure. There is a real possibility that you will be asked to put your arm into the wrong size cuff. One of the most common mistakes made by doctors and nurses is using a standard cuff for all comers. A study carried out in one hospital demonstrated that people with "nonstandard" arms were "miscuffed" 72 percent of the time.[11]

Now they're not talking about something weird when they say "nonstandard" arm size. What they mean is that if you've got a large arm—either because you have good muscles or because you've added a few extra pounds here and there—you are not standard. And believe me, this isn't uncommon. Almost half the people in that study should have been tested with a special cuff.

Cuff, schmuff, what's the big deal? How much difference can the cuff make, anyway? We're talking big errors here, folks. According to this team of investigators, "researchers have clearly demonstrated that an undersized cuff *over*estimates and an oversized cuff *under*estimates the true BP by as much as 10 to 30 mm.[12-15] Undercuffing can lead to the overtreatment of hypertension and overcuffing to its undertreatment."[16]

What this means in simple language is that if you have a large arm and the doctor uses a cuff which is too small, you could get treated for a blood-pressure problem you don't really have. If he uses a cuff that is too big on a slender arm, he could miss a true case of high blood pressure. There is nothing like a case history to bring this problem home. Physicians at Duke University Medical Center reported a typical case.

> **A 70-year-old man was referred for treatment of "severe hypertension." He was 5'7" tall, weighed 229 lbs and had an arm circumference of 18". His physician obtained blood pressure of 180/110 mm supine [lying down] and standing using a standard adult cuff. We repeated the measurements using a standard cuff and observed a blood pressure of 170/108 mm. When a large adult cuff was substituted for the standard cuff, the blood pressure was 158/80 mm supine and 150/86 standing. The patient was not severely hypertensive; rather, he was quite normotensive [normal] and required no therapy.[17]**

OK, let's face it, this 70-year-old man was fat. Anyone who is 5'7" and weighs 229 pounds is more than a little overweight; and you better believe his arms were chubby too. But his doctor did not take that circumstance into account. By using a standard-size cuff, he falsely elevated the patient's blood pressure by almost 30 points and was probably ready to zap him with some pretty potent medications until the docs at Duke took another reading with a larger cuff.

Now you don't have to be grossly overweight or thin as a rail to need a special cuff. A handy guide, based on the American Heart Association's recommendations for blood pressure measurement, will tell you what cuff you need for the most accurate reading.[18,19]

Arm Circumference	Cuff Size
Less than 9.5 in.	small adult cuff
9.5 in. to 12.5 in.	standard adult cuff
13 in. to 16.5 in.	large adult cuff

But how do you use this information to make sure the doctor is using the right kind of cuff? First you must measure your arm to learn the circumference. Put this book down and go dig up a tape measure right now. Get a friend or relative to measure the roundness of your arm halfway between your shoulder and elbow. Anything between 9.5 and 12.5 inches is "standard." If that's where you fit, you can relax and keep relying on the regular old cuff the doctor has probably been using for years. But if your arm measures under 9.5 or over 13 inches, you will want to make sure that your doctor also owns a nonstandard cuff. Otherwise she could underestimate or overestimate your true blood pressure. The last thing you want is to be falsely diagnosed hypertensive.

All right, you've measured your arm. For argument's sake let's say your arm circumference is somewhere around 14 inches. Now what do you do? The next time you go to the doctor's office, mention to the nurse or doctor that you need a large adult cuff instead of the standard size. You also need to take along a ruler or a 3 × 5 card. If you want to make sure that they are indeed using the right cuff for you, whip out your ruler (or if you want to be sneaky, surreptitiously grab your 3 × 5 card) and start measuring. A large adult cuff should be a little over 6.5 inches wide, which is significantly more than the long side of your 3 × 5 card. If the cuff is around 5 inches wide (about the same size as your card length), that means it's a standard size and is not appropriate for someone with a large arm. The larger cuff will also be longer, insuring that the arm is almost completely surrounded by the rubber air bladder, allowing extra fabric for overlap. If you're a string bean with thin arms (less than 9.5 inches in circumference), you need a small cuff, one that is no more than 4.5 inches wide.

Lest you think this is all a lot of trouble for nothing, remember that if your arms are a little on the heavy side, a standard size cuff could falsely elevate your blood pressure by 10 to 30 points. And that misreading could fool your doctor into thinking that you have hypertension, which in turn could lead to unnecessary treatment with drugs.

One final word of caution. A recent study has demonstrated that arm *position* is also extremely important when blood pressure is being measured. If the doctor has you sitting up in a chair with your arm resting at your side, in your lap, or on a low table or arm rest (a common procedure), there is a good possibility your blood pressure will be falsely elevated. A recent article in the *British Medical Journal* concludes:

> **Our results confirm that changing the position of the arm has a substantial influence on the blood pressure recorded in that arm by a sphygmomanometer. We believe that the magnitude of this difference, first reported in 1909, has been overlooked and underestimated . . . Our experience shows that both systolic and diastolic blood pressures may be changed by 20mm Hg simply by moving the arm through 90°. . .**

> **Variations in recorded blood pressure are particularly important when a decision has to be made on whether to treat patients with so called mild or borderline hypertension or to modify treatment regimens in patients with poorly controlled hypertension . . .**

> **On the basis of our finding we recommend that the patient should usually be sitting, with the arm in a roughly horizontal position at heart level supported on a desk.[20]**

It's hard to believe that simply changing arm position could make the difference in whether a person is considered to have blood pressure high enough to be treated, or blood pressure that is nearly normal. Don't just take my word for it. Do the experiment yourself: Take your blood pressure with your arm at your side, wait a few moments, then take it again with your arm supported at heart level. I think you'll be amazed by how much the two readings can vary.

Is Your Doctor Giving You High Blood Pressure?

Now you're really on your toes. You've measured your arm to find out what kind of blood pressure cuff should be used. You've informed your doctor or nurse accordingly. And you've noted with satisfaction that they are using a mercury sphygmomanometer, the instrument most likely to be accurate. You insisted that your arm be out almost straight and even with your heart to minimize error. Sounds like your worries are over.

Not so quick. None of these cautions may make much difference when the doctor walks into the room. All other sources of error, while important, can pale by comparison with the mistake a doctor makes when he relies on the office blood-pressure reading alone.

There is no such thing as a single uniform blood pressure. Over the course of a normal day your pressure will bounce up and down like a ping-pong ball. Take Art for example. He's 48, an executive in a small computer-software company, and in darn good shape for someone his age. Art has no medical problems and is only about 10 pounds overweight. He plays tennis twice a week and eats carefully, shying away from salt and fatty foods. Art does *not* have high blood pressure.

I asked him to do me a favor and take his own blood pressure periodically throughout the day with one of those fancy new digital machines. The first reading was taken just after he shaved and brushed his teeth. It was excellent—118/76. Next Art took his blood pressure at 9:45, about half an hour after he got to the office; it was up to 128/84. When I asked him to describe what had happened that might have accounted for the mild increase, he mentioned that he was caught in a rush-hour traffic jam and was a little upset about getting in late. Upon questioning, he also admitted to having had three cups of coffee that morning, two more than usual. The third reading was taken in the middle of the afternoon, after a business lunch with an important client which had not gone as well as expected; this time Art's reading was 134/86. After work Art had a tennis date, which he described as a tough match that really had him working. He took his blood pressure in the locker room right after he finished. It was way up there—152/84. That evening after supper he was back down to 124/78.

Art is not unique. Numerous studies have shown that blood pressure is not static, but will vary up and down over 24 hours depending upon your state of mind and activity level.[21–24] Caffeine, for example, can jack the pressure up far more than most people think. One snazzy study published in the *New England Journal of Medicine* showed a startling 14 percent increase in blood pressure after 250 mg. of caffeine (two to three cups of coffee).[25] This relatively modest dose raised systolic pressure 14 points and diastolic pressure 10 points in healthy medical students. The elevation was seen within 30 minutes and lasted over 3 hours.

It's hardly any wonder that Art's blood pressure was up after an aggravating commute and three cups of coffee. If he was a smoker, it would probably have been even worse. Just by smoking 2 cigarettes it is possible to increase blood pressure almost 10 points.[26] The effect "only" lasts about 15 minutes, but if you smoke *and* drink coffee, the blood pressure elevation is substantial and may last several hours.

But if you think those figures are impressive, hold onto your hat. Going to the doctor is one of those activities that could be somewhat hazardous to the health of hypertensive patients—and maybe a lot of normal people as well. Articles in the medical literature have acknowledged for over 40 years that a "visit to a physician's office for evaluation of blood pressure may itself elevate the pressure."[27,28] But until recently no one really had a good understanding of how dramatic that increase could be.

Researchers in Milan, Italy, performed an elegant study on 48 hospitalized people. Some had high blood pressure, while others were perfectly normal.[29] Now this was no run-of-the-mill investigation. A catheter was placed in the artery of each subject for continuous blood-pressure monitoring over a 24-hour period. This is without a doubt *the* most accurate way of measuring blood pressure. In addition, once in the morning and once in the afternoon a physician took a reading with a traditional sphygmomanometer applied to the other arm. Here is what was found.

No sooner did the doctor walk into a patient's room than blood pressure started skyrocketing. Within two minutes systolic pressures rose by an average of 27 points and diastolic by 15 points. Many people reacted even more dramatically, with at least one person showing a gain of 75 mm in systolic blood pressure because of the doctor's presence. Pulse, too, was elevated. The average increase in heart rate was 15 beats a minute, and some subjects' hearts jumped up as much as 45 beats. What made these results so fascinating was that the increases in blood pressure occurred across the board in almost everyone (47 out of 48), regardless of whether they started with a normal blood pressure.

It doesn't take a genius to run the numbers. Say you arrive at the doctor's office with an actual blood pressure of 126/84—nice and normal. But after a frustrating wait and a little anxiety associated with having the doctor or nurse take your blood pressure, it could easily jump to 150/98. Now add 8 systolic and 5 diastolic points for undercuffing. Throw in another 7 for improper arm position—and voilá, you are up to 165/110. When the doctor sees those figures, he may be ready to label you hypertensive and start you on medication, even though your pressure may stay within a normal range 95 percent of the time.

The researchers who discovered the extraordinary effect doctors can have on their patients' blood pressure offer some conclusions.

Our study shows that the usual procedure for measuring blood pressure (i.e., the use of a sphygmomanometer by a doctor) is commonly associated with rises in systolic and diastolic blood pressures . . . it is reasonable to assume that the doctor's

> visit and the expectation of having the blood pressure mea-
> sured cause an alarm reaction in the patient. . . .
>
> A single blood-pressure measurement or even multiple mea-
> surements during the first few minutes of the visit might
> frequently lead to overestimated blood-pressure values. . . .
>
> The current trend toward treating so-called mild hyperten-
> sion is likely to extend treatment (and its disadvantages) to a
> large section of subjects whose blood pressure rises to the
> mild hypertensive levels during measurements only. Blood-
> pressure values obtained by a doctor are often greater than
> those obtained in the same subjects by self measurements.[30]

Now a lot of physicians are aware of this phenomenon. But many
prefer to ignore its importance. In fact, some doctors grow very uncomfortable at the idea of patients taking their own blood pressure at home.
For one thing, it confuses them. What should they do, for example,
when a patient has normal readings at home but elevated readings in the
office? Exactly such a question was directed to a consultant for the
American Medical Association.

> Q. A 64-year-old man has had consistently high office BP
> [blood pressure] readings (152/96 to 200/110) over the past
> five years. However, his home readings are consistently nor-
> motensive [normal] (116/70 to 130/82). His BP is monitored
> at home every two weeks and is considered reliable. It is
> checked at my office every three to four months. He has been
> maintained on various combinations of antihypertensive ther-
> apy in the attempt to reduce his office BP levels, with no
> detectable response. Currently he is receiving Inderal, 20
> mg three times a day, and Aldoril, 25 mg twice a day. Should
> I treat his hypertension less aggressively because of his home
> normotensive levels, or more aggressively because of the signif-
> icantly higher office levels?[31]
>
> R. Edward Dodge, Jr., M.D.
> Inverness, Fla

It seems clear that Dr. Dodge's patient goes bananas every time he has
his blood pressure taken at the office, even though he is on three heavy-
duty drugs—**Inderal** plus **Aldoril**, which is a combination of methyldopa
and hydrochlorothiazide. Here is good old Doc Dodge asking the AMA
expert if he should cut back or get even more aggressive with the
medications. Guess what the recommendation was? Yup, you get the
cigar, my friend. Aggressive won!
The expert encouraged Dr. Dodge to keep his patient on hydrochloro-

thiazide and, if necessary, to quadruple the dose of methyldopa (**Aldomet**) until the patient registered a normal blood pressure in the office. If that didn't do the job, then he was supposed to add a new powerhouse called **Apresoline** (hydralazine) up to a whopping dose of 300 mg. per day.

I would be surprised if the 64-year-old patient didn't develop side effects at such doses. His problems could include headache, diarrhea, nausea, loss of appetite, rapid heart beat, chest pain, dizziness, weakness, stuffy nose, red face, swollen feet, and blood disorders. And don't forget that **Aldomet** also has the potential to cause side effects, including drowsiness, headache, weakness, lightheadedness, dizziness, dry mouth, forgetfulness, nightmares, swelling of the feet, depression, decreased libido, impotence, and liver disorders. With such a dynamic duo it would be a miracle if Dr. Dodge's patient didn't feel pretty spaced out and uncomfortable, especially at the peak doses suggested.

Why risk such potentially unpleasant side effects to bring down blood pressure which is normal at home but jumps in the doctor's office? Here, in a nutshell, is the expert's answer to Dr. Dodge's question.

> **If he responds positively by a rise in BP on coming into your office, you can be sure that he will respond similarly to any stressful situation; therefore, his therapy should be adequate to prevent spiking of the BP under emotional stress, since most vascular catastrophes occur with spikes in BP.**[32]

Put another way, the AMA's chosen consultant believes that come hell or high water you must get everyone's blood pressure down to normal even when it only goes up temporarily in the doctor's office. He rationalizes this on the grounds that what goes up once can go up twice. So the person whose blood pressure climbs in the doctor's office might also have it go up during an emotionally stressful moment. And that, he claims, is dangerous and cannot be tolerated.

I can't really disagree with this point. Frequent sudden spiking of blood pressure would indeed be cause for concern. But I wonder how many doctors would be so aggressive about treatment if they themselves had their blood pressure recorded continuously throughout the day. I would love to take the expert's blood pressure while he was giving a speech to his colleagues. If he didn't have an elevation, especially during a tough question-and-answer session, I'd be surprised. And what surgeon wouldn't have his pressure go zooming into the stratosphere if he cut an important artery by mistake in the middle of an operation?

And what about sex? If the good doctor were willing to let us monitor his blood pressure during intercourse, we would almost certainly see an extraordinary quick rise at orgasm. Elevations to over 200 are not unusual, though fortunately such increases last only a few seconds.

Would these doctors be willing to start taking antihypertensive medication merely to "prevent spiking of the BP under emotional stress," or give up sex? I sincerely doubt it. Most of the physicians and pharmacologists I know go to great lengths to avoid taking these drugs, especially if they are prescribed on no better grounds than several office readings.

The issue of diagnosing high blood pressure is a hot topic in medicine right now. Not everyone agrees with the AMA's consultant. A recent article published, interestingly enough, in the *Journal of the American Medical Association* nicely summarizes the debate.

> [T]here is considerable controversy regarding the exact level of BP that poses sufficient risk to the patient to warrant long-term drug treatment. The decision to treat is further complicated by the fact that the BP measurement made in the physician's office, which is traditionally used as a guide to therapy, may be unrepresentative of the fluctuating BP levels during the day, and therefore, a misleading indicator of risk in the individual patient. . . .

> If antihypertensive therapy were entirely harmless and inexpensive, treating all persons with even minimal elevation of diastolic or systolic BP might be justified, if it were not for the psychological impact of making asymptomatic persons into patients. However, drug treatment is neither harmless nor inexpensive.[33]

These doctors set out to determine which was most important—the occasional blood-pressure measurement done in a doctor's office (which is often elevated) or the average walking-around pressure (ambulatory blood pressure), which is more typical of people's regular routine. They reviewed 1,076 patients with hypertension over a 10-year period. What they found will doubtless make many doctors uncomfortable.

Their research on ABP (ambulatory blood pressure) demonstrated that repeated measurements taken at home and work can accurately predict the risk of cardiovascular complications in "those groups of patients in whom the decision to treat hypertension is controversial—in the young, in those with borderline hypertension, in women, and in patients without evidence of the harmful effects of hypertension. It is in these groups that the benefit of lowering the BP has been difficult to prove."[34] Other researchers have also reported that frequent blood-pressure determinations done at home or work may be as good as or better than those done in the doctor's office when it comes to predicting problems down the road.[35–38]

Hey, Doc, I'd Rather Do It Myself!

So what's the answer to this blood pressure business? By now you are probably getting the idea that I might be in favor of home blood-pressure measurement. And you'd be absolutely, positively right! I am committed to this concept 100 percent. In fact, I can't imagine how a doctor would prescribe medicine to anyone without first getting some idea of what the home and work numbers look like.

Actually, quite a few physicians agree. As far back as 1940 articles started appearing in the medical literature in support of home blood-pressure readings.[39] Since then a surprising number of hypertension experts have come out in favor of this idea.[40-45] I say "surprising" only because it has taken a long time for the average doctor to accept it, and even today more physicians probably resist home blood-pressure measurements than encourage them.

Now just a cotton-pickin' minute. Here I am telling you that taking blood pressure is complicated and that doctors and nurses make all sorts of mistakes, and now you read that good old Joe is encouraging you to do it yourself. Why should you be any better at it than the doctor?

For one thing, you can make sure that the cuff you have is the right size for your arm. Second, you can take your pressure with your arm resting straight out even with your heart. Another advantage is that you can use a machine with a digital readout, which eliminates observer error and the need for you to master complicated stethoscope skills. And perhaps most important, you won't have to worry about being scared by the doctor or nurse. You can measure your pressure under a wide variety of conditions—stressful and relaxed—so that you get a more accurate picture of your normal readings.

Oh, you still have your doubts? Believe me, it's not that big a deal. Researchers at the University of Michigan School of Medicine have proved that just plain folks can do as good a job as any health professional.

> **The present study shows that patients are not only able to record reproducible readings but that they are also able to detect small changes in response to antihypertensive medication. We believe that the home BP self-determination technique will prove to be an invaluable aid in the management of borderline hypertension. The technique is simple. It takes about 20 minutes for a nurse to explain the principles and train the subjects.[46]**

British researchers have come to exactly the same conclusion.

> **Self-recording of the blood pressure by patients away from hospital or office ("home blood pressure") has been advo-**

cated as providing a better estimate of "true" blood pressure. . . .

This study suggests that home blood pressures are as accurate as clinic readings but may be recorded more frequently and thus provide more useful information.[47]

Still not convinced? Afraid your doctor will get mad? Okay, here is the coup de grace.

Clinical trials to determine the efficacy of anti-hypertensive drugs would do better to rely on patient-recorded blood-pressure readings than on those taken by health professionals outside the home. . . .

Values obtained from patients who monitored their own blood pressures at home, four times a day for 10 days, were much more consistent with intra-arterial blood-pressure recordings than were readings taken in a clinical setting.[48]

So there you have it. Home blood-pressure measurement is the way to go. Now you're convinced? Good. Of course you can do it. And if your doctor is a decent person, she'll back you all the way. But this should not mean that you become obsessed with taking your blood pressure. Some people may misinterpret my enthusiasm for this idea to mean that they have to take their blood pressure every few minutes throughout the day. That is *not* what I am recommending. And I definitely do not want you worrying every time you notice a slight elevation. The whole point of this exercise is to obtain a reasonably accurate impression of what your blood pressure is. By keeping a daily diary, you can give your physician some meaningful information to help plan a rational treatment strategy if you do have hypertension.

But which machine should you buy? Once upon a time it was relatively easy to answer that question. So few were available that there wasn't much choice. Today it seems as if everyone and his uncle has jumped into the business of making blood-pressure monitors. You can buy them in pharmacies, department stores, and through mail-order catalogues.

The wide range of devices on the market makes deciding difficult. There is no doubt that the old-fashioned glass column filled with mercury is still the most accurate and reliable. A model I have always been pleased with is called the **HI/LO Baumanometer**. It costs about $65 and can be ordered from the W. A. Baum Company in Copiague, NY 11726. You will also have to spend an extra $8.50 to get the tote bag in which to store the somewhat cumbersome **HI/LO**. This company (one of the most respected manufacturers of such equipment) would prefer that you buy the product from a medical or surgical supplier in your area but will sell it direct if you are persistent. A small, standard, or large size cuff can be ordered and will be happily exchanged if you make a mistake and order the wrong one to start with.

The problem is that most mercury-column sphygmomanometers are cumbersome and not very portable. They are also hard to use. Even though the **HI/LO Baumanometer** comes with an excellent instruction booklet, it is not easy to master the technique of listening to the sound of blood whooshing through an artery as you let air out of a pressure bulb.

In my experience, anything that isn't easy or portable won't get used as much as it should. But if you are willing to invest the time and effort in learning how to use this equipment properly (with a little help from your doctor), it is an excellent and highly reliable tool.

Alternatively, you could invest in an inexpensive aneroid gauge. These devices (plus a stethoscope) usually run between $20 and $100, depending upon how fancy you want to get. They have a small circular dial face with a needle. You pump up the cuff and watch the needle as it comes down while listening with a stethoscope.

These machines have the advantage of being portable, but they are not much easier to use than the mercury type unless you purchase a more expensive automated version with a flashing light that winks at you or with a tiny beeper that comes on when it detects the systolic pressure and goes off with diastolic pressure. The problem is that aneroid gauges aren't always accurate. They are vulnerable to variations in temperature and altitude and can lose calibration if they get bumped around a lot.[49,50]

That leaves those wonders of modern technology, the offspring of the electronic revolution—whizbang digital machines that make the taking of blood pressure almost as easy as a reading a clock radio. These babies are neat because they're portable, convenient, and make the stethoscope obsolete, which eliminates observer error. Not only do they give you a digital readout in numbers for both systolic and diastolic pressure, but most will tell pulse rate as well.

Some of the really fancy new up-scale machines even come with printers and automatic inflation. All you do is stick your arm in the cuff and push a button. The darn things pump themselves up and then slowly let the air out as they record your pressure. Afterward they print out systolic and diastolic pressure on a piece of paper, along with the time of day and date, so that you have a permanent record to file, plot on a graph, or give to your doctor. Incredible!

Sounds great, but what's the catch? You gue$$ed it; these machines generally do cost more than other types of blood-pressure devices. But as with most electronic advances, the price is falling fast. Used to be that you couldn't lay your hands on a digital machine for less than $200 to $300. Today, Marshall Electronics sells **Astropulse 49** for less than $70 and is planning to introduce **Astropulse 51** for less than $50. Timex sells the **Healthcheck Digital Blood Pressure Monitor** for about $70, and the Lumiscope Company markets a device called **Digitronic** for just about the same price. The Sybron Corporation, a leader in the field of blood-pressure monitoring, markets the **Tycos Self Check Digital Blood Pressure Monitor** for about $80. Norelco has also hopped on the bandwagon with the **HC 3000 Digital Blood Pressure/Pulse Meter** ranging from $80 to $90. And you can bet your boots that lots of other companies will be marketing digital equipment very soon. That's good news for consumers, since such competition usually brings with it better products at a lower price—think of calculators and computers.

Which machine should you buy? I wish I could give you an unequivocal answer. Objective testing and analysis of all the blood-pressure monitors on the market would take months and cost tens of thousands of dollars. Short of that, I have reviewed some of the most popular brands; my findings are summarized in a table at the end of this chapter. The information will, I hope, give you some guidelines for making a wise choice. For a more detailed evaluation, you should check in at your local library and scan *Consumer Reports*. That magazine periodically analyzes blood-pressure machines for ease of operation and accuracy.

Some pitfalls must be avoided, no matter what kind of device you buy. You absolutely *must* read all instructions carefully. I know the temptation to push buttons and start pumping is hard to resist, but I guarantee that you will make some serious mistakes if you do that. Nothing will raise your blood pressure faster than trying to figure out how to use one of these damn machines if you don't know what you're doing. By the way, the most common error is failure to place the built-in microphone (usually identified on the cuff as a painted circle or arrow) over the artery near the inside of your elbow.

A final word of caution. Home blood-pressure determination should not replace proper measurement in your doctor's office. What you need to do is monitor your pressure for several weeks at home, work, and at play. Periodic readings throughout the day will begin to give you a pretty good picture of your body's normal variation in blood pressure. Keep track in a diary of the time, date, and activities that correspond to those readings and bring the whole kit and caboodle along to the doctor's office the next time you have an appointment.

On the day of your visit take your pressure before you leave home. Take it again in the doctor's waiting room. When you finally see the doctor, tell her that you want to check your machine against her accurate mercury sphygmomanometer. First you should take your own pressure without letting the doctor see the results (to keep her objective). After waiting at least five minutes to allow your arm time to relax and return to normal and your nerves a chance to calm down, let the doctor use her stethoscope and mercury meter to compare results.

The numbers may not be exactly the same, but they shouldn't differ by more than 10 to 20 points (if they do, you may want to return the machine for calibration by the company). Now show her the numbers you have been collecting over the last few weeks or months. With this information she will be in an excellent position to evaluate your treatment program.

Help For Hypertension

So you've got high blood pressure. Everyone agrees—the nurse, the doctor and your own machine. Well, join the crowd. I noted at the outset of this chapter that 37 million Americans suffer from hypertension. Some believe that the numbers are even higher and estimate that as many as 60 million people are being stalked by the "silent killer."[51,52] It should come as no surprise to learn that hypertension accounts for more visits to the doctor than any other condition.

Those are the kinds of statistics that make drug-company executives lick their chops. Can you imagine the incredible bonanza they represent? No matter how good you feel, once you are labeled hypertensive, there is a very good likelihood you will be put on at least one medicine, and more likely two or three different medications, to be taken several times a day for the rest of your life. And even if the drugs make you drowsy, forgetful, impotent, depressed, or otherwise miserable, everyone from your doctor to some authoritative television announcer will encourage you to keep taking your medicine!

Multiply a potential 60 million people by four pills a day (a *very* conservative number, I assure you), multiply that figure by 365 days a year, and you get 87,000,000,000 tablets or capsules each year. (Yes, Virginia, that *is* 87 billion.) Would you like to know how much that amounts to in money? Multiply 60 million by $500 per person per year, and you come up with the staggering total of $30 billion as the potential market for blood pressure medicine. And hard as this may be to believe, this conservative figure doesn't even take into account doctor visits, laboratory tests, and other related costs.

Now $30 billion ain't chicken feed. You don't have to be an accountant to know that only a small part of the action would be like tapping into the mother lode. What a deal: millions and millions of otherwise healthy people are exhorted to keep taking billions and billions of pills, year in and year out. It's no wonder the drug companies are drooling all the way to the bank.

But should 60 million Americans be blithely swallowing so many drugs? That is a billion dollar question if ever there was one. There is probably no more controversial issue in medicine right now than when and how to treat high blood pressure. Many fine doctors are agonizing over this problem. Here are just a few of the titles that can be found these days in typically cautious scientific journals.

Should We Treat "Mild" Hypertension?[53]

Conflicting Clinical Trials and the Uncertainty of Treating Mild Hypertension[54]

The Dilemma of 'Mild' Hypertension Another Viewpoint of Treatment[55]

Treatment Reduces Deaths from Hypertension New Study Shows Dramatic Effects of Treating Even Those with Mild Hypertension[56]

Caution in Treating Mild Hypertension Urged[57]

"Mild" Hypertension: The Gray Zone Gets More Confusing[58]

Do you get the idea that doctors are just a bit befuddled about high blood pressure? They still don't know what causes it, and even worse, they aren't even sure what to do about it. Now that's something most physicians would never admit to their patients. But conscientious doctors are struggling with what is a very sticky situation. Don't get me wrong— there is near unanimity within the medical profession that people with moderate to severe hypertension *must* be treated aggressively, and there I won't argue. But how high is "high," and what about that "gray zone" called mild hypertension?

Okay, let's take a look at the numbers. Remember that, according to your doctor, par is 120/80. Even those who are "normal" may go above and below those numbers over the course of 24 hours, especially if they are making love; but overall, that is the ballpark range for young healthy adults. As we get older, the acceptable range climbs a tad, and most doctors don't get too upset if a 70-year-old patient shows up with a pressure of 140/90.

If, however, your true systolic blood pressure is regularly higher than 160 and your diastolic stays above 105 most of the time, you are way over par. Almost everyone I know would agree that something needs to be done to get the reading down. But what about people who consistently average somewhere between 140/90 and 160/105, the so-called mild hypertensives? Somewhere between 25 million and 40 million people fit into this category. These are the folks caught smack-dab in the middle of the doctor's tug-of-war over whether to vigorously treat borderline blood pressure with drugs.

The Gray Zone Gets Grayer

At one end of the rope are the crusaders who believe that any elevation in diastolic blood pressure over 90 requires aggressive treatment. One of the loudest shouters is Dr. Ray W. Gifford, Jr., a hypertension expert from the renowned Cleveland Clinic. He's at the vanguard of those who insist on controlling even mild hypertension. They got a big boost from a $70-million study called HDFP (Hypertension Detection and Follow-up Program).[59] According to Dr. Gifford, the study showed that

> **rigorous treatment of mild hypertension decreases the five-year mortality by 20.3 percent . . . a simple extrapolation from the HDFP results would mean that 325,000 lives will be prolonged in five years by rigorous treatment; this means 65,000 lives saved each year.[60]**

Now that sounds very impressive! Hundreds of thousands of lives prolonged by vigorous blood pressure treatment—and Dr. Gifford is nothing if not vigorous. His "goal is to get the diastolic pressure down to below 85 mm Hg (mercury)."[61] That's a little like asking Arnold Palmer to sink a 20-foot putt every time out, no matter what the conditions. Gifford points with pride to his colleagues who have adopted a similar aggressive approach; "a recent survey in New York State showed that 92 percent of physicians who responded stated that they were treating mild diastolic hypertension with antihypertensive drugs."[62,63]

But equally eminent experts are not at all convinced that such a track record is something to crow about. In fact, they wonder if such aggressive blood-pressure control may not be counterproductive at best and downright dangerous at worst.

Dr. Edward D. Freis could easily be called Mr. High Blood Pressure. He is certainly one of the world's leading authorities on the detection and treatment of hypertension. It was his study, almost 20 years ago, that demonstrated the clear-cut benefits of reducing severe high blood pressure, and he has been a leading advocate of drug therapy ever since. But he is not at all convinced that mild hypertension requires the same degree of drug treatment.

> **There is a growing body of opinion that all patients with hypertension—no matter how mild or uncomplicated—should be treated. . . . In considering drug treatment in such a large segment of the population, the disadvantages must be weighed against the possible advantages. Drug treatment may have toxic effects, especially in patients who do not become normotensive with a simple drug regimen but require a combina-**

tion of drugs. In addition to overt toxicity, most drugs have subjective effects that, though not life-threatening, are disturbing to the person's quality of life.[64]

Dr. Freis has analyzed all the major blood-pressure research carried out in recent years, and except for the HDFP study, he reports that most mild hypertensive patients probably did not benefit from drug therapy. As for the Hypertension Detection and Follow-up Program—which he describes as having become the "chief pillar supporting the aggressive treatment of mild hypertension"—Dr. Freis is not impressed. For one thing, it did not demonstrate that medications were helpful for patients under 50 or white women. And unlike the enthusiastic Dr. Gifford, he finds serious flaws in the design of the study and comes to very different conclusions.

> The most favorable results come from the study of most questionable design, in which interpretation is difficult because the trial was not planned to test drug treatment but rather global medical care. . . .
>
> In view of the uncertainties, we may be doing more harm than good by giving lifelong drug treatment to patients with borderline or mild hypertension.[65]

Dr. Freis's isn't the only voice calling for caution. Many other physicians have started raising a red flag, too. Several Yale epidemiologists who also analyzed recent research cautioned that there is "misinterpretation" of the data, that "excessive enthusiasm for treatment has resulted," and that "mild hypertension is being extensively overtreated."[66] Dr. Neil McAlister, writing in the *Journal of the American Medical Association*, also warns his colleagues to cool it.

> Clinical trials have failed to show significant, reproducible clinical benefits derived from treating uncomplicated, mild hypertension, nor is there much convincing evidence that treatment prevents complications.
>
> In this light and in consideration of the age-old warning *primum non nocere* [first do no harm], we must weigh the potentially negative health effects that could arise from indiscriminate treatment of all mildly hypertensive persons.[67]

High-Blood-Pressure Medicine: Hurting More Than Helping?

In case you missed the point, these experts are tiptoeing around an extremely delicate issue—the potential hazards of medication for high blood pressure. The Hippocratic oath exhorts physicians to first do no harm. Yet many doctors are beginning to worry that, like the plumber who sets out to fix a leaky faucet and ends up flooding the house, they may be doing their patients more harm than good when they aggressively prescribe lifelong drug therapy for mild hypertension.

Put aside for a moment the insult of impotence, the downer of fatigue, and the discomfort of drowsiness, dizziness, and depression (don't forget the beta-blocker blues). These are just some of the side effects that can come with drugs. Doctors have known about these "inconveniences" for years, but they are not what has some physicians worried. What's on their minds these days is the possibility that many commonly prescribed blood-pressure medications may actually be *increasing* the risk of cardiovascular problems and heart attacks in mild hypertensives rather than decreasing them.

Do you remember MRFIT—the Multiple Risk Factor Intervention Trial? We mentioned that it was the most expensive ($100 million plus), most comprehensive study ever undertaken to investigate heart-attack prevention. It took over 10 years to complete and involved more than 12 thousand volunteers. It was supposed to prove once and for all that a carefully designed program that helped people to stop smoking, to lower cholesterol levels, and to reduce high blood pressure would have a profound positive influence on the incidence of heart attacks and mortality.

But, to put it bluntly, MRFIT bombed. The control group (those fellows who received no special intervention) did just about as well as the men who were given intensive supervision and treatment. The researchers tried to explain the unexpected results on the grounds that all America is health-conscious these days and that therefore even the guys in the control group were probably eating better and exercising more.

Maybe so. But another unexpected result of the MRFIT study was a hell of a lot harder to explain. Some of the men in the intervention group with abnormal electrocardiograms had received blood-pressure medication. Nothing surprising there—it happens every day. What was astonishing, however, was the discovery that they seemed to be dying faster than the men who got no special treatment. Whoops! What gives? Could it be that the drugs actually doubled the death rate? This bombshell should have shaken the medical establishment to its foundation. And indeed, a number of doctors have paid attention. A group of Norwegian hypertension experts asked their American counterparts some tough questions.

Why has drug treatment of hypertension no preventing effect on CHD [coronary heart disease]? And what is new and really alarming: Why had antihypertensive drug treatment a possible adverse effect when hypertension was associated with a high cholesterol level or with resting ECG [electrocardiogram] abnormalities?[68]

American researchers had no easy answers. Instead of reassurance, Dr. Norman Kaplan, an authority on hypertension from the University of Texas in Dallas, added his own words of caution.

> **MRFIT should bring about a reassessment of the current widespread routine use of drug treatment for most people with mild hypertension, defined as a diastolic BP between 90 and 104 mm Hg. Such patients make up about 75 percent of the hypertensive population, a total of at least 30 million Americans.**

> **The MRFIT results . . . reconfirm the value of antihypertensive drug therapy for those with diastolic BP *above* 100 mm Hg. However, for the large number, the majority of mild hypertensives who have diastolic BPs in the 90- to 100-mm Hg range, these results confirm the need for a more cautious, conservative approach toward drug therapy.**[69]

If ever there was a hot potato, this is it. Dr. Ray Gifford and his colleagues are adamant that mild elevations in blood pressure *must* be treated. But equally respected investigators in hypertension research, Dr. Edward Freis and Dr. Norman Kaplan, have expressed doubts that the benefits of drug therapy outweigh the risks.

Depletion and Disruption With Diuretics

But what *are* the risks? Let's deal with diuretics—or "water pills," as my mother calls them. Almost inevitably the new patient with raised blood pressure will receive one of these drugs as the first step in any treatment program. (By the way, these *were* the medications primarily used in the MRFIT study.)

Hydrochlorothiazide (HCTZ) is by far the most popular. Over ten million generic prescriptions are written each year for HCTZ, and countless millions more are dispensed in such brand-name preparations as **Esidrix**, **HydroDIURIL**, **Hydro-Aquil**, **Hydrozide-Z-50**, **Lexor**, **Oretic**, and **Thiuretic**. We better not forget the even more popular combination products that include hydrochlorothiazide along with additional medicine, such as **Aldactazide**, **Aldoril**, **Apresoline-Esidrix**, **Dyazide**, **Esimil**, **Hydralazide**, **Hydropres**, **Hydro-Serp**, **Hyperserp**, **Inderide**, **Moduretic**, **Oreticyl**, **Salupres**, **Ser-Ap-Es**, **Timolide**, and **Unipres**.

Other commonly prescribed medications that contain diuretics include bendroflumethiazide (**Naturetin**, **Rauzide**), benzthiazide (**Aquastat**, **Aquatag**, **Aquex**, **Exna**, **Hydrex**), chlorothiazide (**Aldoclor**, **Diupres**, **Diuril**, **Saluric**), chlorthalidone (**Combipres**, **Demi-Regroton**, **Hygroton**,

Regroton, Thalitone), cyclothiazide (**Anhydron, Fluidil**), hydroflumethiazide (**Diucardin, Saluron, Salutensin**), methyclothiazide (**Aquatensen, Diutensen, Enduron, Enduronyl**), polythiazide (**Minizide, Renese**), and trichlormethiazide (**Metahydrin, Metatensin, Naqua, Naquival**).

Diuretics are considered benign drugs by most physicians. Ask about side effects, and you may get an indignant upraised eyebrow in response, almost as if the question were impudent in regard to such safe medicine. You might be told that these drugs will make you pee a little more often or may deplete your body of potassium, (**Dyazide** and **Aldactazide** can be exceptions). But such adverse reactions are considered minor, and patients are often told simply to eat bananas and drink orange juice to replace lost potassium.

But is the matter really so simple? Well, my friend, I'm here to tell you a slightly different story. First, I am not at all convinced that diuretics are as supersafe as most docs like to think. It's not that these drugs produce obvious adverse reactions. Oh, there may be some dryness of the mouth and a little thirst, some weakness, nausea, or impotence. But the majority of people seem to tolerate diuretics surprisingly well. It's the subtle stuff that has me concerned—changes that most people probably wouldn't pick up without special lab tests.

You see, diuretics can screw up body chemistry something fierce. There are few other drugs that have such a profound impact on so many different biochemical systems. Insulin and blood sugar can be affected, and that reaction may turn someone who is on the borderline into an out-and-out diabetic. Uric-acid levels tend to increase, and that can bring on gout in susceptible individuals. Diuretics can also alter calcium, zinc, and magnesium balances. It is also possible that such drugs temporarily increase cholesterol levels. This finding has led some physicians to wonder whether the benefits derived from lowering blood pressure now may be counterbalanced by an increased risk of arteriosclerosis in the future.[70–72]

But the biggest problem, really, is potassium. And I am not at all sure that you can correct the damage by drinking a little orange juice and eating a banana. Potassium loss is a complication that may be more serious than previously recognized. Symptoms of inadequate potassium include muscle cramps, weakness, and irregular heart rhythms (arrhythmias). And that last one can spell big trouble.

Abnormal heart beats are something we can all do without, but they are especially serious for anyone with underlying heart trouble. An arrhythmia at the wrong time can conceivably lead to fibrillation, which means the heart stops pumping blood. When that happens, the ball game's over unless someone is standing by ready to zap you with a defibrillator. Dr. Kaplan has speculated that diuretic-induced potassium depletion may have been partly responsible for the excess of coronary deaths seen in the MRFIT program.[73]

Now, I don't want to scare people into worrying that the water pills they have been taking for granted all these years are suddenly going to kill them. If there is a danger, it seems to be primarily to those people who already have abnormal electrocardiograms. Nevertheless, there is growing evidence that diuretics may be associated with heart-beat irregularities.[74-79]

Replacing Potassium: The Plot Thickens

So why not just take in some extra potassium and stop worrying? Easier said than done, good buddy. Even if you don't mind overdosing on bananas and orange juice (they *can* get boring), there is still a good chance that these foods won't provide enough to replace what is lost. Unfortunately doctors rarely receive good nutrition training in medical schools, which is why they seem fixated on bananas and orange juice. Someone told them that these are the right foods, and they never bothered to check further.

It just so happens, however, that there *are* other foods which can supply reasonable amounts of potassium. They include apricots, avocados, blackstrap molasses, Brazil nuts, broccoli, brussels sprouts, cantaloupe, carrots, chicken, cocoa powder (not alkali-processed), dates, flounder, hamburger, halibut, kidney beans, lentils, lima beans, liver, milk, oatmeal, peaches, peanuts, pecans, pork chops, potatoes (baked with skin), pot roast, prunes, prune juice, raisins, salmon, shrimp, spinach, tomatoes, tuna, veal, wheat germ, yeast, and yogurt.

The key to success is to mix and match. Don't rely on one or two foods to supply necessary nutrition. A high-potassium breakfast might include oatmeal with wheat germ, molasses, and a few cut-up dates. Lunch could consist of several carrots, a tuna salad, and prunes. If you finished the day with a supper of halibut and a baked potato, and a few apricots for dessert, you would be getting a heck of a lot more potassium than you would from the banana and orange juice the doctor recommended.

Some physicians don't even bother with dietary recommendations. They think they can get around the potassium problem by prescribing a supplement. It used to be that they relied almost exclusively on liquid preparations of potassium chloride, such as **K-Lyte, Kaochlor, Kaon-Cl, Kay Ciel, Klor-Con, Klorvess,** or **Kolyum,** but patients often objected. Liquid potassium can leave a nasty aftertaste that just won't quit. Trying to swallow a yucky-tasting liquid once or twice a day, day in and day out, can become a living hell. Then there is the nausea, vomiting, stomach pain, and diarrhea. Not a pleasant prospect for the rest of one's life.

Enter stage left the slow-release solid potassium tablets and capsules.

Zowee, hooray, and whoopdee-doo! No bad aftertaste, and rarely any nausea. Products like **Slow-K, Micro-K Extencaps, K-Tab, Kaon-CL Tabs,** and **Klotrix** have made docs look like heroes and have become very big sellers. Everyone was happy—or so it seemed. But there was a cloud on the horizon. As far back as 1975 the highly respected journal, *Medical Letter on Drugs and Therapeutics*, urged caution.

> **A recent letter to physicians from the Ciba Pharmaceutical Company announced the marketing of Slow-K—slow-release potassium chloride tablets—and claimed the product is an "important new advance in potassium supplement therapy. . . ."**
>
> **In spite of the slow release, small bowel ulceration and stricture have been reported. . . .**
>
> **CONCLUSION—Slow-release potassium tablets such as Slow-K and Kaon-Cl Tabs are dangerous and should not be used. Supplementation of the regular diet with potassium-rich foods is the safest way to prevent hypokalemia [potassium depletion] in patients taking diuretics.[80]**

Unfortunately almost nobody was listening. Even though occasional reports in the medical literature mentioned ulceration, perforation, obstruction, and hemorrhage of the digestive tract, most physicians considered these products safe. **Slow-K** went on to become one of the most commonly prescribed drugs on the doctors' hit parade, and over nine million people have taken it since it was introduced in 1975.

Concern with digestive-tract irritation seemed unimportant until 1982, when Dr. Gilbert McMahon at Tulane University School of Medicine announced some shocking findings. He found that this "wax-matrix" preparation produced a high incidence of digestive-tract irritation when compared to **Micro-K** (which appeared far safer).[81] What was so insidious was that most patients were unaware of the damage, since they felt no pain.

The danger was even greater for people who were taking other drugs that slow down the digestive tract. According to Dr. McMahon such antidepressants as **Elavil** (amitriptyline), **Limbitrol** (chlordiazepoxide and amitriptyline), **Tofranil** (imipramine), and **Triavil** (perphenazine and amitriptyline) could make solid potassium more dangerous. So could such antihistamines as **Benadryl** (diphenhydramine), **Dimetane** (brompheniramine), and **Contac** (chlorpheniramine and phenylpropanolamine). But worst of all are the medications used to calm a "nervous" digestive tract—like **Bentyl** (dicyclomine), **Combid** (isopropamide and prochlorperazine), **Donnatal** (hyoscyamine, atropine, scopalomine, and phenobarbital), **Librax** (chlordiazepoxide and clidinium), and **Pro-Banthine** (propantheline). According to the new research, such drugs combined with **Slow-K** significantly increase the risk of digestive-tract irritation.

Belatedly the FDA awoke from its stupor. A letter went out from the agency to all manufacturers of slow-release solid potassium pills commenting on Dr. McMahon's research.

> **The results are dramatic showing a high frequency of gastric irritation (erosion and even ulceration) in Slow-K treated patients. The study raises serious questions regarding the safety of Slow-K and, by implication, all wax-matrix, solid dosage forms of potassium.**[82]

Dr. McMahon found that **Micro-K Extencaps** seemed significantly safer than the wax-matrix **Slow-K**-type products. He has candidly admitted to me that if *his* mother had to take a potassium supplement, he would rather have her on **Micro-K** than on **Slow-K**. The Food and Drug Administration, in its infinite wisdom, has required additional testing for *all* solid-potassium formulations. As of this writing, however, the results are not yet in. If I absolutely had to take a potassium supplement, though, I would put my money on **Micro-K**, based on the information currently available.

Having Your Cake and Eating It, Too

So where does all this leave the person with mild high blood pressure? Well, if your doctor has prescribed a diuretic, like **HydroDIURIL** or **Hygroton**, you're probably feeling like you've been caught in a colossal catch-22. First you read that many authoritative experts on hypertension doubt that treatment is even necessary. Then you learn that the nice and simple diuretic you've been taking can cause complex biochemical changes, including potassium depletion, which can be quite serious, especially if you have disturbances of your heart rhythm. But taking a solid-dose potassium supplement, like **Slow-K,** has risks all its own. *Help!*

All right, I grant you that the outlook seems bleak. But believe me, it's not as bad as it appears. First, a word about *serious* high blood pressure—that is, anything over 160/104. Yes, the risks are real, and the condition requires vigorous treatment. On that everyone agrees. Here's a case where the benefits of drug therapy far outweigh the dangers. For an analysis of commonly prescribed blood-pressure medications, turn to the appendix to this chapter.

But what about mild hypertension? Should you just ignore it and hope that it will go away? Not as far as I'm concerned. If you aspired to play par golf, would you settle for 40 over par? Of course not. There is little doubt in my mind that, as in golf, lower blood-pressure numbers are best. That doesn't mean you need to become obsessed; worrying about your blood pressure can in itself probably make it go up.

Let us, then, figure out a strategy to keep your numbers nice and normal if they are already in the 120/80 range or to bring them down if they are starting to climb over 140/90. Okay now, hunker down and pay close attention, this is important.

You *can* lower blood pressure without drugs. And if you're on medicine, it doesn't have to continue for the rest of your life. Dr. Jeremiah Stamler is Chairman of the Department of Community Health and Preventive Medicine at Northwestern University in Chicago. He and his researcher wife, Rose, proved that they could successfully wean almost two-thirds of their mild hypertensive patients off drugs.[83]

How did they do it? No big secret—weight loss of at least ten pounds, salt restriction, increased exercise, and two drinks or less per day. Now I would be the first to admit that such changes are far easier said than done, especially if you aren't getting a lot of support from your doctor. Very few physicians take the time to really work with their patients when it comes to changing life-styles.

I have an excellent doctor, but when I went to him and asked for help in losing *my* extra ten pounds, all he could suggest was that I take up jogging. He might as well have suggested I take up flying (without an airplane). I hate running, and I've got flat feet, weak knees, and a bad back. No, I need some other kind of exercise, like swimming. And I need lots of encouragement. So do you.

First, some facts to spur you on. If you stop smoking, that alone will probably reduce your risk of having a heart attack as much as a lifetime of high-blood-pressure medication. If you lose ten pounds, your blood pressure will almost assuredly come down at lease five points.

Answer me this—if you were a man, and someone told you that your punishment for not losing weight would be castration, would you be motivated to slim down? You bet you would! Yet millions of men allow themselves to be chemically castrated with blood-pressure medicine without so much as a whimper. To be honest, of course, most of these drugs do not actually affect fertility or do anything bad to the family jewels, but many can lead to loss of libido, impotence, and inability to ejaculate. If men were told that losing weight could make the drugs unnecessary, many might indeed be prompted to shed excess pounds.

The Sodium Controversy: Stickier Than You Thought

What about salt? It's bad for you, right? After all, in 1982 *Time* magazine ran a cover story titled, **"Salt: A New Villain?"** The answer: *"Yes, say the doctors, and the country scrambles to change its eating habits."*[84] Boy, I wish it was really that simple. This is another issue that is far more controversial than most people would ever imagine. Two weeks after the *Time* story hit the newsstands, an article appeared in the highly respected journal *Science* with the headline **"Value of Low-Sodium Diets Questioned."** The report was subtitled, *"Some experts say that low-sodium diets are of no benefit to the general public."*[85]

These are just two of the most recent shots fired in the seemingly endless salt wars. Experts on hypertension have been battling for decades over the benefits of salt restriction, and believe me, the fight is far from over. Over the last several years a surprising number of conflicting articles have appeared in medical journals. What follows is merely a random sample.

A survey of 3,566 people in Connecticut found little to worry about.

> **It is unlikely dietary salt intake has a clinically significant effect on BP in the majority of individuals . . . CONCLUSION: On the basis of current evidence, it does not appear justifiable or appropriate to undertake large-scale salt restriction in the general population to prevent hypertension.[86]**
>
> *JAMA,* **July, 1983**

A study examined 476 newborns, half of whom were put on a low-sodium diet and half on a "normal" sodium diet. Blood pressure was monitored for six months. The findings

> **support the view that sodium intake is causally related to the level of BP. Moderation of sodium intake, starting very early in life, might perhaps contribute to prevention of high BP and of rise of BP with age.[87]**
>
> *JAMA,* **July, 1983**

A major review article analyzed the current medical literature.

> **There is no evidence to indicate that a widely applied, moderate reduction of salt intake could prevent the development of hypertension. The evidence suggesting that such moderate salt intake would significantly lower blood pressure in the patients with sodium-sensitive essential hypertension is weak . . . . Sodium deprivation, like other forms of therapy, should be applied only to those patients in whom its effectiveness has been established.[88]**
>
> *Annals of Internal Medicine,* **May, 1983**

A different review of the medical literature came to completely opposite conclusions.

> [E]vidence has shown that moderate restriction of sodium to
> 70–100 mmol/day [about one teaspoon] does cause a fall in
> blood pressure in patients with mild to moderate essential
> hypertension and its effect is additive to that of blood-pressure-
> lowering drugs. This moderate reduction in sodium intake
> has approximately the same blood-pressure-lowering effect as
> a single antihypertensive drug, such as a diuretic or beta-
> blocker.[89]
>
> *The Lancet,* April, 1983

If you think you're confused, imagine my dilemma. I have to sift
through these tea leaves and try to make sense out of contradiction.
Well, it's murky all right, but not hopeless. I won't bore you with the
details of dozens of studies, but here are some of my conclusions after
reviewing much of the conflicting data.

Most people probably don't need to be obsessive about their salt
intake. Somewhere between 70 and 80 percent of the American public
seems able to eat salt without experiencing a rise in blood pressure. That
doesn't mean these people won't benefit from cutting back. We all eat
far too much salt, and moderation can't hurt. But the point is that the
majority can probably indulge occasionally in pickles and pretzels without suffering any obvious ill effects.

The other 20 percent, however, had better watch out. These sodium-
sensitive individuals seem more susceptible to hypertension, and cutting
back on salt can make a significant difference. The trouble is that there's
no good way to tell whether you're in the critical 20 percent. Until they
come up with some snazzy blood test, then, here is a very crude guide for
you to consider.

If one or both of your parents has high blood pressure, chances are
very good that you are at risk yourself. If you are over 50, you have a 40
percent chance of developing hypertension. According to the actuarial
tables, 1 out of every 2 black males will develop high blood pressure.
And anyone with kidney trouble faces a 95-percent risk. Now there is no
guarantee that cutting back on salt will prevent hypertension, or even
bring it down once you've got it. But what have you got to lose?
Throwing away the salt shaker sure beats a lifetime of drugs and the
possibility of impotence.

Unfortunately skipping the shaker isn't the whole answer. Would it
were that easy! Even those physicians who believe that salt is indeed a
"villain" have a hard time agreeing on a "safe" level. Some insist that
anything less than total abstinence is futile, since there are no benefits
unless you restrict yourself to nothing but rice, fruit, and vegetables—a
course that isn't practical for most people. But others are convinced that
moderate sodium reduction *is* worthwhile. These researchers suggest that

high blood pressure can be reduced by keeping salt intake around one teaspoonful per day or approximately 1,150 mg. to 2,300 mg.[90-94]

Oh, I can hear you already: "One teaspoonful of salt—no sweat." On the surface it would seem as if one teaspoon is a lot of salt, and anyone with even a little self-control ought easily to be able to keep below that amount. You'd be wrong. Staying under one teaspoon of salt (2,000 mg. of sodium) a day is a challenge that takes constant vigilance and considerable dedication.

That's because sodium is everywhere. Even if you don't cook with salt and never use it at the table, you are only halfway home; 50 percent of your sodium comes from processed foods and other surprising places. And I'm not talking sauerkraut, anchovies, or potato chips—everyone knows those are salty. Seemingly innocent food will do you in just as fast as the obvious culprits.

You decide, for example, to skip the ham and eggs in favor of a nice, light, salt-free breakfast of Wheaties, one homemade biscuit, and jam. Whoops—you lose. A one-ounce serving of Wheaties has 365 mg. of sodium, one cup of lowfat milk has 244 mg. of sodium, one homemade (from mix) biscuit has 272 mg. of sodium, and one tablespoon of low-calorie jam has 19 mg. of sodium. Total amount of sodium by 9:00 A.M. is 900 mg. Since you were so very good at breakfast (or so you thought), you indulged in a doughnut during your coffee break; add 160 mg. sodium.

For lunch you watch calories—tuna salad (3 oz.) with a slice of rye toast, a glass of V-8 juice (6 oz.), and lemon Jell-O (½ cup) for dessert. Sounds sensible and healthy. Wrong again. The tuna salad has 445 mg. of sodium (303 mg. from the tuna, 117 mg. from 1½ tbsp. of mayonnaise, and 25 mg. from one stalk of celery). The rye toast adds 139 mg. sodium, and the V-8 juice zapped you to the tune of 555 mg. The Jell-O added a measly 75 mg., but even so, your luncheon total came to a whopping 1214 mg. of sodium.

You congratulate yourself on being such a careful eater all day, so you decide to live a little for supper. First a nice hot bowl of chicken-noodle soup (8 oz. of Campbell's finest), followed by a tossed salad, steak, and baked potato. You resist temptation and avoid using the salt shaker, but you do put two tablespoons of A-1 sauce on the steak and a pat of butter on the potato. You wash it all down with a beer, and for dessert you have a piece of German chocolate cake.

Want to hear the bad news? The soup provided 820 mg. of sodium. The salad itself added very little sodium, but the dressing (3 tbsp. of Good Seasons Low-Calorie Italian) added 450 mg., and the croutons (.5 oz. Pepperidge Farm Onion-Garlic) supplied 135 mg. The steak wasn't too bad—it only added 100 mg. for a 6-oz. portion. But two tablespoons of A-1 kicked in 550 mg. The baked potato by itself has virtually no sodium, but the butter gave you 116 mg. The beer (Miller) was only 25 mg., but the chocolate cake (Betty Crocker) weighed in with 420 mg. The supper total was 2,616 mg. of sodium.

Ready for the grand total? Wait just a minute. Let's not forget the **Alka-Seltzer**—after all, you did overdo just a tad. One regular dose (two tablets of the plop-plop, fizz-fizz medicine) will supply 1102 mg. Okay, strap on your seat belt. Your "low-salt" diet for the day provided you with 5992 mg. of sodium, or approximately three teaspoons of salt. Without once picking up a salt shaker, you managed to consume more than three times the maximum amount recommended by the experts. And most of the food didn't taste salty; that's what makes this whole low-sodium trip so difficult.

Say you have a Big Mac attack. You go to McDonald's and order up a quarter-pounder with cheese, a vanilla shake, and an apple pie. You skip the salty french fries because you know that they're the troublemaker. Boy, are you wrong. The fries (with salt added) are the lowest on the list, with 109 mg. Your quarter-pounder nails you with 1,236 mg. The shake has twice as much sodium, and the apple pie four times as much, as the fries.

One final example. A handful of potato chips (15, to be exact) has about 115 mg. of sodium. But one slice of Arnold/Oroweat Bran'nola bread is worse, with 188 mg., and a medium-sized portion of cottage cheese (4 oz.) contains 457 mg. You wouldn't think cottage cheese is a veritable salt mine, would you? But the fact that it is just goes to prove that you can't judge a food by its taste.

So what do you do? First, read labels. Many food companies are responding to pressure from the FDA and consumers to list the sodium content on the label. Next, buy a good reference book from among the several on the market. The Center for Science in the Public Interest has published a fine one titled *Salt: The Brand Name Guide to Sodium Content*. You should be able to get it in any good bookstore for around $6, or order it direct from CSPI, 1755 S St. N.W., Washington, DC 20009. To avoid confusion, make sure you mention the title of the book, since CSPI publishes a number of other food-oriented books. Another reasonable choice is *Low Salt Secrets for Your Diet* by Dr. William Vaughan. It's in paperback and is nicely portable. Warner Books publishes this one, and it should be available in most bookstores.

Even if you read labels and have a reference book handy at all times, you still have a hard road ahead. First you have to train your taste buds to like low-sodium foods. Not easy, but it can be done. I used to be one of those people who reached for the salt shaker before I even tasted my food. Now even moderate amounts of salt taste terrible to my tongue. So you *can* reeducate your mouth. Next, you have to watch where you eat—most restaurants will do you in every time.

But even if you eat at home, you don't have it made. Sodium-free foods are hard to find and often more expensive than regular brands. Ah, but I have a trick for you. A simple solution is as close as the kitchen sink. If you want to reduce the sodium content of some of the foods you eat by 35 to 75 percent, it could be as simple as washing things off before you eat or cook them.

Three researchers at Duke University discovered that a surprising amount of unwanted salt can be rinsed off food simply by running it under tap water.[95] They tested canned green beans, cottage cheese, and canned tuna. All three showed substantial reductions, but tuna was by far the biggest winner. Fresh from the can, the water-packed tuna contained an average of more than 360 mg. of sodium per 100 grams (about 4 oz.) of tuna. When the fish was drained and rinsed for one minute in tap water, the sodium content of the tuna dropped an astounding 76 to 79 percent.

The results were almost as spectacular with cottage cheese—which, as you remember, contains a whopping dose of sodium. Dump the curds and whey into a plastic measuring cup, rinse for a minute, and suddenly you're looking at a 56 percent reduction in salt content. For green beans the rinse wasn't as productive, but it still helped a lot, with about 40 percent of the salt disappearing when the beans were drained, (rinsed for a minute, and then heated to boiling in tap water) rather than the sodium-rich liquid contained in the can.

The bottom line on all this salt stuff is that, while it's easy for doctors to hand out diets calling for lowered sodium levels, most people rapidly discover that such diets are unrealistic, unpalatable, or unattainable, given the realities of a lifestyle that necessarily includes processed foods. The obstacles make you want to throw up your hands in disgust and walk away. Rather than give up the task as hopeless, however, you now have a new and easy option. By both watching and washing what you eat, you should be able to greatly reduce sodium intake without having to make drastic alterations in your customary diet.

One final word of caution—be wary of drugs. It is shocking how many medications are loaded with sodium. **Alka Seltzer**, **Bromo Seltzer**, **Brioschi**, **Eno**, and **Sal Hepatica** each have over 700 mg. of sodium per dose. **Rolaids** has only 53 mg. per tablet, but I know some people who easily put away a pack of **Rolaids** a day, and at that rate you've got problems. Even a simple cough medicine like **Vicks Formula 44** has over 100 mg. of sodium. So remember, vigilance and diligence are the keys to success.

Cashing Out on Caffeine

Sodium isn't the only substance that can cause you trouble; let's not forget caffeine. As little as two or three cups of coffee can raise blood pressure by 14 percent.[96] While this effect probably wears off with heavy coffee drinking because the body adapts to caffeine, for some people it could be a problem, especially for people who may not drink coffee every day. Caffeine also triggers the release of massive amounts of adrenaline into the blood stream (an increase of over 200 percent). This may be why it can cause heart palpitations and irregular heart beats.

One impressive study by Ohio State researchers, published in the *New England Journal of Medicine*, showed that as little as two cups of brewed coffee can produce profound rhythm changes.[97] Dr. Stephen Schaal, the principal investigator, is convinced that "there is absolutely a cause-and-effect relationship here. Caffeine does, in fact, have an effect on the electrical system of the heart."[98] For most of the volunteers in the study these disturbances were worrisome but not life-threatening. But two of the subjects developed ventricular tachyarrhythmia—a rapid ventricular heart rate. According to Dr. Schaal, "This is a rhythm change that can cause sudden death."[99] People with heart trouble *and* high blood pressure should probably avoid coffee.

And that ain't all. A recent study from Norway suggests that heavy coffee drinkers may "increase cholesterol levels enough to more than double the risk of heart disease."[100,101] This humongous study concentrated on 7,368 men and 7,213 women between the ages of 20 and 54. Cholesterol levels were 5 percent higher among moderate coffee drinkers (one to four cups a day) than among people who drank no coffee. Heavy coffee drinkers (five to eight cups) had an increase of 9 percent, and really heavy java junkies (nine or more cups per day) had cholesterol levels 12 percent higher than nondrinkers. These results even shocked the researchers.

> Our attitude toward the present finding of a coffee-cholesterol association changed from suspicious surprise to guarded belief as the relation seemed to withstand all adjustments. The association is strong and consistent, and its magnitude makes coffee one of the strongest determinants of serum cholesterol levels in the present population.[102]

Still not convinced? Well, if the threat of high blood pressure and coronary artery disease isn't enough to dissuade you, how about the fear of cancer?

> Coffee has again been linked to bladder cancer—and by evidence suggesting that even moderate consumption is hazardous. . . .
>
> Interviews with 412 bladder cancer patients and 493 controls indicate that the odds of getting cancer jump 62 percent if a man drinks eight to 20 cups of coffee a week and higher with additional cups.[103]

This isn't the first time coffee has been linked with cancer. Animal and human studies have shown an association with pancreatic cancer as well.[104] Research suggests that the more people drink, the higher the risk.

Simple Nondrug Steps to Success

Okay, I'll stop, I'll stop! Enough already. You have every right to be sick and tired of reading about things *not* to do. You've heard all the don'ts before—*don't smoke, don't overeat, don't use salt, don't drink coffee,* and on and on ad nauseam. I must admit that as logical and reasonable as all these strictures sound, the lifestyle changes are hard as hell to implement. And believe me, I'm no goodie-goodie myself. Yes, I did stop smoking, but I still have an occasional cup of coffee, and every once in a while I indulge in one of my all-time favorite vices— Philadelphia soft pretzels (with salt!). I've even been known to have a Big Mac Attack.

If you are as tired as I am of lectures and don'ts, would you like to find out about some easy stuff? It's coming right up.

Simple Nondrug Step to Success #1: Potassium. Many researchers are beginning to believe that excess sodium is only half the hypertension story. Inadequate potassium may also contribute to this condition. Simple solution: be sure to get more potassium. A number of fascinating reports have started cropping up in the medical literature which suggest that a low-sodium high-potassium diet can have a major influence on blood pressure.

One group of investigators at the London Hospital Medical College performed a fascinating experiment. They located two groups of male medical students. All the students had basically normal blood pressure, but one group had parents with hypertension, while the other group's family history was normal. They then tried various diets—high sodium, low sodium, and low-sodium high-potassium.

Results were predictable: moderate salt restriction lowered blood pressure in both groups, and high salt diets increased it. What was surprising was the finding that the men from hypertensive families had the greatest reduction in blood pressure (about 10 points) when they cut back on salt and simultaneously increased their potassium intake.[105] Other studies confirm that the ratio of sodium to potassium may be far more important than sodium restriction alone.[106–109]

So how do you get more potassium? First, be very careful about taking potassium supplements. Remember my words of caution earlier in the chapter. Besides the risk of digestive-tract irritation, this is an easy way to get too much potassium, which is just as bad (if not worse) than too little, and much harder to detect. Symptoms are subtle, often appearing only when toxicity has become critical. Signs of excessive potassium include mental confusion; unexplained anxiety; unusual tiredness; muscle twitches; numbness or tingling in hands, feet, and lips; weak or heavy legs; difficulty breathing; and worst of all, irregular heart beats. These arrhythmias can become life-threatening. But since muscle cramps and twitches, fatigue, and irregular heart beats can also result from too little potassium, don't rely on do-it-yourself diagnosis. If you have any symptoms, see your doctor and get blood tests.

How in the world do you walk the tightrope between too much and too little potassium? Probably the best way is through diet. Potassium-rich foods like those in the table below can make a real difference, since it's hard to overdose on them.

Potassium-Rich Foods

Apricots	Oatmeal
Avocados	Oranges
Bananas	Peaches
Blackstrap molasses	Peanuts
Brazil nuts	Pecans
Broccoli	Pork chops
Brussels sprouts	Potatoes (baked in skin)
Cantaloupe	Pot roast
Carrots	Prunes
Chicken	Prune juice
Cocoa powder (not alkali-processed)	Raisins
Dates	Salmon
Flounder	Shrimp
Hamburger	Spinach
Halibut	Tomatoes
Kidney beans	Tuna
Lentils	Veal
Lima beans	Wheat germ
Liver	Yeast
Milk	Yogurt

Now you're probably thinking that the list contains several of your least favorite foods—maybe brussels sprouts, wheat germ, yeast, and yogurt. Isn't there any other way to get potassium besides becoming a health food nut? How about all those salt substitutes on the market, like **Lite Salt**, **Salt Substitute**, **Nu-Salt**, and **Nosalt**? The answer is both yes and no. Most salt substitutes do contain potassium chloride. Some, like **Morton's Lite Salt**, are half sodium and half potassium; while others, like **Sweet'n Low Nu-Salt**, are pure potassium chloride.

The problem is that most potassium-chloride salt substitutes taste bitter (though the taste bothers some folks more than others). If you don't have high blood pressure, haven't been put on a low-sodium diet, have no problems with your kidneys, and just want to cut back a little on sodium, you may want to give **Morton's Lite Salt** a try. It tastes pretty good, and each teaspoon contains "only" 1,200 mg. of sodium instead of the 2,200 mg. in regular salt. You will also be getting extra potassium.

If, on the other hand, you are taking a diuretic like **HydroDIURIL** (hydrochlorothiazide), which drains potassium from your body, or if you want to eliminate sodium from the salt shaker and replace it with potassium, you may want to consider a pure potassium-chloride salt substitute. Taste testers for *Consumer Reports* note that two brands scored highest— **Estee For Meats** and **Sweet'n Low Nu-Salt**. They also recommended **Adolph's Salt Substitute** and **Estee For Vegetables**.[110]

An article in the *Journal of the American Medical Association* of several years ago suggested that one teaspoonful of potassium chloride a day can replace lost potassium for 80 percent of the patients taking a diuretic like **HydroDIURIL**.

> **Potassium salt substitutes available without prescription have excellent uniformity of potassium content, are essentially sodium free, represent a considerable cost savings to the patient requiring potassium replacement, and have adequate patient acceptance. They deserve a more prominent role in potassium replacement.[111]**

Now that's a pretty enthusiastic endorsement coming from doctors, and I have no quarrel with their recommendation. If you need extra potassium and can tolerate the taste, salt substitutes are probably a lot safer than solid potassium pills like **Slow-K**, **K-Tab**, or **Klotrix**. But if I had my druthers, I would still stick with high-potassium food rather than any "artificial" substitute. Never ever forget that too much potassium can be dangerous, especially if your kidneys are not up to snuff. Here is an example of what happened when one person overdosed on a salt substitute.

> **A 75-year-old woman was admitted to our hospital for progressive shortness of breath over four weeks. Six weeks before admission her daughter purchased some Lite Salt at a local store and told her mother it was "O.K." to use since it contained "half the salt of regular salt." The patient, over the next several weeks, appears to have used the product ad lib. . . . During the ensuing weeks increasing ankle edema and shortness of breath developed, and she arrived in our emergency room in serious . . . heart failure.[112]**

My final word on potassium is, eat sensibly! If you can, start gorping more of those fruits and vegetables mentioned in this chapter, and you can't go wrong. If you must stay on a diuretic that depletes your body of potassium, a salt substitute is worth considering before you start popping **Slow-K**. In any event, you should have periodic blood tests for kidney function and potassium levels just to stay on the safe side.

Simple Nondrug Step to Success #2: Calcium. I love this one. Who could ever imagine that ice cream, cheese, and milk would help to lower blood pressure? Sure, it sounds ridiculous, but there are a number of lovely little studies which suggest that calcium may indeed play an important role in regulating blood pressure.

Dr. David McCarron, chief of the hypertension program at Oregon Health Sciences University in Portland, discovered that a group of people with high blood pressure took in 39 percent less dairy calcium and 20 to 25 percent less total calcium than normal controls.[113] Another study by Dr. McCarron showed that hypertensive patients have lower blood calcium levels than do normal folks.[114] He has not yet published any research to demonstrate that calcium supplements will bring blood pressure down, but he relates, "I know about a doctor in the East that's giving calcium tablets to people with mild hypertension. It's frightening how fast some of their blood pressures come down."[115]

Johns Hopkins researchers in collaboration with colleagues at the Institute of Nutrition of Central America gave calcium supplements to students and employees between the ages of 18 and 35. Their findings were dramatic.

> **Supplementation with 1 g. [gram] of calcium produced a significant reduction in diastolic BP in young healthy persons of both sexes. The effects were stabilized in the ninth week for women and in the sixth week for men. The reduction in diastolic BP . . . was approximately 5 percent in women and 9 percent for men.**
>
> **These findings confirm the relationship between calcium intake and BP described for rats and support the epidemiologic observations of the association between low calcium intake and hypertension during pregnancy and among hypertensive human subjects . . . high calcium intake, which is associated with lower BP, may produce a protective effect against hypertension.[116]**

I would be jiving you if I said these findings are anything more than tantalizing. The work is too preliminary to take to the bank. Nevertheless, calcium is an essential nutrient that an awful lot of people miss out on—older folks especially. One survey of over 5,000 women who were

45 years old and more uncovered the shocking fact that they were averaging only about 450 mg. of calcium per day.[117] This is only about half the recommended dietary allowance.

Many individuals have trouble digesting milk as they get on in years. The reason is that they seem to lose the activity of a crucial enzyme called lactase, which breaks down milk sugar. Without this enzyme dairy products can bring on abdominal pain, cramping, diarrhea, and gas.

It doesn't take a whole lot of flatulence to discourage milk consumption. This is unfortunate, because calcium is essential for strong bones and possibly as an aid in controlling blood pressure. After women pass through menopause, they are at much greater risk of osteoporosis (weakened bones). A diet high in calcium (1,000 to 1,500 mg. a day), vitamin D, and regular exercise may be helpful in slowing or preventing this very serious deterioration. (By the way, it takes a quart of skim milk and a cup of cottage cheese to add up to 1,423 mg. of calcium.)

But if you can't digest milk or dairy products, what can you do? Well, there are three possibilities. Yogurt is a good source of calcium and, best of all, carries its own lactase. As a result, many people who have a hard time with dairy products can usually digest yogurt with little or no trouble.[118] The other possibility is **LactAid,** a product that contains the enzyme. When 4 to 10 drops are added to a quart of milk, it will predigest almost all the milk sugar overnight. Once the milk sugar is gone, most people have no more trouble. If you can't find **LactAid** at your local pharmacy or health-food store, you can order it directly from LactAid Inc.; 600 Fire Road, Pleasantville, N.J. 08232-0111.

The last possibility, especially if you are avoiding high fat foods, is calcium supplementation, which may be the best solution of all because you can make sure that you are getting a sufficient amount of calcium each day. There are lots of preparations, so you may want to discuss this issue with your doctor. Products like **Calcet**, **Os-Cal**, **Cal-M**, or **Caltrate 600**, **Biocal**, or **Fosfree** should be available from your pharmacy. Antacids like **Tums**, **Alka-2**, **Alkets**, **Dicarbosil**, **Gustalac**, or **Titralac** also contain calcium. Bone meal and dolomite are controversial sources, because some brands have been contaminated with lead, and many health professionals are suggesting that people avoid these sources. My own favorite brand of calcium is supplied by Bronson Pharmaceuticals (4526 Rinetti Lane; La Canada, CA 91011). Each tablet supplies 375 mg. of calcium and 150 mg. of magnesium. I take three tablets a day. And that brings us to

Simple Nondrug Step to Success #3: Magnesium. There is a growing recognition that magnesium is also terribly important in the regulation of blood pressure and heart physiology. A deficiency in this essential mineral may lead to hypertension, cardiac rhythm disturbances, and heart problems. This could conceivably explain why soft water (low in calcium and magnesium) may predispose people to heart disease. It is also interesting to note that many diuretics deplete the body of magnesium as well as of potassium.

A recent study published in the *British Medical Journal* suggests that magnesium supplementation may be helpful in reversing hypertension, especially for people taking diuretics. It's been reported that after six months of magnesium treatment, 19 of the 20 treated patients had decreases of systolic and diastolic blood pressure averaging 12 mm HG and 8 mm Hg respectively.[119,120]

Admittedly all these investigations are preliminary. But even if potassium, calcium, and magnesium don't bring blood pressure down dramatically, they are still essential for good health. I make sure that my family gets an adequate amount, just in case. There are no guarantees that these nondrug approaches will work for you, but they are worth discussing with your doctor.

Simple Nondrug Step to Success #4: Eat like a vegetarian. If you check back to the list of high-potassium foods, you'll probably notice how many fruits and vegetables are high in potassium.

> **Researchers at Rokach Hospital [Tel Aviv, Israel] find 98 vegetarians around 60 years-old registered average blood pressure of 127/77 vs. 147/88 for non-vegetarians. Comparison of individuals of same weight in both groups confirms blood pressure of vegetarians consistently lower. . . . Potassium excretion 26 percent higher in vegetarians due to consumption of fruits, vegetables high in potassium content. Findings confirm usefulness of potassium in 1) regulation of blood pressure; 2) protection against hypertension.[121]**

This isn't the first study that suggests vegetarian fare can lower blood pressure.[122–126] It's unclear whether an increased diet of fruits and vegetables is beneficial because it lowers sodium and raises potassium or because of some other nutritional factors. Investigators have proposed everything from increased fiber and magnesium to a decrease in fat. A group of Finnish researchers believes that it's the lowered fat that really matters. They put 57 couples on a special diet low in saturated fat for six weeks and measured blood pressure. They found an average decrease from 138/89 to 129/81 during the course of the study.[127] When people switched back to their normal diets, blood pressure returned to initial levels.

Gone Fishin'

Simple Nondrug Step to Success #5: Relaxation. There is absolutely no doubt that stress can elevate blood pressure. Remember the research from Italy, where the doctors raised their patients' blood pressure almost 25 points just by walking into the room? Well, there are all sorts of things that will jack your blood pressure up—arguing with your boss, your spouse, or your kids; giving a speech; getting a speeding ticket; paying bills; balancing the checkbook; taking a test; getting divorced. The list is almost endless.

The problem with stress is that it's hard to measure. You can look calm as a cucumber on the outside but be a seething volcano inside. Lots of people do their best to ignore or override their body's stress signals. Just like the idiot who sticks a nickel in a fuse box to bypass a bad wiring system, the person who doesn't listen to his internal alarms may end up blowing out a blood vessel or blocking a coronary artery.

What are the early warning symptoms to be on the alert for? One of my favorites is cold hands. Whenever I'm feeling anxious—deadlines, arguments, speeches, TV shows—my fingers turn to ice. My heart rate goes up, I start talking very fast, and, of course, my blood pressure follows right along. When that happens, I know I'm heading for trouble, and I do my best to take corrective action.

First I try to avoid people who make me feel that way. If I have to shake hands with someone whose very presence makes my hands turn cold, I know I have a problem. It's not always possible to avoid these individuals, but I try to get away as fast as possible. Then I seek support from friends who calm me down. If I feel myself starting to speed up, I try to slow down, take deep breaths, and talk slowly. I guarantee that if you breathe deeply from your diaphragm, your blood pressure *will* come down.

If I am really stressed out, I will try to find time to sit quietly and meditate for 20 minutes or listen to a relaxation tape. If I were really dedicated, I would do this twice a day, come hell or high water. Dr. Herbert Benson has written a wonderful little book called *The Relaxation Response* (available in most bookstores and published by Avon Books for about $2.95). It's as good as anything around if you want to learn a very easy technique for nonreligious meditation.

If you want to sit back, calm down, and get your act together I can think of no better way than to listen to Emmett Miller on tape. This man has one of the all-time great soothing voices. My favorite is *The Healing Journey*. There is also one called *Letting Go of Stress*. (They can be ordered from Medical Self Care Catalogue; P.O. Box 717, Inverness, CA 94937.) The investment, a little more than $10, is a whole lot cheaper than seeing a shrink, and in some cases it may be just as good for relaxation.

Another good tape comes from Dr. Richard Surwitt, a professor at the Behavioral Physiology Laboratory of Duke University. For $9.95 you will receive a "Progressive Relaxation" tape and manual. Make your check payable to Duke University Medical Center and send it to Dr. Richard Surwitt; Box 3926; Duke Medical Center; Durham, N.C. 27710.

But if you *really* want to relax, go fishin'. Catching fish is not the point—sittin' and relaxin' is. There is *no way* to stay uptight if you have your back against a nice old tree and a fishing pole in your hands. Oh, you don't like fishing? Not to worry, I've got the next best thing.

Watching fish swim in a tank has a calming effect and may even offer a means of treating high blood pressure, according to three University of Pennsylvania researchers. Petting a dog or a cat is a known stress reducer and the researchers decided to see if interactions with other animals produced similar results. Fish were selected for the study because more than 10 million American homes have aquariums. The blood pressure of volunteers dropped as they watched fish in an aquarium; it dropped even more significantly for subjects with high blood pressure. The researchers suggest that a home aquarium may be one way to treat high blood pressure without drugs. They say it might work in much the same way as meditation.[128]

There is no doubt that watching fish will relax you. But if you don't think a fish will make a good pet, why not consider a dog or a cat? An article in *The Wall Street Journal* announced that "Talking to Your Dog Can Help Lower Your Blood Pressure." It was based on a scientific meeting held at the University of Pennsylvania. The conference chairman, Dr. Aaron H. Katcher, a psychiatrist, reported, "when people stroke and talk to dogs, the human's blood pressure goes down. (When talking to other humans, it always went up.)"[129]

Tying Up the Loose Ends

We have covered an awful lot of material in this chapter. You learned about all the pitfalls of measuring blood pressure, including the fact that your doctor may be hazardous to your health just by walking into the room. You also learned that there are an awful lot of things to watch out for, like the cuff size on the sphygmomanometer and the position of your arm (relaxed and resting straight out, level with your heart). You were also encouraged to consider investing in a home blood-pressure device. At the end of the chapter is an analysis of some popular brands.

You also got an inside peek into one of the hottest questions in medicine right now—to treat or not to treat mild hypertension. And you learned that diuretics may not always be as safe as doctors would like them to be. We looked at all the don'ts—don't eat sodium, don't drink coffee, don't overeat, don't smoke, and so on. We looked at the dos, too—do get potassium, calcium, and magnesium in your diet; do try a vegetarian way of eating; and *do* learn how to relax. It *is* possible to get high blood pressure down without drugs. And that's a damn good thing, because a lot of these chemicals doctors so casually prescribe have some pretty unpleasant consequences.

But when all else fails, medications have their place. High blood pressure is dangerous. Not everyone can play par golf, and not everyone has to have a reading of 120/80. But if your blood pressure starts creeping up and staying up, it's time to take action and that may mean medicine. For a review of some of the most commonly prescribed high-blood-pressure drugs, turn to the table immediately following the analysis of home blood pressure devices.

Maybe some day we will know exactly what causes hypertension and researchers will find a cure. But until that day arrives, good luck, and keep on truckin'.

Home Blood-Pressure Devices

Astropulse: *Marshall Electronics Inc.*
5425 W. Fargo Avenue
Skokie, IL 60077
(800)323-1482

Marshall was among the first to recognize the potential of the home health-care market. The firm has been supplying all sorts of excellent equipment for years, including the "Black Bag Kit," which comes with an otoscope for looking in ears and noses, a magnifying dental reflector, an aneroid sphygmomanometer, and many other goodies.

But where Marshall has really taken off has been in blood-pressure devices. The company makes so many different models (from the **Astropulse 10** automatic aneroid to the **Astropulse 99** digital) that I couldn't possibly list them all here. Prices range from about $15 to $225 for the most sophisticated automatic machines.

I personally like the **Astropulse 77** model, which costs $90 to $100 and is very compact. If you want to go first-class, the **Astropulse 90** fully automatic, self-inflating, print-out for $225 is impressive. It runs on batteries or AC and is especially attractive to novices because placement of the cuff is not as critical as with most other machines. The best thing to do is write to Marshall for a catalogue and price list. One warning, though: because the company doesn't recommend use of a large adult-size cuff with all the digital machines, if you have a large arm (more than 13 inches circumference), you will need either the **Astropulse 10** (an aneroid model listing for about $55) or the digital **Astropulse 70-P** (about $150).

Digitronic: *Lumiscope Co.*
Customer Service Dept.
375 Raritan Center Parkway
Edison, N.J. 08837
(800) 221-5746

The Lumiscope Company is a relative newcomer to the health-care market. But that hasn't stopped the firm from marketing a wide range of successful devices. The **Digitronic IV** runs around $70, and the top-of-the-line **Digitronic** automatic inflater and printer costs about $250.

"The "deluxe" machine, like so many of the digital devices, is manufactured in Japan. Interestingly, an almost identical model is sold by quite a few different companies, including Copal, Norelco, Labtron, Nelkin/Piper, and Taylor.

It's nice and compact and easy to use and comes with a one-year warranty (as do most of the digital devices). But is the convenience worth the money? Most people don't need the extra bells and whistles on these superduper self-inflating models, especially since the extra cost may just buy you extra things to go wrong.

The company claims that a large-size cuff is available by writing to the Customer Service Department.

Healthcheck: *Timex Medical Products*
Waterbury, CT 06720

for service:
Timex Medical Products
P.O. Box L
7000 Murray Street
Little Rock, AR 72203

The **Timex Healthcheck Digital Blood Pressure Monitor** may have been the main catalyst behind the explosive growth in digital blood-pressure development. It was one of the first really inexpensive ($70) machines on the market, and Timex was a name that people were familiar with.

A few competitors have grumbled that some of the early devices weren't as reliable as they should have been, but I have used the **Healthcheck Monitor** repeatedly and found it to work reasonably well. The instructions are relatively easy to follow, and it is highly portable and convenient. You can order a large-size cuff, if necessary, by sending $8.00 to the service department listed above.

My major complaint is that the automatic air-deflation system is very slow, especially at the low end of the scale. This can make for impatience and a tired arm. One of the big advantages of Timex, however, is that it can be found almost everywhere—pharmacies, department stores, you name it. It, too, carries a one-year warranty.

Norelco: *North American Philips Corp.*
Consumer Relations
High Ridge Park
P.O. Box 10166
Stamford, CT 06904
(800) 243-7884

Norelco is also a familiar name to Americans. The company markets a variety of blood-pressure monitors under the **Healthcare (HC)** logo. The top-of-the-line **HC 3500 Deluxe Digital Blood Pressure/Pulse Meter** inflates itself, deflates itself, and prints out automatically. It is virtually identical (same Japanese manufacturer) to the comparable Lumiscope **Digitronic** machine, but the price is a little less, ranging from $170 to $200, depending on where you buy it.

Remember, though, more gimmicks on a gadget make for more things to break down.

The basic digital machine (**HC 3000**) at $80 seems comparable to similar machines on the market. A large-size adult cuff should become available and will probably be priced between $10 and $20 (at this writing the price hasn't been determined). It can be ordered from Consumer Relations. The plastic carrying cases for all the Norelco products are superb and make storage a snap.

Tycos: *Ritter-Tycos Sybron*
P.O. Box 1
Glenn Bridge Road
Arden, N.C. 28704
(800) 438-6045

The Sybron Corporation has been making sphygmomanometers for 75 years under the Taylor trademark. These folks have a reputation for a quality product. They moved into the digital market with careful deliberation, and I must say that the wait was worth it. I am impressed with the **Tycos Self Check.** It is a dandy little machine, about as compact as anything on the market, but not a lightweight. I was definitely impressed with its accuracy and ease of operation.

One of the elements that makes this unit more attractive than many of its competitors is the audio cassette that comes with it. No blood-pressure monitor will work correctly if you don't read the instructions, but if you are like most folks, taking time to wade through a booklet is tough. The verbal instructions provided on the cassette are excellent and make using this machine quite easy.

The unit costs somewhere between $65 and $80, depending on where you buy it, which makes the **Tycos** competitive with most other devices on the market. A large-size cuff is also available for a modest fee. My only complaint: the carrying case is not as convenient as some I've seen.

If you want to buy the most impressive model (designed for physicians' use), you should inquire about the **Taylor Acoustic Sphygmomanometer A-10**. It's even more portable than the **Tycos** and can be ordered with a large-size adult cuff, which makes it especially good for anyone with an arm over 13 inches in circumference. I think this may be just about the most accurate digital on the market for people with large arms. Unfortunately it carries a hefty price tag of $245.00.

TABLE OF HIGH-BLOOD-PRESSURE MEDICATIONS

This table will provide some practical information about side effects, precautions, and dangerous drug reactions. It is not possible to list every adverse reaction nor all potential drug interactions. Those side effects that may be serious are preceded by an asterisk (*). Contact your physician *immediately* if any occur. Other side effects should not be ignored. They, too, should be brought to the doctor's attention without undue delay.

The information is merely intended to provide some overall guidelines for effective drug use and is not meant to substitute for good communications between you and your physician and pharmacist.

Aldactazide *(hydrochlorothiazide 25 mg + spironolactone 25 mg tablets)*

MFR: G. D. Searle & Co.; also available generically.

USUAL DOSE: one to eight tablets daily.

The two mild diuretics combined in this medication act on the kidneys to increase the flow of urine and the elimination of sodium. The hydrochlorothiazide component also seems to have blood-pressure-lowering properties not related to the diuretic effect. Fixed combinations of diuretics are *not* indicated for the initial treatment of hypertension, but they are frequently used as such. The rationale behind this mixture is that spironolactone supposedly counteracts the tendency of hydrochlorothiazide to cause the body to lose potassium. Also, using the theory that two heads are better than one, these two diuretics are touted as being more effective than either one alone. In reality, spironolactone doesn't always protect against potassium loss, nor will the hydrochlorothiazide protect against excess potassium buildup. Blood potassium levels should be checked regularly. As with any multiple-drug product, the chances of an adverse drug reaction are somewhat increased.

WARNING: Spironolactone has caused cancer in laboratory animals. It is unclear whether there is a similar danger to humans, but to be on the safe side, use this product only if completely necessary.

PRECAUTIONS:
- Do not take if you are allergic to sulfa-containing medicines.
- Do not take potassium supplements while using this product.
- Blood potassium levels should be checked regularly.
- Take with food or milk.
- The correct dose of this medication should be periodically reevaluated.
- May aggravate gout or diabetes.
- Do not take OTC decongestants, diet aids, or asthma medications without first consulting your doctor; they may aggravate high blood pressure.

PREGNANCY AND BREAST-FEEDING:
- Do not use this product if pregnant unless absolutely necessary. Both spironolactone and hydrochlorothiazide cross the placenta and enter the baby's circulation.
- Thiazides and metabolic by-products of spironolactone are found in breast milk. Although no problems have been reported thus far, use with caution if breast-feeding or consider bottle-feeding.

(continues next page)

Aldactazide, *(continued)*

COMMON SIDE EFFECTS:
- Increased frequency of urination (in almost everyone).
- Upset stomach, diarrhea, cramps, loss of appetite.
- Headache, dizziness, drowsiness, lethargy.
- Irregular menstrual cycle (more common after several months of treatment).
- Breast enlargement or tenderness in men and women (quite common, especially after taking **Aldactazide** for several months).
- Sweating.
- *■ Hyperkalemia (high blood potassium levels). This effect occurs in up to 26% of patients taking spironolactone, even when it is combined with hydrochlorothiazide. It may occur more frequently in the elderly. (See page 303.)

UNCOMMON SIDE EFFECTS:
- *■ Hypokalemia (low blood potassium levels). (See page 303.)
- Dizziness and faintness when you stand up too fast.
- *■ Very severe abdominal pain with nausea and vomiting (rare).
- *■ Rash, hives, shortness of breath (allergic reactions; rare).
- *■ Unexplained fever and sore throat (rare).
- *■ Unexplained bruising, bleeding (rare).

SEXUAL SIDE EFFECTS:
- Impotence (probably less than 5%).
- Decreased libido.
- Decreased vaginal lubrication.

DRUG INTERACTIONS:
- Aspirin and other salicylates may decrease effectiveness of spironolactone.
- Potassium supplements (**K-lor**, **Kaon**, **Slow-K**, **K-Lyte**, **Klotrix**, **Micro-K**, **K-Tab**, and many others): may cause hyperkalemia (high blood potassium).
- **Questran** (cholestyramine), **Colestid** (colestipol) decrease hydrochlorothiazide absorption.
- **Lanoxin** (digoxin) and other digitalis drugs: *dangerous* in combination with **Aldactazide** if hypokalemia (low blood potassium) is present. May cause abnormal heart rhythms and can be fatal. (See page 303.)
- **Florinef** (fludrocortisone), **Cortone** (cortisone), **Cortef**, and **Hydrocortone** (hydrocortisone), **Meticorten**, **Deltasone**, and others (prednisone), and **Delta-Cortef** and others (prednisolone) can contribute to potassium loss and hypokalemia. (See page 303).
- **Indocin** (indomethacin) decreases effectiveness of hydrochlorothiazide.

* *These side effects may be serious. Contact your physician immediately if they occur.*

Aldactazide, *(continued)*

- **Eskalith, Lithobid** (lithium): hydrochlorothiazide may cause serious lithium toxicity.
- **Orinase** (tolbutamide), **Dymelor** (acetohexamide), **Tolinase** (tolazamide), and **Diabinese** (chlorpropamide): hydrochlorothiazide may decrease the effectiveness of these oral diabetes drugs.
- **Dyrenium** (triamterene), **Midamor** (amiloride), **Dyazide** (contains triamterene), **Aldactone** (spironolactone), or other potassium-sparing diuretics may cause hyperkalemia.
- Salt substitutes may contain large amounts of potassium and may contribute to hyperkalemia.

Aldactone *(spironolactone 25 mg, 50 mg, and 100 mg tablets)*

MFR: G. D. Searle & Co.; also available generically

USUAL DOSE: 50 to 100 mg daily

Aldactone is a mild diuretic that causes the body to retain potassium. Rarely used alone to treat high blood pressure, it is most often combined with another diuretic whose tendency is to cause the body to lose potassium (see **Aldactazide**, above). The idea is to balance the potassium loss with the gain and to arrive at a net unchanged potassium blood level. This balancing act is pretty tricky, and blood pressure and potassium levels should be checked regularly. **Aldactone** is definitely not the first choice in the treatment of hypertension. In fact, the manufacturer states, "Aldactone is indicated for patients who cannot be treated adequately with other agents or for whom other agents are considered inappropriate." However, certain hypertensive patients may benefit from the addition of **Aldactone** to their diuretic regimen, especially those taking **Lanoxin** or any of the digitalis heart drugs (low potassium levels can be very dangerous to these persons), or those on steroid therapy (steroids tend to cause the body to lose potassium). Since hypokalemia can aggravate diabetes, diabetics can be added to the list.

WARNING: Spironolactone has caused cancer in laboratory animals. It is unclear whether there is a similar danger to humans, but to be on the safe side, use this product only if completely necessary.

PRECAUTIONS:
- Do not take potassium supplements while using this product.
- Blood potassium levels should be checked regularly.
- Do not use this product if pregnant.
- Take with food or milk.
- The correct dose of this medication should be periodically reevaluated.

(continues next page)

Aldactone, *(continued)*

- Do not take OTC decongestants, diet aids, or asthma medications without first consulting your doctor; they may aggravate your high blood pressure.

PREGNANCY AND BREAST-FEEDING:
- Do not use this product if pregnant unless absolutely necessary. Spironolactone crosses the placenta and enters the baby's circulation.
- Metabolic by-products of spironolactone are found in breast milk. Although no problems have been reported thus far, use with caution if breast-feeding or consider bottle-feeding.

COMMON SIDE EFFECTS:
- Increased frequency of urination (in almost everyone).
- Upset stomach, diarrhea, cramps, loss of appetite.
- Headache, dizziness, drowsiness, lethargy.
- Irregular menstrual cycle (more common after several months of treatment).
- Breast enlargement or tenderness in men and women (very common, especially after taking **Aldactone** for several months).
- Sweating.
*- Hyperkalemia (high blood potassium levels): This side effect occurs in up to 26% of patients taking spironolactone, even when it is combined with hydrochlorothiazide (see **Aldactazide**, above). It may occur more frequently in the elderly (See page 303).

UNCOMMON SIDE EFFECTS:
- Dry mouth and thirst.
- Dizziness and faintness when you stand up too fast.
*- Itching and rash, hives (allergic reactions).
*- Unexplained fever.

SEXUAL SIDE EFFECTS:
- Impotence (probably less than 5% incidence).
- Decreased libido.

DRUG INTERACTIONS:
- Aspirin and other salicylates may decrease effectiveness of spironolactone.
- Potassium: may cause hyperkalemia in presence of spironolactone.
- **Dyrenium** (triamterene), **Midamor** (amiloride), **Dyazide** (contains triamterene), **Aldactazide** (contains spironolactone), or other potassium-sparing diuretics may cause hyperkalemia.
- Salt substitutes may contain large amounts of potassium and may contribute to hyperkalemia.

* *These side effects may be serious. Contact your physician immediately if they occur.*

Aldomet *(methyldopa 125 mg, 250 mg, and 500 mg tablets, and 250 mg/5 ml oral suspension)*

MFR: Merck Sharp & Dohme

USUAL DOSE: 500 to 2,000 mg daily

Even though it is rarely indicated as the first choice for treating hypertension, **Aldomet** remains a popular and probably overprescribed medication. There is no doubt, however, that it is indeed effective in lowering blood pressure. It acts on the central nervous system to inhibit nerve messages that tend to raise blood pressure. Major or life-threatening adverse reactions are rare, but annoying minor ones are quite common. The elderly are especially prone to the drowsiness and fatigue caused by **Aldomet**. Postural hypotension (getting dizzy from standing up too fast) is also common, but may be lessened by getting out of bed or up from the chair slowly. One side effect your doctor probably won't mention is impotence, with an incidence of anywhere between 1% to 53% of men treated with **Aldomet**, depending on whose study data you choose to believe. The real occurrence rate is likely to be somewhere in the middle. Because of the many undesirable side effects, **Aldomet** should be prescribed only when other, more benign drugs have failed.

PRECAUTIONS:
- **Aldomet** may cause the urine test for pheochromocytoma (a rare disorder) to appear falsely positive.
- **Aldomet** causes the Coomb's Test to become positive in 10–20% of persons using the drug for six months or more. This is usually of minor significance and does not require the discontinuation of the drug. Very rarely this is associated with hemolytic anemia, a potentially fatal blood disorder.
- Do not take OTC decongestants, diet aids, or asthma medications without first consulting your doctor; they may aggravate your high blood pressure.

PREGNANCY AND BREAST-FEEDING:
- Use in pregnancy or while breast-feeding has not been proven safe.

COMMON SIDE EFFECTS:
- *■ Edema (swelling of ankles and feet as the result of water retention).
- ■ Sedation, especially in the elderly or after a dosage increase (incidence more than 5%).
- *■ Mental confusion, especially in the elderly.
- ■ Dry mouth (incidence more than 5%).
- ■ Headache (incidence more than 5%).

(continues next page)

*** These side effects may be serious. Contact your physician immediately if they occur.**

Aldomet, *(continued)*

UNCOMMON SIDE EFFECTS:
  *■ Hemolytic anemia (increased red-blood-cell destruction, character-
     ized by weakness and fatigue, and pink or red urine; rare).
  *■ Jaundice, liver problems (rare).
  WARNING: Your physician should take periodic blood counts and liver
function tests to check for these conditions. Notify your doctor if you
start feeling unusually weak or if you develop an unexplained fever.
  ■ Dizziness and faintness when you stand up too fast.
  *■ Slow heart rate (infrequent).
  ■ Breast enlargement, tenderness in women (infrequent).
  ■ Nausea, vomiting, diarrhea.

SEXUAL SIDE EFFECTS:
  ■ Impotence (see above).
  ■ Decreased libido (reported incidences widely variable).
  ■ Difficulty in ejaculation (probably uncommon).

DRUG INTERACTIONS:
  ■ uncommon

Aldoril *(15 mg or 25 mg hydrochlorothiazide + 250 mg methyldopa),*
Aldoril D *(30 mg or 50 mg hydrochlorothiazide + 500 mg methyldopa)*

MFR: Merck Sharp & Dohme

USUAL DOSE: 2 to 4 tablets daily, given once in the morning or in divided
doses (widely variable because of the variety of strengths of individual
ingredients).

  Aldoril is not indicated for the initial management of high blood
pressure and should be used only if both component drugs are appropriate and if the correct doses just happen to be those present in this
fixed-combination product. That's a lot of ifs. Since hypertension is a
changeable condition, the correct doses of all high-blood-pressure drugs
should be periodically reassessed. But a big problem with **Aldoril** and
all combination products is that you can't adjust the dose of one of
the ingredients without changing the others. Also, the potential for having an adverse reaction is increased every time you add a new drug to
the regimen. If you do need both drugs, and in doses available in this
combination medicine, **Aldoril** may be appropriate. (See also **Aldomet**
and **Diuril** for more details on how the individual components work.)

---

* These side effects may be serious. Contact your physician immediately if they occur.

Aldoril, Aldoril D *(continued)*

PRECAUTIONS:
- Do not take if you are allergic to sulfa-containing medicines.
- Blood potassium levels should be checked regularly.
- The correct dose of this medication should be periodically reevaluated.
- May aggravate gout or diabetes.
- Do not take OTC decongestants, diet aids, or asthma medications without first consulting your doctor; they may aggravate your high blood pressure.
- Methyldopa may cause the urine test for pheochromocytoma (a rare disorder) to appear falsely positive.
- Methyldopa causes the Coomb's Test to become positive in 10–20% of persons using the drug for six months or more. This is usually of minor significance and does not require the discontinuation of the drug. Very rarely this is associated with hemolytic anemia, a potentially fatal blood disorder.

PREGNANCY AND BREAST-FEEDING:
- Use in pregnancy or while breast-feeding has not been proven safe. Both methyldopa and hydrochlorothiazide cross the placenta and enter the baby's circulation. Use if pregnant only if no safer alternative exists.
- Both methyldopa and hydrochlorothiazide are found in breast milk. Although no problems have been demonstrated, use with caution or consider bottle-feeding.

COMMON SIDE EFFECTS:
- *■ Hypokalemia (low blood potassium levels) (See page 303).
- Increased frequency of urination (in almost everyone).
- Sedation, especially in the elderly or after a dosage increase (incidence more than 5%).
- Mental confusion, especially in the elderly.
- Dry mouth (incidence more than 5%).
- Headache (incidence more than 5%).

UNCOMMON SIDE EFFECTS:
- *■ Hemolytic anemia (increased red-blood-cell destruction, characterized by weakness and fatigue, and pink or red urine; rare).
- *■ Jaundice, liver problems (rare).

WARNING: Your physician should take periodic blood counts and liver function tests to check for these conditions. Notify your doctor if you start feeling unusually weak or if you develop an unexplained fever.

(continues next page)

* *These side effects may be serious. Contact your physician immediately if they occur.*

Aldoril, Aldoril D *(continued)*

- Dizziness and faintness when you stand up too fast.
- Slow heart rate (infrequent).
- Breast enlargement, tenderness in women (infrequent).
- Upset stomach, nausea, vomiting, diarrhea.
- Loss of appetite.
*- Very severe abdominal pain with nausea and vomiting (rare).
*- Rash, hives, shortness of breath (allergic reactions; rare)
*- Unexplained fever, sore throat (rare).
*- Unexplained bruising, bleeding (rare).

SEXUAL SIDE EFFECTS:
- Decreased vaginal lubrication.
- Impotence (methyldopa can cause up to 53% incidence; hydrochloro-thiazide may contribute a little to this side effect).
- Decreased libido (reported incidences widely variable).
- Difficulty in ejaculation (probably uncommon).

DRUG INTERACTIONS:
- **Questran** (cholestyramine), **Colestid** (colestipol) decrease hydrochlo-rothiazide absorption.
- **Lanoxin** (digoxin) and other digitalis drugs: *dangerous* combination if hypokalemic. May cause abnormal heart rhythms and can be fatal. (See page 303.)
- **Florinef** (fludrocortisone), **Cortone** (cortisone), **Cortef**, and **Hydro-cortone** (hydrocortisone), **Meticorten**, **Deltasone**, and others (pred-nisone), and **Delta-Cortef** and others (prednisolone) can contribute to potassium loss and hypokalemia. (See page 303.)
- **Indocin** (indomethacin) decreases effectiveness of hydrochlorothiazide.
- **Eskalith**, **Lithobid** (lithium): hydrochlorothiazide may cause serious lithium toxicity.
- **Orinase** (tolbutamide), **Dymelor** (acetohexamide), **Tolinase** (tolaza-mide), and **Diabinese** (chlorpropamide): hydrochlorothiazide may de-crease the effectiveness of these oral diabetes drugs.

Apresoline *(hydralazine 10 mg, 25 mg, 50 mg, 100 mg tablets)*

MFR: Ciba; also available generically

USUAL DOSE: Start low, then increase to 50 mg four times a day (sometimes given as 100 mg twice daily instead). Should be given in lowest effec-tive dose. Increases may be needed over time to retain effectiveness.

* *These side effects may be serious. Contact your physician immediately if they occur.*

Apresoline, *(continued)*

Apresoline is not generally used in the first-line treatment of hypertension and is rarely used alone. Because it can cause sodium and water retention, a diuretic is commonly added. The "vasodilating" action (dilating the small arteries, thus decreasing the blood pressure) causes a reflex increase in heart rate, so a beta blocker like **Inderal** is generally prescribed to keep the heart rate normal. **Apresoline** is properly used when almost everything else has failed to control blood pressure.

An unusual and serious adverse reaction associated with hydralazine is the induction of a syndrome much like SLE (Systemic Lupus Erythematosus). This drug-induced lupus is manifested by arthritislike joint pain, skin rashes, blisters, weakness, sore throat, and fever. Although it usually occurs in persons who take large doses (400 mg daily or more) for long periods of time, it has occurred with as little as 75 mg a day for less than three weeks. The symptoms usually disappear quickly after the drug is discontinued, but occasionally last months or even years. The predisposition to this side effect is genetically controlled and relates to the speed with which the body metabolizes the hydralazine (slow metabolizers get it more often). Caucasians, Blacks, Scandinavians, and Middle Easterners tend to be at higher risk than Orientals, American Indians, and Eskimos. Your doctor should take periodic blood tests to check for drug-induced SLE, especially if you are taking larger doses or are on the drug for a long time.

PRECAUTIONS:
- Contraindicated in patients with coronary artery disease. May worsen symptoms of angina and could possibly trigger a heart attack in these patients.
- Do not take OTC decongestants, diet aids, or asthma medications without first consulting your doctor; they may aggravate your high blood pressure.
- Take with food or milk for better absorption.
- If **Apresoline** therapy is to be discontinued, taper off gradually to avoid a sudden increase in blood pressure.
- Side effects may be lessened by increasing doses gradually.
- Certain patients may require **Vitamin B$_6$** (pyridoxine) supplementation, 100 mg to 200 mg daily, to treat "peripheral neuropathy" (see side effects, below).
- The physician should take periodic blood tests to check for hydralazine-induced lupus (see above).

PREGNANCY AND BREAST-FEEDING:
- Hydralazine causes birth defects in animals. Whether there is a similar threat to humans is not clear; avoid taking this medication while pregnant if at all possible.

(continues next page)

Apresoline, (continued)

- No problems have yet been seen in breast-fed babies whose mothers were taking **Apresoline.**

COMMON SIDE EFFECTS:
*■ Exacerbation of angina.
- Nausea, vomiting, diarrhea.
- Headache.
- Loss of appetite.
*■ Rapid heart rate, palpitations.

UNCOMMON SIDE EFFECTS:
*■ Drug-induced lupus (see above).
*■ Peripheral neuropathy; characterized by numbness or tingling in lips, hands, feet, etc. Thought to be caused by interferences by hydralazine of **Vitamin B$_6$** (pyridoxine).
*■ Edema (swelling of ankles and legs caused by excess sodium and water retention).
*■ Swelling of lymph nodes.
- Dizziness and faintness when you stand up too fast (orthostatic hypotension).
- Constipation.
- Watery, itching eyes.
- Stuffy nose.

SEXUAL SIDE EFFECTS:
- Uncommon.

DRUG INTERACTIONS:
- Uncommon.

Blocadren (timolol 10 mg and 20 mg tablets)
See Beta Blockers, p. 195.

Capoten (captopril 25 mg, 50 mg, and 100 mg tablets)

MFR: E. R. Squibb & Sons, Inc.

USUAL DOSE: 25 mg to 150 mg, three times daily.

Capoten is a most unusual drug, unlike any other antihypertensive medication currently on the market. The history of its development reads a lot like a detective thriller. The venom of the deadly Brazilian jararaca

* *These side effects may be serious. Contact your physician immediately if they occur.*

Capoten, *(continued)*

snake, which can cause fatal bleeding, played a key role. Investigators suspected that the kidney was crucial in controlling blood pressure. Hypertension, they speculated, resulted from a chemical chain reaction beginning in the kidney and leading to the production of an enzyme which constricts blood vessels and raises blood pressure. An extract of the jararaca venom inhibits the enzyme and interrupts the chain, lowering blood pressure. This discovery ultimately led to the synthesis of other compounds, including **Capoten**, which represent an entirely new direction in hypertension management.

Because **Capoten** works on a different principle from other blood-pressure medicines, it may be effective when others have failed. This drug is particularly helpful for patients with severe congestive heart failure. However, **Capoten** can almost be considered a drug of last resort in treating hypertension. Because it has so many potentially serious and relatively common side effects, almost all else should be tried first. Your doctor should periodically test your urine and blood for early signs of these adverse reactions.

PRECAUTIONS:
- Because of the many side effects common to this drug, it should be used only after other multidrug regimens have been proven ineffective.
- Do not take OTC decongestants, diet aids, or asthma medications without first consulting your doctor; they may aggravate your high blood pressure.
- Take one hour before meals; taking with food decreases absorption.
- Do not use potassium supplements while taking this drug.

PREGNANCY AND BREAST-FEEDING:
- Use in pregnancy has not been proven safe.
- Since **Capoten** is excreted into breast milk, it is inadvisable to nurse while taking this drug.

COMMON SIDE EFFECTS:
- *▪ Rash and itching (up to 10%).
- ▪ Loss of taste perception (up to 7%). Usually goes away by itself.
- *▪ Protein in the urine shows up in about 2% of people taking captopril. Although usually not a serious adverse reaction, in some persons this may develop into more severe kidney problems. People with prior renal disease may be at higher risk.
- *▪ Chest pain (about 1%).
- *▪ Fast or irregular heartbeat, palpitations (about 1%).
- *▪ Swelling of feet, hands, mouth (about 1%).

(continues next page)

* These side effects may be serious. Contact your physician immediately if they occur.

Capoten, *(continued)*

UNCOMMON SIDE EFFECTS:
* ** Decrease in white blood cells (neutropenia); characterized by fever, sore throat.
* ** Severe low blood pressure upon initiation of **Capoten** therapy, especially in persons already taking diuretics or who are salt- and water-depleted. Diuretics may be added at a later date with relative safety. Excessively low blood pressure is much less common in hypertensive patients than in persons treated for congestive heart failure.

SEXUAL SIDE EFFECTS:
* None noted to date, but this is a fairly new drug.

DRUG INTERACTIONS:
* Potassium may cause hyperkalemia in presence of **Capoten**.
* **Dyrenium** (triamterene), **Midamor** (amiloride), **Dyazide** (contains triamterene), **Aldactone** or **Aldactazide** (spironolactone), or other potassium-sparing diuretics may cause hyperkalemia.
* Salt substitutes: these may contain large amounts of potassium and may contribute to hyperkalemia.
* **Indocin** (indomethacin) may reduce the effectiveness of **Capoten**.
* Diuretic therapy may cause severe low blood pressure when captopril is first given. Diuretics may be cautiously added at a later date; and in fact, this combination is common.

Catapres *(clonidine 0.1 mg, 0.2 mg, and 0.3 mg tablets)*

MFR: Boehringer Ingelheim Ltd.

USUAL DOSE: 0.1 mg to 0.2 mg, two to four times daily.

Catapres isn't often the first choice for treating hypertension but is a pretty good second or third choice. It acts on the central nervous system to inhibit nerve messages that tend to raise blood pressure. **Catapres** is usually used in conjunction with a diuretic to minimize sodium and water retention and to enhance the blood-pressure-lowering effects. The big worry is the sometimes serious rebound increase in blood pressure that occurs when **Catapres** is abruptly stopped or a few doses are missed. The pulse may jump from 70 beats a minute to over 90 beats per minute and abnormal heart rhythms may become a problem. Nausea, vomiting, and flushing can also result if the drug is discontinued too fast. Don't let your prescription run too low, or you might find yourself in trouble on a weekend when the pharmacy isn't open and your doctor has gone fishing.

* *These side effects may be serious. Contact your physician immediately if they occur.*

Catapres, *(continued)*

It would be a good idea to *always* have a spare bottle of **Catapres** on hand just to prevent this situation from ever arising. If it becomes necessary to stop **Catapres,** phase it out gradually over several days or weeks under a doctor's careful supervision.

Several unique applications of **Catapres** have started appearing in the scientific literature. There is experimental evidence the drug may be extremely useful in preventing the terrible withdrawal symptoms of narcotic addiction. People who have become physically dependent on such drugs as **Percodan**, **Dilaudid**, **Demerol**, morphine, or heroin can suffer terribly if they are forced to go "cold turkey." Symptoms such as sweating, crying, yawning, sneezing, irritability, nausea, vomiting, insomnia, tremor, weakness, depression, loss of appetite, flushing, gooseflesh, increased heart rate, and hypertension can make people question whether life is worth living. **Catapres** seems to provide a parachute that makes withdrawal from narcotics tolerable.

Another amazing use of **Catapres** may be in the treatment of spinal cord injuries. Preliminary experiments suggest that this medication might be helpful immediately after certain kinds of serious back injuries to reduce or prevent paralysis and spasticity. One other unusual application for this high-blood-pressure drug could be in the treatment of Tourette's syndrome. People with this condition often experience tics (arm movements, blinking, facial grimaces, and shoulder shrugging). Uncontrollable speech problems may also occur such as grunting, shouting, or swearing. The major tranquilizer **Haldol** has often been prescribed in the past, but adverse reactions can limit treatment. If **Catapres** proves to be effective it will be an important breakthrough.

PRECAUTIONS:
- Do not abruptly stop taking this medicine because of the possibility of severe rebound high blood pressure. Be sure to take your medicine regularly.
- Correct dosage should periodically be reevaluated, since tolerance to the beneficial blood-pressure-lowering effects may occur.
- Eye problems have been noted in animal studies. Your doctor should periodically examine your eyes.
- Since **Catapres** can cause drowsiness, be careful when driving or performing any other attention-demanding task.
- Do not take OTC decongestants, diet aids, or asthma medications without first consulting your doctor; they may aggravate your high blood pressure.

(continues next page)

Catapres, (continued)

PREGNANCY AND BREAST-FEEDING:
- Safety for use during pregnancy is questionable. Do not take this drug when pregnant if at all possible.
- No problems with breast-feeding have been noted.

COMMON SIDE EFFECTS:
- Slight slowing of heart rate in most people.
- Dry mouth (very common; about 40%).
- Drowsiness and sedation (very common, especially in the elderly; about 35% and 8% respectively).
- Dizziness (common; about 15%)
- Nausea, vomiting, constipation (up to 5%).
- Dizziness and light-headedness when standing up too fast (orthostatic hypotension; up to 5%).

UNCOMMON SIDE EFFECTS:
- * Mental depression, nightmares, delirium, anxiety.
- * Edema (swelling of ankles and legs caused by excess sodium and water retention).
- * Rash, hives (hypersensitivity reaction; rare).
- * Unexplained coldness and paleness in fingers and toes (Raynaud's phenomenon; rare).

SEXUAL SIDE EFFECTS:
- Impotence (infrequent).

DRUG INTERACTIONS:
- Tricyclic antidepressants: **Desyrel** (trazodone; not really tricyclic), **Elavil** and **Endep** (amitriptyline), **Tofranil** and **Janimine** (imipramine), **Adapin** and **Sinequan** (doxepin), **Surmontil** (trimipramine), **Aventyl** and **Pamelor** (nortriptyline), **Norpramin** and **Pertofrane** (desiprimine), **Vivactil** (protriptyline), **Asendin** (amoxapine), and probably **Ludiomil** (maprotiline) can decrease the effectiveness of **Catapres**.
- Beta blockers **Inderal** (propranolol), **Tenormin** (atenolol), **Lopressor** (metoprolol), **Corgard** (nadolol), **Visken** (pindolol), and **Blocadren** (timolol) can severely worsen the rebound hypertension seen when **Catapres** is discontinued abruptly. In addition, the combination, although frequently used, may rarely cause a paradoxical rise in blood pressure (both interactions likely but unconfirmed).
- Alcohol and other sedating drugs may worsen the drowsiness commonly seen with **Catapres**.

---

* These side effects may be serious. Contact your physician immediately if they occur.

Corgard *(nadolol 40 mg, 80 mg, 120 mg, and 160 mg tablets)*
See Beta Blockers, p. 198.

Diuril *(chlorothiazide 250 mg and 500 mg tablets, and 250 mg per 5 ml liquid suspension)*

MFR: Merck Sharp & Dohme; also available generically.

USUAL DOSE: 500 mg to 1,000 mg daily in single or divided doses (most people take it only once daily)

Diuril and the other "thiazide diuretics" are quite often used as the first choice for newly diagnosed hypertensives and are frequently combined with other blood-pressure-lowering drugs to enhance their effects. They act on the kidney to increase excretion of sodium and water. Fixed-combination products should be discouraged because it is impossible to change the dose of one without changing the dose of the other. The thiazide diuretics (including **Diuril**) compose a large class of pretty much interchangeable drugs such as **Anhydron**, **Aquastat**, **Aquatag**, **Aquatensen**, **Enduron**, **Esidrix**, **Exna**, **Fluidil**, **Hydrex**, **Hydro-Aquil**, **HydroDIURIL**, **Metahydrin**, **Naqua**, **Naturetin**, **Oretic**, **Renese**, and **Saluron**. They are relatively mild diuretics, and all of them cause the body to lose potassium. For this reason patients taking thiazides are encouraged to eat foods high in potassium or are sometimes prescribed potassium supplements. Even though their diuretic action is well understood, this doesn't seem to be the sole reason for their effectiveness in lowering blood pressure. While diuresis happens quickly after taking a thiazide, the full antihypertensive activity may not be obvious for three or four weeks.

Some physicians have recently become concerned that commonly prescribed thiazide diuretics will increase triglyceride and cholesterol levels in the blood. They fear that many years of therapy with such drugs may increase the risk of atherosclerosis and coronary artery disease. As a result, the benefit of reduced blood pressure may be partially compromised by this adverse effect. As of this writing we have no definitive answer to such a question and it is of greater theoretical than practical concern.

PRECAUTIONS:
- Blood potassium levels should be checked regularly.
- May aggravate gout or diabetes.
- Do not take OTC decongestants, diet aids, or asthma medications without first consulting your doctor; they may aggravate your high blood pressure.

(continues next page)

Diuril, *(continued)*

- If given in a single daily dose, take in the morning so you won't be getting up all night to go to the bathroom.
- Three or four weeks may be necessary before you see the full antihypertensive effect of **Diuril** and the other thiazide diuretics.
- Do not take if you are allergic to any sulfa-containing drugs.

PREGNANCY AND BREAST-FEEDING:

- Use in pregnancy has not been proven safe. Thiazide diuretics cross the placenta and are found in the baby's circulation.
- Thiazides are found in breast milk. Although no problems have yet been reported, breast-feeding should probably be stopped if thiazide therapy is necessary.

COMMON SIDE EFFECTS:

- Increased frequency of urination (in almost everyone).
- Upset stomach, diarrhea, cramps, loss of appetite (relatively common).
- *Hypokalemia (low blood potassium levels) (See page 303).

UNCOMMON SIDE EFFECTS:

- *Rash, hives, shortness of breath (allergic reactions; rare).
- *Unexplained sore throat with fever (rare).
- *Unexplained bleeding, bruising (rare).
- Dizziness and faintness when you stand up too fast.
- *Very severe abdominal pain with nausea and vomiting (rare).
- *Liver damage characterized by jaundice (yellow skin and eyes).

SEXUAL SIDE EFFECTS:

- Decreased vaginal lubrication.

DRUG INTERACTIONS:

- **Questran** (cholestyramine), **Colestid** (colestipol) decrease hydrochlorothiazide absorption.
- **Lanoxin** (digoxin) and other digitalis drugs: *dangerous* combination if hypokalemic. May cause abnormal heart rhythms and can be fatal (See page 303).
- **Florinef** (fludrocortisone); **Cortone** (cortisone); **Cortef** and **Hydrocortone** (hydrocortisone); **Meticorten**, **Deltasone**, and others (prednisone); and **Delta-Cortef** and others (prednisolone) can contribute to potassium loss and hypokalemia (See page 303).
- **Indocin** (indomethacin) decreases effectiveness of hydrochlorothiazide.
- **Eskalith, Lithobid** (lithium): hydrochlorothiazide may cause serious lithium toxicity.

* *These side effects may be serious. Contact your physician immediately if they occur.*

Diuril, *(continued)*

- **Orinase** (tolbutamide), **Dymelor** (acetohexamide), **Tolinase** (tolazamide), and **Diabinese** (chlorpropamide): hydrochlorothiazide may decrease the effectiveness of these oral diabetes drugs.

Dyazide *(hydrochlorothiazide 25 mg plus triamterene 50 mg capsules)*

MFR: Smith Kline & French

USUAL DOSE: One or two capsules twice daily.

Dyazide has become the second most prescribed drug in this country—right up there next to **Inderal.** One prescription drug survey even suggests that **Dyazide** has become big number-one, surging *past* **Inderal**. Hundreds of millions of dollars are spent on this combination diuretic each year in the hope that it will lower blood pressure while simultaneously sparing potassium. Physicians have become keenly aware of the importance of potassium. Supplements can taste terrible, and as a result patients often complain bitterly. The prescribing of a combination product which contains one diuretic that "preserves" to counteract the other that "wastes" potassium seems logical.

There's only one problem. The formulation that SmithKline produced in the early 1960s had some flaws. According to Dr. Raymond Lipicky, an FDA expert, **Dyazide** "is a terrible pharmaceutical preparation." Dr. Robert Temple, FDA's Acting Director of Drug Research and Review, agrees: "It is a poor pharmaceutical preparation . . . by which I mean it's not a high bioavailability preparation."

In other words, the way the capsule is physically prepared does not allow for the optimum amount of drug to get into the body. The FDA has been very concerned about this problem and has encouraged both SmithKline and generic manufacturers to come up with a better mousetrap—or more precisely, a better **Dyazide**. SmithKline is hard at work trying to put together the ideal combination of hydrochlorothiazide and triamterene to improve upon its commercially successful product. Meanwhile at least one other drug manufacturer has beaten the master to the finish line. **Maxzide,** marketed by Lederle, appears to provide significantly better bioavailability than the original **Dyazide**. If it's cheaper too, **Maxzide** could be an excellent alternative to **Dyazide**, at least until SmithKline fixes its formula.

PRECAUTIONS:
- Do not take if you are allergic to sulfa-containing medicines.

(continues next page)

Dyazide, *(continued)*

- Do not take potassium supplements while using this product unless under careful supervision of a doctor.
- Blood potassium levels should be checked regularly.
- May aggravate gout or diabetes.
- Do not take OTC decongestants, diet aids, or asthma medications without first consulting your doctor; they may aggravate your high blood pressure.
- The correct dose of this medicine should be periodically reevaluated.
- Take with food or milk if it upsets your stomach.

PREGNANCY AND BREAST-FEEDING:
- Use in pregnancy has not been proven safe. Thiazide diuretics and triamterene cross the placenta and are found in the baby's circulation.
- Thiazides and triamterene are found in breast milk. Although no problems have yet been reported, breast-feeding should probably be stopped if **Dyazide** therapy is necessary.

COMMON SIDE EFFECTS:
- Upset stomach, diarrhea, cramps, loss of appetite (relatively common).
- Increased frequency of urination (in almost everyone).

UNCOMMON SIDE EFFECTS:
- Blue color in urine (uncommon but apparently harmless).
- Dizziness and faintness when you stand up too fast.
- Sunlight sensitivity, sunburn (infrequent).
- * Hypokalemia (low blood potassium levels), (See page 303).
- * Hyperkalemia (high blood potassium levels) (See page 303).
- * Rash, hives, shortness of breath (allergic reactions; rare).
- * Unexplained sore throat with fever (rare).
- * Unexplained bleeding, bruising (rare).
- * Very severe abdominal pain with nausea, vomiting (rare).
- * Very severe flank pain (rare).
- * Anemia characterized by weakness, diarrhea, bright red and burning tongue, dry cracked lips and mouth (rare).
- * Liver damage characterized by jaundice (yellow skin and eyes).

SEXUAL SIDE EFFECTS:
- Decreased vaginal lubrication.

DRUG INTERACTIONS:
- Potassium supplements (**K-Lor**, **Kaon**, **Slow-K**, **K-Lyte**, **Klotrix**, **Micro-K**, **K-Tab**, and many others) may cause hyperkalemia in presence of triamterene despite the inclusion of hydrochlorothiazide in **Dyazide.**

* These side effects may be serious. Contact your physician immediately if they occur.

Dyazide, *(continued)*

- **Questran** (cholestyramine), **Colestid** (colestipol) decrease hydrochlorothiazide absorption.
- **Lanoxin** (digoxin) and other digitalis drugs: *dangerous* combination if hypokalemic. May cause abnormal heart rhythms and can be fatal (See page 303).
- **Florinef** (fludrocortisone); **Cortone** (cortisone); **Cortef** and **Hydrocortone** (hydrocortisone); **Meticorten, Deltasone**, and others (prednisone); and **Delta-Cortef** and others (prednisolone) can contribute to potassium loss and hypokalemia. (See page 303.)
- **Indocin** (indomethacin) decreases effectiveness of hydrochlorothiazide. Can also interact with triamterene to cause deterioration of kidney function (unconfirmed).
- **Eskalith, Lithobid** (lithium): hydrochlorothiazide and triamterene may cause serious lithium toxicity.
- **Orinase** (tolbutamide), **Dymelor** (acetohexamide), **Tolinase** (tolazamide), and **Diabinese** (chloropropamide): hydrochlorothiazide may decrease the effectiveness of these oral diabetes drugs.
- **Dyrenium** (triamterene), **Midamor** (amiloride), **Aldactone** (spironolactone), **Aldactazide** (contains spironolactone), or other potassium-sparing diuretics may cause hyperkalemia.
- Salt substitutes may contain large amounts of potassium and may contribute to hyperkalemia.

Enduron *(methyclothiazide 2.5 mg and 5.0 mg tablets)*

MFR: Abbott Laboratories; also manufactured as **Aquatensin** by Wallace Laboratories (5.0 mg tablets only).

USUAL DOSE: 2.5 mg to 5.0 mg once daily.

See **Diuril** for description of thiazide diuretics.

HydroDIURIL *(hydrochlorothiazide 25 mg, 50 mg, and 100 mg tablets)*.

MFR: Merck Sharp & Dohme; also available generically and as **Esidrix** (Ciba), **Oretic** (Abbott Laboratories), and others.

USUAL DOSE: 25 mg to 100 mg once daily or as a divided dose.

See **Diuril** for description of thiazide diuretics.

Hydropres *(hydrochlorothiazide 25 mg or 50 mg plus reserpine 0.125 mg tablets)*

MFR: Merck Sharp & Dohme; also available generically and as **Serpasil-Esidrix** (hydrochlorothiazide 25 mg or 50 mg plus reserpine 0.1 mg tablets).

USUAL DOSE: One or two tablets once or twice daily (lower strength) or one tablet once or twice daily (higher strength).

Reserpine, one of the components in **Hydropres,** is an old-time medication, and newer, better, and stronger drugs should be tried first. One of the more frightening of reserpine's many potential adverse reactions is the onset of severe mental depression. It can, and has, led to suicide. Although the incidence of this unusual side effect is low if the dose is kept under 0.25 mg per day, **Hydropres** should be immediately stopped if any of the signs of depression or emotional disturbance occur (see *Common Side Effects*). In 1974 there was a flurry of media attention and genuine concern when three European studies seemed to show an increased incidence of breast cancer in women who took reserpine. Fortunately these results were never substantiated, and the studies themselves were found to be faulty. It now appears that reserpine carries little if any potential risk of cancer.

Hydropres is a combination medication and is therefore not indicated for the initial treatment of high blood pressure. Although thiazide diuretics are often prescribed in conjunction with reserpine, the fixed doses in this proprietary mixture allow for no flexibility in dosage.

PRECAUTIONS:
- Do not take if you are allergic to sulfa-containing medicines.
- Blood potassium levels should be checked regularly.
- May aggravate gout or diabetes.
- Do not take OTC decongestants (even though reserpine frequently causes a stuffy nose), diet aids, or asthma medications without first consulting your doctor; they may aggravate your high blood pressure.
- The correct dose of this medicine should be periodically reevaluated.
- Take with food or milk if it upsets your stomach.
- May aggravate asthma.
- May worsen ulcer or ulcerative colitis.
- Do not take if you have a history of depression or emotional illness.
- Do not take if you have Parkinson's disease.
- May precipitate biliary colic (a very painful blockage of the bile duct) in persons with gallstones.

PREGNANCY AND BREAST-FEEDING:
- Reserpine can have adverse effects on the fetus. Do not use this drug if pregnant.

Hydropres, *(continued)*

- Both reserpine and hydrochlorothiazide are found in breast milk. Although no problems have yet been reported, breast-feeding should probably be stopped if **Hydropres** therapy is necessary.

COMMON SIDE EFFECTS:
- Drowsiness.
- Increased frequency of urination (in almost everyone).
- Diarrhea, upset stomach, nausea, vomiting, loss of appetite.
- Dizziness and faintness when you stand up too fast (common; occurs more often in the elderly).
- Stuffy nose and dry mouth. Do not take decongestant medications for this condition; they can increase blood pressure.
- Conjunctivitis (irritated eyes).
*- Hypokalemia (low blood potassium levels) (See page 303).
*- Unusual drowsiness, lethargy, and weakness (more common at higher doses and in the elderly).
*- Mental depression (more common at higher doses and in the elderly).
*- Anxiety, early-morning insomnia, nervousness, nightmares (more common at higher doses and in the elderly).

UNCOMMON SIDE EFFECTS:
*- Palpitations, slow heart beat, chest pain (relatively uncommon).
*- Unusual bruising, bleeding (rare).
*- Parkinsonismlike symptoms: tremor, shaking, stiffness, and rigidity (infrequent).
*- Difficulty in breathing.
*- Rash, hives, itching (allergic reactions; rare).
*- Unexplained sore throat with fever (rare).
*- Very severe abdominal pain with nausea and vomiting (rare).

SEXUAL SIDE EFFECTS:
- Impotence (relatively common).
- Decreased libido (relatively common).
- Decreased vaginal lubrication.

DRUG INTERACTIONS:
- **Questran** (cholestyramine), **Colestid** (colestipol) decrease hydrochlorothiazide absorption.
- **Lanoxin** (digoxin) and other digitalis drugs: *dangerous* combination if hypokalemic. May cause abnormal heart rhythms and can be fatal. (See page 303).

(continues next page)

* *These side effects may be serious. Contact your physician immediately if they occur.*

Hydropres, *(continued)*

- **Florinef** (fludrocortisone); **Cortone** (cortisone); **Cortef** and **Hydrocortone** (hydrocortisone); **Meticorten, Deltasone**, and others (prednisone); and **Delta-Cortef** and others (prednisolone) can contribute to potassium loss and hypokalemia. (See page 303).
- **Indocin** (indomethacin) decreases effectiveness of hydrochlorothiazide.
- **Eskalith, Lithobid** (lithium): hydrochlorothiazide may cause serious lithium toxicity.
- **Orinase** (tolbutamide), **Dymelor** (acetohexamide), **Tolinase** (tolazamide), and **Diabinese** (chlorpropamide): hydrochlorothiazide may decrease the effectiveness of these oral diabetes drugs.
- General anesthetics: reserpine can cause an excessively slow heart rate and low blood pressure.

Hygroton *(chlorthalidone 25 mg, 50 mg, and 100 mg tablets)*

MFR: USV Pharmaceutical Corp.; also available generically and as **Thalitone** (25 mg tablets only; Boehringer Ingelheim Ltd.)

USUAL DOSE: 25 mg to 100 mg once daily.

Although chlorthalidone is technically not a thiazide diuretic, its action on the kidneys and efficacy in hypertension is the same. The main difference is that chlorthalidone stays in the body much longer than the thiazides, and some lucky persons need take it only every other day as a result. (See **Diuril** for a further description of thiazide diuretics.)

PRECAUTIONS:
- Blood potassium levels should be checked regularly.
- May aggravate gout or diabetes.
- Do not take OTC decongestants, diet aids, or asthma medications without first consulting your doctor; they may aggravate your high blood pressure.
- If given in a single daily dose, take in the morning so you won't be getting up all night to go to the bathroom.
- Three or four weeks may be necessary before you see the full antihypertensive effect of **Hygroton**.
- Do not take if you are allergic to any sulfa-containing drugs (chlorthalidone has been used in some persons who have had reactions to thiazides, but since it, too, is related to sulfa, it can't be relied upon to be completely safe).

PREGNANCY AND BREAST-FEEDING:
- Use in pregnancy has not been proven safe. Thiazide diuretics (and probably chlorthalidone) cross the placenta and are found in the baby's circulation.

Hygroton, *(continued)*

- Thiazides (and probably chlorthalidone) are found in breast milk. Although no problems have yet been reported, breast-feeding should probably be stopped if chlorthalidone therapy is necessary.

COMMON SIDE EFFECTS:
- Increased frequency of urination (in almost everyone).
- Upset stomach, diarrhea, cramps, loss of appetite (relatively common).
*- Hypokalemia (low blood potassium levels). (See page 303.)

UNCOMMON SIDE EFFECTS:
*- Rash, hives, shortness of breath (allergic reactions; rare).
*- Unexplained sore throat with fever (rare).
*- Unexplained bleeding or bruising (rare).
- Dizziness and faintness when you stand up too fast.
*- Very severe abdominal pain with nausea and vomiting (rare).
*- Liver damage characterized by jaundice (yellow skin and eyes).

SEXUAL SIDE EFFECTS:
- Decreased vaginal lubrication.
- Possible decreased libido.

DRUG INTERACTIONS:
- **Questran** (cholestyramine), **Colestid** (colestipol) decrease chlorthalidone absorption.
- **Lanoxin** (digoxin) and other digitalis drugs: *dangerous* combination if hypokalemic. May cause abnormal heart rhythms and can be fatal. (See page 303).
- **Florinef** (fludrocortisone); **Cortone** (cortisone); **Cortef** and **Hydrocortone** (hydrocortisone); **Meticorten**, **Deltasone**, and others (prednisone); and **Delta-Cortef** and others (prednisolone) can contribute to potassium loss and hypokalemia. (See page 303).
- **Indocin** (indomethacin) decreases effectiveness of chlorthalidone.
- **Eskalith**, **Lithobid** (lithium): chlorthalidone may cause serious lithium toxicity.
- **Orinase** (tolbutamide), **Dymelor** (acetohexamide), **Tolinase** (tolazamide), and **Diabinese** (chlorpropamide): chlorothalidone may decrease the effectiveness of these oral diabetes drugs.

Inder al (propranolol 10 mg, 20 mg, 40 mg, 80 mg, and 90 mg tablets)
See Beta Blockers, p. 199.

---

* *These side effects may be serious. Contact your physician immediately if they occur.*

Inderide *(propranolol 40 mg or 80 mg plus hydrochlorothiazide 25 mg tablets)*

MFR: Ayerst Laboratories

USUAL DOSE: One or two tablets twice daily (either strength).

This combination of blood-pressure drugs seems to be the doctor's favorite second step for persons whose blood pressure wasn't controlled by a diuretic alone. The idea is good, and both drugs are quite effective, but take a look at the sheer volume of precautions, side effects, and potential drug interactions in the list that follows. Despite these dire warnings, thousands of people have good blood-pressure control, with relatively few adverse reactions, using these two drugs.

Because so many physicians were prescribing propranolol and hydrochlorothiazide simultaneously I guess Ayerst decided to join the party and market **Inderide**. The problem here is the standard complaint against fixed-combination drugs; you can't change the dose of one without changing the dose of the other. One difficulty with this particular product is that propranolol should be taken twice or even three times daily, while hydrochlorothiazide is usually taken just once a day. When you take a diuretic later in the afternoon, you run the considerable risk of having to wake up in the middle of the night to run to the bathroom. After all, a diuretic is supposed to increase the flow of urine. If you need both propranolol and hydrochlorothiazide, it's probably best to take them separately. That way you can take them on an appropriate schedule, and the doses of each can be individualized to your specific needs.

Also see: Beta Blockers, p. 194.

PRECAUTIONS:
- Blood potassium levels should be checked regularly.
- May aggravate gout or diabetes.
- May mask the signs and symptoms of dangerously low blood sugar.
- May decrease your tolerance for strenuous exercise.
- Do not take OTC decongestants, diet aids, or asthma medications without first consulting your doctor; they may aggravate your high blood pressure.
- Do not take if you are allergic to any sulfa-containing drugs.
- Do not abruptly stop taking this drug. Doing so may aggravate heart conditions or, rarely, may precipitate a heart attack.
- Do not take if you are asthmatic or have respiratory difficulty.

PREGNANCY AND BREAST-FEEDING:
- Use in pregnancy has not been proven safe. Thiazide diuretics cross the placenta and are found in the baby's circulation. Possible adverse effects to the baby from propranolol are unclear.

Inderide, *(continued)*

- Thiazides (and to a small extent, propranolol) are found in breast milk. Although no problems have yet been reported, breast-feeding should probably be stopped if **Inderide** therapy is necessary.

COMMON SIDE EFFECTS:
- Drowsiness (fairly common, especially at higher doses).
- Fatigue, decreased tolerance of exercise.
- Dry skin, eyes, mouth.
- Increased frequency of urination (in almost everyone).
*- Very slow heart rate (less than 50 beats per minute).
- Upset stomach, nausea, diarrhea, cramps, loss of appetite (relatively common).
- Tingling sensation in fingers, toes.
*- Hypokalemia (low blood potassium levels); (See page 303.)
*- Excessive faintness or dizziness from low blood pressure.

UNCOMMON SIDE EFFECTS:
- Nightmares, vivid dreams, hallucinations.
- Anxiety, insomnia, nervousness.
- Constipation.
- Dizziness and faintness when you stand up too fast.
- Headache.
*- Mental depression, excess drowsiness, confusion (occurs more commonly with higher doses and in the elderly).
*- Breathing difficulty (much more common in persons with asthma or other respiratory condition).
*- Unusually cold hands, toes, fingers.
*- Rash, hives, shortness of breath (allergic reactions; rare).
*- Unexplained sore throat with fever (rare).
*- Unexplained bleeding, bruising (rare).
*- Very severe abdominal pain with nausea, vomiting (rare).

SEXUAL SIDE EFFECTS:
- Decreased vaginal lubrication.
- Impotence (not uncommon).

DRUG INTERACTIONS:
- **Questran** (cholestyramine), **Colestid** (colestipol) decrease hydrochlorothiazide absorption.

(continues next page)

* These side effects may be serious. Contact your physician immediately if they occur.

Inderide, *(continued)*

- **Lanoxin** (digoxin) and other digitalis drugs: *dangerous* combination if hypokalemic. May cause abnormal heart rhythms and can be fatal. (See page 303).
- **Florinef** (fludrocortisone); **Cortone** (cortisone); **Cortef** and **Hydrocortone** (hydrocortisone); **Meticorten**, **Deltasone**, and others (prednisone); and **Delta-Cortef** and others (prednisolone) can contribute to potassium loss and hypokalemia. (See page 303).
- **Indocin** (indomethacin) decreases effectiveness of both propranolol and hydrochlorothiazide.
- **Eskalith**, **Lithobid** (lithium): hydrochlorothiazide may cause serious lithium toxicity.
- **Orinase** (tolbutamide), **Dymelor** (acetohexamide), **Tolinase** (tolazamide), and **Diabinese** (chlorpropamide): hydrochlorothiazide may decrease the effectiveness of these oral diabetes drugs.
- **Alurate** (aprobarbital), **Amytal** (amobarbital), **Butisol** (butabarbital), **Gemonil** (metharbital), **Lotusate** (talbutal), **Luminal** (phenobarbital), **Mebaral** (mephobarbital), **Mysoline** (primidone), **Nembutal** (pentobarbital), **Seconal** (secobarbital), **Tuinal** (amobarbital and secobarbital), and others (all barbiturates) decrease the effectiveness of propranolol.
- **Thorazine** (chlorpromazine) increases the levels of propranolol in the blood, and possibly vice-versa.
- The effects of a dose of insulin are increased by propranolol. Of more concern is the ability of propranolol to block most of the characteristic symptoms of dangerously low blood sugar. Diabetics beware!
- The beneficial effects of **Theo-Dur**, **Bronkodyl**, **Respbid** and dozens more (all theophylline); **Choledyl** (oxtriphylline), **Aminodur**, **Somophylline** and others (all aminophylline); and **Neothylline** and others (dyphylline) are decreased by propranolol. An increased dose of the above drugs may be necessary to maintain desirable asthma control.
- **Minipress** (prazosin) effects may be markedly increased by propranolol. Adding **Minipress** to a blood-pressure treatment regimen already containing propranolol may cause acutely low blood pressure.
- **Tagamet** (cimetidine) can markedly enhance the levels of propranolol in the blood. Excessively slow heart rate and low blood pressure may result. (Note: these are two *very* commonly prescribed drugs!)
- Birth-control pills can increase the blood levels of propranolol.
- **Rimactane** (rifampin) decreases the amount of propranolol absorbed into the blood stream.

Ismelin *(guanethidine 10 mg and 25 mg tablets)*

MFR: Ciba-Geigy

USUAL DOSE: 10 mg once daily. May be increased *gradually* every 7–10 days to 25 mg to 50 mg once daily.

Ismelin is not one of the easiest drugs to take. It causes some side effects in just about everyone, and they are often quite uncomfortable. Perhaps the most common adverse reaction is "orthostatic hypotension," that dizziness and faintness you feel when you stand up too quickly. The drug also causes difficulty in ejaculation for many men. Guanethidine is quite effective at lowering blood pressure, however, and may be necessary in the most resistant cases. It is most often prescribed along with a diuretic to minimize guanethidine's tendency to cause fluid retention. **Ismelin** lowers your blood pressure more when you stand up than when you are lying down. For this reason your doctor should always take your blood pressure in both standing and supine positions. Note all of the drug interactions that can decrease **Ismelin's** effectiveness and beware!

PRECAUTIONS:
- Do not take OTC decongestants, diet aids, or asthma medications without first consulting your doctor; they may aggravate your high blood pressure. This is especially true for **Ismelin;** the beneficial blood-pressure-lowering properties of guanethidine may be completely blocked by this combination (see *Drug Interactions*).
- May aggravate congestive heart failure or other heart problems.
- Use caution when standing or getting up from a lying position. Guanethidine may make you dizzy or faint.
- May aggravate asthma.

PREGNANCY AND BREAST-FEEDING:
- Although no problems have been documented in pregnant or nursing women, there should be careful consideration of possible risks and benefits before taking any drug while pregnant or nursing.

COMMON SIDE EFFECTS:
- Faintness and dizziness when you stand up too fast (orthostatic hypotension; quite common). This adverse reaction occurs more frequently in the elderly and with higher doses. It is made worse by strenuous exercise, alcohol, and hot weather.
- Weakness and fatigue (quite common).
- Diarrhea.
- Slow heart rate.
- Stuffy nose.
*- Edema (swelling of feet and ankles because of salt and water retention).

(continues next page)

* *These side effects may be serious. Contact your physician immediately if they occur.*

Ismelin, *(continued)*

UNCOMMON SIDE EFFECTS:
- Nausea, vomiting.
- Drooping eyelids, blurred vision.
- Hair loss.
- Increased frequency of urination during the night or incontinence (not a true diuretic effect).
- Rash, skin problems.
- Headache.
*- Mental depression.
- Muscular tremors, muscle pain.
*- Very severe diarrhea.
*- Exacerbation of angina, chest pain.
*- Difficulty in breathing because of fluid accumulation in the lungs.

SEXUAL SIDE EFFECTS:
- Difficulty in erection and ejaculation (quite common).

DRUG INTERACTIONS:
- Guanethidine's blood-pressure-lowering effects are blocked by such prescription diet aids as **Benzedrine** (amphetamine), **Biphetamine** (amphetamine and dextroamphetamine), **Dexedrine** (dextroamphetamine), **Desoxyn** (methamphetamine), **Didrex** (benzphetamine), **Tenuate** (diethylpropion), **Pondimin** (fenfluramine), **Voranil** (clortermine), **Pre-Sate** (chlorphentermine), **Ionamin** (phentermine), **Preludin** (phenmetrazine), **Plegine** (phendimetrazine), **Mazanor** and **Sanorex** (mazindol), and OTC diet drugs such as **Dexatrim**, **Dietac**, and others (phenylpropanolamine). Avoid them!
- **Haldol** (haloperidol) may decrease the effectiveness of guanethidine.
- **Ritalin** (methylphenidate) also decreases the antihypertensive effects of guanethidine.
- Tricyclic antidepressants—**Elavil** and **Endep** (amitriptyline), **Tofranil** and **Janimine** (imipramine), **Surmontil** (trimipramine), **Aventyl** and **Pamelor** (nortriptyline), **Norpramin** and **Pertofrane** (desipramine), **Vivactil** (protriptyline), **Asendin** (amoxapine), probably **Ludiomil** (maprotiline), and to a lesser extent **Adapin** and **Sinequan** (doxepin) can decrease the effectiveness of guanethidine.
- Prescription and OTC decongestants, cold preparations, and asthma remedies containing phenylpropanolamine, pseudoephedrine, or ephedrine can block the effects of guanethidine. Worse yet, blood pressure can actually increase. Out of hundreds, some examples are **Sudafed**, **Sinutab**, **Ornade**, **Drixoral**, **Actifed**, **Dristan**, **Contac**, **Propadrine**, **Primatene**, **Tedral**, and **Marax**. Read the labels on all

These side effects may be serious. Contact your physician immediately if they occur.

Ismelin, *(continued)*

OTC medications before you purchase them or ask your pharmacist for advice.

- "Major tranquilizers" (used for some mental disorders or to prevent nausea and vomiting), such as **Thorazine** (chlorpromazine), **Sparine** (promazine), **Vesprin** (triflupromazine), **Mellaril** (thioridazine), **Quide** (piperacetazine), **Serentil** (mesoridazine), **Trilafon** and **Triavil** (perphenazine), **Tindal** (acetophenazine), **Compazine** (prochlorperazine), **Permatil** and **Prolixin** (fluphenazine), and **Stelazine** (trifluoperazine) can block the blood-pressure-lowering effects of guanethidine.
- The MAO (monoamine oxidase) inhibitors also block the effects of guancthidine. They are **Marplan** (isocarboxazid), **Nardil** (phenelzine), **Parnate** (tranylcypromine), **Eutonyl** (pargyline), and **Furoxone** (furazolidone), an antibiotic with MAO-inhibiting properties.
- **Loniten** (minoxidil) and guanethidine can cause seriously low blood pressure.

Lasix *(furosemide 20 mg, 40mg, and 80 mg tablets, and 10 mg per 1 ml oral solution)*

MFR: Hoechst-Roussel Pharmaceuticals Inc.; also available generically (except the 80 mg tablet or the oral solution).

USUAL DOSE: 40 mg twice daily.

PRECAUTIONS:
- Use with caution if you are allergic to sulfa-containing medications.
- Blood potassium levels should be checked regularly.
- May aggravate gout.
- Do not take OTC decongestants, diet aids, or asthma medications without first consulting your doctor; they may aggravate your high blood pressure.
- Keep in a dark container. Discoloration (harmless and inconsequential) may occur if **Lasix** is exposed to light.

PREGNANCY AND BREAST-FEEDING:
- Use in pregnancy has not been proven safe. Furosemide crosses the placenta and is found in the baby's circulation. Although no problems have yet been reported in humans, animal studies show a possibility of kidney damage to the fetus. Avoid if pregnant unless absolutely necessary.

(continues next page)

Lasix, *(continued)*

- **Lasix** is found in breast milk. Although no problems have yet been reported, breast-feeding should probably be stopped if furosemide therapy is necessary.

COMMON SIDE EFFECTS:
- *▪ Dizziness and faintness when you stand up too fast (more common with excessive doses).
- *▪ Hypokalemia: (low blood potassium levels). (See page 303). May cause less hypokalemia than the thiazide diuretics when given in moderate doses.

UNCOMMON SIDE EFFECTS:
- ▪ Diarrhea.
- ▪ Upset stomach, decreased appetite.
- *▪ Ringing in the ears (tinnitus; more likely to occur with large doses and in persons with preexisting kidney damage). Permanent hearing loss has occurred.
- *▪ Rash or hives (allergic reactions; rare).
- *▪ Unexplained bleeding, bruising (rare).
- *▪ Exacerbations of symptoms of gout.
- *▪ Severe nausea, vomiting with stomach pain (rare).
- *▪ Liver damage, jaundice (yellowing of the skin and eyes; rare).

SEXUAL SIDE EFFECTS:
- ▪ Uncommon.

DRUG INTERACTIONS:
- **Lanoxin** (digoxin) and other digitalis drugs: *dangerous* combinations if hypokalemic. May cause abnormal heart rhythms and can be fatal. (See page 303.)
- **Florinef** (fludrocortisone); **Cortone** (cortisone); **Cortef** and **Hydrocortone** (hydrocortisone); **Meticorten**, **Deltasone**, and others (prednisone), and **Delta-Cortef** and others (prednisolone) can contribute to potassium loss and hypokalemia. (See page 303.)
- **Indocin** (indomethacin) decreases effectiveness.

Lopressor *(metoprolol 50 mg and 100 mg tablets)*
See Beta Blockers, p. 203.

---

* These side effects may be serious. Contact your physician immediately if they occur.

Loniten *(minoxidil 2.5 mg and 10 mg tablets)*

MFR: Upjohn Company

USUAL DOSE: Start at 5 mg daily and increase to 10 mg to 40 mg daily as necessary. 100 mg is the recommended daily maximum. Higher doses may be split into a twice daily reigmen.

Loniten is a drug of last resort because of its many serious side effects. One unique adverse reaction is the growth of excess hair on the face, arms, and back, occurring in about 80% of patients. This can be particularly distressing, as you can imagine, especially to women and children. Depilatories can help. Some researchers are even testing minoxidil (in cream form) for use in baldness. Minoxidil is almost always combined with both a strong diuretic and a beta blocker to help control some of the side effects.

WARNING: **Loniten** has caused heart damage in animals and humans. Use only when all other treatment methods have failed.

PRECAUTIONS:
- May aggravate angina pectoris.
- Do not take OTC decongestants, diet aids, or asthma medications without first consulting your doctor; they may aggravate your high blood pressure.

PREGNANCY AND BREAST-FEEDING:
- Minoxidil crosses the placenta in humans and has caused toxicity in animal studies (although no human problems have yet been reported). Avoid during pregnancy if at all possible.
- Problems have not been reported in humans, but it may be prudent not to breast-feed while taking this drug.

COMMON SIDE EFFECTS:
- Excessive growth of unwanted hair on face, back, and arms (up to 80% of people). It may take up to six months after discontinuation of **Loniten** for this condition to disappear.
- * Extreme edema (swelling of feet and ankles because of fluid retention). May cause rapid weight gain. Some edema (at least 7%).
- * Rapid heart rate (in almost everyone), angina, palpitations.
- * Flushed red skin.
- * Pericardial effusions (excess fluid around the heart; up to 3%).

UNCOMMON SIDE EFFECTS:
- Breast tenderness (less than 1%).
- Headache.
- * Exacerbation of angina, chest pain.

(continues next page)

* **These side effects may be serious. Contact your physician immediately if they occur.**

Loniten, *(continued)*

*▪ Rash and itching (allergic reactions; rare).
*▪ Tingling sensation in hands or feet (rare).
*▪ Difficulty in breathing (result of pulmonary hypertension; rare).

SEXUAL SIDE EFFECTS:
  ▪ Uncommon, but this is a relatively new drug and we may have to await further word.

DRUG INTERACTIONS:
  ▪ The use of minoxidil and **Ismelin** (guanethidine) together may cause seriously low blood pressure.

Minipress *(prazosin 1 mg, 2 mg, and 5 mg capsules)*

MFR: Pfizer Laboratories Inc.

USUAL DOSE: start with 1 mg two or three times daily, then increase as necessary to an average of 6 mg to 15 mg twice daily. Occasionally doses of 20 mg or 40 mg daily are needed.

Minipress, a good antihypertensive agent, is now confined to the second or third rung in the treatment ladder. Because of its relative lack of side effects (the one major exception is listed below) and its effectiveness, it could well be used as first-line therapy (this is mild heresy!).

One reason that I like **Minipress** is that it does not appear to affect triglyceride levels or blood fats adversely. It may in fact be beneficial by lowering these bad guys. Beta blockers like **Inderal** and diuretics such as **HydroDIURIL** or **Hygroton** on the other hand may elevate triglycerides and a nasty form of cholesterol called LDL. While we don't know what this means for an individual patient, there has been some concern raised that many commonly prescribed beta blockers and diuretics may actually increase the risk of coronary artery disease down the road. If it turns out that **Minipress** does not have this liability it may become a more attractive alternative as a first-line antihypertensive agent. One other big plus is that there are very few reports of adverse sexual reactions, and one study actually showed a marked decrease in sexual dysfunction in diabetic men who used **Minipress** as compared to **Aldomet.**

The one major drawback to using prazosin is the occurrence of "first-dose syncope," but with a little forethought this can be minimized. This still unexplained reaction occurs when the first dose is given or when the dose is increased and is manifested by sometimes extreme dizziness and occasional fainting about thirty minutes to two hours after medication is

* *These side effects may be serious. Contact your physician immediately if they occur.*

Minipress, *(continued)*

taken. For this reason prazosin therapy is started in small doses, and upward adjustments are made carefully. The first dose or increased dose is best given at night, when you're lying down anyway. Except for this transient reaction, **Minipress** is usually very well tolerated.

PRECAUTIONS:
- May aggravate angina pectoris.
- Do not take OTC decongestants, diet aids, or asthma medications without first consulting your doctor; they may aggravate your high blood pressure.
- Be cautious of dizziness, faintness, and drowsiness when the first dose is given or when the dose is increased (see above).

PREGNANCY AND BREAST-FEEDING:
- Safety in pregnancy or breast-feeding has not been established. No adverse reactions have occurred in animal studies, nor have any problems been reported in humans. As with any drug, use during pregnancy only if clearly necessary.

COMMON SIDE EFFECTS:
- *■ "First-dose syncope" (see above).
- *■ Dizziness and faintness when you stand up too fast (about 10%).
- *■ Aggravation of symptoms of angina, chest pain (less than 10%).
- *■ Edema (swelling of feet and ankles because of fluid retention).
- Headache (about 8%).
- Drowsiness and lethargy (about 8% and 7%, respectively).
- Palpitations (about 5%).
- Nausea and vomiting (about 5%).

UNCOMMON SIDE EFFECTS:
- *■ Incontinence (rare).
- *■ Tingling sensation in hands, feet (rare).

SEXUAL SIDE EFFECTS:
- Decreased libido (rare).

DRUG INTERACTIONS:
- Prazosin can cause unexpected and overly low blood pressure when the first dose is given or when the dose is increased. The beta blockers **Inderal** (propranolol), **Lopressor** (metoprolol), **Tenormin** (atenolol), **Corgard** (nadolol), **Visken** (pindolol), and **Blocadren** (timolol) may make the "first-dose syncope" much worse.

These side effect may be serious. Contact your physician immediately if they occur.

Ser-Ap-Es *(reserpine 0.1 mg plus hydralazine 25 mg plus hydrochlorothiazide 15 mg tablets)*

MFR: Ciba-Geigy; also available generically.

USUAL DOSE: One to two tablets three times daily.

This triple-drug combination is one of my least favorite blood pressure medicines. Two-drug combinations are bad enough, but this is extreme. True, some cases of hard to treat hypertension require several drugs, but the chance that this fixed combination provides all the right drugs in all the correct doses for all patients is pretty slim. If you take the maximum dose recommended by the manufacturer you will be getting a *whopping* dose of reserpine and exposure to potentially serious risks. Taking a diuretic like hydrochlorothiazide three times a day may also cause problems. Diuretics taken in the afternoon or evening tend to keep you up at night going to the bathroom. Before you take **Ser-Ap-Es**, be sure to scan the lengthy list of potential side effects and drug interactions. Whenever you take more than one medication, the potential for suffering an adverse reaction increases dramatically.

For more information on the individual drugs in this mixture, see **Diuril** (also discusses hydrochlorothiazide), **Apresoline,** and **Hydropres**.

PRECAUTIONS:
- Do not take if you are allergic to sulfa-containing medicines.
- Blood potassium levels should be checked regularly.
- May aggravate gout or diabetes.
- Do not take OTC decongestants (even though reserpine frequently causes a stuffy nose), diet aids, or asthma medications without first consulting your doctor; they may aggravate your high blood pressure.
- The correct dose of this medicine should be periodically reevaluated.
- May aggravate asthma.
- May worsen ulcer or ulcerative colitis.
- Do not take if you have a history of depression or emotional illness.
- Do not take if you have Parkinson's disease.
- May precipitate biliary colic (a very painful blockage of the bile duct) in persons with gallstones.
- Contraindicated in patients with coronary artery disease. May worsen symptoms of angina and could possibly trigger a heart attack in these patients.
- Take with food or milk for better absorption and to decrease stomach upset.
- If therapy is to be discontinued, taper off gradually to avoid sudden increase in blood pressure.
- Certain patients may require **Vitamin B$_6$** (pyridoxine) supplementation, 100 mg to 200 mg daily, to treat "peripheral neuropathy" (see side effects, below).

Ser-Ap-Es, *(continued)*

- The physician should take periodic blood tests to check for hydralazine-induced lupus (see discussion under **Apresoline**).

PREGNANCY AND BREAST-FEEDING:
- Thiazide diuretics cross the placenta and are found in the baby's circulation. Hydralazine causes birth defects in animals. Reserpine can have adverse effects on the fetus. Definitely do not take if pregnant.
- Both reserpine and hydrochlorothiazide are found in breast milk. Breast-feeding should be stopped if **Ser-Ap-Es** therapy is necessary.

COMMON SIDE EFFECTS:
- Drowsiness.
- Increased frequency of urination (in almost everyone).
- Diarrhea, upset stomach, cramps, nausea, vomiting, and loss of appetite (relatively common).
- Dizziness and faintness when you stand up too fast (common; occurs more often in the elderly).
- Stuffy nose and dry mouth. Do not take decongestant medications for this condition, as they can increase blood pressure.
- Conjunctivitis (irritated eyes).
- Headache.
- Hypokalemia (low blood potassium levels). (See page 303.)
*- Unusual drowsiness, lethargy, and weakness (more common at higher doses and in the elderly).
*- Mental depression (more common at higher doses and in the elderly).
*- Anxiety, early-morning insomnia, nervousness, nightmares (more common at higher doses and in the elderly).
*- Exacerbation of angina.
*- Palpitations or slow heart beat.

UNCOMMON SIDE EFFECTS:
- Constipation.
*- Unusual bruising, bleeding (rare).
*- Parkinsonismlike symptoms: tremor, shaking, stiffness, and rigidity (infrequent).
*- Difficulty in breathing.
*- Unexplained sore throat with fever (rare).
*- Very severe abdominal pain with nausea, vomiting (rare).
*- Rash, hives, shortness of breath (allergic reactions; rare).

(continues next page)

***** These side effect may be serious. Contact your physician immediately if they occur.**

Ser-Ap-Es, *(continued)*

*■ Drug-induced lupus (see discussion under **Apresoline**).
*■ Peripheral neuropathy characterized by numbness or tingling in lips, hands, feet. Thought to be caused by interference by hydralazine of **Vitamin B₆** (pyridoxine).
*■ Edema (swelling of ankles and legs caused by excess sodium and water retention).
*■ Swelling of lymph nodes.

SEXUAL SIDE EFFECTS:
■ Impotence (relatively common).
■ Decreased libido (relatively common).
■ Decreased vaginal lubrication.

DRUG INTERACTIONS:
■ **Questran** (cholestyramine), **Colestid** (colestipol) decrease hydrochlorothiazide absorption.
■ **Lanoxin** (digoxin) and other digitalis drugs: *dangerous* combination if hypokalemic. May cause abnormal heart rhythms and can be fatal. (See page 303.)
■ **Florinef** (fludrocortisone); **Cortone** (cortisone); **Cortef** and **Hydrocortone** (hydrocortisone); **Meticorten, Deltasone,** and others (prednisone); and **Delta-Cortef** and others (prednisolone) can contribute to potassium loss and hypokalemia. (See page 303.)
■ **Indocin** (indomethacin) decreases effectiveness of hydrochlorothiazide.
■ **Eskalith, Lithobid** (lithium): hydrochlorothiazide may cause serious lithium toxicity.
■ **Orinase** (tolbutamide), **Dymelor** (acetohexamide), **Tolinase** (tolazamide), and **Diabinese** (chlorpropamide): hydrochlorothiazide may decrease the effectiveness of these oral diabetes drugs.
■ General anesthetics: reserpine can cause an excessively slow heart rate and low blood pressure.

Tenormin *(atenolol 50 mg and 100 mg tablets)*
See Beta Blockers, p. 205.

Visken *(pindolol 5 mg and 10 mg tablets)*
See Beta Blockers, p. 209.

---

* *These side effects may be serious. Contact your physician immediately if they occur.*

SIGNS AND SYMPTOMS OF EXCESSIVE POTASSIUM BUILDUP (HYPERKALEMIA)
- Palpitations and abnormal heart rhythms.
- Slow heart rate.
- Difficulty breathing.
- Confusion or anxiety.
- Numbness or tingling sensation in hands, feet, lips.
- Weakness, lethargy.
- Electrocardiographic disturbances.
- Serum potassium higher than 5 meq/1.

SIGNS AND SYMPTOMS OF INADEQUATE POTASSIUM (HYPOKALEMIA)
- Weakness, lethargy.
- Muscle cramps.
- Difficulty breathing.
- Irregular heart rhythms.
- May not have any symptoms, especially if it occurs gradually.
- Serum potassium lower than 3.5 meq/1; levels lower than 3.0 meq/1 are considered severe hypokalemia.

NOTE: Hypokalemia is always serious. It is especially hazardous for those persons taking **Lanoxin** (digoxin) or other digitalis heart medicine. Hypokalemia in these persons can cause digitalis toxicity which may be fatal.

WARNING: The symptoms of too much or too little potassium are deceptively similar, even for experienced clinicians. Furthermore, many symptoms do not appear until the potassium imbalance is dangerously advanced.

Your doctor should be monitoring the level of potassium in your blood on a regular basis. However, if you notice these symptoms, by all means do not delay. Contact your doctor immediately for an assessment of your electrolyte balance.

SIGNS AND SYMPTOMS OF DIGITALIS TOXICITY
- Upset stomach, nausea, vomiting, diarrhea.
- Headache.
- Visual disturbances, such as seeing yellow "haloes" around objects.
- Palpitations, abnormal heart rhythms.
- Fatigue.
- Loss of appetite.
- Excessively slow pulse.

Table References

Meyers, Frederick H.; Jawetz, Ernest; and Goldfein, Alan. *Review of Medical Pharmacology*, 7th ed. Los Altos: Lange Medical Publications, 1980.

Papadopoulos, Chris. "Cardiovascular Drugs and Sexuality—A Cardiologist's Review." *Arch. Intern. Med.* 140:1341–1345, Oct. 1980.

Lipson, Loren G. "Treatment of Hypertension in Diabetic Men: Problems With Sexual Dysfunction." *Am. J. Cardiol.* 53:46A–50A, 1984.

Kastrup, E. K.; Boyd, James R.; and Olin, Bernie R., eds. *Facts and Comparisons*. Philadelphia: J. B. Lippincott Co., 1984.

Mangini, Richard J., ed. *Drug Interaction Facts*. Philadelphia: J. B. Lippincott Co., 1984.

USP Dispensing Information; Drug Information for the Health Care Provider, vol. I. The United States Pharmacopeial Convention, Inc., 1984.

USP Dispensing Information; Advice for the Patient, vol. II. The United States Pharmacopeial Convention, Inc., 1984.

Physicians' Desk Reference, 38th ed. Oradell: Medical Economics Co., 1984.

References

1. American Heart Association. *Heart Facts*, 1983.

2. AMA News Features. "High Blood Pressure is Major American Health Problem." May 20, 1981.

3. Burke, M. J., et al. "Sphygmomanometers in Hospital and Family Practice: Problems and Recommendations." *Br. Med. J.* 285:469–471, 1982.

4. Conceicao, Sergio, et al. "Defects in Sphygmomanometers: An Important Source of Error in Blood Pressure Recording." *Br. Med. J.* 3:886–888, 1978.

5. Thompson, David, R. "Recording Patients' Blood Pressure: A Review." *J. Adv. Nursing* 6:283–290, 1981.

6. Eilertsen, E., and Humerfelt, S. "The Observer Variation in the Measurement of Arterial Blood Pressure." *Acta Med. Scand.* 184:145–157, 1968.

7. Chapman, John M., et al. "Problems of Measurement in Blood Pressure Surveys: Inter-observer Differences in Blood Pressure Determinations." *Am. J. Epidem.* 84:483–494, 1966.

8. Seligman, S. A. "Observer Error in Blood Pressure Recording." *Br. Med. J.* 1:1076, 1976.

9. Rose, G. A., et al. "A Sphygmomanometer for Epidemiologists." *Lancet* 1:296–300, 1964.

10. Richardson, J. F., and Robinson, D. "Variations in the Measurement of Blood Pressure Between Doctors and Nurses." *J. Roy. Col. Gen. Pract.* 21:698–704, 1971.

11. Manning, Dennis M., et al. "Miscuffing: Inappropriate Blood Pressure Cuff Application." *Circulation* 68:763–766, 1983.

12. Ragan, C., and Bordley, J., III. "The Accuracy of Clinical Measurement of Arterial Blood Pressure." *Bull. Johns Hopkins Hosp.* 69:504, 1941.

13. Berliner, K., et al. "Blood Pressure Measurements in Obese Persons: Comparison of Intraarterial and Ausculatory Measurements." *Am. J. Cardiol.* 8:10, 1961.

14. Trout, K. W., et al. "Measurement of Blood Pressure in Obese Persons." *JAMA* 162:970, 1956.

15. Nielson, P. E., and Janniche, H. "The Accuracy of Ausculatory Measurement of Arm Blood Pressure in Very Obese Subjects." *Acta Med. Scand.* 195:403, 1974.

16. Manning. Op cit.

17. Feussner, John R., et al. "Blood Pressure Measurement: Getting the Right Cuff." *North Carolina Med. J.* 44(4):241, 1983.

18. Manning. Op cit.

19. Kirkendall, Walter M., et al. "AHA Committee Report: Recommendations for Human Blood Pressure Determination by Sphygmomanometers." *Circulation* 62:1146A–1155A, 1980.

20. Webster, J., et al. "Influence of Arm Position on Measurement of Blood Pressure." *Br. Med. J.* 288:1574–1575, 1984.

21. Pickering, Thomas G., et al. "Blood Pressure During Normal Daily Activities, Sleep, and Exercise." *JAMA* 247:992–996, 1982.

22. O'Brien, Eoin T., and O'Malley, Kevin. "ABC of Blood Pressure Measurement. Reconciling the Controversies: A Comment on 'the Literature.' " *Br. Med. J.* 2:1201–1202, 1979.

23. Perloff, D., and Sokolow, M. "The Representative Blood Pressure: Usefulness of Office, Basal, Home, and Ambulatory Readings." *Cardiovascular Medicine* 3:655–668, 1978.

24. Raftery, J. B. "The Methodology of Blood Pressure Recording." *Br. J. Clin. Pharmacol.* 6:193–201, 1978.

25. Robertson, David, et al. "Effects of Caffeine on Plasma Renin Activity, Catecholamines and Blood Pressure." *N. Engl. J. Med.* 298:181–186, 1978.

26. Freestone, S., and Ramsay, L. E. "Effect of Coffee Drinking and Cigarette Smoking on Blood Pressure of Untreated and Diuretic-treated Hypertensive Patients." *Am. J. Med.* 73:348–353, 1982.

27. Pickering, Thomas G., et al. Op. cit.

28. Ayman, D. and Goldshine, A. D. "Blood Pressure Determinations by Patients with Essential Hypertension: I. The Difference Between Clinic and Home Readings Before Treatment." *Am. J. Med. Sci.* 200:465–474, 1940.

29. Mancia, Giuseppe, et al. "Effects of Blood-Pressure Measurement by the Doctor on Patient's Blood Pressure and Heart Rate." *Lancet* 2:695–698, 1983.

30. Ibid.

31. Questions and Answers. "Normotensive Home BP Readings v Hypertensive Office Readings." *JAMA* 248:1642–1643, 1982.

32. Ibid.

33. Perloff, Dorothee, et al. "The Prognostic Value of Ambulatory Blood pressures." *JAMA* 249:2792–2798, 1983.

34. Ibid.

35. Ibid.

36. Floras, J. S., et al. "Cuff and Ambulatory Blood Pressure in Subjects with Essential Hypertension." *Lancet* 2:107–109, 1981.

37. Rowlands, D. B., et al. "Assessment of Left Ventricular Mass and its Response to Antihypertensive Treatment." *Lancet* 1:467–470, 1982.

38. Ibrahim, M. M. et al. "Electrocardiogram in Evaluation of Resistance to Antihypertensive Therapy." *Arch. Intern. med.* 137:1125–1129, 1977.

39. Ayman. Op cit.

40. Freis, Edward D. "The Discrepancy Between Home and Office Recordings of Blood Pressure in Patients Under Treatment with Pentapyrrolidinium. Importance of Home Recordings in Adjusting Dosages." *Med. Ann. D.C.* 23:363–414, 1954.

41. Julius, S., et al. "Home Blood Pressure Determination: Value in Borderline ('Labile') Hypertension." *JAMA* 229:663, 1974.

42. Smith, W. J., et al. "The Evaluation of Antihypertensive Therapy Cooperative Clinical Trial Method." *Ann. Intern. Med.* 61:829, 1964.

43. Schroeder, H. A. "Management of Arterial Hypertension." *Am. J. Med.* 17:540, 1954.

44. O'Brien. Op. cit.

45. Gould, Brian A., et al. "Assessment of the Accuracy and Role of Self-recorded Blood Pressures in the Management of Hypertension." *Br. Med. J.* 285:1691–1694, 1982.

46. Cottier, Christopher, et al. "Usefulness of BP Determination in Treating Borderline Hypertension." *JAMA* 248:555–558, 1982.

47. Gould. Op. cit.

48. News. "At-Home BP Readings Prove Best in Drug Trials." *Medical World News* 24(19):52, 1983.

49. Conceicao. Op. cit.

50. Burke. Op cit.

51. Freis, Edward. D. "Should Mild Hypertension Be Treated?" *N. Engl. J. Med.* 307:306–309, 1982.

52. United States Department of Health and Human Services, Public Health Service. "Health United States 1980 With Prevention Profile." Washington, D.C.: Government Printing Office, 1981:35. DHHS publication no. (PHS) 81–1232.

53. McAlister, N. H. "Should We Treat 'Mild' Hypertension?" *JAMA* 249:379–382, 1983.

54. Toth, Patrick J., and Horwitz, Ralph I. "Conflicting Clinical Trials and the Uncertainty of Treating Mild Hypertension." *Am. J. Med.* 75:482–488, 1983.

55. Gifford, Ray W. Jr., et al. "The Dilemma of 'Mild' Hypertension: Another Viewpoint of Treatment." *JAMA* 250:3171–3173, 1983.

56. Kolata, Gina Bari. "Treatment Reduces Deaths from Hypertension: New Study Shows Dramatic Effects of Treating Even those with Mild Hypertension." *Science* 206:1386–1387, 1979.

57. "Caution in Treating Mild Hypertension Urged." AMA News Release, January 21, 1983.

58. Marwick, Charles. " 'Mild' Hypertension: The Gray Zone Gets More Confusing." *Medical World News* 23(6):66–85, 1982.

59. Hypertension Detection and Follow-up Program Cooperative Group. "The Effect of Treatment on Mortality in 'Mild' Hypertension." *N. Engl. J. Med.* 307:976–980, 1982.

60. Gifford. Op. cit.

61. Marwick. Op. cit.

62. Gifford. Op. cit.

63. Thompson, G. E., et al. "High Blood Pressure Diagnosis and Treatment: Consensus Recommendations vs. Actual Practice." *Am. J. Public Health* 71:413–416, 1981.

64. Freis. Op. cit.

65. Ibid.

66. Toth. Op. cit.

67. McAlister. Op. cit.

68. Oslo Study Group. "MRFIT and the Oslo Study." *JAMA* 249:893–894, 1983.

69. Kaplan, Norman M. "Therapy for Mild Hypertension Toward a More Balanced View." *JAMA* 249:365–367, 1983.

70. Kaplan, Norman M. "New Choices for the Initial Drug Therapy of Hypertension." *Am. J. Cardiol.* 51:1786–1788, 1983.

71. Editorial. "Antihypertensive Drugs, Plasma Lipids, and Coronary Disease." *Lancet* 2:19–20, 1980.

72. Ogilvie, R. I. "Diuretic Treatment in Essential Hypertension." *Curr. Med. Res. Opin.* 8(Suppl. 3): 53–58, 1983.

73. Kaplan. Op. cit.

74. "New Trial Tightens Link Between Thiazides and Cardiac Arrhythmia." *Medical World News.* 24(2):32, 1983.

75. Perez-Stable, E., and Caralis, P. V. "Thiazide-Induced Disturbances in Carbohydrate, Lipid, and Potassium Metabolism." *Am. Heart J.* 106:245–251, 1983.

76. Hollifield, J. W., and Slaton, P. E. "Thiazide Diuretics, Hypokalemia and Cardiac Arrhythmias." *Acta Med. Scand.* (Suppl.) 647:67–73, 1981.

77. Ogilvie. Op. cit.

78. Cembrowski, G. S., et al. "Probable Fatal Cardiac Dysrhythmia Secondary to Diuretic-Induced Hypokalemia." *Am. J. Forensic Med. Pathol.* 2(3):243–248, 1981.

79. Solomon, R. J., et al. "Importance of Potassium in Patients with Acute Myocardial Infarction." *Acta Med. Scand.* (Suppl.) 647:87–93, 1981.

80. "Who Needs Slow-Release Potassium Tablets?" *Medical Letter* 17:73–74, 1975.

81. McMahon, Gilbert F., et al. "Upper Gastrointestinal Lesions After Potassium Chloride Supplements: A Controlled Clinical Trial." *Lancet* 2:1059–1063, 1982.

82. Lipicky, Raymond J., Acting Director, Division of Cardio-Renal Drug Products. FDA; Letter to Dr. Robert Keenan, A. H. Robins. NDA 18–238, May 25, 1982.

83. Marwick. Op. cit.

84. Wallis, Claudia, et al. "Salt: A New Villain?" *Time*, March 15, 1982, pp. 64–71 (emphasis in original).

85. Kolata, Gina. "Value of Low-Sodium Diets Questioned." *Science* 216:38–39, 1982 (emphasis in original).

86. Holden, Robert A., et al. "Dietary Salt Intake and Blood Pressure." *JAMA* 250:365–369, 1983.

87. Hofman, Albert, et al. "A Randomized Trial of Sodium Intake and Blood Pressure in Newborn Infants." *JAMA* 250:370–373, 1983.

88. Laragh, John H., and Pecker, Mark S. "Dietary Sodium and Essential Hypertension: Some Myths, Hopes, and Truths." *Ann. Int. Med.* 98:735–743, 1983.

89. MacGregor, Graham A. "Dietary Sodium and Potassium Intake and Blood Pressure." *Lancet* 1:750–753, 1983.

90. Scribner, Belding H. "Salt and Hypertension." *JAMA* 250:388–389, 1983.

91. Parijs, J., et al. "Moderate Sodium Restriction and Diuretics in the Treatment of Hypertension." *Am. Heart J.* 85:22–34, 1973.

92. Morgan, T., et al. "Hypertension Treated by Salt Restriction." *Lancet* 1:227–230, 1978.

93. MacGregor, G. A., et al. "Double-Blind Randomised Crossover Trial of Moderate Sodium Restriction in Essential Hypertension." *Lancet* 1:351–355, 1982.

94. Beard, T. C., et al. "Randomised Controlled Trial of a No-added-sodium Diet for Mild Hypertension." *Lancet* 2:455–458, 1982.

95. Vermeulen, Rita T., et al. "Effect of Water Rinsing on Sodium Content of Selected Foods." *J. Am. Dietet. Assoc.* 82:394–396, 1983.

96. Robertson. Op. cit.

97. Dobmeyer, David, J., et al. "The Arrhythmogenic Effects of Caffeine in Human Beings." *N. Engl. J. Med.* 308:814–816, 1983.

98. UPI. "Caffeine Danger to Heart Reported." San Francisco *Examiner*, April 5, 1983, p. A9.

99. Ibid.

100. "Coffee Consumption and Cholesterol." *Internal Medicine Alert* 5(12):45, 1983.

101. Thelle, Dag S., et al. "The Tromso Heart Study: Does Coffee Raise Serum Cholesterol?" *N. Engl. J. Med.* 308:1454–1457, 1983.

102. Ibid.

103. "Coffee Tied to Bladder Cancer Again, But Skeptics Still Unpersuaded." *Medical World News* 24(7):61, 1983.

104. MacMahon, Brian, et al. "Coffee and Cancer of the Pancreas." *N. Engl. J. Med.* 304:630–633, 1981.

105. Parfrey, P. S., et al. "Blood Pressure and Hormonal Changes Following Alterations in Dietary Sodium and Potassium in Young Men with and without a Familial Predisposition to Hypertension." *Lancet* 1:113–117, 1981.

106. Skrabal, F., et al. "Low Sodium/High Potassium Diet for Prevention of Hypertension: Probable Mechanisms of Action." *Lancet* 2:895–900, 1981.

107. Henningsen, Nels-Christian, et al. "Potassium/Sodium Ratio and Thermogenes." *Lancet* 1:591–592, 1983.

108. MacGregor, Graham A., et al. "Moderate Potassium Supplementation in Essential Hypertension." *Lancet* 2:568–570, 1982.

109. MacGregor, Graham, A. "Dietary Sodium and Potassium Intake and Blood Pressure." *Lancet* 1:750–752, 1983.

110. "Salt and Your Health: Salt Substitutes." *Consumer Reports* 49(1):21, 1984.

111. Sopko, Joseph A., and Freeman, Richard M. "Salt Substitutes as a Source of Potassium." *JAMA* 236:608–610, 1977.

112. Snyder, Edward L., et al. "Abuse of a Salt 'Substitute.' " *N. Engl. J. Med.* 292:320, 1975.

113. McCarron, D. A., et al. "Dietary Calcium in Human Hypertension." *Science* 217:267–269, 1982.

114. McCarron, D. A., et al. "Low Serum Concentrations of Ionized Calcium in Patients with Hypertension." *N. Engl. J. Med.* 307:226–228, 1982.

115. Steiman, Harvey. "The Sodium Theory." San Francisco *Chronicle*, Aug. 15, 1982, Scene, p. 2.

116. Belizan, Jose M. "Reduction of Blood Pressure With Calcium Supplementation in Young Adults." *JAMA* 249:1161–1165, 1983.

117. Albanese, Anthony A., et al. "Osteoporosis: Effects of Calcium." *American Fam. Physician* 18(4):160–167, 1978.

118. Kolars, Joseph C. "Yogurt—An Autodigesting Source of Lactose." *N. Engl. J. Med.* 310:1–3, 1984.

119. "Magnesium Replacement May Improve Blood Pressure in Patients on Long Term Diuretic Therapy." *Internal Medicine Alert* 5(12):47, 1983.

120. Dycker, T., and Wester, P. O. "Effect of Magnesium on Blood Pressure." *Br. Med. J.* 286:1847–1849, 1983.

121. Gallagher, Bernard, P., ed. "Potassium Protects Against High Blood Pressure." *Gallagher Medical Report* 1(20):4, 1983.

122. Rouse, Ian L., et al. "Blood-Pressure Lowering Effect of a Vegetarian Diet: Controlled Trial in Normotensive Subjects." *Lancet* 1:5–9, 1983.

123. Sacks, F. M., et al. "Blood Pressure in Vegetarians." *Am. J. Epidemiol.* 100:390–398, 1974.

124. Armstrong, B., et al. "Urinary Sodium and Blood Pressure in Vegetarians." *Am. J. Clin. Nutr.* 32:2472–2476, 1979.

125. Rouse, I. L., et al. "Vegetarian Diet, Lifestyle and Blood Pressure in Two Religious Populations." *Clin. Exp. Pharmacol. Physiol.* 9:327–330, 1982.

126. Sacks, Frank M., et al. "Effect of Ingestion of Meat on Plasma Cholesterol of Vegetarians." *JAMA* 246:640–644, 1981.

127. Puska, Pekka, et al. "Controlled, Randomised Trial of the Effect of Dietary Fat on Blood Pressure." *Lancet* 1:1–5, 1983.

128. "Quantum Sufficit." *American Fam. Physician.* 25(5):24, 1982.

129. Helyar, John. "Talking to Your Dog Can Help to Lower Your Blood Pressure." *The Wall Street Journal,* Oct. 16, 1981, p. 1.

CHAPTER 8

Coping with Pain

Pain Relief—Too Often, Too Little, or Too Late?
• *The Private Experience of Pain* • *Measuring Pain: Easy as Capturing Moonbeams* • *Fear of Addiction* • *How to Treat Something with Nothing: The Placebo Response* • *How the Brain Fights Pain: Endorphins and Enkephalins* • *Treating Pain with Pills* • *Aspirin and Acetaminophen:* **Anacin, Anacin-3, Tylenol, Datril,** *and* **Panadol** • *When Aspirin Won't Work:* **Dolobid, Motrin, Rufen, Naprosyn, Clinoril, Anaprox, Feldene, Tolectin, Nalfon, Tylenol No. 3, Empirin No. 3, Fiorinal No. 3, Darvocet-N, Percodan, Talwin, Demerol, Dilaudid, Dolophine** *and* *morphine* • *Watch Out for* **Phenergan** • *Banishing Pain: The Nondrug Alternatives* • *Pain Clinics, Biofeedback, TENS, Behavior Mod, Acupuncture, Hypnosis* • *The Future of Pain Relief.*

"Take two aspirin and call me in the morning" used to be a standing joke. But I'm not laughing any more, for two reasons. First, pain is no laughing matter. Whether it's a "minor" problem like a headache or hemorrhoids, or something as serious as arthritis or a heart attack, pain takes over your consciousness and makes it hard to think about anything else. Chronic pain can come to dominate your life.

Another reason I'm not laughing is that too many doctors have a hard time helping their patients in pain. A study of 526 patients who had just had major surgery and were suffering acute pain came to some shocking conclusions.

> **A substantial number of patients who suffered pain during the postoperative period received less than the maximal dose of narcotic analgesic ordered by their physicians. During the first 24 hours, the average dose was 30% less than the maximum prescribed. This suggests that the patients, the nurses, or both are responsible for undertreatment.**[1]

Not only the patients (who didn't always ask for pain medication when they needed it) and the nurses (who gave less pain reliever than the doctor ordered when they had a choice), but the doctors, too, are to blame. ''Physicians also prescribed drugs in doses that were often inadequate and at inflexible fixed time intervals that may not have been appropriate for all patients.''[2]

What in the world is going on here? Why are patients being expected to ''bite the bullet'' and bear up, with inadequate pain relief? And make no mistake, the patient who moans with pain or complains that the medication isn't doing the job is likely to be seen as a problem—a moaner, a whiner, a crybaby.

The words alone express the widespread disdain health professionals have for anyone who doesn't follow the old Yankee example of suffering in stoical silence. And then there is the common belief that suffering is good for the soul. *BULL!* Suffering may indeed offer spiritual benefits for some people—that's not my field of expertise—but it's also likely to be physically debilitating and emotionally demoralizing.

In most cases pain is a symptom of some underlying disorder, and the best medical approach is to treat the cause. Once you get at that, the pain usually goes away. Relying on potent painkillers without a good diagnosis is both foolish and dangerous. Aesop's mouse didn't scurry off to fetch an aspirin; instead, it pulled the thorn out of the lion's paw.

But when the condition can't be cured readily, surely a patient deserves some relief, at least. And often even while the disease is being treated, people need help to cope with the pain. But the answers to the critical questions—what kind of help? how much? how often? for how long?—may well vary from one individual to another, since no two people suffer alike.

The Private Experience of Pain

Pain is very personal. We've all experienced some type of pain at one time or another, from the fleeting sting of a scraped knee to the day-in, day-out pain of arthritis. And because it *is* so intensely personal, so rooted in each individual's private experience, it is very, very difficult for anyone else to understand. I am the only one who knows what my pain is like; trying to tell *you* about it is an exercise in approximation and, often, in futility.

My particular weakness is a bad back. When it goes out on me, walking is torture, but getting out of a bed or a chair is inhuman punishment. Even sitting on the john becomes almost unbearable, and something as simple as getting dressed and putting on my shoes becomes a major undertaking. No one wants to hear what agony I'm going through, and even if my wife lends a sympathetic ear, there's no way that I can communicate how totally the pain interferes with everything I do. No matter how much I want to put it out of my mind and concentrate on other things, the back is always there, nagging, persistent—painful.

Not only does each of us experience pain differently, people also have very different ways of dealing with pain. Few ideas, save maybe politics and religion, are so firmly entrenched for most people as their "philosophy" about pain. Perhaps pain, like politics and religion, should be banned as a topic fit for discussion in polite company.

For the "tough it out" school, admitting something hurts is tantamount to failure. Cut to the bone, such a person insists, "It's nothing. Let's keep playing." At the other extreme are those who believe that crying out or talking about it makes the pain easier to bear, and they use this tactic until their listeners become bored and annoyed. As a result of these contradictory approaches and the emotional importance we give them, it is hard to study pain objectively.

Even more to the point, these attitudes often get in the way of effective treatment for pain. One attending physician tells about two young doctors, fresh out of medical school,

> each treating a patient with the same kind of fracture. One physician gave his patient no pain medication, whereas the other prescribed large doses of narcotics. Afterward, they were asked to explain the reasoning behind their choices.

> The one who gave no medication said, "Well, I knew the pain would last only 24 hours, so I didn't see any need for medication." . . . The other young physician said, "Well, I knew the pain would last only 24 hours, so why not use the short-term pain killer so the patient doesn't feel any pain?"[3]

Measuring Pain: Easy as Capturing Moonbeams

If I tell you that I have a cup of water in a container, you know pretty exactly how much water that is. You can visualize the amount, you know it's eight ounces, you know just about how big a puddle it will make if I spill it. But we can't even come close to that kind of accuracy when we're talking about pain, and that's where the trouble begins.

Pain can't be quantified. We have no yardsticks to compare yours and mine, and that fact can frustrate medical researchers used to nailing everything down with a measurement. "The experience of pain," notes one research team, "cannot be measured directly: precise studies are therefore not possible."[4]

Think you'd know pain if you saw it? Most people, doctors and nurses included, think they would. As it turns out, a lot of the time you can't rely on appearances. In one experiment volunteers were injected with a solution known to cause pain, and their reactions were videotaped. Almost half turned out to be true stoics who did not moan, groan, whine, nor wince to show they were in pain, though all stated when asked that the injection had been painful.[5]

"Restlessness, moaning, or grimacing can be misleading," state two pain researchers. "The patient who appears to be resting comfortably may be struggling not to show pain or trying not to aggravate the pain by moving."[6]

For years researchers have been hoping to find a way to measure pain reliably. They've tried about everything you can think of, and a few things I'll bet would never occur to you, to come up with some neat and nifty scale that would allow them to say, "Patient Y was suffering a grade 9.3 pain in the left rumpus-grumpus muscle." And all in vain. Take a temperature, yes, take a pain measurement, no. It can't be done.

If doctors can't tell by looking at a person how much he or she hurts, then, how can they know how bad the pain is and how much medication is needed? Simple: just ask the person who's hurting! That may sound revolutionary, even heretical, but it's not really a very original idea. More than a century ago a British doctor said, "Not only degrees of pain, but its existence, in any degree, must be taken upon the testimony of the patients."[7]

The *only* way to find out for sure if someone hurts is to ask; the only way to find out reliably how much the person hurts is to ask and to believe the answer. And the only way to find out if enough pain-relieving medication has been given is to ask if the person still hurts. This method is elegant in its simplicity, utterly reliable, and too often overlooked by doctors and nurses who think they know better.

In the eyes of such practitioners, all appendix incisions or heart attacks, or whatever, are created equal. You'll get 10 mg. of morphine every four hours, because that's what everyone gets for what you've got. This is a sad relic of the "doctor knows best" philosophy, and it's something no patient should have to put up with. Nobody knows a patient's pain experience except the patient, and the patient deserves a lot more respect for that experience than many medical people seem willing to offer.

You have a right to full pain relief. If it isn't offered, ask for it. Then demand it! Get your family to demand it. If you've been hospitalized under the care of a specialist and you have an understanding personal physician, ask her to go to bat for you. Or copy the articles by Kampon Sriwatanakul and his colleagues, D. S. Shimm and his coworkers, and J. B. Reuler's group, all listed in the reference section for this chapter, and wave them under the doctors' noses. Kick up a fuss. Call in the cavalry if you have to. But don't suffer in silence unless that is what you really want to do.

And if you *don't* want to suffer, for goodness sake don't wait until the pain is intense before you tell the nurse. Nurses are busy people and may have a lot of other patients they need to care for first. As one nurse who has looked into the problem put it, "Patients who wait until they are really hurting to ask for relief are assured another wait. Thirty minutes was the norm, I found—an eternity to those in pain."[8]

Now that doesn't mean demanding whopping doses as to produce oblivion. These drugs have many side effects, including constipation, nausea, lethargy, respiratory problems, and difficult concentration. After surgery, it's usually a good idea to be up and moving as soon as possible, to prevent blood clots from forming or fluid from collecting in the lungs. You don't want to be so blotto that you can't move, just as you shouldn't be in such pain that you're unwilling to move. Obviously, the answer here is a careful balance, and you'll have to be the one guiding the doctors and nurses about how much pain relief is appropriate for you.

Fear of Addiction

Besides their trouble with assessing a patient's pain objectively and scientifically, medical people have one other big problem that keeps them from providing adequate relief. We might as well face this bogeyman right now and get it out of the way. When killing pain means administering narcotic drugs, everyone is afraid of addiction. The idea that people may become addicted to pain medication terrifies both doctors and patients, suggesting as it does an image of some poor unsuspecting individual who comes into the hospital as a respectable pillar of the community and goes out the door a hopeless junkie.

Considering how pervasive this fear of addiction to narcotic medications is, you might think that doctors and nurses see it happen every day, or at least a dozen times a week. But the truth, according to an experienced burn-ward nurse, is quite different.

> Addiction very rarely happens. I've been in burn care for nearly 10 years and have never had a patient leave the hospital addicted to morphine and we give it by the truckload. Actually, fewer than 0.1 percent of patients who are given narcotics while in acute pain become addicted and once the source of the pain is no longer present, there's no trouble weaning them off narcotics.[9]

The figure she cites of 1 in 1,000 is not merely hyperbole, by the way, or even a good guess. It comes from an actual clinical study of the problem.[10] If only the medical establishment got as excited about other severe drug reactions among hospitalized patients as it does about addiction, a lot of pain and suffering could be avoided. But though side effects are far more common and medically more serious, the fear of addiction dominates when it comes time to prescribe heavy-duty pain relievers. It's actually a very emotional reaction from professionals who pride themselves on being rational and objective. "Fear of dependence or addiction is incredibly overblown," claims University of Utah pharmacy professor Arthur Lipman. "People in pain aren't junkies looking for a fix."[11]

The idea that a few shots of morphine are the first steps on the road to hell seems to be slowly diminishing, but according to pain expert Dr. Ned Cassem, "narcotics may still intimidate their prescribers."[12] The result is often needless anguish, as one of our newspaper column readers relates.

> **My mother is dying from breast cancer which has spread through her body, especially into her bones. It makes me furious that the nurses insist on sticking to a rigid schedule for her pain medication.**
>
> **Why should my mother have to suffer, gritting her teeth with tears in her eyes for up to an hour, while she waits anxiously for them to bring her next shot? This dignified lady has been reduced to begging for relief, but it just seems to fall on deaf ears.**

In the grand scheme of things addiction is the last of this woman's worries. Yet because of that fear, her doctors failed to prescribe effective pain relief, just as many doctors don't provide adequate relief for the millions who suffer with acute pain, which may be intense, but is expected to last "just" a short time.

Acute pain results from such things as surgery, limited illness, and injury. Throwing everything we've got at such pain is reasonable and justified, and there's little to be feared from drug dependency in the case of acute pain, since the medications shouldn't be needed long enough for that problem to develop. Using pain medication properly—in big enough doses and often enough to keep the patient comfortable all the time—actually results in the need for *less* narcotic medicine in the end, as well as making the patient more comfortable.[13,14]

For the terminally ill patient, like our reader's mother, dependence is simply not an issue, as the Health and Public Policy Committee of the American College of Physicians underscores in its official position on the treatment of pain.

> **Although fear of patients becoming dependent on narcotics has limited the effective use of morphine and other narcotic drugs, such fear is unfounded, because dependence is of little consequence in the context of terminal illness.[15]**

This committee endorses the goal of controlling the pain experienced by dying patients as much as possible through flexible, individually adjusted dosages and schedules of such narcotics as morphine, methadone, **Demerol** (meperidine), and **Dilaudid** (hydromorphone). What the American College of Physicians is saying in careful medical language is that there is simply no excuse for withholding any available pain relief from the patient with chronic pain caused by terminal illness.

Unfortunately the common chronic pain resulting from a lot of different conditions is much harder to deal with. Sometimes it accompanies an on-going, intractable condition, like lower back problems. Sometimes it can't be linked to any obvious physical problem, leading to a nasty situation where the patient insists that he or she hurts, and the doctor insists that there is no reason for the pain, implying (and sometimes saying) that the pain is the patient's fault. "Chronic pain means when the patient comes in the front door, I want to go out the back," one doctor candidly admits.[16] Chronic-pain patients rarely get better, and as a result many doctors dread treating them.

Prescribing drugs to ease chronic pain can become complicated, for in this case fears of drug dependency are much better founded. One study conducted at the Mayo Clinic showed that 65 percent of the noncancer chronic-pain patients developed a drug dependency problem. "Physicians are becoming more aware that for non-cancer patients, narcotic use does not lend itself to anything but futility," according to Dr. Rick Schwettmann, director of the Anesthesia Block Clinic at the University of Wisconsin.[17]

Fortunately, however, narcotics are not the only avenue to relief from chronic pain. The way patients think and feel about their conditions can offer valuable clues to coping with the problem, as Meg Bogin demonstrates in her valuable book, *The Path to Pain Control* (Houghton Mifflin, 1982). A number of techniques can help some people, as can a variety of other drugs that are not narcotics. We'll take a look at many of them in the rest of the chapter, starting with one far more useful than you might think: a good, healthy dose of nothing.

How to Treat Something with Nothing: Placebo Power

Can a pill that contains nothing do something? When it comes to pain, the answer is crystal clear: *yes*. The nothing pill really does do something, and it has led to the discovery of how the body marshals its own resources to deal with the problem of pain. Doctors call a medication or treatment containing no known therapeutic agent a *placebo*. They've been handing them out almost as long as they've been seeing patients. As Thomas Jefferson wrote, "One of the most successful physicians I have ever known has assured me that he used more of bread pills, drops of colored water, and powders of hickory ashes, than of all other medicines put together."[18]

No wonder; such things work remarkably well. In a frequently cited review of studies involving more than 1,000 patients with a variety of painful conditions, H. K. Beecher found that an average of 35 percent of the people experienced relief from pain when they were given a placebo—a pill that presumably did nothing![19]

That study, conducted in 1955 and published in the *Journal of the American Medical Association,* got a lot of attention and set off a good deal of research into the "placebo effect." The power of placebos turned out to be a lot more complicated than the common notion that "it's all in a patient's head," though the latest research suggests that the old saw may be literally true.

One of the things Beecher noted in his study was the wide range of conditions in which the placebo effect showed up and the consistency with which it appeared to relieve 35 percent of the people of their discomfort. It didn't seem to matter whether the pain came from angina, wounds, headache, or the common cold. Give patients a pill or injection, and around one-third of them will feel better.

When Beecher finished, no one could really doubt the existence of the placebo effect. The problem was that nobody could predict who would or wouldn't respond. Research showed that some people reacted to the way the doctor behaved; the color, shape, or taste of medication; the number of diplomas on the doctor's wall; or the ritual involved in making the diagnosis.[20] Yet suggestible patients, as measured by other types of tests, aren't always placebo responders.[21]

For those who do respond, the effect can be incredibly powerful. Syrup of ipecac is widely used to induce vomiting in people who have swallowed poisons, and it does its job with monotonous regularity. In an experiment to test the placebo effect, Stewart Wolf gave syrup of ipecac to a 28-year-old woman who had been suffering from pregnancy-related nausea for two days straight. The woman was "told it was medicine which would abolish her nausea. Within 20 minutes the nausea had subsided completely and did not recur until the following morning."[22] He later repeated the experiment on another woman, with the same results. This is like making the river run backward! Here's a drug known to make people throw up, yet when you tell people it will stop them from throwing up, they stop. Have you ever heard of a better example of mind over matter?

But that's not all. Placebos are so powerful that they can do more than cure—they can cause side effects! We're talking about powerful medicine here, that's for sure. In his study of other studies, Beecher found that placebos had caused dry mouth in 9 percent of the subjects; nausea in 10 percent; headache in 25 percent; and drowsiness in an amazing 50 percent. Keep in mind that these effects were experienced by people who mistakenly thought they were taking a real drug and were reported to doctors who didn't know that what they'd given the patients was a placebo. But despite all this scientific evidence that placebos *do* work, it has taken until very recently for researchers to work out just *how* they work.

How the Brain Fights Pain

Scientists have known for a long time that in doing its complex job, the brain churns out a wide variety of chemicals. But when researchers announced in the mid-1970s that the brain makes its own narcotics, the news landed like a gift-wrapped package of dynamite. "The discovery of endogenous endorphin led to a research explosion whose consequences are altering our understanding of pain, mental health, and drug addiction," wrote one observer.[23]

Answers led to questions, which produced more answers. Almost faster than you could say "pain," scientists found not only that the brain was in the narcotics business, but that brain cells also possessed "opiate receptors", which were uniquely responsive to these natural narcotics, called *endorphins* (from *endo*genous m*orphine*.) The naturally produced substances were found to be hundreds of times more powerful in their pain-relieving effects than morphine derived from the opium poppy, long considered the heaviest gun in the pain-reliever arsenal.

Just as the Rosetta Stone allowed for the deciphering of ancient, previously mysterious writings, the discovery of endorphins caused a lot of pieces of the pain puzzle to suddenly fall into place. For example, it provided a promising hypothesis for the placebo effect. Many people are apparently able to produce endorphins in response to their belief that what's being given them will do some good, or by those diplomas on the wall, or by the impressiveness of the machinery being used to administer the treatment. These natural painkillers quickly find their way to the opiate sites, bind there, and reduce the pain.

The endorphin discovery also provided a plausible explanation for Western medical practitioners struggling to understand how (or even *if*) Chinese acupuncture could effectively relieve pain or produce anesthesia sufficient to allow surgery. Since sticking needles in people seemed more likely to cause pain than prevent it, most physicians were extremely skeptical about the use of acupuncture. It suddenly became reasonable to suggest that acupuncture did work, by stimulating the release of endorphins. Needle meets nerve, East meets West, and the patient feels no pain. Even some doctors felt a bit of relief, since this explanation permitted a "scientific" explanation of what had seemed to many of them medical hocus-pocus. The Chinese merely smiled politely.

Other tantalizing connections between endorphins and pain are still being discovered. Researchers suspect that abnormalities in one or more of the endorphins play a role in such diseases as schizophrenia, since schizophrenics and others with mental illness have abnormal pain responses.[24] Recent studies also show that a significant relationship exists between the level of endorphins in the spinal fluid and depression in pain patients; in addition, patients with high endorphin levels had higher pain thresholds and pain tolerance than did those with a low level of the natural painkiller.[25]

Endorphins and the related enkephalin compounds certainly offer hope for new approaches to the treatment of pain. The initial step in that direction was taken in late 1983, when the Food and Drug Administration approved the first clinical trial of a synthetic derivative, met-enkephalin.

The day is still far off when most of us will be able to produce our own painkilling compounds at will, but several physicians at UCLA believe that we can already learn how to do this. Drawing on their experience in teaching pain self-management without drugs, these doctors remarked, "It is clear that many patients have a dramatic ability to learn to turn on their inner pain-control circuits."[26] However, until more doctors become familiar with these nonpharmacologic techniques, the first line of defense against pain will continue to be medication.

Treating Pain with Pills

If I were somehow advised in advance that I'd be shipwrecked on an island far from civilization and allowed to bring only two painkilling drugs along, my choice would be easy. Codeine gets the nod for severe pain. And number two? For most pain, I'd opt for a bottle of aspirin.

Yes, good old unadulterated, unadorned, plain-Jane aspirin. Though it's been around for over 80 years, "the pain reliever doctors recommend most" is actually little short of a wonder drug. I'd put it in my black bag with full confidence that it can provide relief for a lot of different kinds of pain. And as you've already read, the possibility exists that a little aspirin a day may keep a stroke or heart attack at bay. There is even some preliminary evidence to indicate that aspirin slows or halts the progression of cataracts.

Each year Americans swallow over 20 billion pills containing that old tongue-twister, acetylsalicylic acid, also known as aspirin; that's equal to around 100 tablets for every man, woman, and child in the country. And for good reason. "Aspirin, given in doses of 650 mg [two tablets] every four to six hours, remains the most effective mild analgesic and the standard of comparison for all other drugs'' writes one research group that examined pain relief.[27] Study after study has found that aspirin does what it's supposed to do as well as or better than a lot of other pills claiming to be stronger medicine, such as **Darvon** (propoxyphene), **Clinoril** (sulindac), **Tolectin** (tolmetin), **Motrin** (ibuprofen), or **Naprosyn** (naproxen). But with a pain-reliever market that amounts to more than $1 billion every year, drug companies aren't likely to stop trying to top "the standard."

In such a competitive market, each advertiser does its best to make its brand stand out from all the others. One product is touted as faster-acting, another as gentler to the stomach, and yet a third is ballyhooed as the most potent pain reliever you can buy without a prescription. But the primary ingredient in most of these products is aspirin, and nearly all the aspirin on pharmacy shelves, regardless of the label on the bottle, originally came from one of two manufacturers, Dow or Monsanto. (Sterling, maker of **Bayer**, and Norwich-Eaton are the exceptions by creating their own.) It should come as no surprise to learn that when researchers at Consumers Union examined nine widely purchased brands of plain aspirin, they found no significant differences among them.

Nationally advertised brands, such as Bayer and Squibb, as well as the cheaper house brands sold by K Mart, A & P, Safeway, and Kroger, all contained almost exactly the same amount of aspirin in each tablet, and all met strict government standards. All the tablets dissolved at virtually the same speed; the rate of dissolution is important because it determines how quickly aspirin can be absorbed into the bloodstream to begin providing relief. The net results of these studies were that all aspirin is pretty much the same.

Of course some products have special formulas containing more than aspirin. The maker of **Anacin**, for example, has for years touted "a special combination of medical ingredients" (nothing more exotic than aspirin and caffeine) and "more pain reliever" (additional aspirin).

A wise consumer is suspicious of claims for buffered aspirin, too. Aspirin can, undeniably, irritate the stomach and cause gastric bleeding, which can be a problem for arthritis victims and other chronic pain sufferers who have to take massive amounts of aspirin all the time. Some manufacturers of over-the-counter pain relievers brag that their buffered aspirin products, containing antacids, cause less irritation than regular aspirin, but the evidence is weak. Buffered as well as unbuffered aspirin can produce severe damage to the stomach lining when taken in quantity.

This points to the value of comparative shopping. Aspirin is aspirin, and even jazzing it up with extra ingredients does not seem to make much difference in the pain relief you will get; it therefore makes sense to look for the least expensive brand of USP aspirin you can find. The "USP"—for United States Pharmacopeia—means that the tablets meet quality standards no matter what their cost. Careful shopping can save you as much as 1,000 percent.

For some people, though, saving money is not the only name of the game. One reader wrote us an indignant letter.

> I am mad at my pharmacist and don't feel I can trust him any more. He recently talked me out of buying Bayer aspirin, because he said I could buy the house brand for less and it would work just as well.

> That really was a bum steer. True, it was a lot cheaper, but what good is saving money on pills that don't work? My headache definitely did not go away with the generic aspirin. How could he ever have thought an ordinary aspirin would be as good as Bayer?

Who's right here? They *both* are! There is absolutely no chemical difference at all between Bayer and generic aspirin. But remember the power of the placebo effect? Two British researchers have discovered that

> patients' expectations that medication will help them increases the likelihood of response. . . . Such expectations and beliefs are influenced by non-active aspects of the medication, such as color, taste, dosage, and size of tablets.[28]

In this study people were given aspirin, a placebo, and a placebo made to look like a popular brand-name aspirin. The scientists found that headache pain was substantially reduced even in 40 percent of the people given the unimpressive-looking inactive placebo. The placebo which resembled a brand-name product was significantly more effective. But the clear winner was the true brand-name aspirin. The authors of the study report that the aspirin itself accounted for about two-thirds of the pain relief experienced. As much as one-third of the benefit could be attributed to appearance of a familiar name on the tablet and people's belief that it would work better.

If you have a favorite nonprescription pain reliever, then, use it. As long as you believe in it, you may notice how much better it works. And if it's that much better, it's probably worth the premium you'll have to pay for a widely advertised brand. If you don't have a favorite, you're in luck, because for you the cheapest no-name aspirin should work just as well as the fancy brand-name pills. In any case, there's certainly no sense taking anything you don't believe in. Remember, this kind of placebo effect is definitely *not* imaginary and shouldn't be denigrated. Anything that can boost the potency of analgesic medication is a real boon to people in pain.

Aspirin-containing products aren't the only nonprescription pain pills reaping the benefits of big-budget advertising campaigns, of course. **Tylenol, Anacin-3, Datril,** and **Panadol** all rely on acetaminophen instead of aspirin as their active ingredient, and their manufacturers have made the most of this difference.

In its television advertising, the maker of **Tylenol** tried hard to convince the public that aspirin is much less safe than acetaminophen. Using the slogan, "**Trust Tylenol. Hospitals do**," the ads imply that hospitals do not trust aspirin—which must have come as quite a surprise to the hospital pharmacists dispensing it by the ton every year. In a direct pitch to doctors, McNeil Laboratories (the folks who bring you **Tylenol**) stressed the dangers of aspirin. "**Tylenol** acetaminophen at recommended doses is unlikely to produce the adverse reactions associated with aspirin, which makes it the logical non-prescription analgesic to recommend to your patients."

Are **Tylenol, Datril, Panadol,** and the rest really better than aspirin? That, as you may guess, is a hotly debated issue. Acetaminophen is about as good as aspirin at relieving pain and bringing fever down. It doesn't produce the stomach irritation and even ulcers which aspirin can cause in sensitive people, and it's somewhat less likely to bring on a dangerous allergic reaction.

However, aspirin boosters claim that acetaminophen has problems of its own. Large acetaminophen overdoses can result in serious liver damage and can possibly be fatal. There has been considerable controversy about the toxic potential of therapeutic doses.[29,30] An editorial in the *Journal of the American Medical Association* reported that "serious liver disease has developed in some patients with the long-term use of relatively small amounts of the drug, 2.9 to 6.5 G [grams] daily" (6 to 13 extra-strength **Tylenol** tablets).[31] Evidence is gradually building to prove that chronic use of large doses of acetaminophen in combination with alcohol or other drugs metabolized in the liver may spell trouble.

The manufacturers of **Tylenol** disagree strongly, of course, characterizing the known cases of acetaminophen toxicity as "medical curiosities." They maintain that even mild side effects associated with the recommended use of acetaminophen are extremely rare; they believe that liver damage resulting from the use of alcohol and their medicine occurs only when both substances are abused.

There seems little question, though, that alcohol and acetaminophen really don't mix well. One researcher studying acetaminophen toxicity advocates a prudent precaution warning people not to take acetaminophen if they have been using alcohol, barbiturates, antianxiety agents—like **Valium, Librium,** and **Dalmane**—or such epilepsy drugs as **Dilantin** (phenytoin), all of which are metabolized through similar routes in the liver.[32] The alcohol interaction is paradoxical, since it leaves the heavy drinker with nothing to help his or her hangover. Aspirin and alcohol are an equally bad combination since alcohol dramatically increases the stomach irritation caused by aspirin.

Regardless of the eventual outcome of this controversy, it is clear that for pain and fever any difference between the two drugs is minimal and that moderate use poses little danger. But do not use these drugs simultaneously. I know one woman who thought that by taking aspirin together with **Tylenol** she could increase her pain relief. Big mistake! There is a growing fear that products which combine more than one analgesic—aspirin, acetaminophen or salicylamide, for example—may increase the risk of kidney damage.

A number of countries have banned multi-ingredient painkillers and it boggles my mind that at the time of this writing the FDA still hasn't taken any action. Products which have combined more than one analgesic include **Vanquish**, **Extra-Strength Excedrin** and "headache powders" such as **Goody's**, **BC**, and **Stanback**. You would be best to pick one kind of pain reliever and then stick with it.

Arthritis sufferers will probably benefit more from aspirin, while people with sensitive stomachs or allergies to aspirin should stick to acetaminophen. Enteric-coated aspirin tablets—such as **Encaprin** (my favorite), **Ecotrin, Easprin,** and **Asa Enseals**—designed to dissolve in the small intestine rather than in the stomach, are another option for people who have difficulty handling regular aspirin.

When Aspirin Won't Work

Aspirin may be a wonderful drug, but there are times when it's not enough on its own. At that point it's best to have a talk with your doctor. **Motrin** and **Rufen** (ibuprofen) are now available without a prescription under the names **Nuprin** and **Advil,** but all the other possibilities require a prescription.

The next step may be **Dolobid** (diflunisal), a new nonnarcotic analgesic. In some ways this drug could be described as a better mouse trap—or actually, a better aspirin. It is a chemical cousin to aspirin, but instead of lasting only 4 hours, one pill provides relief almost three times longer—up to 12 hours. It's also stronger. In two well-controlled studies **Dolobid** was shown to be as good or better than **Tylenol** with codeine (**Tylenol No. 3**) or **Darvocet-N 100** for relieving postoperative dental pain.[33,34] Another advantage is that you don't have to keep increasing the dose to maintain relief. Because it's not a narcotic, the addiction problem doesn't arise, either.

Like aspirin, **Dolobid** can be irritating to the digestive tract; 3 to 9 percent of those taking the drug may experience nausea, indigestion, pain, or diarrhea, but such side effects may be less common than with aspirin.[35–37] **Dolobid** shouldn't be used by anyone who is allergic to aspirin and develops a rash, runny nose, or asthma or by anyone who has kidney problems.

A handful of other drugs may also be prescribed for pain. Besides **Motrin** and **Rufen,** there are **Naprosyn** and **Anaprox** (naproxen), **Clinoril** (sulindac), **Feldene** (piroxicam), **Tolectin** (tolmetin), and **Nalfon** (fenoprofen). All are essentially similar. They were developed as antiarthritis medications, but they may also be used to combat other types of pain.

None stands out above the others in analgesic power; all are roughly as good as aspirin. Their advantage lies in the lower likelihood of side effects, but even here a fair proportion of people will experience digestive complaints, including nausea, diarrhea, indigestion, and abdominal pain. All have been known to cause peptic ulcers, though this is a relatively uncommon complication. Allergic reactions, showing up first as rashes or itchy skin, can also be a major problem for an unlucky few.

Of greater concern is the growing awareness that many of these drugs (**Clinoril** may be the exception) seem to put a small minority of people at risk of developing kidney damage. Anyone who notices fluid buildup (edema), back pain, increased urination, or a change in color of the urine must contact a doctor immediately, since such symptoms could be warnings of kidney damage.

The next step up the ladder of pain relief is a mild narcotic, codeine. This is rarely prescribed by itself, although it can be. It is, however, the powerhouse behind the punch of such popular products as **Tylenol No. 3**, **Empirin No. 3**, **Phenaphen No. 3**, and **Fiorinal No. 3**. (By the way, the No. 3 stands for 30 mg. of codeine; analgesics designated No. 1 contain 7.5 mg. of codeine; No. 2 equals 15 mg. of codeine; and No. 4 is equivalent to 60 mg. of codeine.) The popularity of such products probably results from the fact that the combination of codeine and aspirin or acetaminophen reduces pain more effectively than any one alone could.

The possibility of becoming physically addicted to codeine is very low, but if you use it every day, you may discover that you become tolerant to it after a while. This means that to do the job on your pain, you'll need to keep increasing the dose—plainly not a good idea if you'll be taking it a long time.

Some people—especially those who have had problems with alcohol or other drugs—may develop a psychological dependence on codeine-containing analgesics which can be hard to shake. Like other narcotics, codeine can cause constipation, and some people find that it causes nausea or vomiting, especially after the first few doses. Lying down for a while may get you past this problem, but if it continues, you'll need to check with your doctor.[38]

Propoxyphene, another mild narcotic, comes in two forms, **Darvon** and **Darvocet-N**. Because these drugs require a prescription, many people think of them as strong medicine. However, the authoritative *AMA Drug Evaluations* remarks that the usual dose of propoxyphene ''is no more effective, and usually less so, than 650 mg of aspirin or acetaminophen.''[39] That's to say, if two tablets of aspirin don't make you comfortable, don't expect **Darvon** to work wonders. **Darvocet-N 100** may be slightly better because it contains acetaminophen in addition to propoxyphene, but there's little reason to choose it above any of the other medications I've discussed.

For pain so severe that it will not respond to any of these drugs, your doctor will probably turn to the heavy-duty narcotics. These include **Percodan** (oxycodone and aspirin), **Tylox** (oxycodone and acetaminophen), **Talwin** (pentazocine), **Demerol** (meperidine), **Dilaudid** (hydromorphone), **Dolophine** (methadone), **Levo-Dromoran** (levorphanol), and morphine. All are relatively similar in terms of the pain relief they can offer, the side effects you may risk, and the kinds of things you should avoid while you are using them.

Because most of these drugs can cause nausea, they should not be taken on an empty stomach. They may also produce drowsiness, dizziness, disorientation, weakness, vomiting, sweating, constipation, and shortness of breath. Children and older people may be especially sensitive to the breathing difficulties these medicines can produce.[40] You should not take any of them if you have to drive or work with machinery unless you have enough experience with the drug to be certain that it won't make you sleepy, absurdly euphoric, or mentally fuzzy. You may avoid some dizziness and light-headedness if you make it a point to stand up slowly when you have been sitting or lying down.

Such symptoms as extreme nervousness, severe dizziness, or drowsiness, cold clammy skin, pinpoint pupils, seizures, unconsciousness, very low blood pressure, very slow heartbeat, and slow breathing are a signal of overdose. Call your doctor, ambulance service, or poison-control center immediately!

You won't want to mix these medications with anything that could make the side effects worse. What this basically means is a ban on alcohol, sleeping pills, muscle relaxants, antihistamines in cough and cold remedies, anticonvulsants, and some types of antidepressants. While I'm on the topic of interactions, you should know that quite a few doctors prescribe **Phenergan** (promethazine) along with a narcotic. It is an antihistamine that often causes extreme drowsiness. Perhaps this practice started because sedated patients don't cause disturbances, but if anyone tries to give you **Phenergan** along with **Demerol**, **Percodan**, **Talwin**, **Dilaudid**, or other narcotic pain medicine, turn it down. I would also avoid combination pain products containing promethazine such as **Compal**, **Maxigesic**, **Mepergan**, or **Stopayne**. If you take analgesics with promethazine, you'd be likely to hurt more, not less, and feel very sleepy or out of it.[42,43]

Regular use of narcotics produces *tolerance*—which means that ever-greater amounts are needed to obtain the same degree of relief. Ultimately your body adjusts to these drugs, and you become dependent. Stop abruptly, and withdrawal symptoms set in—that's addiction.

For years there was no way around this problem but to go through the "cold turkey" experience. Now, however, people who are having trouble getting off one of these painkillers can ask their doctors for **Catapres** (clonidine). Nobody seems to know exactly why, but this blood-pressure drug can give you a parachute to help kick a narcotic habit gently, without serious withdrawal symptoms like anxiety, sweating, sneezing, tearing, yawning, nausea, vomiting, or diarrhea.[44] Although **Catapres** hasn't been approved for this use by the FDA, it is a tremendous improvement over the old way.

Banishing Pain: The Nondrug Alternatives

Because pain *is* such a personal experience, no one prescription, no one drug will provide the answer for every patient. As we saw earlier, one of these drugs in adequate doses is a reasonable approach for short-term pain. But the person in chronic pain simply cannot rely completely on drugs to manage his pain.

Because so much distress is tied up in the meanings pain carries for an individual and the emotions it triggers, learning to use these feelings in coping can be extremely helpful. *The Path to Pain Control* by Meg Bogin (Houghton Mifflin, 1982, $12.95) is excellent, giving the chronic pain sufferer a variety of down-to-earth practical advice on dealing with constant pain, including an excellent "pain emergency kit" that doesn't depend on a doctor's prescription.

When chronic pain gets out of hand, the best place to get help may be at a pain clinic. Though ten years ago there were only a handful of these specialized groups, today more than 800 are scattered around the country. Theoretically the pain clinic looks at the entire picture to try to help the patient find a technique or combination of techniques that will provide relief.

The clinic may succeed where the individual physician has failed because its staff is often quicker to recognize the connection between psychological and physical factors and because they are often willing to spend the time necessary to devise a highly personalized plan of attack. A national directory of pain clinics, Pain Clinic Directory, is available for $15 from the American Society of Anesthesiology, 515 Busse Highway, Park Ridge, IL 60068. At the time of this writing the publication is woefully out of date (1979) and therefore incomplete, but as far as I can tell it is the only reference available.

Some of the techniques a pain clinic might offer include:

Biofeedback. Patients gain control over specific body responses by letting them see the response as it occurs. This is typically accomplished by flashing a light or ringing a buzzer as the patient increases or decreases blood flow to an area or relaxes a particular muscle.

Biofeedback often consists of teaching a person to undo unhealthy behavior that has somehow become part of an unseen, unconscious behavioral pattern. By bringing this automatic behavior to the forefront for a while, a person can learn to act differently, until eventually the new healthier behavior becomes the normal pattern.

The technique has proved of some value in pain control, but it is far from a panacea, and there are substantial questions as to how permanent any gains achieved through biofeedback are. Nonetheless, it's a safe technique that involves no risk and little expenditure. It would therefore be difficult to argue against giving it a try when drugs have failed to do the job, or in tandem with medication to reduce pain to tolerable levels.

Electrical Stimulation—TENS (transcutaneous electrical nerve stimulation) is considered a very new, very modern means of pain relief, but the ancient Egyptians and Greeks who used electric eels to combat pain may have been the first experimenters in putting electricity to work against pain.

The use of TENS involves the electrical stimulation of certain specific nerve fibers believed to be important in the transmission of pain messages from outlying areas to the brain. There's still disagreement about the exact mechanism by which TENS does its job—endorphins, once again, may be involved—but there's no question that the technique can successfully relieve some peoples' pain even when other treatments have failed. One woman I met who experienced unbearable pain across her upper back and across her chest as a consequence of shingles swore that she was only able to return to the world of the living and resume work because of TENS.

A TENS rig consists of an electrical source leading to electrodes which are typically placed right over the painful area or over a nearby nerve source. Since many of the units are battery-powered and portable, a patient can literally get pain relief to go, much like fast-food hamburgers. The electrical current is either high or low frequency, and there is some indication that high frequency usually works better for acute pain, while low frequency more often does the job for chronic pain.[45]

This electrical magic has had some rather dramatic successes in relieving pain that had resisted almost every other attempt at alleviation. TENS appears to work best for postoperative pain, phantom limb pain sometimes suffered by amputees, low back pain, degenerative arthritis of the spine, shingles, and neuralgias of the extremities. It has been less successful with arthritis and cancer pain, but as is often the case in pain relief, the results are highly variable and inconsistent. Some people aren't helped by TENS at all, but sometimes a change in positioning the electrodes or timing the application or amount of stimulation, will help. Simply having the means of pain relief under your own control and being able to experiment with it at your leisure to find the combination that works best for you can make a big difference!

Some people develop a skin reaction to the paste or gel used under the electrodes, but this seems to be the only side effect that is at all common. It should be possible to sidestep this problem without too much trouble, though; one manufacturer suggests that petroleum jelly or hand cream can be used on the electrodes without compromising the efficiency of the unit.[46]

TENS can be used by itself or in combination with pain-relieving medications. Problems of interaction between TENS and drugs don't arise, there is absolutely no impairment of mental function as there often is with strong painkillers, and it's a relatively inexpensive method, particularly for those who require long-term treatment.

At this time probably 90 percent of the TENS units in use are supplied (often rented out) by hospitals and doctors, but people with chronic pain can purchase their own units. In sum, according to one doctor who tested TENS in 375 chronic pain patients, "It is a safe, practical, noninvasive [nonsurgical] means of treating chronic pain patients which should be part of every physician's office armamentarium."[47]

A variety of TENS devices are now on sale under a doctor's prescription. Most, including the Mentor 402 (Mentor Corp. Minneapolis, MN 55411) and the Tenzcare model 6240 (3M Medical Products, 3M Center, St. Paul, MN 55144) cost $400 to $600 and are designed principally for the doctor's office. One, the Wright Care #1012-1000 (Dow Corning Wright, Arlington, TN 38002), is intended as a disposable unit for postoperative pain, and is available in a single-channel model for about $70 or a dual-channel one for approximately $90.

The Therapette NS-105 has been reasonably priced at $96 explicitly for home use by the chronic pain sufferer. For those who wish to experiment, this might be a good model to start with. You can order it directly from the manufacturer (Technical Resources, Inc.; P.O. Box 1613; Waltham, MA 02154), but like all TENS units, it requires a doctor's prescription. If your physician is willing to go along, all he need do is to provide one and you can send it on to the company.

Behavior Modification. The roots of the pain problem can be far removed from the physical hurt. For some people pain becomes a means of getting sympathy, attention, or something else they need or want. Pain can be a symptom of something wrong with a person's social relations as well as with his or her body. One report suggests that many people with severe facial pain (known as TMJ for "tempero-mandibular joint") are members of families in which they are subjected to many stresses and can find no acceptable ways of coping.[48] Family, friends, and coworkers of other people in pain may often unwittingly prolong the pain by their actions.

Behavior modification involves trying to get both the patient and those around him or her to alter the pain-rewarding behavior and replace it with positive feedback for nonpain behavior.

Acupuncture. That acupuncture can work some of the time for some of the people is clear. But whether it works better than anything else is still a topic of debate.

Lots of people get the willies just thinking about having someone stick lots of little needles into them; the idea of causing pain to relieve pain isn't their cup of tea. Yet it appears that acupuncture can be highly effective in some types of pain relief. As I mentioned earlier, there's a strong but unconfirmed suspicion that acupuncture does its work by stimulating production of endorphins, which are by far the strongest painkillers around.

A first cousin to acupuncture is acupressure, which involves pressing on certain points rather than stimulating them by inserting needles. For the squeamish it has some appeal, but evidence on its behalf is still largely anecdoctal.

Hypnosis. Here's a technique that earned a rather bad reputation in its infancy, largely because it became a parlor game and TV gimmick. Slowly but surely, though, hypnosis has established itself as an important and viable tool in skilled hands.

To a greater degree than many of the other techniques hypnosis depends on the individual, who must be hypnotically suggestible. There are wide variations in people's responses to hypnosis, ranging from those who can't be hypnotized at all to those who readily achieve a deep trance. The latter are ideal candidates for pain relief through hypnosis. "These patients," notes Dr. Paul Sacerdote of New York's Montefiore Hospital and Medical Center, "who are capable of reaching the deepest states represent, in my experience, no less than 15 to 20 percent of the general population." He goes on to explain his method. "As soon as I see evidence that hypnosis is developing, I explain to the patient that his brain is activating circuits which will almost automatically permit reinduction of the hypnotic state from then on. This is an important step in preparing him to assume control over his pain."[49] Once again a technique offers the advantage that it lacks risk and side effects and allows the person who hurts to have control over pain relief.

Surgery. This is *the* last-ditch proposition. It should almost never be done until virtually everything else—and I do mean *everything* else—has been tried and found wanting.

Surgical techniques for pain relief usually involve an attempt to cut the nerve or nerves going to or from the painful area or, in extreme cases, to attempt to cut off pain transmission in the spinal cord. The trouble is that, though this seems like a simple and obvious solution, it carries substantial risks and often does not work as well as expected.[50]

In cases of truly intractable pain surgery is sometimes effective. It may even be the only practical means of pain control in some instances. But even for those very few whose pain cannot be controlled by any of the current drugs or other techniques, hope is on the horizon in the form of exciting new discoveries that may truly change the face of pain treatment.

The Future of Pain Relief

For people in pain the discovery of endorphins and enkephalins must unquestionably be the most exciting scientific breakthrough of the past decade. Research on these compounds is generating tremendous excitement because it could eventually lead to the development of potent pain relievers with little or no addiction or abuse potential. Equally important, there would be no need to increase the dose in order to maintain effective relief.

In late 1983 the FDA approved the first clinical trial of such a drug, and you can look forward in the not-too-distant future to being able to obtain a pill that will augment your natural bodily supply of endorphins to alleviate the short-term pain of a headache, toothache, or surgical procedure.

Another promising new compound is under development by Upjohn. Currently known as U-50,488, it may be the first step in relieving severe, chronic pain with little if any risk of addiction. U-50,488 (which we can eventually expect to see marketed with a somewhat jazzier name) is a unique new drug that differs from most existing painkillers.

Preliminary tests in monkeys show that in addition to being nonaddictive, the drug isn't subject to the tolerance problem that plagues users of narcotic pain relievers. Nor does it slow down the respiratory system as do the narcotic drugs. With any luck this may just be the first in a series of important new breakthroughs for the treatment of chronic pain. Of course a number of other pharmaceutical firms—including Burroughs Wellcome and Hoffmann-La Roche—are also hot on the trail of new, more powerful, nonaddicting analgesic compounds.

It is also possible that someday diet may play a role in pain relief. Researchers are finding that the foods we eat may have an effect on the brain's production of at least some neurotransmitters—the substances responsible for moving messages along from nerve to nerve. At least two of these neurotransmitters have been identified as playing a role in determining pain threshold and the behavioral response to pain.[51] It's still quite a long step from this discovery to actually developing a migraine-preventive diet, for example, but it could someday turn out to be an additional alternative to drugs and offer the advantage of no side effects.

Another interesting link in that chain of brain chemistry leading to pain may be depression. We're now finding that depression and pain are often linked, though there's still disagreement as to whether pain causes depression or whether depression changes the perception of pain.[52] In any event, treating the depression can sometimes help ease the pain, as one researcher points out.

> **[I]mprovement in patients' perception of their pain usually occurs early in the course of tricyclic [antidepressant] therapy and at relatively low doses which would not be thought to be therapeutic for depression. There is the possibility that clinical analgesia and the antidepressant activity of tricyclics are pharmacologically related properties.[53]**

Another positive development on the pain-relief front is an increasing tendency toward giving control over pain to the patient. Most of the nondrug therapies—including TENS, hypnosis, and biofeedback—are designed to make this possible once the technique has been learned. Not only can each individual adjust the level and pattern of pain relief to respond to the unique pain experience; but it also seems that being able to control pain relief independently releases patients from the fear of pain, which can intensify the anguish.

A tool that may make this procedure possible is an infusion pump—a small unit that dispenses a strong pain reliever directly into a vein at the push of a button. Thanks to a sophisticated microprocessor, the unit can be programmed to release a certain amount of the drug at each push of the button, and to be inactive for any given period of time. This device gives the patient control over the time when the drug is given yet places a limit on how much can be self-administered within a given time period.

Such pumps have recently received FDA approval, and there are encouraging signs that they will be welcomed at many medical centers. Although some doctors and nurses fear either the loss of control over their patients or, once again, the bogeyman of addiction, study after study shows that, left to their own devices, people will in fact take the minimum amount of medication required to really relieve their pain.[54] The chance—already small—that the patient in acute pain would become addicted to narcotic medications seems, if anything, to diminish rather than increase with the use of the patient-controlled infusion pump.

Eventually these units, which are not now portable and are therefore restricted to use in hospitals, will without a doubt become miniaturized and mobile, providing another important alternative to thousands of pain sufferers.

We can certainly look forward to the day when potent but nonaddicting pain medicines are within the grasp of everyone who needs them. You don't have to grit your teeth and bear it quietly until then, though. For acute pain, demand relief! Be sure to let the nurses and doctors know if the pain relief they're giving you doesn't relieve *your* pain.

If your problem is long-term, work with your health-care providers until you learn some approaches that are successful for you. The nondrug techniques shouldn't be overlooked. They can be very helpful alone, in combination, or together with drugs. Everyone is different, though, so don't let anyone tell you what you should or shouldn't feel. You are the only judge of your own pain, and you're the only one who can really learn how to cope with it.

References

1. Sriwatanakul, Kampon, et al. "Analysis of Narcotic Analgesic Usage in the Treatment of Postoperative Pain." *JAMA* 250:926–929, 1983.

2. Ibid.

3. Trubo, Richard, and Bankhead, Charles D. "Pain: Assembling the Pieces of a Complex Puzzle." *Medical World News* 24(15):40–59, 1983.

4. Wilson, Peter R., and Yaksh, Tony L. "Pharmacology of Pain and Analgesia." *Anesthesia and Intensive Care* 8:248–256, 1980.

5. Lim, K. S., and Guzman, F. "Manifestations of Pain in Analgesic Evaluation in Animals and Man." Is *Proc. Int. Symp. on Pain,* A. Soulairac et. al. (eds). New York, Academic Press, 1968, pp.119–152.

6. Heidrich, George, and Perry, Samuel. "Helping the Patient in Pain." *Am. J. Nursing* 8:1828–1833, 1982.

7. Latham, P. M. "Lectures on Subjects Connected with Clinical Medicine." 2nd ed. Philadelphia, Barrington and Haskell, 1847, pp. 108–117.

8. Vache, Ellen. "Inadequate Treatment of Pain in Hospitalized Patients." *N. Engl. J. Med.* 307:55, 1982.

9. Kibbee, Ellen. "On Pain Relief." *Emergency Med.* 15(5):141–164, 1983.

10. Miller, R. R., and Jick. H. "Clinical Effects of Meperidine in Hospitalized Medical Patients." *J. Clin. Pharm.* 18:180, 1978.

11. Phillips, Carolyn. "Patient-Controlled Device for Painkillers Meets Some Resistance on Hospital Staffs." *The Wall Street Journal,* February 8, 1984, p. 27.

12. Cassem, Ned H. "Pain." In *Scientific American Medicine*, vol. 1, Current Topics in Med., 1983, pp. 1–14.

13. Shimm, D. S., et al. "Medical Management of Chronic Cancer Pain." *JAMA* 241:2408–2412, 1979.

14. Reuler, J. B., et al. "The Chronic Pain Syndrome: Misconceptions and Management." *Ann. Intern. Med.* 93:588–596, 1980.

15. "Drug Therapy for Severe, Chronic Pain in Terminal Illness." *Ann. Int. Med.* 99:870–873, 1983.

16. Trubo and Bankhead. Op. cit.

17. Ibid.

18. Ford, P. L., ed. *The Writings of Thomas Jefferson.* New York, Putnam, 1898, vol 9. pp. 78–85.

19. Beecher, Henry K. "The Powerful Placebo." *JAMA* 159:1602–1606, 1955.

20. Berg, Alfred O. "The Placebo Effect Reconsidered." *J. Fam. Prac.* 17:647–650, 1983.

21. Fields, Howard L. "Pain II: New Approaches to Management." *Ann. Neur.* 9(2):101–106, 1981.

22. Wolf, Stewart. "Effects of Suggestion and Conditioning on the Action of Chemical Agents in Human Subjects—The Pharmacology of Placebos." *J. Clin. Invest.* 29:100–109, 1950.

23. Bishop, Beverly. "Pain: Its Physiology and Rationale for Management." *Phys. Ther.* 60(1):21–23, 1980.

24. Greenberg, Joel. "Psyching Out Pain." *Science News,* 115:332–333, 1979.

25. Almay, B., et. al. "Endorphins in Chronic Pain. I. Differences in CSF Endorphin Levels Between Organic and Psychogenic Pain Syndromes." *Pain* 5:153–162, 1978.

26. Gagne, James, et. al. "Inadequate Treatment of Pain in Hospitalized Patients." *N. Engl. J. Med.* 307:55, 1982.

27. Luce, John M. et al. "New Concepts of Chronic Pain and Their Implications." *Hosp. Prac.* April 1979, pp. 113–123.

28. Braithwaite, A., and Cooper, P. "Analgesic Effects of Branding in Treatment of Headaches." *Br. Med. J.* 282:1576–1578, 1981.

29. Editorial. "Aspirin or Paracetamol?" *Lancet* 2:287–289, 1981.

30. Murton, K. J. "Aspirin or Paracetamol?" *Lancet* 2:1163–1164, 1981.

31. Craig, Robert M. "How Safe is Acetaminophen?" *JAMA* 244:272, 1980.

32. Personal communication, Gerald M. Rosen, 1983.

33. Forbes, James A., et al. "Difluinsal: A New Oral Analgesic with an Unusually Long Duration of Action." *JAMA* 248:2139–2142, 1982.

34. Forbes, James A., et al. "A 12-Hour Evaluation of the Analgesic Efficacy of Diflunisal, Propoxyphene, a Propoxyphene-Acetaminophen Combination, and Placebo in Postoperative Oral Surgery Pain." *Pharmacotherapy* 2:43–49, 1982.

35. Forbes, et al. Op. cit., *JAMA.*

36. Hannah, J., et al. "Discovery of Diflunisal." *Br. J. Clin. Pharmacol.* 4(suppl 1):7–13, 1977.

37. DeSchepper, P. J., et al. "Gastrointestinal Blood Loss After Diflunisal and After Aspirin: Effect of Ethanol." *Clin. Pharmacol. Ther.* 23:669–676, 1978.

38. USPDI. *Advice for the Patient* 1984, vol. II. "Narcotic Analgesics," p. 591.

39. *AMA Drug Evaluations* 1980, p. 69.

40. USPDI. *Drug Information for the Health Care Provider.* 1984, vol. I. "Opioid (Narcotic) Analgesics," pp. 779–780.

41. Ibid, p. 781.

42. Sriwatanakul. Op. cit, pp. 928–929.

43. Personal communication, David McWaters.

44. Beckert, Charles E. "Pain Relieving Medication Update." Speech, April 11, 1983.

45. Warfield, Carol A., and Stein, Jonathan M. "Pain Relief by Electrical Stimulation." *Hosp. Prac.* 18:207–218, 1983.

46. Personal communication, Joseph Saba, (President Technical Resources, Inc.)

47. Dougherty, Ronald J. "TENS: An Alternative to Drugs in the Treatment of Chronic Pain." Paper presented at the 30th Annual Scientific Assembly, American Academy of Physicians, 1978.

48. Laskin, Daniel M. Reported in *Gallagher Medical Report* 11(4), February 15, 1984.

49. "Pain—Diagnosis and Management." *Guidelines to the Neurosciences* 5(1), 1981.

50. Wepsic, James G. "Neurosurgical Treatment of Chronic Pain." *Int. Anes. Clinics* 21(4):153–163, 1983.

51. Seltzer, Samuel; Marcus, Richard; and Stoch, Russell. "Perspectives in the Control of Chronic Pain by Nutritional Manipulation." *Pain* 11:141–148, 1981.

52. Murphy, Michael F., and Davis, Kenneth L. "Biological Perspectives in Chronic Pain, Depression, and Organic Mental Disorders." *Psych. Clinics N. Am.* 4:223–237, 1981.

53. Edwards, W. Thomas. "Systemic Medications of Use in Pain Treatment." *Int. Anes. Clinics* 21(4):11–25, 1983.

54. Phillips, Carolyn. "Patient-Controlled Device for Painkillers Meets Some Resistance on Hospital Staffs." *The Wall Street Journal*, February 8, 1984, p. 35.

CHAPTER 9

Behind the Scenes with OTCs

Nonprescription Drugs Make Snake Oil Look Good ▪ *The FDAs 21 Year Review* ▪ *Without Prescription But Not Without Power* ▪ *OTC Dangers for Children* ▪ *Pregnant Women Beware* ▪ *Questions About PPA Still Alive* ▪ *The Big Switch: From Prescription to OTC* ▪ *Informed Self-Care: The Wave of the Future.*

Once upon a time virtually all medicines were sold over the counter—or, more literally, over the backboard of the patent-medicine peddler's wagon. There were no regulations; almost any medication could be sold in general stores, at fairs, or even through the mail. Snake-oil vendors put on a great show, and nobody cared much whether they were selling colored water or tincture of opium.

Such old-time favorites as **Professor Lowe's Magnetic Worm Syrup**, **Eskay's Neuro Phosphates**, **Red Raven Water**, and **Pil Damiana et Nux Vomica Cum Phosphori** were widely sold to cure worms or combat pain, hangovers, headaches, mental overwork, general debilitation, and a host of other problems. **Pil Damiana** in particular was touted as a "powerful, permanent and determined aphrodisiac"![1] Today these nostrums are remembered mainly by the archivists of the drug firms they gave rise to—SmithKline and Eli Lilly, in these particular cases. A few patent medicines of the nineteenth century have survived essentially unchanged. Some, such as **Father John's Medicine** or **Mother's Friend Lotion,** are still sold to a small but loyal clientele. Others, like **Listerine,** remain familiar household names.

There's a bewildering array of pharmaceutical products sold over the counter in this country, and until very recently most consumers had no way of knowing whether the pill they picked off the shelf was powerful medicine or just gussied-up snake oil. You see, all these years the drug companies have been selling hundreds of ingredients in hundreds of thousands of preparations, all making claims to shrink your hemorrhoids, knock out your headache, soothe your upset stomach, put the whammy on your athlete's foot, or whatever almost instantly. But from the time of patent medicines on, plenty of over-the-counter drugs have contained ingredients that don't work, and some that have been downright dangerous. If you think this practice amounts to fraud, I won't argue, but nobody's likely to go to jail for it.

These circumstances came to light as a result of what at first seemed innocuous, unobjectionable changes in the law governing the sale of drugs. Believe me, when Congress revised the Food, Drug and Cosmetics Act in 1962, about the last thing on earth the drug companies dreamed was that it would result in public evaluation of what they peddled over the counter and in having much of it declared worthless. But that's exactly what happened, although the process took more than twenty years and has a few years to go before grinding to completion.

In the Beginning . . .

Back before 1962, the FDC Act divided drugs into two categories: prescription and nonprescription, also called OTC (over-the-counter). Anyone could create and market an OTC drug as long as its ingredients were considered safe. In other words, it was legal to market ground-up bats' wings and salamander glands in alcohol as long as somebody would buy it and the stuff normally didn't kill anyone.

If you're laughing, then the joke is on you. Lots of OTC remedies sold through the years were equally silly. Not long ago **Doan's Pills** contained uva ursi and buchu as principal ingredients. It has been reformulated and now relies on magnesium salicylate (an aspirin-like analgesic) to supply backache relief. But if you look for them you will still find some extraordinary products on pharmacy shelves.

In my part of the country **Father John's Medicine** for coughs due to colds is a big seller. You will find Father John's picture right there on the label looking trustworthy and benevolent with a high clerical collar. Unfortunately, the product doesn't contain any approved cough suppressants. It does have cod liver oil, emulsified pure gum, glycerine, sugar, licorice, and flavoring oils. **Father John's** is guaranteed to give your taste buds a run for the money, but hardly anything for your cough.

Another amazing OTC remedy still being sold is **Dr. Kilmer's Swamp Root**. Looking like something from a traveling medicine show it "promotes flow of urine" and is a "mild laxative." Some of the ingredients include rhubarb root, scullcap leaves, and Venice turpentine. Oh, and let's not forget **Swamp Root's** 21 proof alcohol content. You might have thought such a product would have disappeared with the patent-medicine peddler of frontier days. But clearly that has not yet happened. Still laughing?

Under great pressure dozens of states in the last few years passed "lemon laws," forcing car makers to sell cars that actually work as they're supposed to. In 1962 the revision of the FDC Act stated that all new drugs, or old drugs claiming new uses, had to be safe *and effective*. The act was sort of a drug-company lemon law, but the FDA is taking its time about enforcing it. That's why, at this very moment, you can run right over to the corner drugstore and plunk down your hard-earned bucks for a product that can't live up to its advertising claims.

It's hard to believe that adding the two little words "and effective" could cause an earthquake, but that's what happened. The Food and Drug Administration, after sitting around stunned for a while, suddenly realized that *it* was responsible for figuring out which of the hundreds of ingredients in several hundred thousand products actually did what they claimed to do. The officials leaped to the task with all the enthusiasm of a child sitting down to a plateful of liver (which is to say, not a whole lot).

Four years after the law was passed (I told you the agency was enthusiastic), the FDA asked the prestigious National Academy of Sciences to look at a sample of OTC remedies and figure out how effective the ingredients were. The news was startling; In 1969 the review committee reported that only about one-quarter of the ingredients had any effect at all, and not always in the way that was being claimed.

The FDA thought about that finding for a while—until 1972, in fact. (It really was *very* eager to learn which drugs were effective, wasn't it?) Then the agency opened Pandora's box by initiating the Over the Counter Drug Review. A decade after the 1962 law was passed, the FDA finally made a serious move to find out what all those things really were—or weren't—doing in OTC drugs. The agency appointed 17 panels of qualified experts to review 26 categories of drugs. The task, it was estimated, would take three to five years.

Eleven years later—and an incredible 21 years after the revised FDC Act was put on the books—the final panel wandered in with its report. In a performance that must certainly merit the chutzpah award of the year, the FDA actually congratulated itself on this "milestone in drug history." At 21 years per milestone, it's a good thing the FDA doesn't have responsibility for building roads in this country.

"The review," noted Health and Human Services Secretary Margaret Heckler, "has begun to transform the nonprescription drug market."[2] That it certainly had. But the HHS Secretary hadn't spelled out the reason for the transformation very clearly. The panels submitted 58 reports, concluding that only about one-third of the more than 700 ingredients in nonprescription medications could be considered effective. The remaining 70 percent were either ineffective or unsafe, and in many cases there were insufficient data to allow the reviewers to come to any meaningful conclusions.[3]

Long before the final report came in, it was evident that the drug companies were in very serious trouble. As panel after panel produced its findings, the news was consistent. Many of the ingredients in most of the products don't do anything very much. Two-thirds of the individual ingredients lack strong scientific proof to back up the claims made for them. Their use in combination is often irrational and certainly not supported by data in the medical literature. It's hard to escape the conclusion that a lot of the money spent in the multibillion-dollar OTC market has been wasted.

This disheartening news would be bad enough if the ineffective products were going to be yanked off the market in the near future. But the best estimate of FDA insiders is that full implementation of the review process may not be complete until 1990 at the earliest.

Though that's a depressing conclusion, some tangible progress has been made. Many unsafe ingredients have already disappeared from pharmacy shelves. Hexachlorophene—a germ killer once found in soaps, toothpaste, baby powders, and underarm deodorants—was banned because babies were absorbing toxic amounts of it through the skin. Methapyrilene—an antihistamine found in over 1,000 sleeping pills, daytime sedatives, cold and allergy remedies—was eliminated because it was shown to have serious cancer-causing potential.

Ingredients determined to be ineffective by the panels can also be expected to slowly fade away. But the problem is with that limbo category—ingredients the panels couldn't decide on. Anything in this category gets to stay on the market while the drug companies presumably do further testing to prove that the stuff works, and the FDA temporarily delays a final decision in deference to all this good data gathering.

The impression given is that this whole messy 21-year-old business might have caught some poor unwary manufacturer entirely by surprise, so please be understanding if they need just a bit more time to show the worthiness of their snake—uh, of their remedies. Of course a lot of data could have been gathered in the last 21 years, but the FDA seems untroubled by that slight lapse.

Needless to say, the entire OTC review process has been incredibly complex. And this mammoth task is not yet finished. Several more steps remain before all decisions will have been finalized and implemented. The panels were not infallible, of course, and several came up with contradictory recommendations.

The experts reviewing daytime sedatives, for example, found that the antihistamines, bromides, or scopolamine used in products like **Alva-tranquil, Seedate,** and **Nervine** didn't do much except make people a little sleepy, and they concluded that wasn't good enough. The menstrual-product panel, on the other hand, decided that it was just fine for manufacturers to include antihistamines with the claim that their products can relieve nervous tension, irritability, and anxiety. As a result, a product like **Pursettes** contains pyrilamine, though the other panel turned thumbs down on this ingredient for almost exactly the same use. Naturally, before any of these reviews gain the status of enforceable law, the FDA plans to have the final say, and the agency will be ironing out these inconsistencies and contradictions.

You may be thinking that a project of this magnitude can't be cheap, and you'd be right. The FDA estimates that the bill for the first ten years alone comes to about $12 million.[4] But what we taxpayers have gotten for our money may eventually turn out to be almost priceless. For the first time in history, anywhere in the world, someone has taken a careful, systematic look at all the nostrums being sold to make people feel better, and has determined on the basis of scientific evidence whether they work and whether they are relatively safe.

When the review is fully implemented, presumably all the ingredients that were not approved, along with any that were not reviewed, will no longer be marketed. You should be able to walk into any drugstore in the country, pick nearly any product off the shelf and have reasonable confidence that it will do what it says on the label and will be unlikely to cause you serious harm if you follow the instructions. Sure, in an isolated outpost or two you may be able to find **Dr. J. H. McLean's Volcanic Oil Treatment,** with the label that claims it's good for man or beast alike.[5] But by and large the days of the medicine show, old and new, will be gone forever. No more wild claims, no more wasted money— and it's about time!

It would be natural to assume that the makers of all these over-the-counter products fought the OTC review tooth and nail. No doubt some dragged their feet; surely most presented their favorite ingredients with decidedly partisan enthusiasm; but by and large the companies welcomed the review process as a chance to distance themselves and their products from the unsavory reputation the old "patent medicines" had earned.[6] One representative of the Warner-Lambert Company confessed that he'd rather have all the old claims about "infectious dandruff" and the like removed from the **Listerine** label and stick with the statement that has scientific validity.[7] Many other OTC manufacturers would echo the sentiment—they want to see their products taken seriously. And that, friends, is advice we'd all do well to heed.

Potent Medicine Without Prescription

The first thing to understand is that OTC remedies can be very powerful medicine. In addition to their ability to relieve symptoms and ease discomfort, OTC drugs share with their prescription brothers and sisters the potential to interact with food, alcohol, and other drugs and to cause side effects—sometimes very serious ones.

Whoa! How can that be? Aren't "dangerous" drugs always prescription drugs? No, absolutely not. Rarely has there been a fuzzier line than the one separating prescription from nonprescription drugs. In fact, the line is so fuzzy that drugs can sometimes jump right over from one side to the other.

The FDC Act declares that everything is OTC except for the exceptions.

One exception, not surprisingly, is drugs that are habit forming. Fair enough. Now comes the loophole big enough to fly a jumbo jet through— the category "Drugs that are toxic, have a potential for harmful effects, or whose method of use or collateral measures for use make them unsafe for self-medication."[8] Well, most drugs have some potential for harmful effects and almost all are toxic in large enough doses; virtually everything, then, could be made a prescription drug. But not everything is. In the end, it comes down to the situation where a prescription drug is whatever the FDA says is a prescription drug. The agency claims to know one when it sees it.

Perhaps. But a drug's being available over the counter is far from being an ironclad guarantee that it's a weak, wimpy, failsafe product that wouldn't harm a fly. As a matter of fact, there's evidence that many OTC drugs are powerful medicine, which can do plenty of harm under the wrong circumstances.

Major problems can arise when these drugs are given to children. Not only are children smaller, noisier, and more energetic that adults, but their bodies often handle drugs differently. Some of the most frequently used OTC medications can cause severe overdose reactions in children at strengths that might produce no more than mild discomfort in an adult.

Antihistamines found in cold and allergy products such as **Allcrest**, **Chlor-Trimeton**, **Contac**, **Comtrex**, **Dristan**, **Nyquil**, and **Triaminicin** can leave adults feeling drowsy and slightly disoriented; but many children are, instead, stimulated by these medications. They become irritable and nervous and may have trouble falling asleep. According to one concerned pediatrician, "Kids can become bitchy and twitchy on antihistamines. They cry more easily and may have more difficulty paying attention in school." Even worse, accidental overdose is much more serious for children than adults. Excitement, flushing, bad coordination, muscle twitching, and convulsions are symptoms of toxicity and require immediate emergency treatment.

Another OTC drug that has caused more than its share of trouble for children is aspirin, a drug we adults take by the ton. This pain reliever is so familiar that almost nobody thinks of it as posing any real danger. But for a child, aspirin can be poisonous more quickly and in far lower amounts than it would be for an adult.

Most people believe that overdose reactions occur only when children help themselves to extra tablets, but that's not always the case. A well-intentioned parent who is worried about a child's fever may give the medicine every three hours instead of every four. And too many people believe that if two are good, then three must be better. Children are more susceptible to aspirin poisoning when they've had a fever or when they have been taking aspirin for a while, and infants are very sensitive to high doses. Their lives are much more threatened by the side effects of aspirin overdose, which may in some ways mimic the disease being treated. Symptoms of aspirin poisoning include nausea, vomiting, diarrhea, dehydration, high fever, fatigue and changes in body chemistry.

Aspirin belongs to a chemical category called salicylates, and other drugs in this class are also toxic at high doses. But it's not always easy to recognize them. **Pepto-Bismol**, for instance, contains salicylates and should be given to children with caution. Perhaps the most hazardous salicylate is oil of wintergreen—methyl salicylate—which turns up in liniments and arthritis rubs like **Ben-Gay**, **Doan's Rub**, **Heet**, **Icy Hot**, and **Musterole Deep Strength**. Some solutions used in vaporizers also contain oil of wintergreen, which is so strong that any ingestion could be fatal.

Acetaminophen (**Tylenol**, **Liquiprin**, or **Tempra**), too, can be a real problem. Cases have been reported in which well-meaning but overzealous parents have given a child far too much liquid acetaminophen for a fever and then discovered with horror that the drug can cause severe liver damage, sometimes even death. Other OTC drugs that can cause side effects in children include laxatives, nasal sprays, and asthma products. Before you give a child *any* medication, make certain that the drug is safe for pediatric use, and then check and doublecheck the dose. And it makes sense to keep all drugs, including OTCs, out of the grasp of sticky little fingers.

Perhaps the kids who are *most* vulnerable to side effects from nonprescription drugs are the tiniest—the ones who haven't been born yet. It's quite likely that the end of the review process will see warnings on any OTC medicine absorbed into the body reminding pregnant women to check with a doctor, nurse, or pharmacist before taking the medication. Some products pose particular dangers, and unfortunately some of these are often used to combat symptoms pregnant women experience.

Constipation is common during pregnancy, but the stool softener docusate (dioctyl sodium sulfosuccinate) is suspected of possibly causing birth defects. Many popular products—including **Colace**, **Dialose**, **Kasof**, **Correctol**, **Comfolax**, and **Regutol**—which contain docusate, should not be taken by pregnant women. Instead, a diet high in liquids and fiber from bran, fresh fruits, and vegetables should provide the developing baby with much-needed nutrition and help the expectant mother stay regular without endangering her baby.

Sometimes questioning a drug and removing it from the market may give women a false sense of security, making them believe that available medications will not include the controversial ingredient. **Bendectin,** for example, which contained the antihistamine doxylamine, was widely used for morning sickness until it was pulled off the market in response to allegations that it could contribute to birth defects. However, most women aren't aware that **Nyquil, Vicks Formula 44, Consotuss,** and many other cold remedies use the same antihistamine. It's also contained in the sleeping pill **Unisom**—at double the dose **Bendectin** used to supply. Whether or not doxylamine actually causes birth defects, most pregnant women will want to take the precaution of avoiding it.

Besides watching out for children, adults had better watch out for themselves as well. They can get into big trouble, especially if they don't pay attention to the warnings and dosage instructions on the label. Most folks are too impatient to bother reading labels on drugs or on appliances.

Consider the case of PPA (phenylpropanolamine)—a decongestant and appetite suppressant found in such popular products as **Comtrex, Contac, 4-Way Cold Tablets, Dex-A-Diet, Dexatrim, Dietac Capsules** and **Tablets, Sucrets Cold Decongestant Formula, Allerest,** and **Anorexin.** The problem with PPA is that in high doses it can be responsible for driving blood pressure up to dangerous levels. Some experts believe that "clearly the use of phenylpropanolamine poses a danger to the public."[9] The medical literature contains a number of reports that PPA causes side effects ranging from severe headaches to strokes in susceptible people.[10] Needless to say, some of these people took more of the medication than they should have, figuring that they'd lose weight or get rid of their sniffles faster that way. And some may have taken the pill with beer, wine, or a drink which dissolved the time-release capsule and gave them an immediate dose much higher than the pill was supposed to deliver.

But not all the reactions can be blamed on the victim. One young nurse testified before the House Select Committee on Aging that when she decided to lose weight, she read the label on the nonprescription appetite suppressant carefully and noted that each time-release capsule contained 75 mg. of PPA.

> I also noted the warning on the package cautioning people with heart disease, hypertension, diabetes, and thyroid disease not to take the preparation. I considered myself a healthy person, having none of the above-mentioned afflictions, and therefore began to take the drug as directed—one capsule daily.
>
> On the fourth day of my diet regimen, I began to feel unusually and intensely fatigued. . . . I counted my radial pulse, the pulse one feels in the wrist. The total pulse rate counted for one full minute was 40. . . .
>
> I then realized that something terrible was happening to me. I went to the hospital and was admitted to the same coronary care-intensive care unit where I worked . . . the cardiac monitor showed my heart was beating only 36–40 times per minute. . . . My blood pressure was extremely elevated, being 200/120. I realized two distinct dangerous possibilities: First, the electrical conduction system in my heart could become

further arrhythmic and I could die. Secondly, I could have a stroke. I remember thoughts of denial and disbelief that this could happen to me.

I told my physician the only drug I was taking at the time was the *Dietac* preparation. He immediately suspected the PPA caused my blood pressure to elevate. . . .

I assumed that, because a drug is sold over the counter and not by prescription, the drug is safe. How many other people, particularly the elderly, also believe this assumption? The older individual, who statistically stands to have hidden heart disease, and hypertension [is] at great risk when taking any over the counter preparations containing PPA. If something like this can happen to a healthy, young individual, like myself, it can happen to anyone.[11]

This young woman was lucky. She did not, after all, suffer a stroke or have any lasting damage from her PPA-induced crisis. But her story points up an important moral none of us should ever forget: Never assume that a drug is harmless just because you don't have to get a doctor's permission to take it. The FDA is still looking very carefully at PPA, and who knows, it may someday decide that this drug should be available by prescription only.

The Big Switch: from Prescription to OTC

Although the FDA's big review isn't finished yet, it's already having a profound effect on the drugs you can find on your local pharmacy shelves. In the midst of the evaluation some companies saw the handwriting on the wall and acted to remove potentially hazardous ingredients before the FDA imposed a ban. For example, the makers of **Contac** voluntarily removed belladonna from the "tiny time pills" in 1980, long before they would have been legally required to do so. Others, like **Doan's Pills**, reformulated their products in line with the panels' recommendations.

The brands Grandma used in 1943 may still be around, but there are plenty of cases where nothing remains of the original product but the name. **Carter's Little Liver Pills** (now **Carter's Little Pills**), **Sominex**, and **Coricidin** nowadays bear little resemblance to the original products so popular years ago.

And while you're busy thinking that one over, take a look at some of the new brands on the shelf. The OTC drug you buy today may have been a prescription drug yesterday. Turns out that it's not impossible for a tiger to change its stripes—at least when the tiger is a prescription medication.

Knowing that there are no absolute rules for defining what gets sold at the local pharmacy or supermarket and what gets dispensed only with a fancy and expensive prescription from the doctor puts you in a better position to see why in the last few years more than two dozen drugs have suddenly switched from prescription to OTC. Not too long ago, "ethical" drug companies did their best to distance themselves as much as possible from the raucous, undignified arena of OTC remedies, preferring the prestige of prescription medicines.

Often what decides whether a drug will be introduced as prescription or OTC has as much to do with money as with science. In a game that has few rules, drug companies may consider the economics of the goods they market as carefully as they do the chemistry. Sometimes they see a big advantage in marketing a medication by the prescription route. While that procedure usually means a smaller market, it also justifies a much higher price, and it shifts some of the burden for the patient's welfare to the doctor.

But things change, and with the OTC review, quite a few drugs once available "by prescription only" have suddenly been deemed suitable for us ordinary folk to use on our own, much to the financial benefit of the producing companies. "Our success rate with **Afrin** (a nasal spray), **Chlor-Trimeton** (an antihistamine) and **Tinactin** (an antifungal for treating athlete's foot) shows that after a number of years our sales have more than tripled," says the marketing director for the drugs' manufacturer, Schering.[12] Sales of hydrocortisone-containing creams (**Cortaid, Cortef, Lanacort, Rhulicort**, and the like) soared into the stratosphere within a year of the switch on that ingredient.

Given a track record like that, it's no wonder some of the big drug firms are fighting like cats and dogs to get their prestigious prescription drugs switched to OTC status. Some companies have submitted new studies to back up their requests: **Actifed** (triprolidine and pseudoephedrine), **Benylin** (diphenhydramine), and **Drixoral** (pseudoephedrine and dexbrompheniramine), all became nonprescription on the basis of this kind of New Drug Application.

Are these hotsy-totsy products far superior to existing OTC brands? Not as far as I'm concerned. We already have a plethora of antihistamine-decongestants available. Just because Wally Schirra used **Actifed** on his space mission doesn't mean it's any better for your runny nose than any of the other hundreds of brands already on the market.

But many of the prescription-to-OTC switches have been extremely beneficial for consumers. The antihistamine chlorpheniramine had been available OTC for years in such products as **Contac, Coricidin,** and **Dristan**. But it was always combined with other medications, like decongestants, pain relievers, and drying agents. Paradoxically, if you wanted the simple antihistmine by itself to dry up your runny nose, you had to get your doctor to write you a prescription for **Chlor-trimeton.** Finally the FDA greased the skids and allowed Schering to market its successful antihistamine without a prescription. As the man from Schering pointed out, it rapidly became even more successful.

Then there's **Micatin** (miconazole). Once the domain of dermatologists, this powerful antifungal agent recently became available for the likes of you and me. Every dermatologist I've talked to says it's more effective at zapping athlete's foot, crotch rot, and other such grossouts than products like **Desenex** (undecylenic acid) and its predecessor in the Rx-to-OTC sweepstakes, **Tinactin** (tolnaftate).

The prescription-only drug **Benadryl** (diphenhydramine) was, and still is, one of the most frequently prescribed antiallergenics for hives and hay fever. But it often made people feel sleepy. It's now been approved for use in OTC sleeping pills, sold as **Sominex 2**, **Nytol with DPH**, **Compoz**, and **Sleep-Eze 3**. Some smart customers have been using the OTC form marketed as a sleeping pill for their stuffy noses and allergic skin rashes. This way they save a trip to the doctor's office for a prescription and the OTC costs less to boot.

Other drugs that have switched to nonprescription form include doxylamine succinate, a sleep aid in **Unisom;** the antihistamine brompheniramine maleate (**Dimetane**); and a new use for ephedrine sulfate, which has long been used in OTC asthma drugs and also relieves hemorrhoidal swelling (brand names **Pazo**, **Wyanoid**). Check hemorrhoidproduct labels for the ingredients epinephrine and phenylephrine as well. These ingredients are also effective switcheroos and are more likely to shrink hemorrhoids than products like **Preparation H**. Dyclonine, available as **Resolve,** an external pain-reliever for the mouth; pyrantel pamoate (**Antiminth**), a pinworm medicine; and fluoride (**Fluorigard**), a cavity preventer round out the list.

Most of these switches came as a result of suggestions from the official review panels, some of which were heavily stocked with industry representatives. Nonetheless, acting on available scientific evidence, the FDA did carefully review and approve these changes.

The agency grew a bit too exuberant, however, when it decided on its own to recommend placing the asthma drug metaproterenol (sold as **Alupent**) on OTC status. It seems that the FDA didn't consult very carefully with anyone, and when the switch was announced and became fact in one fell swoop, there were wounded egos all over the place. Quite a few doctors who treat asthmatics insisted that some patients would overuse this drug if it were available without prescription and that making metaproterenol available over the counter, was an invitation to disaster. Even the company that manufactured metaproterenol expressed some bewilderment at the sudden switch. Before long a besieged FDA backed off and placed the drug back up on the prescription shelf. "Our

error,'' said FDA commissioner Arthur Hull Hayes, ''was in being mis-
led into believing that no one cared.''[13] A hundred or so angry complaints from doctors later, Hayes had a strong suspicion that someone
did indeed care.

Even though the FDA apparently made a faux pas with metaproterenol
and was forced to pull in its horns, there is a Big Mo (momentum) to
keep moving new products to the customer's side of the pharmacist's
counters for some time to come. While some manufacturers only dream
of making blood-pressure medicine, penicillin, antifungal mouthwashes,
and powerful ulcer drugs like **Tagamet** available OTC,[15] two companies
are battling for the right to sell one of the most popular prescription
arthritis drugs over the counter.

Last year 19 million prescriptions were filled for ibuprofen under the
names **Motrin** and **Rufen**. Now Upjohn would like to have its cake and
eat it, too, in a way; it wants to keep **Motrin** a prescription drug and
sell a lower dose of ibuprofen, under the brand name **Nuprin,** over the
counter. The manufacturers of **Anacin** want to get into the act, too.
Whitehall labs is making ibuprofen available at your friendly local pharmacy (or supermarket) as **Advil**. Better yet, Whitehall is marketing it,
not merely as an antiarthritic medication, but as a general pain reliever.

This move has definitely been a real shocker for the OTC painkiller
market—not to mention for **Tylenol,** which has the lion's share of that
market. At issue is money, safety, and that hazy line between prescription and OTC remedies.

We're talking big dollars here. The market for prescription drugs in
the same class as **Motrin** is estimated to be $1.2 billion annually. You
can bet the other prescription manufacturers aren't happy about the prospect of watching their share of that number drift to **Nuprin** or **Advil** just
because these brands are easier to get. Nor do the makers of **Tylenol** and
other popular OTC pain relievers like seeing a carpet-bagging prescription drug walk off with a piece of their lucrative billion-dollar market.
But competition aside, many companies are made nervous by the idea
that ibuprofen is being marketed, sold, and used like aspirin. If serious
problems resulted from the switch, they could jeopardize people's sense
of safety about all OTC drugs, and no manufacturer wants to see that
happen.

Of course it would be foolish for anyone to imagine that when a
prescription drug changes its stripes to become OTC, it leaves its side
effects behind. But making highly effective medicines more widely
available is a very welcome trend. Most people have good common
sense, and when given clear instructions and supervision from their
pharmacists, they are willing and able to assume greater responsibility
for their own health care.

A tidal wave of interest in informed self-care is sweeping the country.
Simple-to-use diagnostic kits are being sold in pharmacies, while books,

articles, and magazines (my all-time favorite is *Medical SelfCare*—an annual subscription costs $12; P.O. Box 717 Inverness, CA. 94937) are flourishing. It's time for you to join the movement and take advantage of all the new information on staying healthy.

References

1. Kahn, E. J. Jr. "All in a Century: The First 100 Years of Eli Lilly and Company."

2. HHS News Release, October 7, 1983.

3. Ibid.

4. Zimmerman, David, R. *The Essential Guide to Nonprescription Drugs*. Harper & Row, NY, 1983.

5. Klein, Frederick, C. "Wholesale Drug Firm Thrives on Nostalgia, Buyers' Loyalty." *Wall Street Journal*, June 20, 1983.

6. Zimmerman, op. cit.

7. Personal communication, Ed Marlowe, 1984.

8. "What Makes it Prescription?" *FDA Consumer*, July/August, 1983.

9. Blum, A. "Phenylpropanolamine: An Over-the-Counter Amphetamine." *JAMA* 245:1346–1347, 1981.

10. Bernstein, Edward, and Diskant, Barry. "Phenylpropanolamine: A Potentially Hazardous Drug." *Ann. Emerg. Med.* 11:311–315, 1982.

11. Phipps, Janey P. Testimony Before Subcommittee on Health and Long-Term Care, House Select Committee on Aging, July 17, 1983.

12. "More Rx Drugs Moving to OTC Status." *Med. World News*, January 10, 1983.

13. "FDA Defends Metaproterenol Action But Concedes Errors in Judgment." *Med. World News*, July 11, 1983.

14. "FDA Sidesteps Review Process in Prescription-to-OTC Proposals." *Med. World News* 24(22), 1983.

15. Hecht, Anabel. "Drugs that are Rx No More." *FDA Consumer*, July/August, 1983.

CHAPTER 10

A Practical Guide to Drugs of the 1980s

A Revolution in Acne Treatment: **Accutane** *and Those Amazing Retinoids* ▪ *The Quiet Breakthroughs in Allergy and Asthma:* **Beconase, Vancenase, Nasalide, Beclovent, Vanceril, Proventil, Ventolin, Theo-Dur, Slo-Phyllin** ▪ *An Antibiotic Worth Knowing:* **Ceclor** ▪ *Another NSAID for Arthritis:* **Feldene** ▪ *Cutting Back on Cigarettes with* **Nicorette** ▪ *A New Cholesterol Lowering Drug:* **Lopid** ▪ *Fighting Fungi with* **Nizoral** ▪ *Going After Gallbladders with* **Chenix** ▪ *Help for the Heart (and maybe the ears) with* **Tonocard** ▪ *Motion-Sickness Magic:* **Transderm Scop** ▪ **Parlodel** *for Parkinsonism* ▪ *Sedatives and Sleeping Pills:* **Centrax, Halcion, Paxipam, Xanax** ▪ **Zyderm** *for Your Wrinkles.*

Over the last few years there have been some impressive advances on a number of fronts. The following discussion and accompanying tables will provide practical information on how to use some of the new drugs of the 1980s. Because it would be impossible to include every new medication without doubling the size of this book, I have tried to restrict the list to those compounds that have really made an important therapeutic contribution and those that are being prescribed in large numbers.

Unfortunately, the two categories are not always one and the same. Some physicians are easily seduced by manufacturers' reps into prescribing the latest "me-too" drug for anxiety or insomnia, even though it represents relatively little improvement over existing medications. But I figured that you'd better know about these agents, since there is a strong likelihood your doctor will prescribe one within several years.

It is not my intention to include every side effect, precaution, or drug interaction ever discovered. The following list is not meant to tell you everything in the world about these medicines. Rather, it is designed to assist you in using them as wisely as possible in conjunction with the information you have received from your doctor and pharmacist. It is *not* meant to replace either of these health-care providers. When in doubt about any drug, question them carefully until you get the answers you

349

seek. (Once again, potentially serious side effects are marked with an asterisk. Other side effects should not be ignored. They, too, should be brought to the doctor's attention without undue delay.)

A Revolution in Acne Treatment

Time was, not too long ago, if you went to the dermatologist with acne, he told you to give up drinking milk and stop eating chocolate and nuts. You were given a powerful germ-killing soap called **Phisohex,** you were told to wash vigorously several times a day, and then out came the prescription for tetracycline.

Today, about all that's left is the tetracycline, and even that has undergone some radical changes. A quiet revolution in acne therapy has been taking place over the last decade, and it virtually guarantees that no one need suffer with scarred skin ever again.

We now know that acne is not caused by either dirt or diet. You don't need to scrub your face with strong soap. In fact, once or twice a day with a mild soap—**Dove,** for example—is usually all that's necessary. (**Phisohex,** by the way, was banned from OTC use because of the fear that it causes brain damage in babies.) The next myth to die was diet. Turns out you can eat just about anything you want, and it won't make your skin break out.

Okay, now that you know what doesn't cause acne, what does bring it on? Pimples are caused by a buildup of oil secreted by glands around the base of tiny invisible hairs. Even when this fatty substance (sebum) and dead cells block the pores to the surface of the skin, the "oil factory" below keeps on working, leading to the formation of blemishes.

At some time in their lives almost 90 percent of all adolescents will have pimples. But acne can no longer be perceived simply as a teenage problem. In the last 10 to 20 years increasing numbers of adults, especially women, are having persistent acne into their twenties and thirties. Many adults are reporting problems with acne for the first time, having been spared the problem during adolescence. No one knows why we're seeing such an epidemic of skin problems at this time. Some experts theorize that cosmetics and birth-control pills may be responsible, but your guess is probably as good as theirs.

So what to do? Before I tell you all about the hot new stuff of the 1980s, start simple with OTCs. Benzoyl peroxide is widely available in such products as **Panoxyl** 5 and 10 percent, **Benoxyl**, **Clearasil BP**, **Loroxide**, **Oxy-5**, and many more. These OTC products are effective when spread thinly on the face. Since it actually takes three months for an individual acne pimple to evolve into an inflamed lesion, any acne preparation must be used at least that long before its full effect can be judged.

If the acne is tougher than the benzoyl peroxide, it's time to move up a step. In recent years dermatologists have been relying more and more on topical (ointments and creams) antibiotic preparations—**Cleocin T** (clindamycin phosphate); **Eryderm**, **Staticin**, and **Erymax** (erythromycin); **T-Stat** and **Topicycline** (tetracycline hydrochloride); and **Meclan** (meclocycline sulfosalicylate).

Topical antibiotics can be almost as effective as oral medicine for milder forms of acne. And because the ointments are less likely to be absorbed into the body, side effects like stomach upset, allergic rash, and yeast vaginitis are rarely a problem. One word of caution about **Cleocin T,** however. It is probably the most effective of the new-wave skin antibiotics, but a few sensitive souls may absorb enough through their skin to produce severe colitis. Anyone who develops stomach pain or diarrhea while using **Cleocin** should contact a doctor immediately!

The really big news in skin care these days, however, is Vitamin A. Popeye knew a good thing when he saw it; the spinach he downed in such awesome quantities is full of a substance that shows promise in preventing cancer, curing acne, and perhaps offering relief from psoriasis and some types of joint disease.

Spinach, carrots, Brussels sprouts, and lots of other eatables are rich in beta-carotene. When your body gets a hold of this stuff, it promptly turns it into Vitamin A. The A could well turn out to stand for "amazing" when scientists finish figuring out everything this vitamin and its chemical cousins the retinoids can do.

It has been known for years that this naturally occurring vitamin could have beneficial effects on acne. But it took such huge doses (100,000 to 500,000 units) over many weeks that it was far too toxic to use. Because this vitamin is fat-soluble, it is stored in the body and will produce serious side effects, including headaches, weakness, liver damage, dryness of the skin, and hair loss.

In the early 1970s dermatologists began using topical forms of Vitamin A (**Retin-A**) in an attempt to achieve the same beneficial effects. This preparation is effective, but it is also irritating and requires patience and careful supervision by a dermatologist.

But the really big news in acne treatment is a breakthrough drug called **Accutane** (isotretinoin), first approved by the FDA in 1982. A synthetic form of Vitamin A (13-*cis*-retinoic acid), it belongs to a class of compounds called retinoids. These Vitamin-A derivatives hold enormous promise for a variety of medical applications, including treating psoriasis, preventing cancer, and relieving inflammation.

Until now there was no cure for acne. About all you could hope for was to grow out of it or keep smearing or swallowing antibiotics. But dermatologists are enthusiastic about **Accutane;** not only does it provide dramatic benefit for almost everyone treated for cystic acne, but the improvement also persists long after the drug is stopped. Some patients are still free of acne three years after discontinuing the medication, and **Accutane** may very well provide a cure for many.

It is not entirely clear why the benefits of this drug last so long after treatment is stopped. Some researchers believe that oil glands in the skin permanently shrink in size, leading to a dramatic decrease in the production of sebum and shutting down the fuel that fires the acne lesion in the first place.

Unfortunately there's a price to pay for this kind of long-lasting improvement. Almost everyone who takes the drug experiences side effects similar to those that occur when Vitamin A is taken in large doses. More than 90 percent of patients develop severe drying and chapping of the lips. Over 30 percent experience dryness inside the mouth and nose and complain of dry, red eyes. Nosebleeds, muscle aches, pains, rash, loss of hair, headache, fatigue, and susceptibility to sunburn are other adverse reactions.

Because **Accutane** causes birth defects, any woman of childbearing age must use highly effective birth-control techniques if she wants to take this drug. And since it also raises triglyceride levels, patients should cut back on fatty food and undergo blood tests every two to four weeks while they are taking **Accutane**. In rare cases the drug has been reported to cause severe visual disturbances, and anyone who experiences headaches, nausea, vomiting, or changes in vision should stop the medicine immediately.

By now you are probably saying that no one in his right mind would ever take **Accutane.** You'd be wrong. It is certainly not to be used by anyone with garden-variety acne. But for severe, recalcitrant cystic acne— the kind that leads to deep pitting and scarring of the face, neck, and back if left untreated—physicians may prescribe **Accutane** for a patient who hasn't responded to other therapies. All the side effects seem to be reversible when the drug is discontinued—all, that is, except the damage to your pocketbook. Treatment over several months may range between $750 to $1,000 for the pills, lab tests, and office visits.

Whether there will ever be a place for **Accutane** in the treatment of less severe but very persistent forms of acne will take a long time to determine. Clearly the risks are great, but the benefits are also impressive. At this point the only thing we can say with certainty is that for patients with untreatable cystic acne, **Accutane** comes very close to being a miracle.

Accutane *(isotretinoin 10 mg, 20 mg, and 40 mg capsules)*

MFR: Roche Laboratories

FDA APPROVED USES: Treatment of severe cystic acne that is not responsive to other agents.

Accutane, *(continued)*

USUAL DOSE: Cystic acne: 1 mg to 2 mg per kg body weight per day, divided into two daily doses, for 15 to 20 weeks. Improvement may occur in one or two months and may continue even after the drug has been stopped.

PRECAUTIONS:
- **Accutane** is *very* expensive.
- **Accutane** should not be frivolously used for the common nonserious garden-variety of acne because of its significant side effects; it should be used *only* after other methods have failed.
- Since **Accutane** is related to **Vitamin A,** do not take vitamin supplements containing this vitamin while using **Accutane**.
- Take with meals.
- Acne may be temporarily exacerbated when first starting **Accutane**.
- **Accutane** may make you abnormally sensitive to sunlight. Avoid overexposure.
- Side effects are quite common with **Accutane**, but most disappear after treatment is stopped.

PREGNANCY AND BREAST-FEEDING:
- Do not, under any circumstances, use during pregnancy. **Accutane** can cause birth defects. If you are a woman of childbearing age, take precautions against pregnancy while using **Accutane** and for at least one month after stopping the drug.
- Although it is not known whether **Accutane** is found in breast milk, because of the potential for serious adverse reactions, do not breast-feed if you are using this drug.

COMMON SIDE EFFECTS:
- Dry itching skin, dry mouth and nose with occasional nose bleeds (about 80%).
- * Dry, cracked, inflamed lips (about 90%).
- * Irritated eyes and conjunctivitis (about 50%).
- * Mild to moderate muscle pain (about 16%).
- Loss or thinning of hair (less than 10%).
- Photosensitivity (about 5%).
- Lethargy and fatigue (less than 10%).
- Headache (about 5%).
- Fragile skin; peeling of skin from hands, face, feet (up to 31%).
- * Skin infections (about 5%).
- * Skin rash (less than 10%).
- * Nausea, vomiting, stomach pain (up to 20%).
- Loss of appetite (about 4%).

(continues next page)

* These side effects may be serious. Contact your physician immediately if they occur.

Accutane, *(continued)*

UNCOMMON SIDE EFFECTS:
* ** Headache, blurred vision, or other visual disturbance.
* ** Severe stomach pain, diarrhea, or rectal bleeding.

SEXUAL SIDE EFFECTS:
* ▪ None yet reported.

DRUG INTERACTIONS:
* ▪ Avoid or minimize alcohol consumption while being treated with **Accutane**. Both increase triglyceride levels in the blood, which may increase the risk of cardiovascular disease.
* ▪ Do not take **Vitamin A** while using **Accutane** (see Precautions, above).

Allergy and Asthma: More Treatable Than Ever

Most drug breakthroughs are announced with a great deal of fanfare certainly most severe acne victims learned about **Accutane** within weeks of its introduction. Such has not been the case for asthma and allergy patients; a quiet revolution has been taking place in the treatment of both these ailments, but it has gone largely unnoticed.

Until recently many of the six million asthmatics in this country were caught in a terrible bind. They either suffered periodic attacks of wheezing or they depended on powerful medications that had the potential to produce serious side effects.

One old standby that goes back at least 2,000 years to ancient China is ephedrine (found in such products as **Bronkotabs**, **Quibron**, **Mudrane**, **Quadrinal**, and **Tedral**). It can open constricted airways but it can also cause nervousness, insomnia, dizziness, irregular heart beats, nausea, tremor, difficult urination, and increased blood pressure.

Aerosol inhalers containing adrenaline known as epinephrine (**Asthmanefrin, Bronitin Mist, Bronkaid Mist, Primatene Mist, Vaponefrin**) and isoproterenol (**Isuprel, Mucomyst, Duo-Medihaler, Medihaler-Iso, Norisodrine**) are not nearly as old as ephedrine, but they, too, can cause increased heart rate, palpitations, tremors, anxiety, restlessness, and insomnia.

When things got really rough, out came the cortisone. It did the job, but at a substantial price. Side effects of drugs like **Prednisone** include lowered resistance to infection, stomach ulceration, fluid retention, potassium depletion, risk of cataracts, and muscle weakness—and those are just a few of the adverse reactions seen with cortisone.

* These side effects may be serious. Contact your physician immediately if they occur.

But today use of such powerful drugs is fading fast. So many new options are available that it should be rare for an asthma patient to suffer breathlessness. Bronchodilators—such as metaproterenol sulfate (**Alupent** and **Metaprel**), terbutaline (**Brethine**, **Bricanyl**), and a newcomer called albuterol (**Ventolin** and **Proventil**)—are less likely to affect the heart than previous medications.

These drugs work well for an acute attack. But even more exciting advances have been made in preventing asthma and allergy attacks in the first place. Long-acting theophylline preparations (**Theo-Dur, Slo-Phyllin**) have made such therapy much more practical. Cromolyn sodium (**Intal** and **Nasalcrom**), which prevents histamine from being released from cells, is very effective in forestalling nasal congestion (**Nasalcrom**) and asthmatic attacks (**Intal**).

And then there are the steroid aerosols containing beclomethasone dipropionate (**Beclovent, Vanceril, Beconase, Vancenase**) and flunisolide (**Aero Bid** and **Nasalide**). They deliver cortisone-type medicine to the lungs or the nose, where it's most needed, and very little is absorbed into the rest of the body. As a result typical steroid side effects rarely, if ever, occur.

With all the important new advances now available, there is no longer any need for people to suffer in silence. Any doctor who has patience and is willing to take a cautious, step-by-step approach to therapy should be able to help almost anyone breathe freely. Here are some practical guidelines to some of the newest allergy and asthma medicines.

Beconase and **Vancenase** *(beclomethasone diproprionate nasal spray; 16.8 g containers; about 200 sprays per canister. Each spray delivers approximately 42 mcg.)*

MFR:
- **Beconase:** Glaxo
- **Vancenase:** Schering

FDA APPROVED USES: Symptomatic relief of perennial or seasonal allergic rhinitis ("hay fever").

USUAL DOSE:
- One spray in each nostril two to four times daily.

Steroids are probably the most effective drug in the war against allergies, but when used orally, they often bring on unacceptable and sometimes serious side effects. For this reason they were most often used as a last resort. Now, however, with the advent of locally applied steroid nasal sprays, the systemic side effects are much less prevalent. These sprays represent the first really new therapeutic advance for allergy sufferers in

(continues next page)

Beconase and Vancenase, *(continued)*

many years. About the only common side effect is a stinging sensation after using the spray, but this is a modest inconvenience for most people. Steroid nasal sprays don't have the same rebound congestion and addictive potential seen with the decongestant nasal sprays. Unlike the latter sprays, **Beconase** and **Vancenase** won't unclog a stuffy nose and aren't meant to be used "as needed." They are only effective when used regularly; to work best, they should be used even when you are not suffering from acute allergy symptoms.

PRECAUTIONS:
- Proper administration is essential. Be sure you know how to use the inhaler, or ask your doctor or pharmacist to explain its use to you.
- Do not exceed recommended doses.
- Use on a scheduled basis, even when you are not experiencing acute nasal symptoms. Beclomethasone is not effective for immediate relief of allergy symptoms and should not be used "as needed."
- If you have a stopped-up or runny nose, the medication may not reach the intended area. Use a decongestant nasal spray to open up the nasal passages before using the steroid nasal spray.
- It may take a few days for the full effectiveness of beclomethasone nasal spray to become evident.
- Do not use if you have tuberculosis, ocular herpes, or serious untreated viral, fungal, or bacterial infections.

PREGNANCY AND BREAST-FEEDING:
- Even though the small doses absorbed from steroid nasal sprays are probably not harmful to the baby, their use has not been proven safe during pregnancy. Avoid using steroid nasal sprays while pregnant if possible.
- Steroids are found in breast milk, and in much higher concentrations than would be expected. Steroid nasal sprays have caused suppression of the baby's adrenal glands. Use with caution if nursing.

COMMON SIDE EFFECTS:
- Nasal irritation (fairly common).
- Sneezing.

UNCOMMON SIDE EFFECTS:
*- Recurrent bloody nose.
*- Sore throat.

SEXUAL SIDE EFFECTS:
- None.

---

* These side effects may be serious. Contact your physician immediately if they occur.

Beconase and Vancenase, *(continued)*

DRUG INTERACTIONS:
- None expected.

Nasalide *(flunisolide nasal spray; 25 ml bottles; about 200 sprays per bottle. Each spray delivers approximately 25 mcg.)*

MFR: Syntex

FDA APPROVED USES: Symptomatic relief of perennial or seasonal allergic rhinitis ("hay fever").

USUAL DOSE: Two sprays in each nostril twice or three times daily. About 15% of users can get by with only one spray in each nostril daily.

Nasalide is similar to **Beconase** and **Vancenase** (beclomethasone diproprionate nasal spray). For a description of the use of intranasal steroids in hay fever, see discussion under these. Unlike the beclomethasone sprays, **Nasalide** contains no fluorocarbon propellant.

PRECAUTIONS:
- Throw away any medication remaining after three months.
- Proper administration is essential. Be sure you know how to use the inhaler, or ask your doctor or pharmacist to explain its use to you.
- Do not exceed recommended doses.
- Use on a scheduled basis, even when you are not experiencing acute nasal symptoms. Flunisolide is not effective for immediate relief of allergy symptoms and should not be used "as needed."
- If you have a stopped-up or runny nose, the medication may not reach the intended area. Use a decongestant nasal spray to open up the nasal passages before using the steroid nasal spray.
- It may take from a few days to three weeks for the full effectiveness of **Nasalide** to become evident.
- Do not use if you have tuberculosis, ocular herpes, or serious untreated viral, fungal, or bacterial infections.

PREGNANCY AND BREAST-FEEDING:
- Even though the small doses absorbed from steroid nasal sprays are probably not harmful to the baby, their use has not been proven safe during pregnancy. Avoid using steroid nasal sprays while pregnant if possible.
- Steroids are found in breast milk (in much higher concentrations than would be expected). Steroid nasal sprays have caused suppression of the baby's adrenal glands. Use with caution if nursing.

(continues next page)

Nasalide, *(continued)*

COMMON SIDE EFFECTS:
- Nasal irritation (fairly common).
- Sneezing.

UNCOMMON SIDE EFFECTS:
- Loss of sense of smell or taste.
- Stuffy nose.
*▪ Recurrent bloody nose.
*▪ Sore throat.

SEXUAL SIDE EFFECTS:
- None.

DRUG INTERACTIONS:
- None expected.

Proventil and Ventolin *(albuterol 2 mg and 4 mg tablets, and as an aerosol inhaler in 17 g canisters; each puff delivers approximately 90 mcg.)*

MFR:
- **Proventil:** Schering.
- **Ventolin:** Glaxo.

FDA APPROVED USES: Bronchodilation (opening of the airways in the lung) in persons with asthma and other reversible obstructive airway diseases.

USUAL DOSE:
- Bronchodilation (inhaler): Two inhalations every four to six hours.
- Bronchodilation (oral): 2 mg to 4 mg three or four times daily, up to 8 mg four times a day (32 mg total daily dose).

Albuterol is a mimic. It fools the body into believing it is acting like adrenaline in the lungs and thus opens constricted airways. Unlike adrenaline and many other asthma medications, albuterol leaves the heart and blood vessels relatively unaffected. This is a great advantage because the side effects—such as a racing heart beat and an increase in blood pressure—seen with less selective imitators, like ephedrine, are infrequent.

Albuterol is available as an inhaler as well as the more familiar tablets. This enables the medication to be delivered right to the site of action rather than having to approach it through the back door via the blood stream. Consequently whole-body side effects are further decreased and

---

* These side effects may be serious. Contact your physician immediately if they occur.

Proventil and Ventolin, *(continued)*

the total dose needed to open up the breathing passages is much less than the comparably effective oral dose.

All these advantages make albuterol or the similar drug **Alupent** (metaproterenol) most likely the drugs of first choice in treating asthma and other reversible airway diseases. These two inhaler medications represent a significant advance in the treatment of asthma.

PRECAUTIONS:
- Do not use if you have a heart condition causing an increased pulse.
- The onset of action is about 30 minutes after taking a tablet and within 5 to 15 minutes after using an inhaler.
- Proper use of the inhaler is essential for the medication to be maximally effective (many people use it incorrectly).
- Wait one full minute between inhalations.
- If relief is not obtained after using the inhaler, call your doctor immediately.
- Do not use more medication than is prescribed. Excessive and prolonged use of the inhaler may cause a rebound airway spasm. Overuse may also lead to a loss of effectiveness.
- If you are using a steroid inhaler as well (see **Beclovent** and **Vanceril**), use the bronchodilator 15 to 30 minutes prior to the steroid. This enables the airways to open up and to get the steroid more effectively down into the lungs.
- The inhaler contains fluorocarbon propellant. Do not use if you are sensitive to this ingredient.

WARNING: One animal study showed an increased risk of benign tumors when very high doses of albuterol were administered. No human data are available, and the implications of the animal study are unknown.

WARNING: Overuse of bronchodilating aerosol sprays has been associated with an increased death rate. Although the cause is unclear, and there is probably less risk with albuterol than with **Isuprel** (isoproterenol), immediately notify your physician if your normal doses do not improve breathing.

PREGNANCY AND BREAST-FEEDING:
- Safety for use during pregnancy is questionable. Animal studies show an increased risk of birth defects, but no human data are available. Do not use during pregnancy unless the benefit clearly outweighs the possible dangers.
- It is not known whether albuterol is found in breast milk. Since its safety is not clear, use while breast-feeding only if absolutely necessary.

(continues next page)

Proventil and Ventolin, *(continued)*

COMMON SIDE EFFECTS:
- Nervousness, restlessness, agitation, anxiety, tremor, shaking (the jitters).
- Fast heart rate.
- Insomnia.
- Nausea (vomiting less frequent).
- Coughing and bronchial irritation (inhaler only).

UNCOMMON SIDE EFFECTS:
*- Dizziness and faintness.
- Headache.
*- Dry mouth or bad taste in mouth.
*- Heartburn.
*- Chest pain.

  NOTES: These side effects are more prominent with the oral dosages than with the inhaler. Overdose causes these side effects to become more pronounced. Do not exceed the prescribed dosage and notify your doctor if any adverse reaction becomes especially bad.

SEXUAL SIDE EFFECTS:
- Probably none.

DRUG INTERACTIONS:
- Albuterol is a "sympathomimetic" agent and its side effects are additive with other sympathomimetic or similar drugs such as **Brethine** (terbutaline), **Isuprel** (isoproterenol), **Alupent** and **Metaprel** (metaproterenol), **Bronkosol** (isoetharine), ephedrine, **Sudafed** (pseudoephedrine), and OTC and prescription combination products containing these ingredients.
- The beta blockers **Inderal** (propranolol), **Blocadren** (timolol), **Visken** (pindolol), **Corgard** (nadolol), and in large doses **Lopressor** (metoprolol) and **Tenormin** (atenolol) can block the bronchodilating effects of albuterol.
- The MAO inhibitors may increase the cardiac effects of albuterol. They are: **Marplan** (isocarboxazid), **Nardil** (phenelzine), **Parnate** (tranylcypromine), **Eutonyl** (pargyline), and **Furoxone** (furazolidone), an antibiotic with MAO-inhibiting properties.
- The tricyclic antidepressants **Elavil** and **Endep** (amitriptyline), **Tofranil** and **Janimine** (imipramine), **Surmontil** (trimipramine), **Aventyl** and **Pamelor** (nortriptyline), **Norpramin** and **Pertofrane** (desiprimine), **Vivactil** (protriptyline), **Asendin** (amoxapine), probably **Ludiomil** (maprotiline), and **Adapin** and **Sinequan** (doxepin) may also increase the cardiac side effects of albuterol.

* *These side effects may be serious. Contact your physician immediately if they occur.*

Proventil and Ventolin, *(continued)*

- The xanthine medications, although commonly prescribed together with albuterol, may increase the possibility of adverse reactions. The xanthines are: **Bronkodyl, Theo-Dur, Theobid, Slo-Phyllin, Theolair, Sustaire, Theovent** and many others (theophylline), and **Somophyllin, Aminodur,** and others (aminophylline), and **Neothylline, Droxine,** and others (dyphylline).

NOTE: Many of these drug interactions are more likely to occur with the oral dosage form than with the inhaler.

Beclovent and Vanceril *(beclomethasone diproprionate inhalers; each puff provides approximately 42 mcg; 16.8 g containers delivering about 200 doses)*

MFR:
- **Beclovent:** Glaxo
- **Vanceril:** Schering

FDA APPROVED USES: Bronchial asthma.

USUAL DOSE: Two puffs three or four times a day.

Steroids are extremely effective in treating asthmatics. The multitude of unfortunate and almost unavoidable adverse reactions associated with long-term oral use, however, greatly limit their application to last-resort situations. Steroids are essential body hormones and participate in stress reactions, influence electrolyte (sodium, potassium, etc.) and water balance, fat, protein, and carbohydrate metabolism, and many other crucial processes. The body's adrenal gland manufactures its own steroids, but when you take additional steroids, the adrenals stop making their own. After a while they actually shrivel up from disuse. When some big-time stress comes along and whopping doses of steroid are needed by the body to cope with the extra burden, the adrenal glands aren't in a position to help. It may take months for them to fully recover their function. For this reason it is important not to suddenly stop taking any steroid medication when you have been taking it longer than a couple of weeks.

It would be great if you could deliver the steroid right to the lungs and bypass the total circulation and avoid all those side effects. **Beclovent** and **Vanceril** are designed to do just that, and this makes them an important improvement in asthma treatment. They are not totally free from adverse reactions, however, and some of the beclomethasone is

(continues next page)

Beclovent and Vanceril, *(continued)*

absorbed into the body through the lung tissue. For those asthmatics who aren't controlled on the more benign medications, steroid inhalers are probably much safer than the orally taken steroids. Used with caution, they are quite effective and usually don't cause many problems.

PRECAUTIONS:
- If you are using a bronchodilator inhaler as well (see **Proventil** and **Ventolin**), use the bronchodilator 15 to 30 minutes prior to the steroid. This enables the airways to open up and to get the steroid more effectively down into the lungs.
- This product is not for use "as needed." It should be used on a scheduled basis, whether or not symptoms of acute asthma are present.
- This product is *not* a bronchodilator. It will not help in an acute asthmatic attack and may even exacerbate the condition.
- Do not suddenly discontinue using this product.
- To prevent fungal mouth infections (usually not terribly serious), rinse mouth with mouthwash after using the inhaler.
- The inhaler must be used properly to be of benefit. Be sure you know the correct procedure for use.
- The inhaler contains fluorocarbon propellant. Do not use if you are sensitive to this ingredient.

PREGNANCY AND BREAST-FEEDING:
- Beclomethasone has caused birth defects in animals. Although no data exists for humans, use only if absolutely necessary during pregnancy.
- Some related drugs are found in breast milk, although it is not known whether this is the case for beclomethasone. Since steroids can have adverse effects on the baby's growth and adrenal-gland function, if you must use beclomethasone, it is prudent not to breast-feed.

COMMON SIDE EFFECTS:
- Fungal mouth infections (see precautions, above).

UNCOMMON SIDE EFFECTS:
*- Exacerbation of acute asthma attack (your doctor may want you to temporarily discontinue use of steroid inhalers during an acute attack).
*- Cough, hoarsness, throat irritation (minor).
*- Suppression of adrenal gland function (see discussion above).

SEXUAL SIDE EFFECTS:
- Probably none with proper use.

---

* *These side effects may be serious. Contact your physician immediately if they occur.*

Beclovent and Vanceril, *(continued)*

DRUG INTERACTIONS:
- None significant.

Theo-Dur *(theophylline 100 mg, 200 mg, and 300 mg sustained-release tablets)* and
Slo-Phyllin *(theophylline 60 mg, 125 mg, and 250 mg sustained-release capsules)*

MFR:
- **Theo-Dur:** Key
- **Slo-Phyllin:** Rorer

FDA APPROVED USES: Bronchodilation (opening of the airways in the lung) in persons with asthma and other reversible obstructive airway diseases.

USUAL DOSE: Adults only: In nonemergency cases, start with 4 mg per kg body weight every eight to twelve hours. Increase slowly to a maximum of 13 mg per kg total daily dose or 900 mg total daily dose, whichever is less. Most persons should have blood levels of theophylline determined, especially those who need higher doses or prolonged treatment. Doses should be individualized for each person on the basis of these blood levels.

PRECAUTIONS:
- Absorption of these sustained-release products may be erratic if you have diarrhea.
- Theophylline may aggravate abnormal heart rhythms and other cardiac disorders. Use with caution.
- Theophylline may aggravate fibrocystic breast disease.
- Blood levels of theophylline should be periodically checked to reassess the correct dose.
- Not all persons are adequately controlled with sustained-release theophylline and may need more frequent dosing.
- Do not take more of this medication than prescribed. It is quite toxic in doses only moderately larger than normal.
- Use with caution if you have liver disease or hyperthyroidism uncontrolled by medication.
- Theophylline may aggravate ulcers.
- Do not change from one product to another. All theophyllines are not alike.

(continues next page)

Theo-Dur and Slo-Phyllin, *(continued)*

PREGNANCY AND BREAST-FEEDING:
- Do not use during pregnancy if at all possible. Although no human data exist, one animal study indicates an increased risk of birth defects. Theophylline crosses the placenta and is found in the baby's circulation. Newborns whose mothers have taken theophylline may be irritable or show other signs of theophylline toxicity.
- Theophylline is found in the milk of nursing mothers and is passed on to the infant. Do not breast-feed if you need to take theophylline.

COMMON SIDE EFFECTS:
- Nervousness, jitters.
- Nausea.

UNCOMMON SIDE EFFECTS:
*■ Bloody vomit, tarry stools (exacerbation of ulcer).
*■ Heartburn.

SIGNS OF TOXICITY: Side effects become quite common if too much theophylline is taken. If you experience any of these adverse reactions, call your doctor immediately.
*■ Unusually fast heart rate.
*■ Vomiting, severe nausea, stomach pain.
*■ Diarrhea.
*■ Unusual headache.
*■ Irritability, mood changes, insomnia.
*■ Palpitations.
*■ Seizures.
*■ Tremor, twitching muscles.
*■ Unusually rapid breathing rate.
*■ Increased urination.
*■ Loss of appetite.
*■ Dizziness, faintness, vertigo.
*■ Unusual fatigue, weakness.
*■ Unexplained fever, flushing, redness.

SEXUAL SIDE EFFECTS:
- Probably none.

DRUG INTERACTIONS:
- Smoking (tobacco or marijuana) can increase the metabolism of theophylline and decrease its effects; you may need a larger dose as a result. It may take up to one year after you have stopped smoking for your metabolism to return to normal.

* *These side effects may be serious. Contact your physician immediately if they occur.*

Theo-Dur and Slo-Phyllin, *(continued)*

- **Alurate** (aprobarbital), **Amytal** (amobarbital), **Butisol** (butabarbital), **Gemonil** (metharbital), **Lotusate** (talbutal), **Luminal** (phenobarbital), **Mebaral** (mephobarbital), **Mysoline** (primidone), **Nembutal** (pentobarbital), **Seconal** (secobarbital), **Tuinal** (amobarbital and secobarbital), and others (all barbiturates) may decrease the effectiveness of theophylline.

- The beta blockers **Inderal** (propranolol), **Blocadren** (timolol), **Visken** (pindolol), **Corgard** (nadolol), and in large doses **Lopressor** (metoprolol) and **Tenormin** (atenolol) can block the bronchodilating effects of theophylline.

- **Tagamet** (cimetidine) decreases the metabolism of theophylline and increases its effects. This combination can be quite dangerous. Watch for the signs of theophylline toxicity, above.

- **E-Mycin, E.E.S., Ilosone,** and many others (erythromycin) and **TAO** (troleandomycin) decrease the metabolism of theophylline and can significantly raise its blood levels, leading to possible toxicity. The effectiveness of the erythromycin may also be decreased.

- Halothane anesthesia can cause disturbances of heart rhythm in persons taking theophylline.

- Theophylline and the anticonvulsant drugs **Dilantin** (phenytoin), **Peganone** (ethotoin), and **Mesantoin** (mephenytoin), mutually inhibit each other's effectiveness. Dosage increases in both drugs may be necessary.

- Influenza vaccine decreases the metabolism of theophylline, and a temporary dose reduction in the latter may be necessary. This interaction does not occur in most persons.

- Birth-control pills decrease the metabolism of theophylline and may cause theophylline toxicity.

- Theophylline may decrease the effectiveness of **Eskalith** and others (lithium) by increasing lithium excretion. Higher lithium doses may be necessary.

An Antibiotic Worth Knowing: Ceclor

If you have young children you will probably come into contact with **Ceclor** (cefaclor) at least once each winter. Ear infections are getting tougher and tougher to treat because of resistant strains of bacteria. Not too long ago penicillin, ampicillin, and amoxicillin would have done the trick. Now pediatricians have to turn to **Ceclor** or **Bactrim** or **Septra** (trimethoprim and sulfamethoxazole). It's time you got acquainted.

Ceclor *(cefaclor 250 mg and 500 mg capsules, and 125 mg and 250 mg per 5 ml oral suspensions)*

MFR: Eli Lilly and Company

FDA APPROVED USES: Many bacterial infections.

USUAL DOSE:
- Adults: 250 mg three times a day. More serious infections may require 500 mg three times a day. Maximum 4 gm total daily dose.
- Children: 20 mg per kg daily, up to 40 mg per kg daily, divided into doses given every eight hours. Maximum 1 gm total daily dose.

Ceclor is one of the rapidly growing members of the family of cephalosporin antibiotics, all derivatives of a compound produced by a fungus found in the ocean near Sardinia. These antibiotics are generally grouped into "generations," indicating pretty much the order in which they were developed but, more importantly, what bacteria they counteract. So far there are three generations on the market, but I understand that some fifth-generation cephalosporins are now on the drawing boards. **Ceclor** is the only second-generation cephalosporin that can be taken orally. Only two first-generation cephalosporins are available as oral preparations, and all third-generation antibiotics are used by injection only.

Ceclor has a broader spectrum of activity than the first-generation cephalosporins and the penicillins, but the quite considerable cost prohibits it from being the antibiotic of choice unless laboratory tests show that it is the most effective drug against your particular infecting bug. It has proven helpful in both upper- and lower-respiratory tract infections, urinary tract infections, and some skin infections. **Ceclor** is often used to treat *Hemophilus influenzae* infections, a common cause of childhood otitis media (middle ear infections). While most pediatricians would start out using ampicillin or amoxicillin in these children, **Ceclor** is a good alternative if resistant bacteria seem present. The biggest danger is that it will probably be prescribed for lots of children for whom the much less expensive ampicillin would be just as good.

PRECAUTIONS:
- Cephalosporins crossreact somewhat with the penicillin antibiotics. If you are allergic to penicillin, you have about a 15% chance of being allergic to the cephalosporins.
- Antibiotics should be used only if absolutely necessary, in order to prevent the emergence of resistant strains of bacteria.
- Take the complete course of antibiotics, even though you may feel better before the medication is finished.
- You may take **Ceclor** with food or milk if it upsets your stomach.
- Diabetics: a false positive urine sugar test may occur with **Clinitest Tablets**, although this does not occur with **Tes-tape** or **Clinistix**.

Ceclor, *(continued)*

PREGNANCY AND BREAST-FEEDING:
- Although **Ceclor** is probably safe for use in pregnant women, there is no conclusive proof to that effect. As with all drugs, use during pregnancy only if the probable benefits outweigh any potential risks.
- Cephalosporins are found in small amounts in the milk of nursing mothers. Use while breast-feeding only if necessary.

COMMON SIDE EFFECTS:
- Nausea and vomiting (about 1%).
- Diarrhea (about 1.5%).
*- Rash, itching (allergic reaction; about 1.5%).
*- Sore mouth (fungal growth).

UNCOMMON SIDE EFFECTS:
*- Itching of rectal, genital region (fungal growth; rare).
*- Severe watery diarrhea, severe nausea, vomiting, bloody stools, unexplained tiredness, weakness, weight loss (all may be symptoms of antibiotic-associated "psuedomembranous colitis"; very rare).

SEXUAL SIDE EFFECTS.
- None.

DRUG INTERACTIONS:
- **Benemid** (probenicid) inhibits the excretion of cephalosporins, increasing their concentration in the blood stream.
- "Bacteriostatic" antibiotics (which inhibit bacterial growth rather than killing bacteria directly) such as the tetracyclines **Achromycin V** and **Sumycin** (tetracycline), **Terramycin** (oxytetracycline), **Vibramycin** (doxycycline), **Declomycin** (demeclocycline), **Minocin** (minocycline), and **Rondomycin** (methacycline) can decrease the effectiveness of the cephalosporins, which depend on having actively growing bacteria to kill.

Not Another NSAID: Feldene

In Chapter 4 you learned more than you ever wanted to about NSAIDs (non-steroidal anti-inflammatory drugs). Here comes **Feldene,** the latest entry to join the lucrative sweepstakes.

* *These side effects may be serious. Contact your physician immediately if they occur.*

Feldene *(piroxicam 10 mg and 20 mg capsules)*

MFR: Pfizer Laboratories

FDA APPROVED USES: Rheumatoid arthritis and osteoarthritis.

USUAL DOSE: 10 mg twice daily or 20 mg once daily.

Feldene is another in a long series of medicinal agents known as the nonsteroidal anti-inflammatories. Drugs like **Motrin, Clinoril, Indocin, Naprosyn, Tolectin,** and **Nalfon** are used primarily to decrease the inflammation associated with arthritis and other disorders and to alleviate mild to moderate pain. What makes **Feldene** new and different is its once-a-day dosage. This makes the drug slightly more convenient, though naturally you will pay for this "luxury." If you have to take lots of other medicine on precise schedules, the extra ease of **Feldene** may make the extra price worthwhile.

PRECAUTIONS:
- Piroxicam can aggravate ulcers or create them in susceptible individuals. Use with caution if you have gastrointestinal problems. (By the way, for reasons that are not clear people with type O blood seem more susceptible to this kind of problem.)
- It may take up to 12 weeks before the full effects of **Feldene** are evident.
- Take with food, milk, or antacids if your stomach is upset by **Feldene**.
- If you have had an allergic reaction to aspirin or any other non-steroidal anti-inflammatory agent, you may be sensitive to piroxicam.
- This drug should be taken with caution if you have poor kidney function.
- Use with caution if you have any bleeding disorder.
- May aggravate asthma.

PREGNANCY AND BREAST-FEEDING:
- Do not take during pregnancy. Animal studies have demonstrated the possibility of birth defects.
- Do not take if breast-feeding. Although no problems have yet been reported in humans, animal studies show an inhibition of milk production.

COMMON SIDE EFFECTS:
- Stomach upset, nausea (at least 3 to 6%).
- * Edema (swelling of the feet and ankles because of water retention) and water-weight gain. This may aggravate high blood pressure or certain heart conditions (about 1 to 3 %).
- * Tinnitus (ringing in the ears; 1 to 3%).

* These side effects may be serious. Contact your physician immediately if they occur.

Feldene, *(continued)*

*■ Unusual sore throat, fever because of decrease in white blood cell count (1 to 3%).
*■ Rash, itching (allergic reaction; 1 to 3%).
*■ Unusual sores in mouth (1 to 3%).

UNCOMMON SIDE EFFECTS:
*■ Gas, heartburn, indigestion, diarrhea, constipation, loss of appetite, vomiting.
 ■ Drowsiness, dizziness, faintness.
 ■ Headache.
 ■ The "blahs."
 ■ Nervousness.
 ■ Red, swollen, irritated eyes.
*■ Blood in urine, stool (stool may be black and tarry).
*■ Blood or coffee-ground type material in vomit (usually from an aggravated or new ulcer).
*■ Unusual bruising, bleeding (rare).
*■ Unusual lethargy, weakness (rare).
*■ Psychological depression (rare).
*■ Blurred vision (rare).

SEXUAL SIDE EFFECTS:
 ■ None significant.

DRUG INTERACTIONS:
 ■ **Eskalith, Lithobid** (lithium): Piroxicam may cause lithium toxicity.
 ■ Alcohol, aspirin, and nonsteroidal anti-inflammatories may exacerbate stomach pain and irritation.
 ■ Aspirin decreases the amount of piroxicam in the bloodstream and thus decreases its effectiveness.
 ■ **Athrombin-K** (warfarin potassium). **Coumadin, Coufarin,** and **Panwarfin** (warfarin), **Dicoumarol** (dicoumarol or bishydroxycoumarin), **Liquamar** (phenprocoumon), **Hedulin** (phenindione), and **Miradon** (anisindione), are all oral anticoagulants that "thin" the blood. Since **Feldene** inhibits platelet activity (important in blood lotting), the combination may lead to excessive anticoagulation and possible unexpected bruising and bleeding.

Cutting Back on Cigarettes With Nicorette

Cigarette smoking is far and away the number-one preventable cause of death in the United States. There is absolutely, positively, no doubt

* These side effects may be serious. Contact your physician immediately if they occur.

that smoking causes cancer, respiratory disease, and cardiac disease, despite what the tobacco industry wants you to believe.

But have you ever tried to stop smoking? It's hell! It took me ten years and an awful lot of fear to finally kick the habit. A lot of folks never seem to make it.

If you're one of the vast majority of smokers who have tried to quit and failed, you realize that cigarettes are *very* addicting and *very* difficult to give up. Doctors and behavioral psychologists are more and more looking at cigarette smoking as not only a social addiction, but also a true physical drug addiction. Unlike the heroin or alcohol abuser, a smoker needs a fix every half-hour or so to avoid withdrawal symptoms. Because you need it so often, the act of smoking is a quite powerful psychological reinforcer. The difficulty of quitting is reflected in the dismally consistent statistics that only about 20 to 25 percent of those who try to quit succeed for any length of time.

But now nicotine addicts have a crutch—**Nicorette,** nicotine chewing gum. Although several other brands on the market sound like nicotine, this is really the first product that actually delivers.

Each piece of gum contains 2 mg. of nicotine—about equal to the content of an average cigarette. By relieving the craving for nicotine, it's supposed to allow the beleaguered smoker to concentrate on eliminating the behavioral patterns that are an intimate part of the smoking pattern. Does the stuff work? Dr. Jack Henningfield, a pharmacologist and professor at Johns Hopkins, calls it "one of the most important, fundamentally new types of treatment."

In preliminary tests the gum had a 40 percent long-term success rate (one year or more without cigarettes) when used as part of a formal stop-smoking program. A British study of nicotine gum reported a lower success rate but concluded that there's "a clear increase in the success rate when the advice of general practitioners to stop smoking is accompanied by an offer of treatment with nicotine chewing gum." In a study conducted at UCLA researchers found use of the gum "is a major advantage" in the first few weeks and for up to six months into a stop-smoking program, probably by relieving the bundle of withdrawal symptoms that so often make people vulnerable when they first quit.

If you've been trying to kick your cigarette habit, this gum just may be the motivator you've been waiting for. But pay careful attention to the instructions, precautions, and side effects. Like any drug, nicotine can produce some pretty unpleasant adverse reactions if you absorb too much of it.

Nicorette *(nicotine chewing gum, 2 mg per piece of gum)*

MFR: Merrell Dow Pharmaceuticals, Inc.

FDA APPROVED USES: As a temporary aid in smoking cessation.

Nicorette, *(continued)*

USUAL DOSE: Chew one stick of gum every time you feel the urge to smoke. Chew the gum *slowly* until you taste it or until a tingling sensation is felt in your mouth. This indicates that nicotine is being released. The nicotine is absorbed through the lining of the mouth and is inactivated when swallowed. When the taste or tingling disappears, resume slow chewing. Repeat the process for about one-half hour. You will soon become accustomed to the regimen and can develop the method which is most comfortable to you. As the urge to smoke lessens, divide the pieces in half and chew **Nicorette** less frequently. Don't try to stop until you're down to about two pieces a day. Do not chew more than 30 pieces daily, and do not use for more than six months.

Nicotine seems to be the element in cigarette smoke that is addicting. Studies show that smokers smoke just enough to maintain a certain level of nicotine in their bloodstreams. When you inhale the smoke, nicotine reaches your brain within seconds. Even with the low-nicotine cigarettes, smokers tend to get the same blood nicotine levels by smoking more and inhaling deeper. The idea behind **Nicorette** is that by getting the nicotine in chewing-gum form, you can break all the behavioral links you have with smoking without going through withdrawal at the same time. The gum isn't nearly so psychologically reinforcing as is smoking, and even though you are still consuming the addictive substance, it is a much easier psychological habit to break.

Nicorette can't work alone—it needs your help. You must be motivated to change your behavior and become a permanent nonsmoker. Merrell Dow, the manufacturer of **Nicorette,** also puts out the booklet *Quitting,* which you can obtain from your physician. In it are some tips on how to successfully become an ex-smoker. Good luck!

PRECAUTIONS:
- Smoking cessation is only successful if you break the emotional, psychological, and social bonds you have with cigarettes. Make a *commitment* to stop.
- If at first you don't succeed, try, try again!
- Carry the gum with you at all times.
- Do not use if you have severe angina or severe abnormal heart rhythms.

PREGNANCY AND BREAST-FEEDING:
- **Nicorette** is contraindicated during pregnancy. So is smoking!
- Do not use **Nicorette** while breast-feeding. Nicotine is found in breast milk of nursing mothers.

(continues next page)

Nicorette, *(continued)*

COMMON SIDE EFFECTS:
- Nausea, vomiting (occurs in many persons using **Nicorette,** but probably can be markedly reduced by chewing the gum more *slowly*).
- Hiccups (about 15–22%).
- Sore jaw muscles (very common).

UNCOMMON SIDE EFFECTS:
- Diarrhea, constipation.
- Dry mouth.
- Excess salivation.
- Cough, sneezing.
*• Abnormal heart rhythms (occurs with cigarette smoking as well).

SEXUAL SIDE EFFECTS:
- None significant.

DRUG INTERACTIONS:
- Probably few of significance. Check with your doctor.

Clarifying the Cholesterol Controversy

Medical science works in mysterious ways. It can take scientists a long time to prove something most people thought they already knew—that cholesterol is bad for your arteries. Actually it has been no easy matter to demonstrate a clear-cut relationship between blood cholesterol and heart disease. So many other variables must be ruled out that until recently most doctors were willing to take the connection on faith.

But one major study, supervised by the National Heart, Lung, and Blood Institute, finally demonstrated what had long been strongly suspected by health researchers—that there is a definite relationship between high cholesterol levels and the risk of heart attack. The study, in which more than 3,800 males participated over a ten-year period, initially involved lowering cholesterol levels through changes in diet. Next some of the men were also given the cholesterol-lowering drug **Questran** (cholestyramine resin), while others received a sham preparation.

The cholesterol levels of those who received the real drug dropped an average of 13.4 percent, while the group given a placebo recorded an average decrease of 8.5 percent. The difference was even more dramatic for LDL-cholesterol, a subspecies thought to be the real enemy in the fight against heart disease. LDL-cholesterol levels dropped 20.3 percent in the drug-treated group and 12.6 percent in the others. The effect of

* *These side effects may be serious. Contact your physician immediately if they occur.*

lowered cholesterol on the heart-attack rate was indeed dramatic; the drug-treated group suffered 19 percent fewer heart attacks of all types and 24 percent fewer fatal heart attacks. In a country where half a million people die each year from heart attacks, these percentages could add up to a lot of lives saved.

This finding is leading lots of men, and even a few physicians, to immediately conclude that the answer will be found in a pill; but that's the way a good study can bring about bad conclusions. Once again Americans are being seduced by the idea that if they merely take a pill, they won't have to change their ways. For most people the answer to the cholesterol question is plain—eat sensibly! Cut back on *all* fats! The more vegetables and fruits the better. Vegetarianism is probably the best solution of all. And of course exercise.

But even a healthy diet can't bring down everyone's cholesterol and triglyceride levels. Those with a genetic predisposition to elevated blood fats may need additional help; that's where drugs like **Questran** and **Lopid** may be helpful.

Lopid *(gemfibrozil 300 mg capsules)*

MFR: Parke-Davis

FDA APPROVED USES: Hypertriglyceridemia (high triglyceride levels in the blood).

USUAL DOSE: 600 mg twice daily. Some persons may require only 900 mg daily, while others may require a total daily dose of up to 1500 mg.

Lopid is not for everyone. Despite growing evidence that high cholesterol levels are an important risk factor for coronary artery disease, the question still remains whether we should be trying to prevent heart disease by treating hypertriglyceridemia. Putting this argument aside, does this mean that most or even many persons with high triglycerides should take **Lopid**? Probably not. The first and best treatment for hypertriglyceridemia is dietary change—losing weight and decreasing the saturated fats, sugar, cholesterol, and alcohol in the diet. Only after an honest try at a diet has failed should drug treatment be considered. To quote a recent ad, "**Lopid** is indicated for treatment of adult patients with very high serum triglyceride levels . . . who present a risk of pancreatitis and who do not respond adequately to diet."

Now that we've narrowed down our prospective drug-treatable candidates to those with a high risk of abdominal pain and pancreatitis (disease of the pancreas), *and* who have very high triglyceride levels of a certain type, *and* who can't control them with dietary modification, we might consider **Lopid**. But what are the risks? Studies done on patients without

(continues next page)

Lopid, *(continued)*

heart disease who were given **Atromid-S** (clofibrate), a drug somewhat similar to **Lopid** and used for the same purpose, show a 36% *higher* death rate in those treated with the drug than in those given a placebo. The excess deaths were due to cancer, pancreatitis, and complications of gallbladder surgery. Another study showed no difference in mortality in patients who had suffered a recent heart attack and were given **Atromid-S** and those given placebo, but the drug-treated group developed twice as many cases of gallstones requiring surgery. Clearly drug treatment of high triglyceride levels is controversial. If the aim is to prevent coronary heart disease, treatment must be carefully weighed against the considerable risks and unanswered questions surrounding the drug.

WARNING: Animal studies have shown an increase in cancer in animals given gemfibrozil.Although no cause and effect has been proven, humans given a pharmacologically similar drug, clofibrate, also had an increased incidence of cancers.

PRECAUTIONS:
- Take 30 minutes before morning and evening meals.
- If you become dizzy or have blurred vision, use caution when driving.
- Use with extreme caution if you have gallstones or gallbladder disease.
- Do not use if you have poor liver or kidney function.
- Do not use if you have biliary cirrhosis.

PREGNANCY AND BREAST-FEEDING:
- Do not use during pregnancy. Animal studies show an increased risk of damage to the fetus.
- The risk of breast-feeding while taking gemfibrozil is unknown, but because of the increased risk of cancer demonstrated in animal studies, nursing is inadvisable.

COMMON SIDE EFFECTS:
- Stomach pain (about 6%).
- Diarrhea (about 5%).
- Nausea, vomiting (about 4% and 2%, respectively).
- Gas or heartburn (about 1%).
*- Skin rash and itching (less than 10%).

UNCOMMON SIDE EFFECTS:
*- Dizziness, blurred vision.
- Headache.
*- Muscular or joint pain.
*- Unusual sore throat, fever (rare).
*- Severe stomach pain, vomiting (symptoms of gallbladder disease).

These side effects may be serious. Contact your physician immediately if they occur.

Lopid, *(continued)*

SEXUAL SIDE EFFECTS:
- None significant.

DRUG INTERACTIONS:
- **Athrombin-K** (warfarin potassium); **Coumadin, Coufarin,** and **Panwarfin** (warfarin); **Dicumarol** (dicumarol, also called bishydroxy-coumarin); **Liquamar** (phenprocouman); **Hedulin** (phenindione); and **Miradon** (anisindione) are all oral anticoagulants that "thin" the blood. **Lopid** may increase the effects of these medications, leading to unwanted bruising and bleeding.
- Since **Lopid** can induce gallstones, it may decrease the effectiveness of **Chenix** (chenodiol), an oral gallstone-dissolving agent (**Lopid** is contraindicated in these patients anyway).

New Fungus Fighters to the Rescue: Micatin and Nizoral

Fungus—the very name is revolting. It makes you think of dark, damp, smelly places where all sorts of creepy, crawly things grow. Fungus is just about the last thing you'd want growing in or on your body. Yet it's amazing how many common medical problems are caused by yucky fungi, even in normally healthy people.

Basically two classes of fungi cause all the problems. One is the yeastlike fungus called alternately Candida and Monilia. It is normally found in the mouth, digestive tract, vagina and, under some circumstances, the skin. Ringworm is the other fungus we most commonly come in contact with. It will grow in the outermost layer of the skin when conditions are right. And conditions are almost always right as far as our feet are concerned. Think about it for a minute; could there be a better place for fungi to thrive than in the warm, dark, moist area between the toes? Of course not.

The good news is that there has been steady improvement in the drugs available to deal with these infections. It used to be that undecylenic acid (found in **Desenex, Quinsana, Rid-Itch Cream,** and **Ting**) was the standard treatment. But this antifungal agent smelled sort of rancid, and it wasn't effective in every case. Then along came tolnaftate (**Tinactin** and **Aftate**). This was a real improvement—no unpleasant odor and somewhat greater effectiveness. But the latest development is better still.

Micatin (miconazole) recently went from prescription-only to over-the-counter status. The cream or lotion form is probably more effective than spray or powder, because the cream and lotion allow better penetration through the skin. **Micatin** will knock out athlete's foot, jock itch, and diaper rash caused by fungal infection.

Another topical antifungal agent was recently approved for prescription use in this country. **Loprox** (ciclopirox) is tantalizing, because German researchers report that topically applied, it may be helpful in clearing up fungal infections that hit the fingernails and toenails.

There are two conventional ways to treat fungal infections of the nails. Taking an oral medication like griseofulvin (**Fulvicin, Grifulvin, Grisactin, Gris-Peg**) will get the drug to the nail by the very indirect route of our general circulation. But because it can take six months for a new fingernail and as long as eighteen months for a toenail to grow completely, the medicine needs to be taken for an awfully long time. It can cause side effects (headaches and stomach upset) and is quite expensive. Even with diligent treatment, susceptible people are prone to recurrences. **Loprox** applied topically may offer an alternative.

One other treatment is worth mentioning. In recent years there has been a resurgence in interest in using urea ointments (40 percent concentration). Placed under closed dressings, the urea can help in removing diseased portions of the nails without the trauma of surgery. It has actually been so used in Russia for quite a while. When supervised by a dermatologist, the urea treatment can be quite effective. If your doctor looks at you with a blank stare when you mention the urea treatment, suggest that he look up an article by Drs. David A. South and Eugene M. Farber published in *Cutis*, volume 25, June, 1980. Dr. Farber is Chairman of the Department of Dermatology at Stanford University Medical Center and a real heavyweight in this field. He provides instructions on how to make and use the urea ointment.

If pharmacists in your area have difficulty making the ointment your doctor can order it already formulated from: Dermatological Laboratory and Supply; 201 Ridge Street; Council Bluffs, IA 51501. This company's toll free number is (800) 831-6273.

An oral drug that belongs to the same class of compounds as **Micatin** was recently approved by the FDA. **Nizoral** (ketoconazole) is effective against ringworm and Candida. To women who are prone to recurrent vaginal yeast infections and are tired of inserting vaginal preparations (which can be quite messy) the availability of an oral preparation may seem like a great alternative.

Unfortunately **Nizoral** does have some potentially serious side effects. While quite safe when used for two or three days—usually long enough to clear up vaginitis—it can cause enlargement of the breasts and do damage to the liver with the more extended treatment necessary for other kinds of fungal infection.

Nizoral *(ketoconazole 200 mg tablets)*

MFR: Janssen Pharmaceutica Inc.

FDA APPROVED USES: Many systemic fungal infections.

USUAL DOSE: 200 mg once daily, although higher doses have been used.

Nizoral is quite an effective drug and is useful for many different types of fungal infections, from oral thrush to athlete's foot that has involved the toenails. Especially in the latter case, many months or even years may be required to eradicate these stubborn infections. Ketoconazole isn't an easy drug for many to take, and some of those prescribed **Nizoral** have to discontinue its use because of intolerable side effects. One of the most dangerous adverse reactions is liver damage, and anyone on ketoconazole should be monitored for this problem.

PRECAUTIONS:
- Ketoconazole has, rarely, been associated with severe liver disease. Your doctor should periodically take blood tests to check for this condition.
- **Nizoral** treatment may take months or even years in some cases. It is important for you to take your medicine conscientiously throughout this period.
- May be taken with food or milk (but not antacids) if stomach upset occurs. (Some upset occurs in about one-fourth of those treated with ketoconazole).
- Drive with caution if dizziness or drowsiness occurs.

PREGNANCY AND BREAST-FEEDING:
- Ketoconazole crosses the placenta and enters the baby's circulation. It has caused birth defects in animal studies. Do not use if pregnant.
- Ketoconazole is found in breast milk. Do not nurse if you have to take this drug.

COMMON SIDE EFFECTS:
- Nausea, vomiting (up to 10%).
- Stomach pain (about 1%).
- Itching and rash (about 2%).
- *■ Enlargement of breasts in men (up to 8%).

UNCOMMON SIDE EFFECTS:
- Headache (less than 1%).
- Dizziness, drowsiness (less than 1%).
- Diarrhea (less than 1%).

(continues next page)

* These side effects may be serious. Contact your physician immediately if they occur.

Nizoral, *(continued)*

- Photophobia (increased sensitivity of eyes to bright light; sunglasses may help; less than 1%).
- Insomnia.
*- Hepatitis; signs and symptoms include pale stools, yellow skin and eyes, dark urine, unexplained weakness and lethargy (at least 1 in 10,000, but may be higher).

SEXUAL SIDE EFFECTS:
- Impotence (less than 1%).

DRUG INTERACTIONS:
- **Tums, Rolaids, Maalox, Mylanta, Riopan, Alka-Seltzer,** and any of dozens of antacids can prevent ketoconazole from dissolving in the stomach. An acidic stomach is essential for proper drug absorption.
- **Tagamet** (cimetidine) and **Zantac** (ranitidine) decrease stomach acidity and prevent dissolution of ketoconazole.
- Atropine, Scopolamine, Anaspaz (1-hyoscyamine), **Bellafoline** (belladonna), **Pamine** (methscopolamine), **Valpin 50** (anisotropine), **Quarzan** (clinidium bromide), **Robinul** (glycopyrrolate), **Tral Filmtabs** or **Tral Gradumets** (hexocyclium), **Darbid** (isopropamide), **Cantil** (mepenzolate), **Banthine** (methantheline), **Antrenyl Bromide** (oxyphenonium bromide), **Pro-Banthine** (propantheline), and **Pathilon** (trihexethyl chloride) are all members of a class of "antimuscarinics" (used rather infrequently for ulcers and gastrointestinal hyperactivity) that can decrease stomach acidity and therefore hinder ketoconazole dissolution and absorption.

Loprox *(ciclopirox olamine 1% cream)*

MFR: Hoechst-Roussel

FDA APPROVED USES: Many fungal skin infections.

USUAL DOSE: Apply to affected area twice daily.

There's not that much more to say about **Loprox** except that it appears to be an effective topical agent almost entirely without side effects. It is useful in a number of fungal and yeast skin infections and has about the same spectrum of activity as many already available antifungal preparations. It may be a good alternative if you have sensitivity reactions to other antifungal medications. One German publication suggests that it is helpful for fungal infections that invade the nail and make it crumble and fall apart.

* *These side effects may be serious. Contact your physician immediately if they occur.*

Loprox, *(continued)*

PRECAUTIONS:
- It may take several weeks for the ciclopirox cream to be effective. Use it faithfully for the full prescribed time, even if the symptoms seem to have disappeared.
- If no improvement is seen after one month's use, reconsider the diagnosis.
- Keep the affected area clean; for athlete's foot, wear clean cotton socks.

PREGNANCY AND BREAST-FEEDING:
- There is no evidence to prove conclusively that **Loprox** is safe for use in pregnant women; but because it is topically applied and has caused no problems in animal studies, the risk to the fetus is probably minimal. However, as with all drugs, use during pregnancy only if absolutely necessary.
- It is not known if ciclopirox is found in the breast milk of nursing mothers. Because it is topically applied, the risk to a nursing infant is probably minimal.

COMMON SIDE EFFECTS:
- None significant.

UNCOMMON SIDE EFFECTS:
- Worsening of symptoms of skin disease (rare).

SEXUAL SIDE EFFECTS:
- None.

DRUG INTERACTIONS:
- Probably none.

Going After Gallstones

Chenix *(chenodiol 250 mg tablets)*

MFR: Rowell Laboratories, Inc.

FDA APPROVED USES: Dissolution of gallbladder stones in persons for whom surgery is inadvisable.

USUAL DOSE: 13 to 16 mg per kg body weight, divided into two daily doses.

Gallbladder surgery is a relatively routine and fairly safe procedure in most people, the treatment of choice for removing gallstones. But it is

(continues next page)

Chenix, *(continued)*

not always necessary to remove the gallbladder, even when stones have developed. And some persons are poor candidates for surgery, either because of old age or the presence of other disease states. **Chenix** is the first, and so far the only, drug alternative to surgery. It is only partially effective however, and should be used only in very carefully selected patients. It works best in those persons with small, cholesterol-rich gallstones; it acts by slowly dissolving the stones. It should be reserved for those people who, for one reason or another, would be poor risks on the operating table. Even in those persons in whom **Chenix** treatment is successful (at most about 70% of well-chosen candidates), the chances of new gallstones forming within five years is about 50-50. Clearly **Chenix** is no miracle cure, but it *is* an important alternative to surgery, at least for a chosen few.

PRECAUTIONS:
- **Chenix** should be used only in carefully selected patients. Surgery is the treatment of choice for most people.
- **Chenix** treatment may take up to two years for complete success.
- Studies have shown that doses only slightly smaller than those recommended are not very effective. If you decide to take **Chenix,** you must take this drug regularly and faithfully.
- Your physician should take regular blood tests to monitor for liver damage and should periodically check to see if your gallstones are dissolving.
- Since diarrhea is a very common side effect and seems related to the dosage, a temporary reduction in dose may decrease the diarrhea.

PREGNANCY AND BREAST-FEEDING:
- Chenodiol can cause birth defects. Do not take during pregnancy.
- It is not known whether chenodiol is found in the breast milk of nursing mothers. It would be prudent not to breast-feed if you must take this drug.

COMMON SIDE EFFECTS:
- *■ Diarrhea occurs in 30% to 40% of persons taking **Chenix**. A temporary dosage reduction and antidiarrheal medication may help.
- *■ Stomach pain and cramps, heartburn and gas, constipation, nausea and vomiting, and an increased urge to urinate, all occur, but with less frequency than diarrhea. These side effects must be evaluated to distinguish them from possible biliary colic (pain caused by the blockage of the bile duct), which is usually surgically treated.

UNCOMMON SIDE EFFECTS:
- *■ Severe liver damage.
- *■ Moderate decrease in the number of white cells in the blood.

* *These side effects may be serious. Contact your physician immediately if they occur.*

Chenix, *(continued)*

SEXUAL SIDE EFFECTS:
- None yet seen.

DRUG INTERACTIONS:
- Antacids containing aluminum, such as **AlternaGel**, **Amphojel**, **Camalox**, **Gaviscon**, **Gelusil**, **Maalox**, **Mylanta**, and **WinGel** may reduce the absorption and decrease the effectiveness of **Chenix**. To be on the safe side, before you purchase any OTC antacid preparation, carefully read the label to check for aluminum content.
- **Questran** (cholestyramine) and **Colestid** (colestipol) can interfere with the absorption of chenodiol and reduce its effectiveness.
- Estrogens such as **Premarin** (conjugated estrogens), **Menest** (esterified estrogens), **Ogen** (estropipate), **Estrace** (estradiol), **Estinyl** (ethinyl estradiol), **Estrovis** (quinestrol), **DES** (diethylstilbestrol), and **Tace** (chlorotrianisene) can increase cholesterol secretion in the bile, increasing the chances of new gallstones and decreasing the likelihood of successful **Chenix** treatment.
- Estrogen-containing birth-control pills such as **Ovulen, Ortho-Novum, Norlnyl,** and **Enovid** can interact in the same manner as the estrogens above.
- **Atromid-S** (clofibrate) and perhaps **Choloxin** (dextrothyroxine sodium) and **Lopid** (gemfibrozil) increase the secretion of cholesterol through the bile duct and may increase the chances of developing new gallstones and decrease the effectiveness of **Chenix**.

Help for the Wayward Heart—And Ears?

There is almost nothing more scary than a heart that stops following its normal rhythm. We have a number of drugs to calm it down, but none of them is perfect. **Tonocard** isn't either, but it is a useful addition to the existing list because it can be given orally.

There is one other unique, unapproved use for **Tonocard**. I would never mention it except for the fact that nothing else is available for tinnitus. This is the fancy medical name for ringing in the ears, and it is a constant torment for millions of Americans. Dr. John R. Emmett has been experimenting with **Tonocard** for years in the treatment of this condition, and he claims relatively good results.

I want to emphasize that this is *not* an approved use of the drug and is highly experimental. In addition, **Tonocard** can produce unpleasant side effects for a number of people. Anyone who wants to know more should have his or her physician contact Dr. John R. Emmett, Shea Clinic, 1080 Madison Avenue, Memphis, TN. 38104.

Tonocard *(tocainide)*

MFR: Merck Sharp & Dohme

FDA APPROVED USES: Not yet officially approved at this writing, but is being tested as an oral antiarrhythmic and for use in tinnitus.

USUAL DOSE: No official dosing guidelines currently exist.

Tonocard is a drug designed to decrease or prevent certain abnormal heart rhythms. It is very much like **Xylocaine** (lidocaine), which, although only available for use by injection, has been used for years with much success in hospitalized patients. Since **Tonocard** is available in oral form, this successful type of treatment is, for the first time, available to patients who are not hospitalized. **Tonocard** seems quite effective in reducing or preventing certain "cardiac arrhythmias," especially in those who have responded well to lidocaine while in the hospital. Since tocainide has not yet been released by the FDA, at the time of this writing official dosing guidelines, indications, and contraindications aren't available. Also, since the drug is so new, the incidences of side effects and drug interactions are unclear. Most of the percentages cited below are from one large (369 patients) study on the efficacy of tocainide in persons with life-threatening arrhythmias. As experience with this drug increases, the numbers will undoubtedly change, new side effects will be discovered, and drug interactions will be reported.

PRECAUTIONS:
- Taking tocainide with meals may decrease gastrointestinal symptoms.
- Taking this drug in smaller but more frequent doses may decrease some of the side effects—such as mental confusion, memory loss, and tremors—associated with the central nervous system.

PREGNANCY AND BREAST-FEEDING:
- It is unknown whether **Tonocard** is safe for use during pregnancy. Do not use if pregnant.
- It is unknown whether **Tonocard** is safe for use while breast-feeding. Until further data become available, do not use if you are nursing an infant.

COMMON SIDE EFFECTS:
- Nausea, vomiting, other gastrointestinal problems (up to 34%).
- Dizziness, light-headedness (up to 31% dizziness and 24% light-headedness).
*- Vertigo.
*- Memory loss.
*- Mental confusion (up to 15%).

* *These side effects may be serious. Contact your physician immediately if they occur.*

Tonocard, *(continued)*

*■ Blurred or double vision.
*■ Decreased blood pressure.
*■ Palpitations (up to 17%).
*■ Tremor, incoordination (up to 22%).
 ■ Numbness, tingling sensations (up to 16%).
 ■ Anxiety, nervousness (up to 13%).
 ■ Constipation.
 ■ Night sweats.
*■ Rash (up to 12%).

UNCOMMON SIDE EFFECTS:
*■ Pericarditis with fever.
*■ Possible bone-marrow supression and anemia.

SEXUAL SIDE EFFECTS:
 ■ Not enough data to determine the presence or absence of any sexually related side effects.

DRUG INTERACTIONS:
 ■ One case report indicated a possible interaction between **Inderal** (propranolol) and **Tonocard,** causing personality changes and severe paranoia.

Motion Sickness Magic: Transderm-Scop

Transderm-Scop *(scopolamine 1.5 mg in a transdermal patch that delivers 0.5 mg over three days)*

MFR: Ciba-Geigy Pharmaceutical Company

FDA APPROVED USES: Prevention of motion sickness.

USUAL DOSE: Apply one patch behind ear at least four hours before you are going to need it. One patch is good for three days.

PRECAUTIONS:
 ■ Use with caution if you have narrow-angle glaucoma, an enlarged prostate, pyloric obstruction, or urinary or intestinal obstruction.
 ■ Use with caution if you have impaired kidney or liver function.
 ■ May cause drowsiness. Use caution when driving or performing any attention-requiring task. Do not drink alcohol or take other drugs that cause drowsiness.

(continues next page)

* *These side effects may be serious. Contact your physician immediately if they occur.*

Transderm-Scop *(scopolamine 1.5 mg in a transdermal patch that delivers 0.5 mg over three days)*

- Do not touch your eyes with the patch or your hands. Wash your hands after applying the patch.

PREGNANCY AND BREAST-FEEDING:
- This antinausea drug is not designed to relieve the nausea and vomiting associated with pregnancy. Animal studies have shown equivocal results in tests for birth defects. No human data are available. Do not use during pregnancy if at all possible.
- It is not known whether scopolamine is found in breast milk of nursing mothers. Do not use while breast-feeding if at all possible.

COMMON SIDE EFFECTS:
*■ Blurred vision.
- Dry mouth.
- Drowsiness.

UNCOMMON SIDE EFFECTS:
*■ Mental and mood changes, giddiness, disorientation, confusion, memory loss, and hallucinations.

SEXUAL SIDE EFFECTS:
- None reported.

DRUG INTERACTIONS:
- Use with caution when taking other drugs with similar side effects (anticholinergic side effects), such as the antipsychotic agents **Haldol** (haloperidol), **Moban** (molindone), **Loxitane** (loxapine), **Taractan** (chlorprothixene), **Navane** (thiothixene), **Stelazine** and others (trifluoperazine), **Prolixin** and **Permitil** (fluphenazine), **Compazine** (prochlorperazine), **Tindal** (acetophenazine), **Proketazine** (carphenazine), **Trilafon** (perphenazine), **Serentil** (mesoridazine), **Quide** (piperacetazine), **Mellaril** (thioridazine), **Vesprin** (triflupromazine), **Sparine** (promazine), and **Thorazine** and others (chlorpromazine), the antidepressants **Elavil** and others (amitriptyline), **Tofranil** and **Janimine** (imipramine), **Adapin** and **Sinequan** (doxepin), **Surmontil** (trimipramine), **Asendin** (amoxapine), **Pamelor** and **Aventyl** (nortriptyline), **Norpramin** and **Pertofrane** (desipramine), **Vivactil** (protriptyline), and **Ludiomil** (maprotiline); and antispasmotic agents and antiulcer drugs, such as atropine, **Anaspaz** (l-hyoscamine), **Bellafoline** (belladonna), **Pamine** (methscopolamine), **Valpin 50** (anisotropine), **Quarzan** (clidinium bromide), **Robinul** (glycopyrrolate), **Tral** (hexocyclium), **Darbid** (isopropamide), **Cantil** (mepenzolate), **Banthine** (methantheline), **Pro-Banthine** (propantheline),

---

* These side effects may be serious. Contact your physician immediately if they occur.

Pathilon (tridihexethyl), **Bentyl** and others (dicyclomine), **Trest** (methixene), **Daricon** (oxyphencyclimine), and **Trocinate** (triphenamil), and any combination medicine containing any of these ingredients.

Parlodel For Parkinsonism

Parlodel *(bromocriptine 2.5 mg tablets and 5 mg capsules)*

MFR: Sandoz Pharmaceuticals

FDA APPROVED USES: Parkinson's disease, prevention of lactation, female infertility, amenorrhea (lack of menstrual cycle), and galactorrhea (unusual lactation) caused by hyperprolactinemia (excess of the lactation-regulating hormone, prolactin, in the blood).

USUAL DOSE:
- Parkinsonism: 1.25 mg (one-half tablet) twice daily. Dose may be increased every two weeks to one month as needed by 2.5 mg daily. Use lowest possible effective dose.
- Lactation prevention: 2.5 mg twice daily for two to three weeks after delivery.
- Infertility: 2.5 mg twice or three times daily.
- Amenorrhea and galactorrhea: 2.5 mg twice or three times daily for not more than six months.

Parlodel has two distinct actions on the body. It blocks the lactation-regulating hormone prolactin and is used to stop milk production post-partum and to treat infertility or menstrual abnormalities related to an overproduction of this hormone. Because it also stimulates dopamine receptors in the brain, it is very useful for treating Parkinson's disease, which is characterized by a loss of this crucial dopamine function. **Parlodel** can be effective when used by itself to treat Parkinsonism but is most often prescribed with **Larodopa** (levodopa or L-Dopa) or **Sinemet** (levodopa plus carbidopa). Bromocriptine is not indicated, however, for the initial treatment of this disease. It seems especially useful for those patients in whom the beneficial effects of levodopa treatment are beginning to wear off ("end of dose" deterioration) or in whom the "on-off" phenonemon is occurring (characterized by the sudden onset of the inability to move and severe debilitation, followed by an abrupt return of movement and function, although often accompanied by involuntary movements typical of Parkinson's disease).

PRECAUTIONS:
- Take with meals.

(continues next page)

Parlodel, *(continued)*

PREGNANCY AND BREAST-FEEDING:
- **Parlodel** has not been proven safe for use during pregnancy. Although studies in pregnant women have shown birth defects to be in about the same range as for women not taking the drug, use during pregnancy only if absolutely necessary.
- Bromocriptine inhibits lactation. Do not use if you wish to breast-feed.

COMMON SIDE EFFECTS:
- Stuffy nose (up to 60% in Parkinson patients).
- Constipation (up to 60% in Parkinson patients).
*- Tingling sensation in fingers and toes when cold (Raynaud's phenomenon; up to 60% in Parkinson patients).
- Fatigue and drowsiness.
- Stomach pain, nausea, loss of appetite, vomiting.
- Dry mouth.
- Headache.
*- Mental depression, difficulty in sleeping.
- Nocturnal leg cramps.
*- Visual disturbances.
*- The "on-off" phenonemon in Parkinson patients (see discussion above, for definition; about 1%).
*- Shortness of breath.
*- Incoordination, difficulty in keeping balance.
*- Dizziness and faintness, frequently when you stand up too fast ("orthostatic hypotension" caused by a drop in blood pressure).
*- Hallucinations, mental confusion (perhaps 25% of Parkinson patients; may last for days after stopping bromocriptine).
*- Uncontrollable limb, facial, head, and body movements (perhaps 25% of Parkinson patients; may last for days after stopping bromocriptine).

UNCOMMON SIDE EFFECTS:
*- Fainting.
*- Ulcers and internal hemorrhaging, causing bloody vomit or dark tarry stools (rare).
*- Increased blood pressure, seizures, stroke (very rare, but potentially fatal).

SEXUAL SIDE EFFECTS:
- Increased libido in Parkinson patients (may be related to improvement in the symptoms of the disease).

DRUG INTERACTIONS:
- Since **Parlodel** may decrease blood pressure, use with caution when other blood-pressure-lowering drugs are being administered.

These side effects may be serious. Contact your physician immediately if they occur.

Parlodel, *(continued)*

- **Haldol** (haloperidol), **Aldomet** (methyldopa), **Reglan** (metoclo-pramide), **Taractan** (chlorprothixene), **Navane** (thiothixene), and the phenothiazine antipsychotic agents **Stelazine** and others (trifluopera-zine), **Prolixin** and **Permitil** (fluphenazine), **Compazine** (prochlor-perazine), **Tindal** (acetophenazine), **Proketazine** (carphenazine), **Trilafon** (perphenazine), **Serentil** (mesoridazine), **Quide** (piper-acetazine), **Mellaril** (thioridazine), **Vesprin** (triflupromazine), **Sparine** (promazine), and **Thorazine** and others (chlorpromazine); the MAO inhibitors **Marplan** (isocarboxazid), **Nardil** (phenelzine), **Parnate** (tranylcypromine), **Eutonyl** (pargyline), and **Furoxone** (furazolidone), and **Serpasil** and others (reserpine) can all, to some extent, cause an increase in blood prolactin levels and would interfere with bromocriptine treatment aimed at decreasing prolactin levels (all indicated condi-tions except Parkinsonism).

Sedatives and Sleeping Pills

Valium (diazepam) is a household word. It is still the most frequently-prescribed minor tranquilizer around, even though its popularity has slipped dramatically in recent years, probably as the result of a bad press. Over the last decade there have been all sorts of scary reports of prominent people (like Betty Ford) who have become "addicted" to **Valium**.

Now I confess, I am not disappointed that the number of annual **Valium** prescriptions is down. But I fear that instead of finding nondrug alternatives for coping with stress, most people have simply switched to newer, less well-known drugs that don't have the same stigma **Valium** has.

Let's get one thing straight. All these medications are pretty much the same, and I don't care whether you're talking about **Librium** (chlor-diazepoxide), **Ativan** (lorazepam), **Serax** (oxazepam), **Tranxene** (chlora-zepate), or **Valium**. All belong to a class of compounds called ben-zodiazepines and are mostly used for anxiety ("nerves") and insomnia. When differences do exist, they lie in the duration and onset of action.

Many benzodiazepines are converted by the liver into "active meta-bolites"—breakdown products that are also potent drugs. Some of these metabolites can linger in the body for days and can cause unwanted sedation and other side effects. Both the liver and the kidneys are essen-tial in eliminating most of the benzodiazepines, and anyone with poor liver or kidney function should take these drugs with caution.

Several new benzodiazepines have recently been marketed and are trying to move in on the territory already occupied by their older cousins such as **Valium**, **Librium**, and **Dalmane** (flurazepam). All benzo-diazepines are not alike, but the drugs listed in the table below don't offer a great deal that wasn't already available. Much of the information that is provided applies to all benzodiazepines and can be used accordingly.

Centrax *(prazepam 5 mg and 10 mg capsules and 10 mg tablets)*

MFR: Parke-Davis

FDA APPROVED USES: Antianxiety.

USUAL DOSE: 10 mg to 20 mg three times a day, or 20 mg to 40 mg once at bedtime. Geriatric and debilitated persons should receive lower doses.

Centrax is very slowly absorbed into the circulation and doesn't reach a peak of activity for at least six hours after you have taken the medication. For this reason prazepam probably isn't the best choice for relieving acute anxiety, but it is more useful for someone who needs to take it on a scheduled basis for longer-term therapy. Actually prazepam itself is not an active drug but is converted by the liver into two "active metabolites," desmethyldiazepam and oxazepam. The former metabolite is particularly long-acting and can build up to high levels, especially in the elderly or in persons with decreased kidney function. **Centrax** doesn't really offer any significant advantage over any of the other benzodiazepines.

PRECAUTIONS:
- May cause drowsiness. Use caution when driving or performing any attention-demanding activity.
- Do not drink alcohol or take sedating drugs while taking this medication. This combination may lead to oversedation.
- Do not use if you have severe breathing problems. This drug may worsen the condition.
- Do not use if you have narrow-angle glaucoma.
- The benzodiazepines can be addicting and withdrawal symptoms do occur in some persons after cessation of therapy. Use with caution.
- The elderly and debilitated are, in general, more sensitive to the effects of this drug. Lower doses are suggested.
- Do not take more of this drug than prescribed.

PREGNANCY AND BREAST-FEEDING:
- If possible, *do not use if pregnant*.
- Desmethyldiazepam is found in breast milk of nursing mothers. Use of benzodiazepines by the mother may cause sedation in the nursing infant. Do not breast-feed if you need to take this drug.

Centrax, *(continued)*

COMMON SIDE EFFECTS:
- Drowsiness, confusion, sedation, sleepiness (quite common, especially when first taking the medication and in the elderly). Reduce dose under doctor's supervision if these adverse reactions persist.
- Dizziness.
- Tiredness, weakness.
*- Clumsiness, unsteady gait.

NOTE: Many of these side effects are dose-related. Decreasing the dosage may help to alleviate the problem.

UNCOMMON SIDE EFFECTS:
*- Hallucinations, vivid dreams, nervousness, insomnia (rare).
*- Psychological depression.
*- Rash and itching skin (allergic reactions, rare).
- Nausea, vomiting, constipation, diarrhea.
- Stomach pain.
*- Visual disturbances.

SEXUAL SIDE EFFECTS:
- Decreased libido may be a problem for some people.

DRUG INTERACTIONS:
- **Tagamet** (cimetidine) decreases the metabolism of prazepam, and unwanted excessive sedation may occur.
- **Antabuse** (disulfiram) decreases metabolism and increases the sedating effects of prazepam.
- Oral contraceptives probably inhibit the metabolism of prazepam and thus increase the potential for sedation and other related side effects.
- Alcohol and benzodiazepines don't mix! The combination can cause synergistic ($1 + 1 = 3$) sedating effects. This is a common reason for admission to emergency rooms around the country.
- Cigarette smoking may decrease the effects of benzodiazepines.

Halcion *(triazolam 0.25 mg and 0.50 mg tablets)*

MFR: The Uphohn Company

FDA APPROVED USES: Sleeping aid.

USUAL DOSE:
- 0.25 mg or 0.50 mg once at bedtime. The elderly or debilitated may need less.

(continues next page)

* *These side effects may be serious. Contact your physician immediately if they occur.*

Halcion, *(continued)*

Halcion is the shortest-acting benzodiazepine that is approved for use in insomnia. This may be of benefit for those individuals who are still groggy the morning after taking **Dalmane** (flurazepam). Unfortunately its activity may be too short. People who wake up too early with **Halcion** may want to try another, longer-acting variety. If nondrug treatment is ineffective and an alternate sleeping pill is necessary for temporary relief of insomnia, one possibility is **Restoril** (temazepam). It is sufficiently short-acting so that morning-after hangover is rarely seen, and it remains in the body long enough for you to get a full night's rest.

PRECAUTIONS:
- **Halcion** is supposed to cause drowsiness. Use caution when driving or performing any attention-demanding activity.
- Do not drink alcohol or take any sedating drugs while taking this medication. The combination may lead to oversedation.
- Do not use if you have severe breathing problems. This drug may worsen the condition.
- Do not use if you have narrow-angle glaucoma.
- The benzodiazepines can be addicting, and withdrawal symptoms do occur in some persons after cessation of therapy. Use with caution and don't take them if you don't have to.
- The elderly and debilitated are, in general, more sensitive to the effects of this drug. Lower doses are suggested.
- Do not take more of this drug than prescribed.
- This drug is indicated for short-term use only. **Halcion** may become less effective after prolonged use.
- Rebound insomnia may occur for a few nights following discontinuation of **Halcion** use.

PREGNANCY AND BREAST-FEEDING:
- If possible *do not use if pregnant*.
- Triazolam is found in breast milk of nursing mothers. Although no problems have yet been reported, use of other benzodiazepines by nursing mothers has caused sedation in their infants. Do not breast-feed if you need to take this drug.

COMMON SIDE EFFECTS:
- Drowsiness (about 14%—a desired effect in a sleeping pill!).
- Headache (about 10%).
- Dizziness, light-headedness (about 8% and 5%, respectively).
- * Clumsiness, unsteady gait (about 5%).
- Nausea, vomiting (about 5%).

* These side effects may be serious. Contact your physician immediately if they occur.

Halcion, *(continued)*

UNCOMMON SIDE EFFECTS:
* *■ Hallucinations, vivid dreams, nervousness, insomnia (rare).
* *■ Psychological depression (less than 1%).
* *■ Rash and itching skin (allergic reactions; rare).
* ■ Visual disturbances (less than 1%).
* ■ Euphoria (less than 1%).
* *■ Rapid heart rate (less than 1%).
* *■ Confusion, decreased memory (less than 1%).
* ■ Constipation, diarrhea (rare).
* ■ Stomach pain, cramps (less than 1%).

SEXUAL SIDE EFFECTS:
* • Decreased libido in some people.

DRUG INTERACTIONS:
* ■ **Tagamet** (cimetidine) decreases the metabolism of triazolam, and unwanted excessive sedation may occur.
* ■ **Antabuse** (disulfiram) decreases metabolism and increases the sedating effects of triazolam.
* ■ Oral contraceptives probably inhibit the metabolism of triazolam and thus increase the potential for sedation and other related side effects.
* ■ Alcohol and benzodiazepines don't mix! The combination can cause synergistic (1 + 1 = 3) sedating effects. This is a common reason for admission to emergency rooms around the country.
* ■ Cigarette smoking may decrease the effects of benzodiazepines.

Paxipam *(halazepam 20 mg and 40 mg tablets)*

MFR: Schering Corporation

FDA APPROVED USES: Antianxiety.

USUAL DOSE: 20 mg to 40 mg three or four times daily. The elderly or debilitated may need less.

Paxipam is simply another long-acting benzodiazepine. It is broken down in the liver to an "active metabolite," desmethyldiazepam, which is a common product of many of the benzodiazepines. This metabolite is particularly long-lived, especially in the elderly, the debilitated, and persons with kidney trouble; its sedative effects may linger on for days after you have stopped taking the drug.

(continues next page)

* *These side effects may be serious. Contact your physician immediately if they occur.*

Paxipam, *(continued)*

PRECAUTIONS:
- May cause drowsiness. Use caution when driving or performing any attention-demanding activity.
- Do not drink alcohol or take any sedating drugs while taking this medication. The combination may lead to oversedation.
- Do not use if you have severe breathing problems. This drug may worsen the condition.
- Do not use if you have narrow-angle glaucoma.
- The benzodiazepines can be addicting, and withdrawal symptoms do occur in some persons after cessation of therapy. Use with caution and don't take them if you don't have to.
- The elderly and debilitated are, in general, more sensitive to the effects of this drug. Lower doses are suggested.
- Do not take more of this drug than prescribed.

PREGNANCY AND BREAST-FEEDING:
- If possible *do not use if pregnant*.
- Desmethyldiazepam is found in breast milk of nursing mothers. Use of benzodiazepines by the mother may cause sedation in the nursing infant. Do not breast-feed if you need to take this drug.

COMMON SIDE EFFECTS:
- Drowsiness, confusion, sedation, and sleepiness (quite common, especially when first taking the medication and in the elderly). Reduce dose if these adverse reactions persist.
- Dizziness.
- Tiredness, weakness.
*- Clumsiness, unsteady gait.

NOTE: Many of these side effects are dose-related. Decreasing the dosage may help to alleviate the problem.

UNCOMMON SIDE EFFECTS:
*- Hallucinations, vivid dreams, nervousness, insomnia (rare).
*- Psychological depression.
*- Rash, itching skin (allergic reactions; rare).
- Nausea, vomiting, constipation, diarrhea.
- Stomach pain.
*- Visual disturbances.

SEXUAL SIDE EFFECTS:
- Decreased libido in some people.

DRUG INTERACTIONS:
- **Tagamet** (cimetidine) decreases the metabolism of halazepam, and unwanted excessive sedation may occur.

* *These side effects may be serious. Contact your physician immediately if they occur.*

Paxipam, *(continued)*

- **Antabuse** (disulfiram) decreases metabolism and increases the sedating effects of halazepam.
- Oral contraceptives probably inhibit the metabolism of halazepam and thus increase the potential for sedation and other related side effects.
- Alcohol and benzodiazepines don't mix! The combination can cause synergistic $(1 + 1 = 3)$ sedating effects. This is a common reason for admission to emergency rooms around the country.
- Cigarette smoking may decrease the effects of benzodiazepines.

Xanax *(alprazolam 0.25 mg, 0.50 mg, and 1.0 mg tablets)*

MFR: The Upjohn Company

FDA APPROVED USES: Anxiety. Also useful for those in whom anxiety is a component of depression.

USUAL DOSE: 0.25 mg to 0.50 mg three times daily, or up to a maximum of 4.0 mg in one day. The elderly or debilitated may need less.

Xanax has an advantage over **Paxipam** and **Centrax** because it is *not* metabolized to desmethyldiazepam. There is little chance of unwanted drug buildup, even for those with poor kidney function, and any sedation is gone within a few hours after you have stopped taking the drug.

PRECAUTIONS:
- May cause drowsiness. Use caution when driving or performing any attention-demanding activity.
- Do not drink alcohol or take any sedating drugs while taking this medication. This combination may lead to oversedation.
- Do not use if you have severe breathing problems. This drug may worsen the condition.
- Do not use if you have narrow-angle glaucoma.
- The benzodiazepines can be addicting, and withdrawal symptoms do occur in some persons after cessation of therapy. Use with caution and don't take if you don't have to.
- The elderly and debilitated are, in general, more sensitive to the effects of this drug. Lower doses are suggested.
- Do not take more of this drug than prescribed.

PREGNANCY AND BREAST-FEEDING:
- If possible *do not use if pregnant*.
- Although no good data exists for alprazolam, many benzodiazepines are found in breast milk of nursing mothers. Use of benzodiazepines

(continues next page)

Xanax, *(continued)*

by the mother may cause sedation in the nursing infant. Do not breast-feed if you need to take this drug.

COMMON SIDE EFFECTS:
- Drowsiness, confusion, sedation, sleepiness (quite common, especially when first taking the medication and in the elderly). Reduce dose if these adverse reactions persist.
- Dizziness.
- Tiredness, weakness.
*- Clumsiness, unsteady gait.

NOTE: Many of these side effects are dose-related. Decreasing the dosage will probably alleviate the problem.

UNCOMMON SIDE EFFECTS:
*- Hallucinations, vivid dreams, nervousness, insomnia (rare).
*- Psychological depression.
*- Rash, itching skin (allergic reactions; rare).
- Nausea, vomiting, constipation, diarrhea.
- Stomach pain.
*- Visual disturbances.

SEXUAL SIDE EFFECTS:
- Decreased libido.

DRUG INTERACTIONS:
- **Tagamet** (cimetidine) decreases the metabolism of alprazolam and unwanted excessive sedation may occur.
- **Antabuse** (disulfiram) decreases metabolism and increases the sedating effects of alprazolam.
- Oral contraceptives probably inhibit the metabolism of alprazolam and thus increase the potential for sedation and other related side effects.
- Alcohol and benzodiazepines don't mix! The combination can cause synergistic ($1 + 1 = 3$) sedating effects. This is a common reason for admission to emergency rooms around the country.
- Cigarette smoking may decrease the effects of benzodiazepines.

Zyderm for Your Wrinkles

Getting older isn't fun. Watch a four-year-old charge around the house and it looks like a perpetual motion machine. Once you get over thirty the muscles don't seem to take to such activity with the same enthusiasm.

* *These side effects may be serious. Contact your physician immediately if they occur.*

The bones and joints may start to ache, the plumbing doesn't always work as well as it once did, and the ticker may start tocking when it isn't supposed to. But most of that damage is internal and relatively invisible.

The problem lies in the face. We live in a youth-oriented culture, where unfortunately, appearance means almost everything. Our jobs, love lives, and sense of self-esteem often depend on what we look like. Americans fork over billions of dollars trying to recapture youth. We dye our hair, massage in skin conditioners, and exercise to get rid of the paunch. But no matter how hard we work at it, smile lines, frown lines, and crow's feet give us away every time.

Until recently, there wasn't much we could do, short of expensive plastic surgery, to reverse the ravages of Father Time. But now there's **Zyderm,** an injectable collagen preparation, which is supposed to help erase age and frown lines, wrinkles, and even smooth out certain kinds of scars.

Collagen is a natural protein that helps hold your skin up much as a trestle holds up a bridge. Collagen fibers are woven together like a fabric to give the skin its texture and suppleness. If the collagen structure is disturbed, by disease, surgery, or the aging process, the result is creases or scars that can cause anything from discomfort to psychological disability for some people.

In the last few years, a very purified form of collagen (**Zyderm**) has been prepared from cow hides. If that sounds unappealing, don't worry; this material has been processed under extremely refined and exacting conditions. But since this is an animal product, allergic reactions are to be expected. A skin test made by injecting a small amount of material in the forearm one month prior to using it in other areas is mandatory. Three percent of people tested will experience a sensitivity reaction and should not go through with the injections.

Even after screening, some individuals who have a negative skin test (no reaction) will still experience allergic reactions—swelling, redness and itching—to the treatment. Such side effects usually disappear on their own over time, but on rare occasions they have lasted several months or more. This should serve as a reminder that there are no absolute tests for safety and every drug has its hazards. Anyone with a history of autoimmune disease (rheumatoid or psoriatic arthritis, scleroderma, lupus erythematosus, polymyositis) should not have this material injected.

For the majority, however, **Zyderm** has proved quite effective. Over the last several years over 100,000 have been treated for everything from forehead creases and frown lines to facial wrinkles, scars, and other ravages of time. Acne scars that are mildly depressed with gradual sloping margins also respond nicely. "Ice-pick" scars, on the other hand, do not seem to benefit.

The injection technique is relatively simple but does require some experience. If you consider **Zyderm** treatment, make sure the dermatologist or plastic surgeon has had plenty of practice. Unfortunately, even good technique will not guarantee a permanent effect. The collagen tends to fade over time and after a year or so "touch-up" injections may be necessary. After all, smiling and frowning are facial expressions that are part of our daily behavior and will eventually cause the lines and wrinkles to reform.

Although **Zyderm** implants are less expensive and less traumatic than plastic surgery, they aren't cheap. Treatment can range from $300 to $1,200, depending on the number of injections and amount of material that is used. If you throw in "spot welds" every couple of years we are talking about a very big bill. Nevertheless, the investment may be worth it for people whose livelihood or sense of well-being depends upon their appearance.

Zyderm

MFR: Collagen Corp.

FDA APPROVED USES: Facial lines caused by smiling or frowning, minor surgical scars, and shallow acne scars.

USUAL DOSE: Determined by competent dermatologist or plastic surgeon.

Zyderm is made from protein that comes from cattle hide. It has been chemically purified to reduce the likelihood of allergic reactions. Injected superficially into the outermost layer of the skin it can help correct minor age lines that commonly occur after a lifetime of smiling or frowning.

PRECAUTIONS:
- **Zyderm** must never be used unless a skin test has been performed at least one month prior to treatment. Anyone who has a reaction to the test injection should not procede.
- People with a personal or family history of autoimmune disease (rheumatoid arthritis, psoriatic arthritis, lupus erythematosus, dermatomyositis, polymyositis, Hashimoto's thyroiditis, Graves' disease, polyarteritis nodosa, scleroderma, ulcerative colitis, Crohn's disease, Sjogren's Syndrome, Reiter's Syndrome), or any other connective tissue disease must not undergo **Zyderm** treatment.
- Anyone who suffers general allergic reactions (hay fever, for example) should probably not receive treatment as this may predispose to **Zyderm** reactivity.
- Anyone with a history of severe allergic reactions leading to anaphylactic shock must not undergo this treatment.
- Anyone who is allergic to lidocaine must not undergo this treatment.
- **Zyderm** should not be used in reconstructive breast surgery.
- Anyone with skin eruptions (cysts, pimples, hives or rashes) should not consider treatment until these active lesions have disappeared.

Zyderm, *(continued)*

COMMON SIDE EFFECTS:
- Swelling, firmness, itching, bruising, and redness can occur in the immediate area of the injection. Some discomfort may also be felt. These reactions should be temporary. Spreading redness or increased swelling must be reported to the doctor immediately.

UNCOMMON SIDE EFFECTS:
- *■ Increased swelling, spreading redness, firmness, and itching that lasts from two weeks up to several months or more (1%).
- *■ Rarely, herpes may occur at the injection site (less than 1 in 1,000).
- *■ Rash, nausea, muscle aches, headache, dizziness, difficulty in breathing (very rare, less than 3 in 10,000).
- *■ Scab formation in the area of the injection site which may lead to scarring (less than 1 in 10,000).

Wrapping It All Up

And there you have it. From **A (Accutane)** to **Z (Zyderm).** Of course, there are a lot of drugs out there, already in use or still in the pipeline, that we just didn't have room to include.

One that we're especially excited about is **Trental** (pentoxifylline). Although it has been used in Europe for many years, it has only recently become available in his country for circulatory problems. By making red blood cells more flexible, it helps blood flow more readily through narrowed vessels. Trental is being used for the painful leg cramps called "intermittent claudication," though it may turn out to be beneficial for other conditions as well. The best news about **Trental** is that, as of this writing, it appears to produce very few side effects.

One of the more far-fetched possibilities now being investigated is that **Trental** may be helpful in treating some types of senility. Although the studies have not yet been completed, some of the researchers feel that **Trental** may offer some hope for helping this condition.

Investigators at Parke-Davis, Hoffmann-La Roche, and Lederle laboratories are also excited about drugs they are testing for counteracting the effects of aging on learning and memory. Dr. Robert Hodges, Vice-President of Research and Development at Parke-Davis, confided that their compounds are "the most exciting thing we've got." One of them, pramiracetam, has already shown its usefulness in helping "to restore to some extent the short- and long-term memory" of their crotchety and forgetful elderly monkeys. Parke-Davis is now testing the drug in hu-

* *These side effects may be serious. Contact your physician immediately if they occur.*

mans with Alzheimer's disease to see whether it can help arrest this condition.

Ancient cranky monkeys, who get frustrated and rattle their cages when they forget things, are playing a starring role at Lederle Laboratories too, as scientists there test compounds that may improve aging memories as much as 20 percent. The "performance enhancers" being developed at this time may not cure advanced senility, but if they pan out they could improve the lives of millions of older Americans. If the research goes well, one or more of these extraordinary drugs may become available by 1990.

New drug advances also offer great promise for millions of people with psoriasis and related skin conditions. Building upon the research which produced **Accutane** for acne, dermatologists have developed another synthetic cousin of Vitamin A, called etretinate (being used in Europe under the brand name **Tigason**).

Like **Accutane**, etretinate will probably have many side effects similar to those provoked by Vitamin A, but it is being hailed as a major advance in the treatment of psoriasis. It appears to be more convenient and effective than many conventional psoriasis therapies; and unlike the more recent ultraviolet light treatment (PUVA), which helped many psoriasis patients, it does not appear to pose a risk of cancer. In fact, etretinate and **Accutane** are being tested for their activity against certain cancers.

Perhaps even more exciting, the psoriasis research is producing some important insights into the biochemical processes that trigger this condition. Dr. John Voorhees, chairman of the Department of Dermatology, University of Michigan, believes that the next important advance in the treatment of this disease will be drugs which can inhibit the leukotrienes, compounds which regulate inflammation and overproduction of skin cells. It's not inconceivable that a diet rich in fish oil or linseed oil will be shown to improve psoriasis by influencing leukotriene production. Combined with refinements of conventional psoriasis therapies, these new advances should make the heartbreak of psoriasis a thing of the past.

Diabetics may also benefit from current research and new medications. The oral drugs glyburide (**Micronase** and **DiaBeta**) and glipizide (**Glucotrol**) offer longer-lasting effects than previous oral diabetes medicines. Perhaps more significant is sorbinil, being tested at twelve medical centers around the country. According to one of the investigators, Dr. Mark Feinglos of Duke University, the new agent should help control diabetic neuropathy (nerve damage) and "could offer relief to thousands of people." Sorbinil may also reduce the risk of cataracts and retinopathy, serious complications of diabetes.

Ultimately, the long-sought-for cure for a diabetes could come from space—but not from little green men in flying saucers. The space shuttle missions have already made room for machinery designed to purify pancreatic beta cells which could be injected into the diabetic, where they would hopefully start producing insulin in a natural manner.

If all this sounds like science fiction, remember that the advances of the past decade would have seemed even more unbelievable in 1950. And there are, or soon will, be vaccines for hepatitis (**Heptavax-B**), pneumonia (**Pneumovax 23**), and chickenpox; new blood pressure medications as **Vasotec** (enalapril); heart medicines like milrinone for congestive heart failure; and antihistamines, including **Seldane** (terfenadine) and astemazole, which are far less likely to produce drowsiness than currently available remedies.

We are still far from being able to cure—or even treat—all the ills of humankind. But the drug advances of the 80s should go a long way towards making life better for millions of people.

Although it was impossible to discuss every new drug development, we have hit on some of the more interesting compounds. Never forget that every medicine has the potential for good as well as harm and that it is up to you to become as informed as possible before starting any therapy. We hope the information in this book will help you get a good headstart down that road.

AFTERWORD

We enjoyed working on this book more than anything else we've ever written. We hope you found it provocative, entertaining, informative, and helpful. We would appreciate any comments, criticism and suggestions. Since we get a lot of mail from our syndicated newspaper column as well as from the readers of our other books, we may not be able to answer each letter personally. Nevertheless, your questions and ideas are valued and may well be incorporated in a future book.

All correspondence will be forwarded to us if addressed to:

Joe and Terry Graedon
The New People's Pharmacy
Bantam Books
666 Fifth Avenue
New York, NY 10103

For information about the authors, turn to page 429.

INDEX